Understanding Movies

Second Canadian Edition

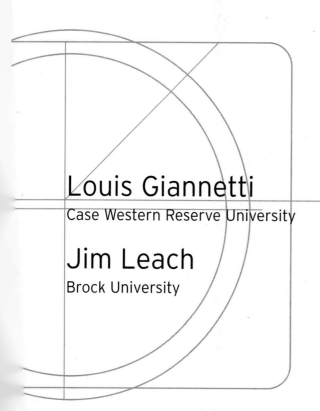

Louis Giannetti
Case Western Reserve University

Jim Leach
Brock University

Prentice
Hall

Toronto

Canadian Cataloguing in Publication Data

Giannetti, Louis D.,
    Understanding movies

Second Canadian Edition

Includes index.
ISBN 0-13-027386-4

1. Motion pictures.   I. Leach, Jim.   II. Title.

PN1994.G47 2001   791.43   C00-930595-5

ISBN 0-13-027386-4

Vice-President, Editorial Director: Michael Young
Acquisitions Editor: Kathleen McGill
Marketing Manager: Christine Cozens
Developmental Editor: Madhu Ranadive
Associate Editor: Tammy Scherer
Copy Editor: Cheryl Cohen
Production Editor: Susan Adlam
Production Coordinator: Peggy Brown
Permissions: Susan Wallace-Cox
Art Director: Julia Hall
Cover Design: Sputnik Design
Cover Image: From *The Red Violin*, Rhombus Media/Bob Marshak
Page Layout: Heather Brunton/ArtPlus Limited

    4 5   05 04 03

Printed and bound in Canada

CONTENTS

PREFACE

The Canadian adaptation of Louis Giannetti's highly successful film studies textbook is intended for use in Canada in introductory film courses. In addition to chapters dealing with the basic issues of film language and film criticism, it includes a chapter on Canadian cinema and provides examples from Canadian films throughout.

In his preface, Giannetti stressed the urgent need for "cineliteracy" because "the average American family watches about seven hours of television per day." Canadian families watch a lot of movies and television, but most of the images they see originate in the United States. As a result, Canadian students need to develop not only media literacy but also an understanding of the distinctive ways in which Canadian movies and television communicate. The focus in this book is on film rather than television. Although television uses moving images in much the same way as film, its variety of formats and its technological and organizational complexity raise more difficult issues that are best tackled after an introduction to film studies.

The overall goal is not to teach students to change their viewing habits, but to make them more aware of the reasons why people respond to movies as they do. In preparing a Canadian edition, my aim has been to make students more aware of their own national cinema and to suggest some of the reasons why people respond to Canadian movies in particular ways.

NEW TO THE SECOND CANADIAN EDITION

* The new opening chapter focuses on the *film medium*, including discussion of the roles of the director, screenwriter, and spectator in the film experience.
* The chapter on *Story* (Chapter 2) has been moved forward in recognition of the need to introduce students to the principles of narrative structure at an early stage.

* The chapter on *Canadian Cinema* (Chapter 10) has been updated.
* The chapters on ideology and theory have been combined into one *Theory* chapter (Chapter 11) and thoroughly revised to take recent trends into account.
* Giannetti's *Synthesis* chapter, focusing on *Citizen Kane*, has been reinstated (Chapter 12) and reorganized to conform to the new arrangement of the earlier chapters.
* New stills have been inserted throughout the book.

ORGANIZATION

This edition of *Understanding Movies* begins with two chapters designed to introduce the basic properties of the medium and the principles of narrative structure. Chapters 3 to 8 deal with the elements of film language and technique used by filmmakers and with how these elements affect the spectator's experience. Chapter 9 discusses the specific uses of film language in nonfiction film, because of the importance of the documentary tradition in Canada, while Chapter 10 focuses on Canada as an example of national cinema. Chapter 11 deals with broader issues of film theory, and Chapter 12 uses *Citizen Kane* as an example to synthesize the topics discussed in the earlier chapters (except chapters 9 and 10). The chapters are fairly self-contained and can be read in a different sequence to meet the needs of specific courses.

FEATURES

* Chapters begin with brief, provocative quotations that can be used as a basis for class discussion.
* Chapter summaries at the beginning of each chapter outline the topics that will be discussed.
* A Glossary of selected terms appears at the back of the text. Terms are boldfaced the first time they appear in each chapter.
* A list of suggested further readings is included at the end of each chapter.
* A list of Web links to Internet sites relevant to film studies is included after the Preface.

SUPPLEMENTS

* An *Instructor's Manual* is available as is a *Test Item File*.

A NOTE ON STILLS

Giannetti generally preferred to use publicity photos rather than frame enlargements because of their superior quality when reproduced. Frame enlargements were used only when close analysis was required, as in the extracts from *The Seven Samurai* (**1–24**) and *Battleship Potemkin* (**6–16**). This edition, somewhat reluctantly, follows Giannetti's lead, partly because of concern for clear reproduction and partly because of the difficulty in obtaining suitable frame enlargements from Canadian films.

ACKNOWLEDGMENTS

The following individuals and institutions graciously allowed use of materials under their copyright: Andrew Sarris, for permission to quote from "The Fall and Rise of the Film Director," in *Interviews with Film Directors* (New York: Avon Books, 1967); Kurosawa Productions, Toho International Co., Ltd., and Audio Brandon Films for permission to use the frame enlargements from *The Seven Samurai*; Albert Maysles, in *Documentary Explorations*, edited by G. Roy Levin (Garden City: Doubleday & Company, Inc., 1971); Herbert Read, "Towards a Film Aesthetic," *Film: A Montage of Theories*, edited by Richard Dyer MacCann (New York: E.P. Dutton & Co., Inc. 1966); Vladimir Nilsen, *The Cinema as a Graphic Art* (New York: Hill and Wang, a Division of Farrar, Straus and Giroux); Marcel Carné, from *The French Cinema*, by Roy Armes (San Diego, Cal.: A. S. Barnes & Co., 1966); Richard Dyer MacCann, "Introduction," *Film: A Montage of Theories* (New York: E. P. Dutton & Co., Inc.) copyright © 1966 by Richard Dyer MacCann, reprinted with permission; V. I. Pudovkin, *Film Technique* (London: Vision, 1954); Akira Kurosawa, from *The Movies as Medium*, edited by Lewis Jacobs (New York: Farrar, Straus and Giroux, 1970); John Grierson, *Grierson on Documentary* (Berkeley: University of California Press, 1966); Margaret Atwood, *Survival: A Thematic Guide to Canadian Literature* (Toronto: Anansi, 1972); Robert Lapsley and Michael Westlake, *Film Theory: An Introduction* (Manchester: Manchester University Press, 1988); Maya Deren, "Cinematography: The Creative Use of Reality," in *The Visual Arts Today*, edited by Kyorgy Kepes (Middletown, Conn: Wesleyan University Press, 1960).

I would like to thank the staff at Pearson Education Canada. Special thanks to the following reviewers, whose feedback was extremely valuable in the development of the Canadian edition of *Understanding Movies*: William Beard, University of Alberta; Peter Morris, York University; Zuzana Pick, Carleton University; Paul Salmon, University of Guelph; Stuart Donovan, St. Thomas University; Richard Epp, University of Lethbridge; Eric Savoy, University of Calgary; and Angela Stukator, University of Western Ontario.

J.L.

WEB LINKS

There are thousands of sites on the Internet devoted to movies and to the media. They include permanent and growing databases, institutional sites for studios and film organizations, publicity for new releases, and fan sites devoted to favourite stars. The following list is just a selection of some of the most useful addresses.

Information

All Movie Guide:
    www.allmovie.com
Cine Media:
    www.cinemedia.org
Excite Movies:
    movies.excite.com
Internet Movie Database:
    imdb.com
Mr Showbiz:
    mrshowbiz.go.com

Archives and research sources:

American Film Institute:
    www.afionline.org
Cinematheque Ontario:
    www.bell.ca/filmfest/cinematheque
Cinémathèque québécoise:
    www.cinematheque.qc.ca
Media History Project: Film History:
    www.mediahistory.com/movies.html
National Film Board of Canada:
    www.onf.ca

Film industry

Academy of Canadian Cinema and Television:
    www.academy.ca
Academy of Motion Picture Arts and Sciences:
    www.oscars.org
National Screen Institute — Canada:
    www.nsi-canada.ca/nsi/
Telefilm Canada:
    www.telefilm.gc.ca

On-line film journals

Bright Lights:
    www.brightlightsfilm.com
indieWIRE:
    www.indiewire.com
Rough Cut:
    www.roughcut.com
24 Frames per Second:
    www.24framespersecond.com

Film Studies

Cyber Film School:
    cyberfilmschool.com

Film Studies Association of Canada:
    www.film.queenu.ca/FSAC/Home.html

International Festival Directory for Students:
    www.temple.edu/ufva/dirs/directories.html

ScreenSite:
    www.tcf.ua.edu/screensite

MEDIUM | 1

The film is the art of space-time: it is a space-time continuum.
—HERBERT READ

SUMMARY

The three styles of film: realism, classicism, and formalism. Three broad types of cinema: documentaries, fiction films, and avant-garde movies. The signified and the signifier: how form shapes content in movies. Subject matter plus treatment equal content. The role of the director. The role of the screenwriter. The role of the spectator: co-creator of meaning. How time, space, and language are used in film. Figurative comparisons: motifs, symbols, metaphors, allegories, and allusions. Point of view.

REALISM AND FORMALISM

From the very early days of the medium, movies began to develop in two major directions: the realistic and the formalistic. In the mid-1890s in France, the Lumière brothers delighted audiences with their short movies dealing with everyday occurrences. Such films as *The Arrival of a Train* (**6–2**) fascinated viewers precisely because they seemed to capture the flux and spontaneity of events as they were viewed in real life. At about the same time, Georges Méliès was creating a number of fantasy films that emphasized purely imagined events. Such movies as *A Trip to the Moon* (**6–3**) were typical mixtures of whimsical narrative and trick photography. In many respects, Louis and Auguste Lumière can be regarded as the founders of the realist tradition of cinema, and Méliès of the formalist tradition.

Realism and **formalism** are general rather than absolute terms. When used to suggest a tendency toward either polarity, such labels can be helpful, but in the end they're just labels. Few films are exclusively formalist in style, and fewer yet are completely realist. There is also an important difference between realism and reality, although this distinction is often forgotten. Realism is a particular style, whereas physical reality is the source of all the raw materials of film, both realistic and formalistic. Virtually all movie directors go to the photographable world for their subject matter, but what they do with this material—how they shape and manipulate it—is what determines their stylistic emphasis.

Generally speaking, realistic films attempt to reproduce the surface of reality with a minimum of distortion. In photographing objects and events, the filmmaker tries to suggest the copiousness of life itself. Both realist and formalist film directors must select (and hence, emphasize) certain details from the chaotic sprawl of reality. But the element of selectivity in realistic films is less obvious. Realists, in short, try to preserve the illusion that their film world is unmanipulated, an objective mirror of the actual world. Formalists, on the other hand, make no such pretence. They deliberately stylize and distort their raw materials so that only the very naive would mistake a manipulated image of an object or event for the real thing.

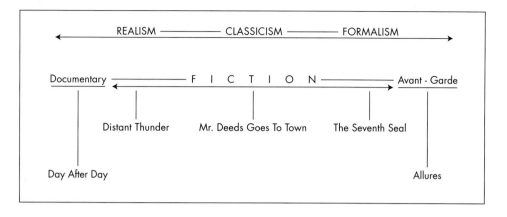

1-1. Classification chart of styles and types of film.
Critics and scholars categorize movies according to a variety of criteria, few of them defini-tive. Two of the most common methods of classification are by style and by type. The three principal styles—realism, classicism, and formalism—might be regarded as a continuous spectrum of possibilities, rather than airtight categories. Similarly, the three types of movies—documentaries, fiction, and avant-garde films—are also terms of convenience, for they often overlap. Realistic films like *Distant Thunder* can shade into the documentary; for-malist movies like *The Seventh Seal* have a personal quality suggesting the traditional domain of the avant-garde. Most fiction films, especially those produced in the United States, tend to conform to the classical paradigm. Classical cinema can be viewed as an intermediate style that avoids the extremes of realism and formalism—though most movies in the classical form lean toward one or the other style.

We rarely notice the style in a realistic movie; the artist tends to be self-effacing. Such filmmakers are more concerned with *what* is being shown rather than how it's manipulated. The camera is used conservatively. It's essentially a recording mechanism that reproduces the surface of tangible objects with as little commentary as possible. Some realists aim for a rough look in their images, one that doesn't prettify the materials with a self-conscious beauty of form. "If it's too pretty, it's false," is an implicit assumption. A high premium is placed on simplicity, spontaneity, and directness. This is not to suggest that these movies lack artistry, however, for at its best, the realistic cinema special-izes in art that conceals art.

Formalist movies are stylistically flamboyant. Their directors are con-cerned with expressing their unabashedly subjective experience of reality, not how other people might see it. Formalists are often referred to as **expressionists,** because their self-expression is at least as important as the subject matter itself. Expressionists are often concerned with spiritual and psychological truths, which they feel can be conveyed best by distorting the surface of the material world. The camera is used as a method of commenting on the subject matter, a way of emphasizing its essential rather than its objective nature. Formalist movies have a high degree of manipulation, of re-forming of reality. But it's pre-cisely this "deformed" imagery that can be so artistically striking in such films.

Most realists would claim that their major concern is with content rather than form or technique. The subject matter is always supreme, and anything that distracts from the content is viewed with suspicion. In its most extreme form, the realistic cinema tends toward documentary, with its emphasis on photographing actual events and people (1–2). The formalist cinema, on the other hand, tends to emphasize technique and expressiveness. The most extreme example of this style of filmmaking is found in the **avant-garde** cinema (1–6). Some of these movies are totally abstract; pure forms (that is, nonrepresentational colours, lines, and shapes) constitute the only content. Most fiction films fall somewhere between these two extremes, in a mode critics refer to as **classical cinema (1–4).**

1–2. *Jour après jour ("Day after Day,"* **Canada, 1962),** *directed by Clément Perron.*
Documentary realism uses images as evidence of the way things really are. On the basis of this evidence, the filmmaker constructs an argument and encourages us to see reality in a certain way. According to John Grierson, one of the founders of the documentary movement, documentary style conveys a social message: "Men must accept the environment in which they live, with its smoke and its steel and its mechanical aids, even with its rain." However, documentaries can make powerful arguments for change, as Perron does in *Jour après jour*, a film about the lives of workers in a Quebec paper mill. The rhythms of the editing and a poetic commentary convey the subjective experience of working long hours at repetitive but often dangerous tasks.   *(National Film Board of Canada)*

Even the terms *form* and *content* aren't as clear-cut as they may sometimes seem. In fact, in many respects the terms are synonymous, although they can certainly be useful in suggesting a degree of emphasis. The form of a **shot**—the way in which a subject is photographed—is its true content, not necessarily what the subject is perceived to be in reality. The Canadian communications theorist Marshall McLuhan pointed out that the content of one medium is actually another medium. For example, a photograph (visual image) depicting

1–3.   *Distant Thunder* (India, 1973), *directed by Satyajit Ray.*
In most realistic films, there is a close correspondence of the images to everyday reality. This criterion of value necessarily involves a comparison between the internal world of the movie with the external milieu that the filmmaker has chosen to explore. The realistic cinema tends to deal with people from the lower social echelons and often explores moral issues. The artist rarely intrudes on the materials, however, preferring to let them speak for themselves. Rather than focusing on extraordinary events, realism tends to emphasize the basic experiences of life. It is a style that excels in making us feel the humanity of others. Beauty of form is often sacrificed to capture the texture of reality as it's ordinarily perceived. Realistic images often seem unmanipulated, haphazard in their design. They frequently convey an intimate snapshot quality—people caught unawares. Generally, the story materials are loosely organized and include many details that don't necessarily forward the plot but are offered for their own sake, to heighten the sense of authenticity.   *(Cinema 5)*

a man eating an apple (taste) involves two different mediums: Each communicates information—content—in a different way. A verbal description of the photograph of the man eating the apple would involve yet another medium (language), which communicates information in yet another manner. In each case, the precise information is determined by the medium, although superficially all three have the same content.

In literature, the naive separation of form and content is called "the heresy of paraphrase." For example, the content of *Hamlet* can be found in a college outline, yet no one would seriously suggest that the play and outline are the same "except in form." To paraphrase artistic information is inevitably to change its content as well as its form. Artistry can never be gauged by subject matter alone. The manner of its presentation—its forms—is the true content of paintings, literature, and plays. The same applies to movies.

1–4. *Mr. Deeds Goes to Town* (U.S.A., 1936), *with Gary Cooper (behind tuba), directed by Frank Capra.*
Classical cinema avoids the extremes of realism and formalism in favour of a slightly stylized presentation that has at least a surface plausibility. Movies in this form are often handsomely mounted, but the style rarely calls attention to itself. The images are determined by their relevance to the story and characters, rather than a desire for authenticity or formal beauty alone. The implicit ideal is a functional, invisible style: The pictorial elements are subordinated to the presentation of characters in action. Classical cinema is story-oriented. The narrative line is seldom allowed to wander, nor is it broken up by authorial intrusions. A high premium is placed on the entertainment value of the story, which is often shaped to conform to the conventions of a popular genre. Often the characters are played by stars rather than unknown players, and their roles are sometimes tailored to showcase their personal charms. The human materials are paramount in the classical cinema. The characters are generally appealing and slightly romanticized. The audience is encouraged to identify with their values and goals.   *(Columbia Pictures)*

The great French critic André Bazin noted, "One way of understanding better what a film is trying to say is to know how it is saying it." Bazin was putting forth the theory of organic form—the belief that form and content are mutually dependent in film as well as any other kind of art. The American critic Herman G. Weinberg expressed the matter succinctly: "The way a story is told is part of that story. You can tell the same story badly or well; you can also tell it well enough or magnificently. It depends on who is telling the story."

Realism and realistic are much overtaxed terms—both in life and in movies. We use these terms to express so many different ideas. For example, people often praise the "realism" of the boxing matches in *Raging Bull*. What they really mean is that these scenes are powerful, intense, and vivid. These traits owe very little to realism as a style. In fact, the boxing matches are extremely stylized, almost like cinematic arias. The images are often photo-

1-5. *The Seventh Seal* **(Sweden, 1957),** *with Max von Sydow (right) and Bengt Ekerot, cinematography by Gunnar Fischer, directed by Ingmar Bergman.*
The formalist cinema is largely a director's cinema: Authorial intrusions are common. There is a high degree of manipulation in the narrative materials, and the visual presentation is stylized. The story is exploited as a vehicle for the filmmaker's personal obsessions. Fidelity to objective reality is rarely a relevant criterion of value. The most artificial genres—musicals, sci-fi, fantasy films—are generally classified as formalist. Most movies of this sort deal with extraordinary characters and events—such as this mortal game of chess between a medieval knight and the figure of Death. This style of cinema excels in dealing with ideas—political, religious, philosophical—and is often the chosen medium of propagandistic artists. Its texture is densely symbolic: Feelings are expressed through forms, like the dramatic high-contrast lighting of this shot. Most of the great stylists of the cinema are formalists.   *(Janus Films)*

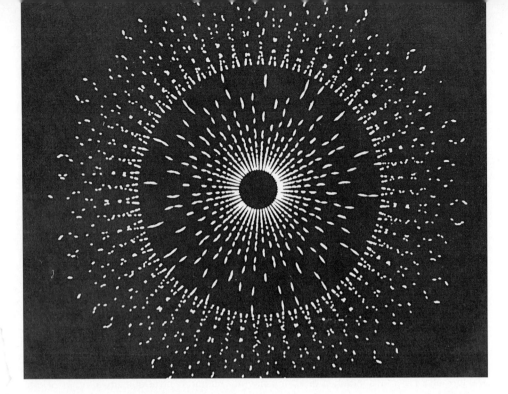

1–6. *Allures* (U.S.A., 1961), *directed by Jordan Belson.*

In the avant-garde cinema, subject matter is often suppressed in favour of abstraction and an emphasis on formal beauty for its own sake. Like many artists in this idiom, Belson began as a painter and was attracted to film because of its temporal and kinetic dimensions. He was strongly influenced by such European avant-garde artists as Hans Richter, who championed the "absolute film"—a graphic cinema of pure forms divorced from a recognizable subject matter. Belson's works are inspired by philosophical concepts derived primarily from Oriental religions, but these are essentially private sources and are rarely presented explicitly in films themselves. Form is the true content of Belson's movies. His animated images are mostly geometrical shapes, dissolving and contracting circles of light, and kinetic swirls. His patterns expand, congeal, flicker, and split off into other shapes, only to reform and explode again. It is a cinema of uncompromising self-expression—personal, often inaccessible, and iconoclastic. *(Pyramid Films)*

---

graphed in dreamy **slow motion**, with lyrical **crane shots**, weird accompanying sound effects (like hissing sounds and jungle screams), staccato **editing** in both the images and the sound, and so forth. True, the subject matter is based on actual life—the brief boxing career of 1940s American middle-weight champion Jake La Motta. But the stylistic treatment of these biographical materials is extravagantly subjective (**1–7a**).

At the opposite extreme, the special effects in *Total Recall* are so uncannily realistic that we would swear they were real if we didn't know better. In the **scene** pictured (**1–7b**), for example, we see a plump bald character magically transformed into Arnold Schwarzenegger after he removes his lifelike headpiece. Such fantasy materials can be presented with astonishing realism thanks to the brilliance of Dream Quest, one of the most prestigious special-effects organizations in the United States.

1–7a. ***Raging Bull** (U.S.A., 1980), with Robert De Niro, directed by Martin Scorsese.* *(United Artists)*

1–7b. ***Total Recall** (U.S.A., 1990), with Arnold Schwarzenegger, directed by Paul Verhoeven.* *(Tri-Star Pictures)*

Realism and formalism are best used as *stylistic* terms rather than terms to describe the nature of the subject matter. For example, although the story of *Raging Bull* is based on actual events, the boxing matches in the film are stylized. In the photo above, the badly bruised Jake La Motta resembles an agonized warrior, crucified against the ropes of the ring. The camera floats toward him in lyrical slow motion while the soft focus obliterates his consciousness of the arena. In *Total Recall,* on the other hand, the special effects are so realistic they almost convince us that the impossible is possible. If special effects look fake, our pleasure is diminished. In short, it's quite possible to present fantasy materials in a realistic style. It's equally possible to present reality-based materials in an expressionistic style.

Form and *content* are best used as relative terms. They are useful concepts for temporarily isolating specific aspects of art for the purposes of closer examination. Such a separation is artificial, of course, yet this technique can yield more detailed insights into the work of art as a whole. By beginning with an understanding of the basic components of the film medium, we will see how form and content in the cinema, as in the other arts, are ultimately the same.

THE DIRECTOR

Film is a collaborative medium, and many individuals—**producers**, directors, screenwriters, actors, technicians—contribute to the final effect. Of these it is the director—whose name usually appears last in the opening credits—and the screenwriter who have usually been seen as the creative artists most responsible for a film's overall meanings.

In the mid-1950s, the French periodical *Cahiers du cinéma* popularized the **auteur theory**, a view that stressed the dominance of the director in film art (see Chapter 11, "Theory"). According to this view, whoever controls the **mise en scène**—the medium of the story—is the true "author" of a movie. The other collaborators are merely the director's technical assistants. No doubt the auteur critics exaggerated the primacy of the director, particularly in the United States, where many film directors were at the mercy of the Hollywood **studio** system, which tended to emphasize group work rather than individual expression and publicized **stars** rather than directors. Nevertheless, the auteur critics were especially interested in certain Hollywood directors, such as John Ford and Alfred Hitchcock, whose films reveal a distinctive personal vision despite the constraints of the studio system.

Even today, the most admired movies—from whatever country—tend to be directors' films. To refer to a movie as "good except for its direction" is as contradictory as referring to a play as "good except for its **script**." Of course we can enjoy a poorly directed movie or a badly written play, but what we enjoy are usually the secondary aspects of the art—a touching performance, a striking set. Such enjoyable elements generally represent the individual triumph of a gifted interpretive artist (actor, set designer, **cinematographer**, etc.) over the mediocrity of the dominant artist—the director in film, the writer in live theatre.

On the stage, the director is essentially an interpretive artist. If we see a poor production of *King Lear*, we don't dismiss Shakespeare's play, but only a specific interpretation of the play. True, the stage director creates certain patterns of movement, appropriate gestures for actors, and spatial relationships, but all of these visual elements take second place to the language of the script, which is created by the playwright. The theatrical director's relation to the text is similar to the stage actor's relation to the role: He or she can add much to what's written down, but what is contributed is usually secondary to the text itself.

On the other hand, screen directors have a good deal more control over the final product. They too dominate the preproduction activities but, unlike the stage director, the filmmaker controls virtually every aspect of the

1–8. *Stagecoach* **(U.S.A., 1939),** *directed by John Ford.*
Ford considered Monument Valley, Utah (pictured), as the "most complete, beautiful, and peaceful place on earth." He shot nine of his westerns here. During his long career, Ford worked for many studios, but most of his films explore the relations between people and nature in a distinctive lyrical style. *(United Artists)*

finished work as well. The degree of precision a film director can achieve is impossible on the stage, for movie directors can rephotograph people and objects until they get exactly what they want. Films communicate *primarily* through moving images, and it's the director who determines most of the visual elements: the choice of shots, **angles**, lighting effects, **filters**, optical effects, framing, composition, camera movements, and editing. Furthermore, the director usually authorizes the costume and set designs and the choice of locales. Even in the Hollywood studio system, when the director was often not involved in the preproduction and postproduction processes, the director's choices tended to determine the film's distinctive qualities.

In the cinema, the director converts three-dimensional space into a two-dimensional image of space. Even with **deep-focus** photography, "depth" is not literal **(1–9)**. But the flat image has certain advantages. A camera can be placed virtually anywhere, so the film director is not confined to a stationary set with a given number of "walls." The eye-level **long shot** more or less corresponds to the theatrical proscenium arch. But in movies, the **close-up** also constitutes a given space—in effect a cinematic "roomlet" with its own "walls" (the **frame**). Each shot, then, represents a new given space with different (and tem-

1–9. *Ikiru,* also known as *To Live* **(Japan, 1952),** *directed by Akira Kurosawa.*
In this deep-focus shot, the materials of three depth planes are precisely aligned to produce an ironic contrast. The protagonist (Takashi Shimura, whose picture adorns the Buddhist altar) was a lowly bureaucrat who did something really significant with his existence only in the final months of his life, when he realized he was dying of cancer. In the flashback portions of the movie, his battered hat is a symbol of his humility and dogged perseverance. His funeral wake (pictured) is a rigid, dismal affair, attended primarily by the deceased's fellow bureaucrats. The placement of the camera in this photo implicitly contrasts the unpretentious hat with the chagrined faces of the office workers and with the formal photograph and altar. *(Brandon Films)*

porary) confines. Furthermore, the movable camera permits the director to rearrange the "walls" many times for maximum expressiveness with no sacrifice of clarity. Thus, in film, a character can enter the frame from below, from above, from any side, and from any angle. By **dollying** or craning, a camera can also take us "into" a set, permitting objects to pass by us.

Most movies average well over a thousand shots. The film director can give us a half-dozen shots of the same object—some emphasizing clarity, others emphasizing expressiveness. Some shots can show a character with his or her back to the camera: The soundtrack guarantees the clarity of the character's speech. A character can be photographed through an obstruction of some kind—a pane of glass or the dense foliage of a forest. Because the cinematic shot need not be lengthy, clarity can be suspended temporarily in favour of expressiveness.

The director does not always have so much control over the film's meanings. In so-called "art cinema," directors like Ingmar Bergman (**1–23**), Akira Kurosawa (**1–9**), and Jean-Luc Godard (**2–3**) used film as a means of personal expression with little outside influence. But only the most successful Hollywood directors were able to exercise such control until the emergence in the 1970s of young filmmakers such as Steven Spielberg, Francis Ford Coppola and Martin Scorsese, who admired the great film artists of the past and achieved a similar command of their medium, often producing and writing as well as directing their films.

Of course, there are many films in which the director functions simply as a craftsman, following established conventions and adding little personal vision to the film. According to the *Cahiers du cinéma* critics, these directors are **metteurs en scène** rather than auteurs. Their films are often undistinguished; but we should not assume that only great directors make great films. As in many **genre** films (see Chapter 2), following the conventions can produce pleasurable and meaningful films, and some screenplays can generate important films with only a competent director.

THE SCREENWRITER

According to the auteur theory, great films are made by directors who use cinematic language much as a writer uses written language. Yet a fiction film usually has its origins in the written words of a screenplay, which includes the dialogue and outlines the action of the film before shooting begins. For this reason, the screenwriter has sometimes been regarded as the main "author" of a film. But generalizing about the writer's contribution in the moviemaking process is an exercise in futility because the writer's role varies immensely from film to film and from director to director. In the first place, some filmmakers have hardly bothered with scripts. Especially in the silent era, improvisation was the rule rather than the exception. Others used only the barest outlines.

Many of the greatest directors have written their own scripts: Cocteau, Eisenstein, Bergman, and Herzog, to name only a few. In the American cinema, there are also many writer–directors: Griffith, Chaplin, Stroheim, Huston, Welles, Mankiewicz, Wilder, Sturges, Woody Allen, and Coppola are among the most famous. The majority of important directors have taken a major hand in writing their scripts, but they bring in other writers to expand on their ideas. Fellini, Truffaut, and Kurosawa all worked in this manner. Surprisingly few major directors depend totally on others for their scripts (1–10).

The American studio system tended to encourage multiple authorship of scripts. Often writers had a certain specialty such as dialogue, comedy, construction, atmosphere, and so on. Some writers were best at doctoring weak scripts. Others were good idea people but lacked the skill to execute their ideas. In such collaborative enterprises, the screen credits are not always an accurate reflection of who contributed what to a movie. Furthermore, although many directors such as Hitchcock, Capra, and Lubitsch contributed a great deal to the final shape of their scripts, they rarely included their names in the credits, allowing the official writer to take it all.

For many years, American critics were inclined to believe that art must be solemn—if not actually dull—to be respectable. Indeed, even in the heyday of the Hollywood studio system, such intellectual writers as Dalton Trumbo, Carl Foreman, and Dore Schary enjoyed tremendous prestige because their scripts were filled with fine speeches dealing with Justice, Brotherhood, and Democracy.

1–10. *Umberto D (Italy, 1952), with Carlo Battisti (right), written by Cesare Zavattini, directed by Vittorio De Sica.*
Zavattini is the most famous scenarist of the Italian cinema, and one of its most important theorists. (See the section on neorealism in Chapter 11.) His best work was done in collaboration with De Sica, including such important works as *Shoeshine, Bicycle Thieves, Miracle in Milan, Umberto D, Two Women, The Garden of the Finzi-Continis*, and *A Brief Vacation*. De Sica worked in close collaboration with his scenarists. For example, the protagonist of this film, a retired government employee (Battisti), is a veiled portrait of the director's father, Umberto De Sica, to whom the film is dedicated.   *(Audio-Brandon Films)*

Not that these values aren't important. But to be effective artistically, ideas must be dramatized with tact and honesty, not parcelled out to the characters like high-sounding speeches on a patriotic holiday. For example, in the novel *The Grapes of Wrath*, John Steinbeck frequently praises the toughness of the Joad family. They have been thrown off their farm during the Great Depression and are forced to seek a new life in California, where conditions are even worse for them.

In John Ford's movie version, there is no narrator, so the characters must speak for themselves. Nunnally Johnson's screenplay is not devoid of ideas, but the ideas are expressed in the words of the characters. A good example is Ma Joad's comments to her husband in the final scene of the movie. They are in their shabby truck, driving to a new job—twenty days as fruit pickers. Pa Joad (Russell Simpson) admits to his wife (Jane Darwell) that for a while he thought the family was finished. She answers, "I know. That's what makes us tough. Rich fellas come up an' they die, an' their kids ain't no good, an' they die out. But we keep a-comin'. We're the people that live. They can't wipe us out. They can't lick us. We'll go on forever Pa, 'cause we're the people."

14

(Quoted from Johnson's script in *Twenty Best Film Plays*, Vol. I, eds. John Gassner and Dudley Nichols; New York: Garland Publishing, 1977.) The final image of the film follows: a thrilling **extreme long shot**, in which the fragile Joad vehicle merges imperceptibly with a procession of other dilapidated trucks and cars, forming an unbroken river of traffic—Ford's visual tribute to the courage and resilience of the human spirit.

Generally speaking, students, artists, and intellectuals are the individuals most likely to discuss ideas and abstractions without a sense of self-consciousness. To be convincing, eloquent language must be dramatically probable. We must believe that the words aren't just the writer's preachments dressed up as dialogue.

But there are always exceptions. *Casablanca*, for example, features a traditional love triangle, in which Ilsa (Ingrid Bergman) is torn between two men—her husband Victor Laszlo (Paul Henreid), a Resistance leader whom she deeply respects and admires, and Rick Blaine (Humphrey Bogart), the man she loves and will always love. Throughout the movie, Rick's comments are generally terse, sardonic, and hard-boiled. He's not a man given to making pretty speeches. But in the airport scene at the end of the film, his remarks to the woman he loves—and must give up—are overtly ideological:

1-11. *Twentieth Century* (U.S.A., 1934), *with John Barrymore and Carole Lombard, written by Ben Hecht and Charles MacArthur, based on their play, directed by Howard Hawks.* The legendary wit and ex-newspaperman Ben Hecht was perhaps the most admired Hollywood screenwriter of the big-studio era. His specialty was comedy—the more outrageous, the better. He delighted in satirizing American hick values. Conventional morality is shown to be as hypocritical as it is dull. Because the censorship code of his era insisted that heroes and heroines had to be upright and moral, he resolved to avoid writing about such paragons of respectability: "The thing to do was to skip the heroes and heroines," Hecht concluded, "to write a movie containing only villains and bawds. I would not have to tell any lies then."

(Columbia Pictures)

Inside of us we both know you belong to Victor. You're part of his work, the thing that keeps him going. If that plane leaves the ground and you're not with him, you'll regret it. . . . Maybe not today, maybe not tomorrow, but soon, and for the rest of your life. . . . Ilsa, I'm no good at being noble, but it doesn't take much to see that the problems of three little people don't amount to a hill of beans in this crazy world. Someday you'll understand that. Here's looking at you, kid. (Quoted from *Casablanca Script and Legend*, script by Julius and Philip Epstein and Howard Koch; Woodstock, N.Y.: The Overlook Press, 1973.)

Some filmmakers are at their best with talky scripts—provided it's scintillating talk, as in the best movies of Lina Wertmüller, Ingmar Bergman, and Woody Allen **(1–12)**. The French, Swedish, and British cinemas are also exceptionally literate. Among the important writers who have written for the screen in Britain are George Bernard Shaw, Graham Greene, Alan Sillitoe, John Osborne, Harold Pinter, David Storey, and Hanif Kureishi **(1–14)**.

1-12. *The Purple Rose of Cairo* (U.S.A., 1985), *with Jeff Daniels and Danny Aiello, written and directed by Woody Allen.*

Woody Allen is widely regarded as the most gifted writer–director of his generation, combining wit with romantic whimsy, poignancy with thought. Almost all of his movies are comedies, of virtually every type—satires, parodies, romantic comedies, fantasies, comedies of manners, and farces. He averages about one film per year. He has also written a number of stage plays and several volumes of humorous essays. Most of his essays originally appeared in the prestigious *New Yorker*, which has published the writings of the finest authors in the United States. The fertility of his invention is nowhere better illustrated than in this movie, a humorous and insightful treatment of the relation of life to art. *(Orion Pictures)*

1–13. *The King of Comedy* **(U.S.A., 1983),** *with Robert De Niro, directed by Martin Scorsese.* Ordinarily, clichés are the deadliest enemies of art. But this movie explores how clichés have become the quintessence of pop entertainment. De Niro plays Rupert Pupkin, an obnoxious egomaniac who's obsessed with becoming a celebrity and is resolutely convinced of his showbiz immortality. His conversations consist almost entirely of talk-show platitudes. His stand-up comedy act (pictured) is devoid of freshness, wit, or originality. Of course, he's a huge success with the public.   *(Twentieth Century–Fox)*

Despite the enormous importance that the script can play in a sound film, some directors scoff at the notion that a writer could be the dominant artist in the cinema. Antonioni once remarked that Dostoyevsky's *Crime and Punishment* was a rather ordinary crime thriller—the genius of the novel lies in how it's told, not in the subject matter per se. Certainly the large number of excellent movies based on routine or even mediocre books seems to bear out such a view.

Movie scripts seldom make for interesting reading, precisely because they are like blueprints of the finished product. Unlike a play, which usually can be read with pleasure, too much is missing in a screenplay. Even highly detailed scripts seldom offer us a sense of a film's mise en scène, one of the principal methods of expression at the director's disposal. With characteristic wit, Andrew Sarris has pointed out how the director's choice of shot—or the way in which the action is photographed—is the crucial element in most films:

> The choice between a close-up and a long-shot, for example, may quite often transcend the plot. If the story of Little Red Riding Hood is told with the Wolf in close-up and Little Red Riding Hood in long-shot, the director is concerned primarily with the emotional problems of a wolf with a compulsion to eat little girls. If Little Red Riding Hood is in close-up and the Wolf in long-shot, the emphasis is shifted to the emotional problems of vestigial virginity in a wicked world. Thus, two dif-

ferent stories are being told with the same basic anecdotal material. What is at stake in the two versions of Little Red Riding Hood are two contrasting directorial attitudes toward life. One director identifies more with the Wolf—the male, the compulsive, the corrupted, even evil itself. The second director identifies with the little girl—the innocence, the illusion, the ideal and hope of the race. Needless to say, few critics bother to make any distinction, proving perhaps that direction as creation is still only dimly understood. (Quoted from "The Fall and Rise of the Film Director," in *Interviews with Film Directors*; New York: Avon Books, 1967.)

Film scripts are rarely autonomous literary products; otherwise they would be published with greater frequency. The screenplays of a few prestigious filmmakers, like Woody Allen, Ingmar Bergman, and Federico Fellini, have reached print. But even these are merely linguistic approximations of the films themselves. Perhaps the worst kind of literary by-products of movies are "novelizations"—commissioned novel versions of popular films that are usually written by hired hacks to cash in on a movie's box-office popularity.

1–14. *My Beautiful Laundrette* **(Britain, 1985),** *with Gordon Warnecke and Daniel Day-Lewis, written by Hanif Kureishi, directed by Stephen Frears.*
One of Britain's most outspoken young writers (plays, fiction, and autobiography as well as screenplays), Hanif Kureishi enjoys shocking the staid literary establishment. His themes characteristically revolve around conflicts between cultures, races, classes, and sexes. Most of his characters are funny as well as bright. Despite being from different classes and ethnic backgrounds, the two leading characters in this film (pictured) are business partners and lovers. They're totally unapologetic about their sexuality, which is not treated as a big deal. Kureishi, who is half English and half Pakistani, is especially interested in minorities, people outside the English mainstream, which is male, white, and heterosexual. "Gay men and black men have been excluded from history," Kureishi has said. "They're trying to understand themselves. Like women, black people and gay people have been marginalized in society, lacking in power, ridiculed."   *(Orion Pictures)*

1–15. *Kolya* **(Czech Republic, 1997),** *with Zdenek Sverak and Andrej Chalimon, directed by Jan Sverak.*
Action and character might almost be viewed as natural enemies in a film's narrative. To get to know a character in depth, it's generally necessary to slow down the story's forward thrust. European filmmakers like Jan Sverak are widely regarded as masters of characterization, in part because the narrative is not forced—it's allowed to move at a realistic pace, as in *Kolya*. American movies are often criticized for piling on too much action, thus shortchanging the audience of any depth or richness or complexity in the characterization. Sometimes the only significant characterization in a routine American action film is provided by a star's iconography, a form of precharacterization that personality stars bring with them. *(Miramax Films)*

Screenplays are often modified by the actors who play the characters. This is especially true in scripts written for personality stars. Naturally their roles will usually include the qualities that make the star popular. For example, screenwriters who wrote for Gary Cooper knew that he was at his best when he said the least. In our own time, Clint Eastwood is famous for his terse one-liners: "Go ahead—make my day." Eastwood's characters, like Cooper's, are usually suspicious of people who are smooth talkers.

On the other hand some screenplays, like those of Joseph L. Mankiewicz, who was one of the most admired writer–directors of the Hollywood big-studio era, revel in the wit and verbal dexterity of highly articulate characters. Mankiewicz's finest work, *All About Eve*, features several brilliantly written roles. One of the best is the acid-tongued theatre critic, Addison Dewitt, played with bitchy *sang-froid* by George Sanders.

Most of the characters in *All About Eve* are well educated and literate. Those in *On the Waterfront*, which was written by Budd Schulberg, are working-class longshoremen. Such characters usually attempt to conceal their emotions behind a macho façade. But in scenes of intense emotions, the words, though simple, are powerful.

Good dialogue is often the result of having a good ear—for catching the correct rhythms of speech, the right choice of words, the length of people's sentences, the jargon, slang, or swear words people use. The foul-mouthed characters in Quentin Tarantino's *Reservoir Dogs* (7–29) speak in torrents of four-letter words, the linguistic equivalent of the violence of their lives. In contexts such as these, polite or laundered prose would constitute bad writing.

THE SPECTATOR

A film's director and its screenwriter are usually the primary (but not the only) creators of its meanings, but the other major collaborator in the production of meaning is the spectator.

It's impossible to understand a movie without being actively engaged in a dynamic interplay with its images and its narrative logic. Most of us have been watching movies and television for so long that we're hardly aware of our instantaneous adjustments to an unfolding **plot**. We absorb auditory and visual stimuli at an incredibly rapid rate. Like a complex computer, our brain click-clicks away in many language systems simultaneously: photographic, spatial, **kinetic**, vocal, histrionic, musical, sartorial, and so on.

But in the American cinema especially, all the other language systems are subordinated to the plot, the structural spine of virtually all American fiction films. Critic David Bordwell and others have explored how the spectator is constantly interacting with a movie's narrative. We attempt to superimpose our sense of order and coherence on the film's world. In most cases, we bring a set of expectations to a movie even before we've seen it. Our knowledge of a given era or genre leads us to expect a predictable set of variables. For example, most westerns take place in the late nineteenth century and are set in the American western frontier. From books, TV, and other westerns, we have a rough knowledge of how frontier people were supposed to dress and behave.

When narratives fail to act according to tradition, **convention**, or our sense of history, as in Mel Brooks's *Blazing Saddles* (1–16), we are forced to reassess our cognitive methods and our attitude toward the narrative. Either we adjust to the author's presentation, or we reject the offending innovation as inappropriate, crude, or self-indulgent.

Our prior knowledge of a film's star also defines its narrative parameters. We wouldn't expect to see Clint Eastwood in a Shakespearean adaptation, or even in a conventional love story. Eastwood's expertise is in action genres, especially westerns and contemporary urban crime stories. With personality stars especially, we can guess the essential nature of a film's narrative in advance. With **actor stars** like Meryl Streep, however, we are less certain about what to expect, for Streep's range is extraordinarily broad.

Audiences also judge a film in advance by the connotations of its title. A movie with a moronic title like *Attack of the Killer Bimbos* is not likely to be chosen as a Gala Presentation at the Toronto International Film Festival. On the other hand, *Lady Windermere's Fan* would probably not play at the local mall the-

1–16. *Blazing Saddles* (U.S.A., 1973), *directed by Mel Brooks.*
Like most of Brooks's works, *Blazing Saddles* is a parody of a popular genre, in this case, the western. Throughout the movie, he constantly undermines the narrative by introducing elements that are out of period, like Madeline Kahn's deadpan performance as Lili von Schtupp, the Teutonic Titwillow, a delicious parody of Marlene Dietrich. At the end of the film, Brooks deliberately sabotages his narrative's shaky credibility by having a cowboy chase spill over into a totally different genre—a sophisticated 1930s-type dance number *à la* Busby Berkeley. *(Warner Bros.)*

atre because of its somewhat effete, aristocratic-sounding title. Of course there are always exceptions. *Sammy and Rosie Get Laid* sounds like a porno film, but it's actually a respected (and sexy) British social comedy. Its title is deliberately aggressive, a bit crude. It's meant to be.

Once a movie begins, we begin to define its narrative limits. The style of the credits and the accompanying score help us to determine the tone of the picture. In the early exposition scenes, the filmmaker sets up the **story** variables and mood, establishing the premise that will drive the narrative forward. The beginning scenes imply how the narrative will be developed, and where it's likely to end up.

The opening expository scenes also establish the internal "world" of the story—what's possible, what's probable, what's not very likely, and so on. In retrospect, there should be no loose threads in a story if the implied author has done a careful job of foreshadowing. In *E.T.: The Extra-Terrestrial,* for example, Spielberg prepares us for the supernatural events that occur in the middle and later portions of the movie because the opening scene (showing us how E.T. got left behind by his spaceship) establishes supernaturalism as a narrative variable (2–23).

When a critic asked the radical innovator Jean-Luc Godard if he believed that a movie should have a beginning, middle, and end, the iconoclastic filmmaker replied: "Yes—but not necessarily in that order." The opening exposition scenes of most movies establish the time frame of the story—whether it will unfold in **flashbacks**, in the present, or in some combination. The exposition also establishes the ground rules about fantasy scenes, dreams, and the stylistic variables associated with these levels of the story (1–17).

An elaborate game is played out between a cinematic narrative and the spectator. While watching a movie, we must sort out irrelevant details, hypothesize, test our hypotheses, retreat if necessary, adapt, formulate explanations, and so on. The spectator is constantly subjecting the narrative to questions. Why does the heroine do that? Why does her boyfriend respond that way? What will the mother do now? And so on.

We can analyze the choices made by a film's director and screenwriter to discover how they want the spectator to respond. Their decisions about camera angles or plot construction, for example, provide cues that allow us to envisage an implied spectator. However, spectators do not always react as they are expected to, and there is now a growing interest in finding out how actual spectators respond to films. Historians investigate archives for evidence of what

1–17. *8¹/₂* (Italy, 1963), *with Sandra Milo, directed by Federico Fellini.*

Although it is one of the most admired movies in the history of the cinema, Fellini's masterpiece features a plot that's diabolically baroque. Most viewers are unable to comprehend it all on first viewing because it's constantly shifting levels of consciousness without warning. Fantasies spill over onto reality, which splashes over memories, which fuse with dreams, which turn into nightmares, which... *(Embassy Pictures)*

1-18. *My Life as a Dog* (Sweden, 1985), *with Anton Glanzelius (centre), directed by Lasse Hallstrom.*

Some movies are so unusual that it's virtually impossible to predict where the plot will lead. In this film, for example, the young hero is separated from his parents and moves in with an eccentric uncle and aunt in a remote village. His escapades in the country are bizarre, funny, and totally unpredictable.   *(Skouras Pictures)*

fans thought of stars and how the studios used audience research to plan their publicity campaigns; other researchers use interviews and devise question-naires to discover how different spectators interpret films to suit their own needs and interests (see Chapter 11).

TIME, SPACE, AND LANGUAGE

The interplay between film and spectator is a complex one but shaped by the properties of the medium in its treatment of time and space. The basic unit of construction in movies is the shot. Because the average shot lasts only ten or fifteen seconds (and can be as brief as a fraction of a second), the cinematic shot can lengthen or shorten our experience of time. Temporal dislocations like the flashback are rare in the live theatre, but commonplace in movies.

In the live theatre, the viewer remains in a stationary position. The distance between the audience and the stage is constant. Of course an actor can move closer to an audience, but compared with the fluid space in the cinema, distance variation in the live theatre is negligible. The film viewer, on the other hand, identifies with the camera's **lens**, which is not immobilized in a chair. This identification permits the viewer to "move" in any direction and from any distance. An **extreme close-up** allows us to count the lashes of an eyelid; the extreme long shot permits us to see several kilometres in each direction. In short, the cinema allows the spectator to feel mobile.

In the live theatre, space is three-dimensional, is occupied by tangible people and objects, and is therefore more realistic; that is, our perception of space is essentially the same as in real life. The living presence of actors, with their subtle interactions—both with other actors and the audience—is impossible to duplicate in film. Movies provide us with a two-dimensional image of space and objects, and no interaction exists between the screen actors and the audience. For this reason, nudity is not so controversial an issue on the screen as in the live theatre, for on stage the naked people are real, whereas in movies they're "only pictures" **(1–19)**.

1–19. *A Winter Tan* (Canada, 1987), *with Erando Gonzalez and Jackie Burroughs, directed by Burroughs, Louise Clark, John Walker, Aerlyn Weissman, and John Frizzell.*

Movies make bodies seem intensely present even though the actors are physically absent. Looking at bodies in ways that we normally cannot in real life is one of the pleasures of film-going. But who gets to look at whom? Sexual conventions change over time; nowadays nudity is fairly common in movies, but women are more likely to be seen nude than men. The naked body can act as a metaphor, as in Burroughs' compelling performance as Maryse Holder, an American woman who died in Mexico, where she had gone in search of sexual adventure. Burroughs' frequently naked body stresses the character's lack of inhibitions and the vulnerability that this brings, while the spectator is left to grapple with the reverse sexism and racism of her treatment of Mexican men as objects.   *(John B. Frizzell)*

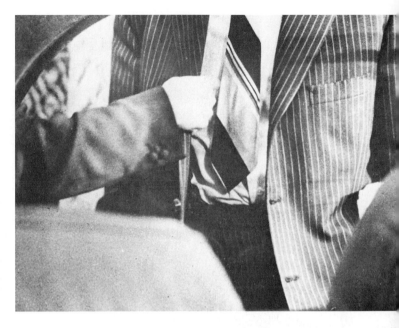

1–20. *Pickpocket* **(France, 1959),** *directed by Robert Bresson.*
In the live drama, if a small prop (like a wallet) is important, it must be highlighted conspicuously or the audience will fail to notice its existence, much less its importance. In the cinema, small articles can be isolated from their context. In this photo, Bresson captures a pickpocket's swift stroke as he lifts a wallet from a pedestrian on a busy walkway. *(New Yorker Films)*

The stage player interacts with viewers, establishing a delicate rapport with each different audience. The screen player, on the other hand, is inexorably fixed on celluloid: He or she can't readjust to each audience, for the worlds of the screen and the viewer aren't connected and continuous as they are in live theatre.

The human being is central to the aesthetic of the theatre: Words must be recited by people, conflicts must be embodied by actors. The cinema is not so dependent on humans. The aesthetic of film is based on photography, and anything that can be photographed can be the subject matter of a movie. One should not assume from this that the best method of adapting a play for the screen is to "open it up"—to substitute exterior locations for interiors. Cinema doesn't always mean extreme long shots, sweeping **pans**, and flashy editing. Hitchcock once observed that many filmed versions of plays fail precisely because the tight, compact structure of the original is lost when the film director "loosens it up" with inappropriate cinematic techniques. Particularly when a play emphasizes a sense of confinement, either physical or psychological—and a great many of them do—the best adapters respect the spirit of the original by finding film equivalents (see **1–21**).

FIGURATIVE COMPARISONS

In his essay "La Caméra-Stylo," Alexandre Astruc observed that one of the traditional problems of film has been its difficulty in expressing thought and ideas. The invention of sound, of course, was an enormous advantage to

1-21.   *Being at Home with Claude* (Canada, 1992), *with Jacques Godin, Roy Dupuis, and Gaston Lepage, directed by Jean Beaudin.*
In the one-act play by René-Daniel Dubois on which this film is based, a male prostitute confesses to the police that he has killed his lover and a detective tries to find out exactly what happened. The play respects the unities of time, space, and action, but Beaudin adds a fast-paced prologue in black and white which shows the bloody killing. Much of the film takes place in the same confined interior setting as the play but, by opening out the action at the beginning, Beaudin shifts the focus of interest away from what happened to why it happened.   *(Alliance Communications)*

filmmakers, for with spoken language they could express virtually any kind of abstract thought. But film directors also wanted to explore the possibilities of the image as a conveyor of abstract ideas. Even before the sound era, filmmakers had devised a number of nonverbal figurative techniques.

A figurative technique can be defined as an artistic device that suggests abstract ideas through comparison, either implied or overt. There are a number of these techniques in both literature and cinema. The most common are **motifs**, **symbols**, and **metaphors**. In actual practice, there's a considerable amount of overlapping between these terms. All of them are "symbolic" in the sense that an object or event means something beyond its literal significance. Perhaps the most pragmatic method of differentiating these techniques is their degree of obtrusiveness. Instead of locking each of these terms into an airtight compartment, however, we ought to view them as general demarcations, with motifs representing the least obtrusive extreme, metaphors representing the most conspicuous, and each category overlapping somewhat with its neighbour.

1–22. *La Nuit américaine ("Day for Night,"* **France, 1973),** *with François Truffaut (leather jacket), directed by Truffaut.*
Film titles are chosen with great deliberation because they are meant to embody the central concept behind a movie. Film titles, in short, are symbolic. The original-language title of this film is *La Nuit américaine,* "The American Night." It reflects Truffaut's great love for American culture, especially its cinema, and deals with the making of an "old-fashioned" kind of movie—the kind they made in Hollywood in the 1940s. (Truffaut even includes a tender homage to *Citizen Kane.*) "La nuit américaine" is also what the French call the day-for-night filter, which converts sunlit scenes into nighttime scenes. The filter transforms reality— makes it magical. For Truffaut, cinema is magic. *(Warner Bros.)*

Motifs are so totally integrated within the realistic texture of a film that we can almost refer to them as submerged or invisible symbols. A motif can be a technique, an object, or anything that's systematically repeated in a movie yet doesn't call attention to itself. Even after repeated viewings, a motif is not always apparent, for its symbolic significance is never permitted to emerge or detach itself from its context **(1–23).**

Symbols can also be palpable things, but they imply additional meanings that are relatively apparent to the sensitive observer. Furthermore, the symbolic meanings of these things can shift with the dramatic context. A good example of the shifting implications of a symbol can be seen in the uncut version of Kurosawa's *The Seven Samurai* **(1–24).** In this movie, a young samurai and a peas-

 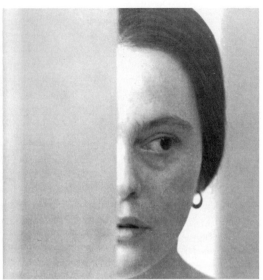

a   b

1–23.   *Cries and Whispers* **(Sweden, 1972),** *with Liv Ullmann (a) and Kari Sylwan (b), writ-ten and directed by Ingmar Bergman.*
A recurrent motif in this movie is the human face split in two, suggesting self-division, the hidden self, the public versus the private self.   *(New World Pictures)*

ant girl are attracted to each other, but their class differences present insurmountable barriers. In a scene that takes place late at night, the two accidentally meet. Kurosawa emphasizes their separation by keeping them in separate frames, a raging outdoor fire acting as a kind of barrier (**a** and **b**). But their attraction is too strong, and they then appear in the same shot, the fire between them now suggesting the only obstacle, yet paradoxically also suggesting the sexual passion they both feel (**c**). They draw toward each other, and the fire is now to one side, its sexual symbolism dominating (**d**). They go inside a hut, and the light from the fire outside emphasizes the eroticism of the scene (**e**). As they begin to make love in a dark corner of the hut, the shadows cast by the fire's light on the reeds of the hut seem to streak across their bodies (**f**). Suddenly, the girl's father discovers the lovers, and the billowing flames of the fire suggest his moral outrage (**g**). He is so incensed that he must be restrained by the samurai chief, both of them almost washed out visually by the intensity of the fire's light (**h**). It begins to rain, and the sorrowing young samurai walks away despondently (**i**). At the end of the sequence Kurosawa offers a close-up of the fire as the rain extinguishes its flames (**j**).

A metaphor is usually defined as a comparison of some kind that cannot be literally true. Two terms not ordinarily associated are yoked together, producing a sense of literal incongruity. "Poisonous time," "torn with grief," "devoured by love" are all verbal metaphors involving symbolic rather than literal descriptions. Editing is a frequent source of metaphors in film, for two shots can be linked together to produce a third, and symbolic, idea. This is the basis of Eisenstein's theory of **montage**. In *October,* for example, he satirized the fears and anxieties of an antirevolutionary politician by **intercutting** shots of a "heavenly choir" of harpists with shots of the politician delivering his cowardly speech. The row of pretty blonde harp players is brought in "from nowhere"; that is, they are certainly not found in the locale (a meeting hall) but are introduced solely for metaphoric purposes. Special-effects cinematography is also used to create metaphoric ideas. For example, through the use of the **optical printer**, two or more objects can be yoked together in the same frame to create ideas that have no literal existence in reality **(1–25)**. Cinematic metaphors are always somewhat obtrusive; unlike motifs and most symbols, metaphors are less integrated contextually, less "realistic" in terms of our ordinary perceptions.

There are two other kinds of figurative techniques in film and literature: **allegory** and **allusions**. The first is seldom used in movies because it tends toward simplemindedness. What's usually involved in this technique is a total avoidance of realism and probability. A correspondence exists between a character or situation and a symbolic idea or complex of ideas. One of the most famous examples of allegory is the character of Death in Bergman's *The Seventh Seal* **(1–5)**. There's not much ambiguity involved in what the character is supposed to symbolize. Allegorical narratives are especially popular in the German cinema. For example, virtually all the works of Werner Herzog deal with the idea of life in general, the nature of the human condition in broadly symbolic terms.

An allusion is a common type of literary analogy. It's an implied reference, usually to a well-known event, person, or work of art. The protagonist of Hawks's *Scarface* was modelled on the gangster Al Capone (who had a well-publicized scar in the shape of a cross on his cheek), an allusion that wasn't lost on audiences of the time. Filmmakers often draw on religious mythology for their allusions. For example, the Judeo-Christian myth of the Garden of Eden is used in such disparate works as *The Garden of the Finzi-Continis* **(4–31)**, *Days of Heaven, How Green Was My Valley* **(4–19)**, and *The Tree of the Wooden Clogs* **(11–4)**.

In the cinema, an overt reference or allusion to another movie, director, or memorable shot is sometimes called a **homage**. The cinematic homage is a kind of quote, the director's graceful tribute to a colleague or established master. Homages were popularized by Godard and Truffaut, whose movies are profuse in such tributes. In Godard's *A Woman Is a Woman,* for example, two decidedly nonmusical characters burst out in spontaneous song and dance while expressing their desire to appear in an MGM musical by Gene Kelly, choreographed by Bob Fosse. Fosse's *All That Jazz* contains many homages to his idol Fellini, and especially to *8½.* Steven Spielberg often pays tribute to his two idols, Walt Disney and Alfred Hitchcock.

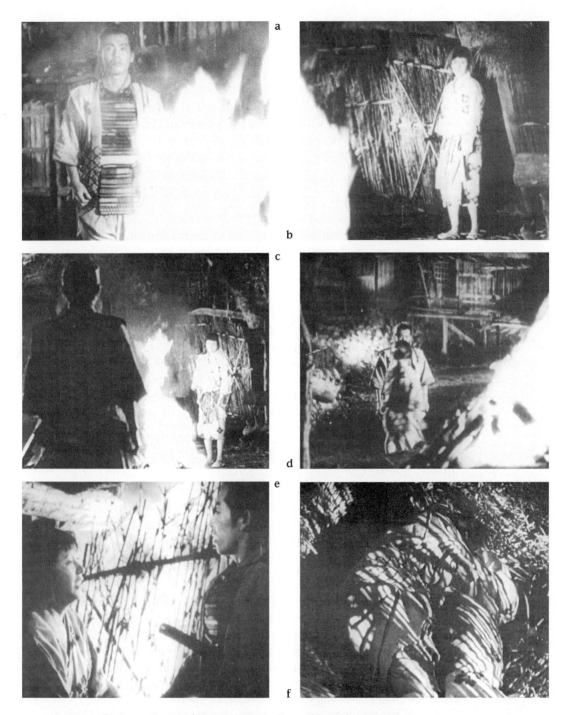

1–24. *The Seven Samurai* (Japan, 1954), *directed by Akira Kurosawa.*
Realistic films tend to use symbols less densely than formalist movies, and the symbolism is almost always contextually probable. For example, in addition to being a symbol, the fire in this scene is also a fire.   *(Toho International)*

g

h

i

j

POINT OF VIEW

The techniques chosen by the filmmakers constitute the film's style and establish its point of view. In films, of course, unlike novels, we actually see the characters and events depicted, and point of view is thus literally a matter of the angle and distance from which we see them. How we see things may also be affected, as in the novel, by the ways in which they are presented to us by a narrator, who should not be confused with the director or the screenwriter.

The first-person narrator tells his or her own story. Many films use first-person narrative techniques, but only sporadically. The cinematic equivalent to the "voice" of the literary narrator is the "eye" of the camera, and this difference is an important one. In literature, the distinction between the narrator and the reader is clear: It's as if the reader were listening to a friend telling a story. In film, however, the viewer identifies with the lens, and thus tends to fuse with the narrator. To produce first-person narration in film, the camera would have to record all the action through the eyes of the character, which, in effect, would also make the viewer the protagonist.

1–25. *Psycho (U.S.A., 1960), directed by Alfred Hitchcock.*
Cinematic metaphors can be created through the use of special effects, as in this dissolve which yields the final shot of the film—the dredging up of a car from a swamp. Three images are dissolved: **(1)** a shot of a catatonic youth (Anthony Perkins) looking directly at us; **(2)** a duplicate shot of his mother's skeleton, whose skull flickers briefly beneath her son's features and whose personality he has now assumed; and **(3)** a heavy chain which seems anchored to his/her heart, hauling up the murder victim's car which contains her corpse.   *(Paramount Pictures)*

In *The Lady in the Lake,* Robert Montgomery attempted to use the first-person camera throughout the film. It was an interesting experiment, but a failure, for several reasons. In the first place, the director was forced into a number of absurdities. Having the characters address the camera was not too much of a problem, for **point-of-view shots** are common in most movies. However, there were several actions where the device simply broke down. When a woman walked up to the hero and kissed him, for example, she had to slink toward the camera and begin to embrace it while her face came closer to the lens. Similarly, when the hero was involved in a fist fight, the antagonist literally had to attack the camera, which jarred appropriately whenever the "narrator" was dealt a blow. The problem with the exclusive use of the first-person camera, then, is its literalness. Furthermore, it tends to create a sense of frustration in the viewer, who wants to see the hero. In fiction, we get to know people through their words, through their judgments and values, which are reflected in their language. But in movies, we get to know a character by seeing how he or she reacts to people and events. Unless the director breaks the first-person camera convention, we can never see the hero, and can see only what he sees.

1–26. *The Lady from Shanghai* (U.S.A., 1948), *with Rita Hayworth, Orson Welles, and Everett Sloane, directed by Welles.*
Voice-over commentaries are commonplace in the genre known as film noir. Movies of this type often feature flashback images of the past accompanied by a present-tense off-screen narrator who tells us how he managed to get himself in such a desperate crisis. This film is narrated by Orson Welles, who plays an innocent and not-very-bright sailor who lives to tell his tale—just barely.   *(Columbia Pictures)*

The **omniscient point of view** is often associated with the nineteenth-century novel. Generally, such narrators are not participants in a story but are all-knowing observers who supply the reader with all the facts he or she needs to know to appreciate the story.

Omniscient narration is almost inevitable in film. Each time the director moves the camera—either within a shot or between shots—we are offered a new point of view from which to evaluate the scene. The filmmaker can cut easily from a subjective point-of-view shot (first person) to a variety of objective shots. He or she can concentrate on a single reaction (close-up) or the simultaneous reactions of several characters (long shot). Within a matter of seconds, the film director can show us a cause and an effect, an action and a reaction. He or she can connect various time periods and locations almost instantaneously (**parallel editing**), or literally superimpose different time periods (**dissolve** or **multiple exposure**). The omniscient camera can be a dispassionate observer, as it is in many of Chaplin's films, or it can be a witty commentator—an evaluator of events—as it often is in Hitchcock's films or those of Lubitsch.

1–27. *Nashville* (U.S.A., 1975), *with Lily Tomlin and Robert Doqui, directed by Robert Altman.* Throughout the 1970s, Altman revolutionized filmmaking with his improvisational techniques. Though the screenplay to *Nashville* is credited to Joan Tewkesbury, in fact she never wrote a conventional script. As she explained, "What you have to do for a director like Bob is to provide an environment in which he can work." For example, *Nashville* is structured mosaically, tracing the activities of twenty-four eccentric characters over a five-day period in the city of Nashville, the heart of the country music industry. One wag referred to the film as "twenty-four characters in search of a movie." Tewkesbury created many of the characters in sketch form, then mapped out what each major character would be doing at any given time. Most of the dialogue and details for the actions were created by the actors. They even composed their own songs. "It's like jazz," Altman explained. "You're not planning any of this that you film. You're capturing."   *(Paramount Pictures)*

While the point of view of the camera is of prime importance in film, many films do employ **voice-over** narrators who provide information and commentary. Some critics regard this technique as uncinematic, and it is usually avoided in classical cinema because it supposedly violates the rule that style should not call attention to itself. Voice-over narration can be first person or omniscient and is often much more than an easy device for providing essential information about the story. In *The Lady from Shanghai,* Orson Welles uses a first-person narrator who reflects on the naive mistakes that led to his involvement in a web of mystery and intrigue **(1–26)**. Since Welles, who directed and wrote the film, also plays the main character and thus speaks the narration, this is an especially complex case of film authorship. Welles also acts as voice-over narrator in *The Magnificent Ambersons*, but in this film he provides an omniscient and detached perspective on the decline of an aristocratic family **(12–36)**.

The arrangement of images and sounds to create a film's point of view involves all the components of film language. In the most familiar kinds of film, film language is used to tell a story and—as the discussion of narration has already shown—it is difficult to separate film language from storytelling in these films. Before looking more closely at the specific technical processes that go into the making of a film, we need to discuss the different forms that film stories can take.

Further Reading

Bordwell, David, *Narration in the Fiction Film* (Madison: University of Wisconsin Press, 1985). The fullest discussion of the role of the spectator.

Braudy, Leo, *The World in a Frame: What We See in Films* (Garden City: Anchor Press, 1976). Thoughtful account of film form.

Harcourt, Peter, *Six European Directors* (Harmondsworth: Penguin, 1974). Discussion of directors in relation to their cultural contexts.

Jacobs, Lewis, ed., *The Movies as Medium* (New York: Farrar, Straus & Giroux, 1970). Collection of essays by critics and filmmakers.

Kawin, Bruce F., *Mindscreen: Bergman, Godard, and First-Person Film* (Princeton: Princeton University Press, 1978). Challenging discussion of storytelling in film.

Nowell-Smith, Geoffrey, ed., *The Oxford History of World Cinema* (Oxford: Oxford University Press, 1996). Exhaustive collection of essays on the history of the medium.

Whittock, Trevor, *Metaphor and Film* (Cambridge: Cambridge University Press, 1990). Discussion of film metaphors using philosophical, linguistic and psychological approaches.

Wilson, George M., *Narration in Light: Studies in Cinematic Point of View* (Baltimore: Johns Hopkins University Press, 1986). Theoretical emphasis.

STORY 2

Narratives are composed in order to reward, modify,
frustrate, or defeat the perceiver's search for coherence.
　　　　　　　　　　　　—DAVID BORDWELL

SUMMARY

Stories: showing and telling. Narratology. Who's telling the story? Voice-over narrators—characters as storytellers. Realistic, classical, and formalist narratives. Story versus plot. Classical narrative structure: shaping the conflict, motivating the action. The narrative elegance of Buster Keaton's *The General*. Realistic narratives. Realism as a style: the illusion of being "lifelike." Slice-of-life, open-ended stories. The pretence of authorial neutrality. Realism's tradition of "shocking" exposés. Formalistic narratives: the importance of pattern and design as values in themselves. Intrusive narrators: brazen manipulation of the storytelling apparatus. Literary adaptations. Genre and myth. Screwball comedies, coming-of-age films, musicals, science fiction. The need to repeat: genre cycles. Primitive, classical, revisionist, and parodic phases of a genre's evolution. Jung and Freud. The social need for myths. Tone: the role of acting, genre, narration, and music in establishing the film's tone.

Since ancient times, people have been intrigued by the seductive powers of storytelling. In *The Poetics*, Aristotle distinguished between two types of fictional narratives: *mimesis* (showing) and *diegesis* (telling). *Mimesis* is the province of live theatre, where the events "tell themselves." *Diegesis*, the province of the literary epic and the novel, is a story told by a narrator who is sometimes reliable, sometimes not. Cinema combines both forms of storytelling and hence is a more complex medium, with a wider range of narrative techniques at its disposal.

NARRATIVE

Scholars in modern times have also studied narrative forms, with most of the focus devoted to literature, film, and drama. Narratology, as this new interdisciplinary field has been called since the 1980s, is a study of how stories work, how we make sense of the raw materials of a narrative, how we fit them together to form a coherent whole. It is also the study of different narrative structures, storytelling strategies, aesthetic conventions, types of stories (**genres**), and their symbolic implications.

In traditional terms, narratologists are interested in the "rhetoric" of storytelling; that is, the forms that "message senders" use to communicate with "message receivers." In cinema, a problem with this triadic communications model is determining who the sender is. The implied author is the filmmaker. However, many stories are not created by a single storyteller. Multiple authorship of scripts is common, especially in the United States, where the story is often pieced together by producers, directors, writers, and **stars**—a truly joint enterprise. Even prestigious filmmakers like Fellini, Kurosawa, and Truffaut preferred collaborating with others in creating the events of a **story**.

2–1. *eXistenZ* **(Canada 1999),** *with Jennifer Jason Leigh, directed by David Cronenberg.*

Many recent films reflect the fragmentation of identity in a society saturated with media images. In these films, the plot often refers to story events that take place on different levels of reality. Modern teenagers find themselves in a 1950s sitcom in *Pleasantville*, a man grows up inside a TV show in *The Truman Show*, characters travel through computer programs in *The Matrix*, and a game designer (Leigh) uses her "bioport" to enter the simulated worlds that she has created in Cronenberg's playful science-fiction film. We are often unsure whether events are taking place inside or outside the game as she seeks to evade the traps laid by her enemies, referred to as "realists."

(Alliance Atlantis)

2–2. *My Left Foot* **(Ireland, 1989),** *with Ruth McCabe and Daniel Day-Lewis, directed by Jim Sheridan.*

The biography film—or biopic, as it's known in the colourful argot of the trade—is a story of a famous and/or interesting real person, in this case, Christy Brown (Day-Lewis), a feisty Irish writer who was born with cerebral palsy and could write only with his left foot. The film is based on Brown's own autobiography and refuses to be the glib purveyor of disease-of-the-week clichés that cheapen many examples of this subgenre. Instead, we get to know a man who is passionate, funny, gifted, hard-drinking, hard-assed, and hard as nails when anyone crosses him or tells him what he can't accomplish.   *(Miramax Films)*

2–3. *Masculin-Féminin* **(France, 1966),** *with Jean-Pierre Léaud and Chantal Goya, directed by Jean-Luc Godard.*
"I considered myself an essayist," Godard said, "producing essays in novel form or novels in essay form: only instead of writing, I film them." Godard's cinematic essays are a frontal attack on the dominance of classical cinema. "The Americans are good at storytelling," he noted, "the French are not. Flaubert and Proust can't tell stories. They do something else. So does the cinema. I prefer to use a kind of tapestry, a background on which I can embroider on my own ideas." Instead of scripts, Godard set up dramatic situations, then asked his actors to improvise their dialogue, as in this interview scene—a technique he derived from the documentary movement called cinéma vérité. He intersperses these scenes with digressions, opinions, and jokes. Above all, he wanted to capture the spontaneity of the moment, which he believed was more authentic when he and his actors had to fend for themselves, without the security of a script. "If you know in advance everything you are going to do, it isn't worth doing," Godard insisted. "If a show is all written down, what is the point of filming it? What use is cinema if it trails after literature?" See also Louis D. Giannetti, "Godard's *Masculine-Feminine:* The Cinematic Essay," in *Godard and Others: Essays in Film Form* (Cranbury, N.J.: Fairleigh Dickinson University Press, 1975). *(Columbia Pictures)*

The problem of the elusive film author is complicated when a movie has a **voice-over** narration **(2–4).** Usually this off-screen narrator is also a character in the story and hence has a vested interest in "helping" us interpret the events. A film's narrator is not necessarily neutral. Nor is he or she necessarily the filmmaker's mouthpiece. Sometimes the narrator—as in the **first-person** novel—is the main character of a movie. (For a fuller discussion of these ideas, see "Point of View" in Chapter 1 and the "Spoken Language" section in Chapter 7).

Narration also differs according to a movie's style. In **realistic** films, the implied author is virtually invisible. The events "speak for themselves," as they do in most stage plays. The story seems to unfold automatically, usually in chronological sequence.

In **classical** narrative structures, we are generally aware of a shaping hand in the storyline. Boring gaps in the narrative are edited out by a discreet storyteller, who maintains a low profile yet still keeps the action on track, moving toward a specific destination—the resolution of the story's central conflict.

In **formalistic** narratives, the author is overtly manipulative, sometimes scrambling the chronology of the story or heightening or restructuring events to maximize a thematic idea. The story is told from a subjective perspective, as in Oliver Stone's polemical *JFK* (**9–1**).

Narratology is often arcane, and occasionally incomprehensible, because of its abstract language and jargon. Exotic terms are often used to describe traditional concepts. For example, the differences between a story and its **plot** structure (that is, between a narrative's content and its form) can be expressed in a bewildering assortment of terms. *Story* versus *discourse* are favoured by many American scholars. Others prefer *histoire* versus *discours*, *mythos* versus *logos*, or *fabula* versus *syuzhet*.

What are the differences between story and plot? The story can be defined as the general subject matter, the raw materials of a dramatic action in chronological sequence. The plot, on the other hand, involves the storyteller's method of superimposing a structural pattern over the story.

The implied author motivates the characters and provides a cause–effect logic to the sequence of events. Peter Brooks defines plot as "the design and intention of narrative, what shapes a story and gives it a certain direction or intention of meaning." In short, plot involves the implied author's **point of view** as well as the structuring of the scenes into an aesthetic pattern.

2–4. *Drugstore Cowboy* (U.S.A., 1989), *with Kelly Lynch, James Le Gros, Heather Graham, and Matt Dillon, directed by Gus Van Sant.*
Set in the 1970s, this movie explores the outlaw lifestyle of four young drug addicts who rob pharmacies to feed their habits. They are almost continuously on the move, not daring to settle down to a fixed routine. Their life has no order, and neither does the narrative structure, which is held together by Dillon's voice-over commentary. Without the explanatory narration, which provides the spectator with drug lore, street wisdom, and psychological insights into the other characters, the events of the story would seem confusing, contradictory, sometimes irrational—just like the lives of the people he describes. See also Sarah Kozloff, *Invisible Storytellers* (Berkeley: University of California Press, 1988), which analyzes voice-over narration in American fiction films. *(Avenue Pictures)*

THE CLASSICAL PARADIGM

The classical paradigm (2–5) is a term invented by scholars to describe a certain kind of narrative structure that has dominated fiction film production ever since the second decade of the twentieth century. It's by far the most popular type of story organization, especially in the United States, where it reigns virtually unchallenged. The model is called "classical" because it's a norm of actual practice, not necessarily because of a high degree of artistic excellence. In other words, bad movies as well as good ones use this narrative formula.

Derived from live theatre, the classical paradigm is a set of conventions, not rules. This narrative model is based on a conflict between a protagonist, who initiates the action, and an antagonist, who resists it. Most films in this form begin with an implied dramatic question. We want to know how the protagonist will get what he or she wants in the face of considerable opposition. The following **scenes** intensify this conflict in a rising pattern of action. This

---

2–5.   The classical paradigm.

Aristotle implicitly suggested the structure of classical drama in *The Poetics*, but it was not until the nineteenth century that the inverted V structure was diagrammed by the German scholar Gustav Freytag. This type of narrative structure begins with an overt conflict, which is increasingly intensified with the rising action of the following scenes. Details that don't relate to this conflict are eliminated or kept incidental. The battle between the main character and his or her antagonists reaches its highest pitch in the climax. In the resolution, the strands of the story are tied up and life returns to normal with a closing off of the action.

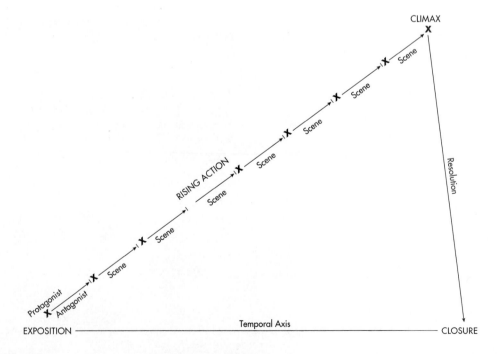

escalation is treated in terms of cause-effect, with each scene implying a link to the next.

The conflict builds to its maximum tension in the climax. Here, the protagonist and antagonist clash overtly. One wins, the other loses. After their confrontation, the dramatic intensity subsides in the resolution. The story ends with some kind of formal closure—traditionally a wedding or a dance in comedies, a death in tragedies, a reunion or return to normal in dramas. The final **shot**—because of its privileged position—is often meant to be a philosophical overview of some kind, a summing up of the significance of the previous material.

The classical paradigm emphasizes dramatic unity, plausible motivation, and coherence of its constituent parts. Each shot is seamlessly elided to the next in an effort to produce a smooth flow of action, and often a sense of inevitability. To add urgency to the conflict, filmmakers sometimes include some kind of deadline, thus intensifying the emotion. During the Hollywood **studio** era especially, classical structures often featured double plot lines, in which a romantic love story was developed to parallel the main line of action. In love stories, a comic second couple often paralleled the main lovers.

Classical plot structures are linear and often take the form of a journey, a chase, or a search. Even characters are defined primarily in terms of what they do. "Action is character," insists Syd Field, the author of several handbooks on screenwriting. "What a person does is what he is, not what he says." Field and other advocates of the classical paradigm are not very interested in passive characters—people to whom things are done. (These types of characters are more typical in other national cinemas.) Classicists favour characters who are goal-oriented so that we can take a rooting interest in their plans of action.

Field's conceptual model is expressed in traditional theatrical terms **(2–6)**. A screenplay is composed of three acts. Act I, "The **Setup**," occupies the first quarter of the **script**. It establishes the dramatic premise: What is the main

2–6. According to Syd Field, the narrative structure of a movie can be broken down into three acts. The story should contain about ten to twenty "plot points," major twists or key events in the action. At the midpoint of the second act, there is usually a big reversal of expectations, sending the action spinning in a new direction. Although the diagram might not be helpful in analyzing most realistic or formalistic narratives, it is surprisingly apt in movies using a classical structure.

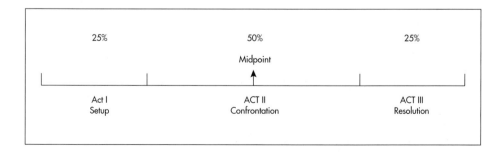

character's goal and what obstacles are likely to get in the way of its attainment? Act II, "The Confrontation," consists of the middle two quarters of the story, with a major reversal of fortune at the midpoint. This portion of the screenplay complicates the conflict with plot twists and an increasing sense of urgency, showing the main character fighting against obstacles. Act III, "The Resolution," constitutes the final quarter of the story. This section dramatizes what happens as a result of the climactic confrontation.

One of the greatest plots in the history of cinema is found in Buster Keaton's *The General*, a textbook example of the classical paradigm (**2–7**). It fits Freytag's inverted V structure as well as Field's three-act play approach. As writer Daniel Moews has pointed out, all of Keaton's feature-length comedies use the same basic comic formula. Buster begins as a sincere but clumsy greenhorn who bungles every attempt to ingratiate himself with a person he holds in awe—usually a pretty girl. At the conclusion of the day, he falls asleep, lonely, depressed, and dispirited. When he awakens, he's a new man. He goes on to succeed, usually at the same or parallel activities of the earlier portions of the movie.

2–7.   An outline of the plot structure of *The General*.
The plot moves forward with such smoothness and poise that we're hardly aware of its dazzling symmetry until the second chase, when most of the earlier gag clusters are triumphantly reprised.

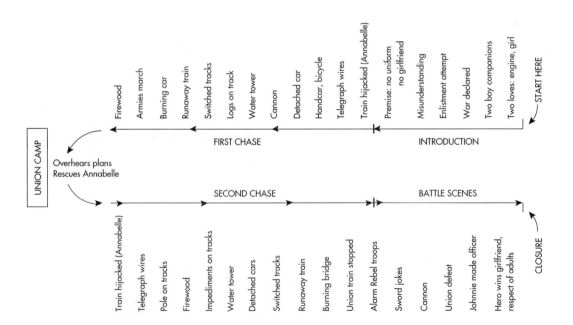

A Civil War comedy loosely based on an actual event, *The General* is laid out with the narrative elegance of a play by Congreve. The first act establishes the two loves in the hero's life: his train, "The General," and Annabelle Lee, his somewhat flaky girlfriend. His only friends, apparently, are two prepubescent boys. (Among other things, the movie is a coming-of-age story.) When war is declared, our hero, Johnnie Gray, trying to impress his girl, attempts to enlist. But he's rejected by the authorities: He's more valuable to the South as an engineer. Through a misunderstanding, Annabelle thinks Johnnie is a coward. "I don't want you to speak to me again until you are in uniform," she haughtily informs him. End of Act I.

A full year is edited out of the story as we begin Act II. (The rest of the movie covers only about twenty-four hours.) We see the plans of the Union officers to hijack a Confederate train, thereby cutting off the supply lines of the Southern army. The Yankee leader's map shows the major stops and rivers along the railroad route. In fact, this map is a geographical outline of Act II.

On the day that the hijacking is to take place, Annabelle Lee boards Johnnie's train to visit her wounded father. She snubs her former suitor. The hijacking of the train sets off the rising action. The second quarter of the movie is a chase sequence: Johnnie pursues the stolen General (with Annabelle on board) as it flees northward. There are a series of gag clusters, each involving

---

2–8.   *The General* (U.S.A., 1927), with Buster Keaton, directed by Keaton and Clyde Bruckman. Silent film comedians were masters of improvisation, capable of spinning off a profusion of gags with a single prop. For example, the gag cluster involving this cannon is a miniature drama, complete with exposition, variations on a theme that constitutes the rising action, and a thrilling climax that serves as a topper to the sequence. Even more extraordinary, Keaton and his regular crew never used written scripts or shooting schedules. They knew only the premise of the film and its conclusion. The rest was improvised. They shot for about eight weeks, making due allowances for baseball games between scenes. Later Keaton viewed all the footage, edited out the dull stuff, and created the narrative structure.   *(United Artists)*

different **props**, such as telegraph wires, switched tracks, a water tower, a cannon (**2–8**), and so on. Johnnie is usually the butt of the jokes.

At the midpoint of the film, our hero sneaks into the enemy's camp, alone and exhausted. Nonetheless, he manages to rescue Annabelle. They fall asleep in the woods in a downpour, discouraged, almost wiped out.

The next day, a second chase begins, reversing the pattern of the previous day, and taking up the third quarter of the plot. Now the jokes are inflicted on the pursuing Yankees as Johnnie and Annabelle speed southward in the recaptured General. The gag clusters are also reversed. Most of them are parallels to those of the first chase: telegraph wires, logs on the tracks, a water tower, a burning bridge, and so on. Just in time, Johnnie and Annabelle arrive at the Confederate camp and warn the troops of an impending Union attack.

Act III is a battle sequence between the two great armies. Johnnie shows himself to be a doggedly perseverant soldier, though not always a successful one. He is rewarded for his heroism with a commission in the army. He also wins back the love of his girl. All ends happily.

Keaton's narrative structure follows an elaborately counterbalanced pattern, in which the earlier humiliations are triumphantly cancelled out on the second day. Described thus schematically, Keaton's plots sound rather mechanical. But as his French admirers have pointed out, his architectural rigour can be likened to the works of the great neoclassical artists of the eighteenth century, with their intricately worked-out parallels and neatly balanced symmetries.

Ordinarily, one would consider such an artificial plot structure as an example of a formalist narrative. However, the execution of each section is rigorously realistic. Keaton performed all his own gags (many of them dangerous), usually on the first **take**. He also insisted on absolute accuracy in the costuming, the sets, and even the trains, which are historically true to the period. This combination of realistic execution with a formally patterned narrative is typical of classical cinema. Classicism is an intermediate style that blends conventions from both stylistic extremes.

2–9. *Chinatown* **(U.S.A., 1974),** *with Jack Nicholson and Faye Dunaway, directed by Roman Polanski.* In genres that depend on mystery and suspense for their effects, the narrative often withholds information, forcing us to fill in the gaps, teasing and tantalizing us with possible solutions to mysteries that aren't totally resolved until the end of the movie. *(Paramount Pictures)*

REALISTIC NARRATIVES

Traditionally, critics have linked realism to "life," formalism with "pattern." Realism is defined as an absence of style, whereas style is a preeminent concern among formalists. Realists reject artifice to portray the material world "transparently," without distortion or even mediation. Conversely, formalists are concerned with fantasy materials or throwaway subject matter to emphasize the world of the imagination, of beauty for its own sake.

Today, these views are considered naive, at least so far as realism is concerned. Contemporary critics and scholars regard realism as a style, with an elaborate set of conventions that are less obvious perhaps, but just as artificial as those used by **expressionists**.

Both realistic and formalistic narratives are patterned and manipulated, but the realistic storyteller attempts to submerge the pattern, to bury it beneath the surface "clutter" and apparent randomness of the dramatic events. In other words, the pretence that a realistic narrative is "unmanipulated" or "lifelike" is precisely that—a pretence, an aesthetic deception.

Realists prefer loose, discursive plots, with no clearly defined beginning, middle, or end. We dip into the story at an arbitrary point. Usually we aren't presented with a clear-cut conflict, as in classical narratives. Rather, the

2-10. *True Love* **(U.S.A., 1989),** *with Kelly Cinnante and Annabella Sciorra, directed by Nancy Savoca.*
True Love is a wry exploration of male-female tensions in an Italian-American working-class community shortly before the marriage of the two main characters. Like most realistic movies, the plot line is loose. The scenes are arranged in apparently random order, and the everyday events are presented matter-of-factly, with no "heightening" for dramatic effect. The dialogue is raw, the language of the streets rather than the genteel living rooms of middle America. The conclusion of the film is ambivalent and ambiguous, with no neat solutions to the complex problems that the movie addresses.   *(United Artists)*

conflict emerges unobtrusively from the unforced events of the exposition. The story itself is presented as a "slice of life," as a poetic fragment, not a neatly structured tale. Rarely is reality neatly structured; realistic art must follow suit. Life goes on, even after the final reel **(2–10)**.

Realists often borrow their structures from the cycles of nature. For example, many of the movies of Yasujiro Ozu are given seasonal titles that symbolize an appropriate human counterpart—*Early Summer, Late Autumn, Early Spring, The End of Summer, Late Spring* **(2–11)**. Other realistic films are structured around a limited period of time, like summer vacation or a school semester. Such movies sometimes centre on **rites of passage**, such as birth, puberty, first love, first job, marriage, painful separations, death.

Often we can't guess the principle of narrative coherence until the end of the movie, especially if it has a circular or cyclical structure, as many realistic films do. For example, Robert Altman's *M*A*S*H* opens with the fresh arrival of two soldier-surgeons, Hawkeye Pierce and Duke Forrest. The movie ends when their tour of duty is over. Yet the M*A*S*H unit will continue saving lives, even after these two excellent surgeons have left. (This same structural principle is used in a later military comedy, Barry Levinson's *Good Morning, Vietnam*.)

2–11. *Late Spring* **(Japan, 1949),** *with Chishu Ryu (seated) and Setsuko Hara (centre), directed by Yasujiro Ozu.*

One of the most common genres in Japan is the home drama. It is the only genre Ozu worked in, and he was one of its most popular practitioners. This type of film deals with the day-to-day routines of domestic life. Although Ozu was a profoundly philosophical artist, his movies consist almost entirely of "little things"—the bitter pills of self-denial that ultimately render life disappointing. Many of Ozu's films have seasonal titles that symbolically evoke appropriate human analogues. *Late Spring*, for example, deals with the attempts of a decent widower (Ryu) to marry off his only daughter (Hara) before she wilts into spinsterhood. *(New Yorker Films)*

The episodic structure of *M*A*S*H* is what appealed to those who adapted it as a television series. Realistic film narratives frequently seem episodic, the sequence of events almost interchangeable. The plot doesn't "build" inexorably, but seems to drift into surprising scenes that don't necessarily propel the story forward. These are offered for their own sake, as examples of "real-life" oddities.

Spectators who like fast-moving stories are often impatient with realistic films, which frequently move slowly. This is especially true in the earlier scenes, while we wait for the main narrative strand to emerge. "Digressions" often turn out to be parallels to the central plotline. But this parallelism must be inferred; it's rarely pointed out explicitly. Other traits of realistic narratives include the following:

1. A nonintrusive implied author who "reports" objectively and avoids making judgments.
2. A rejection of clichés, stale conventions, stock situations and characters in favour of the unique, the concrete, the specific.
3. A fondness for exposé, with "shocking" or "low" subject matter that is often criticized for its grittiness and "bad taste."
4. An antisentimental point of view that rejects glib happy endings, wishful thinking, miraculous cures, and other forms of phony optimism.

2-12. *A Short Film About Killing* **(Poland, 1988),** *directed by Krzysztof Kieslowski.*
Based on an actual case, this movie unflinchingly presents the details of two murders. One is committed by an alienated youth for no apparent motive. The second is perpetrated by the state. The audience is not spared the gruesome details of how the killer is executed by the authorities with even greater cold-bloodedness than the original murder. Ever since the late nineteenth century, when it became a dominant international style in the arts, realism has provoked controversy for its "sordid" or "shocking" subject matter, its preoccupation with details that the conventional majority finds repulsive but fascinating.   *(Film Polski)*

5. An avoidance of melodrama and exaggeration in favour of understatement and dedramatization.

6. A scientific view of causality and motivation, with a corresponding rejection of such romantic concepts as Destiny and Fate.

7. An avoidance of the **lyrical** impulse in favour of a plain, straightforward presentation.

FORMALISTIC NARRATIVES

Formalistic narratives revel in their artificiality. Time is often scrambled and rearranged to hammer home a thematic point more forcefully. The design of the plot is not concealed but heightened. It's part of the show. Formalistic plots come in a wide assortment, but usually they are structured according to the filmmaker's theme. For example, Alfred Hitchcock was obsessed by themes dealing with "doubles" and "the wrong man"—a technically innocent man who is accused of a crime committed by an undetected counterpart.

Hitchcock's *The Wrong Man* is his most explicit treatment of these narrative **motifs**. The entire plot is doubled, structured in twos. There are two

---

2-13. *Rude* (Canada, 1996), *with Sharon M. Lewis, directed by Clement Virgo.*
The plot of this film interweaves three separate stories linked only by the voice of Rude (Lewis), a pirate radio announcer broadcasting on the Easter weekend to the black community. She speaks to people who have been brought from "the land of the Zulu" to "the land of the Ojibway," and her poetic utterances are matched by the atmospheric and dream-like images. The three stories thus become elements of the collective consciousness of people's longing for freedom.   *(The Feature Film Project)*

imprisonments, two handwriting tests, two conversations in the kitchen, two legal hearings, two visits to a clinic, two visits to the lawyer. The hero is arrested twice by two policemen. He is identified (wrongly) by two witnesses at two different shops. There are two transfers of guilt: The main character (Henry Fonda) is accused of a crime he didn't commit, and midway through the movie, his emotionally disturbed wife (Vera Miles) takes on the guilt, requiring her to be committed to an asylum. "People say that Hitchcok lets the wires show too often," Jean-Luc Godard noted. "But because he shows them, they are no longer wires. They are the pillars of a marvellous architectural design made to withstand our scrutiny."

Many formalistic narratives are intruded on by the author, whose personality is part of the show. For example, it's virtually impossible to ignore the personality of Buñuel in his films. He slyly interjects his sardonic black humour into his narratives. He loves to undermine his characters—their pomposity, their self-deception, their mean little souls (**2–14**). Godard's personality is also highly intrusive, especially in his nontraditional narratives, which he called "cinematic essays."

Formalistic narratives are often interrupted by lyrical interludes, exercises in pure style—like the enchanting dance numbers in the Fred Astaire–

2–14.   *Le Charme discret de la bourgeoisie ("The Discreet Charm of the Bourgeoisie,"* **France, 1972),** *directed by Luis Buñuel.*
Most of Buñuel's movies feature bizarre scenes that are left unexplained, as though they were the most natural thing in the world. He delighted in satirizing middle-class hypocrisies, treating them with a kind of affectionate bemusement mingled with contempt. In this film, he presents us with a series of loosely connected episodes dealing with the inane rituals of a group of well-heeled semizombies. Interspersing these episodes are shots of the main characters walking on an empty road (pictured). No one questions why they are there. No one seems to know where they are going. Buñuel doesn't say.   *(Twentieth Century-Fox)*

2–15. *Mon oncle d'Amérique* ("My Uncle in America," France, 1980), *with Gérard Depardieu, directed by Alain Resnais.*
Depardieu portrays a hard-working idealist whose conservative values and faith in God are severely tested. The significance of the title? It's taken from European pop mythology—the proverbial adventurous uncle who left for America, made a fortune, and will someday return loaded with money to solve all their problems. Resnais was also thinking of Samuel Beckett's bitter comedy, *Waiting for Godot*, which revolves around an obscure figure (God?) who's constantly waited for, but never shows up.   *(New World Pictures)*

Ginger Rogers RKO musicals of the 1930s. In fact, stylized genre films like musicals, science fiction, and fantasies offer the richest potential for displays of stylistic rapture and bravura effects. These lyrical interludes interrupt the forward momentum of the plot, which is often a mere pretext anyway.

An excellent example of a formalistic narrative is *Mon oncle d'Amérique* ("My Uncle in America"), directed by Alain Resnais, with a script by Resnais and Jean Gruault (**2–15**). The film's structure is indebted to Godard's essay form, which can combine elements from the documentary and **avant-garde** film with fiction. The ideas in the movie are the stuff of Psychology 101. Resnais **frames** and intersperses his fictional episodes with footage of an actual medical doctor and behavioural scientist, Dr. Henri Laborit, who indulges in the French mania for dissection, analysis, and classification. He wittily discusses the relationship of human behaviour to the makeup of the brain, the conscious and subconscious environment, social conditioning, the nervous system, zoology, and biology. He alludes to the behaviour-modification theories of B.F. Skinner and other theories of human development.

The fictional episodes in the movie are concrete demonstrations of these theories. The characters are autonomous, not mechanized zombies. Nonetheless, they are victims of forces they hardly understand. Resnais focuses on three appealing characters. Each is the product of a unique biological makeup and cultural environment. Their paths intersect by chance. "These people have everything to make them happy," Resnais observed, "yet they're not happy at all. Why?"

Resnais then shows us why through his dazzling **editing** and multiple narratives. In a kaleidoscope of shifting perspectives, Resnais juxtaposes snippets of the characters' lives, dreams, and memories with Dr. Laborit's abstract formulations, statistics, and wry observations. The three main characters are movie freaks, and at various points during the story, Resnais **intercuts** brief clips from the films of their childhood idols—Jean Marais, Danielle Darrieux, and Jean Gabin. Some of these movie clips bear a not-so-coincidental resemblance to the dramatic situations of the characters. Resnais is also paying **homage** to three great stars of the French cinema.

ADAPTATION

A great many movies are adaptations of literary sources. In some respects, adapting a novel or play requires more skill and originality than working with an original screenplay. Furthermore, the better the literary work, the more difficult the adaptation. For this reason, many film adaptations are based on mediocre sources, for few people will get upset at the modifications required in film if the source itself isn't of the highest calibre. There are many adaptations that are superior to their originals: *The Birth of a Nation*, for instance, was based on Thomas Dixon's trashy novel *The Klansman*, which is more blatantly racist than the film. Some commentators believe that if a work of art has reached its fullest artistic expression in one form, an adaptation will

2–16. *Sense and Sensibility* (Britain, 1995), *with Emma Thompson, directed by Ang Lee.*
In the 1990s, virtually all of Jane Austen's six major novels were made into movies and television series, most of them quite fine. *Sense and Sensibility* is perhaps the finest, thanks in part to Emma Thompson's superlative screenplay, which won an Academy Award. It was her first screenplay. Thompson wrote several drafts over a period of four years. "The novel is so complex and there are so many stories in it that bashing out a structure was the biggest labour," she admitted. As an actress, she knew that some of the dialogue in the novel would not translate well to film, so she turned to Austen's letters (Miss Jane was a prodigious letter writer), which contained simpler language. "Some of the sentences in the book go on forever," Thompson says, but in the letters, "Austen's personal style was very clear and elegant. And very funny." In addition to writing the screenplay, Thompson played one of the leading roles, brilliantly. *(Columbia Pictures)*

inevitably be inferior. According to this argument, no film adaptation of Jane Austen's *Pride and Prejudice* could equal the original, nor could any novel hope to capture the richness of *Persona* (**4–29**), or even *Citizen Kane*, which is a rather literary movie. There's a good deal of sense in this view, for we've seen how literature and film tend to solve problems differently, how the true content of each medium is organically governed by its forms.

The real problem of the adapter is not how to reproduce the *content* of a literary work (an impossibility), but how close he or she should remain to the raw data of the *subject matter*, in the sense that these terms have been used throughout this book. This degree of fidelity is what determines the three types of adaptations: the **loose**, the **faithful**, and the **literal**. Of course, these classifications are for convenience only, for in actual practice most movies fall somewhere in between.

The loose adaptation is barely that. Generally, only an idea, a situation, or a character is taken from a literary source, then developed independently. Loose film adaptations can be likened to Shakespeare's treatment of a story from Plutarch or Bandello, or to the plays of ancient Greek dramatists, who often drew on a common mythology. A film that falls into this class is Kurosawa's *Ran*, which transforms Shakespeare's *King Lear* into a quite different tale set in medieval Japan, though the filmmaker retains several plot elements from Shakespeare's original (see also **2–17**).

Faithful adaptations, as the phrase implies, attempt to re-create the literary source in filmic terms, keeping as close to the spirit of the original as possi-

---

2-17. *Clueless* **(U.S.A., 1995),** *with Justin Walker and Alicia Silverstone, written and directed by Amy Heckerling.*

The loose adaptation takes a few general ideas from an original source, then develops them independently. Most of the Jane Austen adaptations exploited the visual appeal of period costumes and settings, but Amy Heckerling's delightfully irreverent comedy transposed the plot of Austen's Emma to contemporary Beverly Hills. The rituals of teenage subculture provide a surprisingly apt parallel to the genteel society of eighteenth-century England, but Heckerling's screenplay freely diverges from the novel to suit the new setting.   *(Paramount Pictures)*

ble. Critic André Bazin likened the faithful adapter to a translator who tries to find equivalents to the original. Of course, Bazin realized that fundamental differences exist between the two mediums: The translator's problem in converting the word *road* to *strada* or *strasse* is not so acute as a filmmaker's problem in transforming the word into a picture. An example of a faithful adaptation is Richardson's *Tom Jones*. John Osborne's screenplay preserves much of the novel's plot structure, its major events, and most of the important characters. Even the witty **omniscient** narrator is retained. But the film is not merely an illustration of the novel. In the first place, Fielding's book is too packed with incidents for a film adaptation. The many inn scenes, for example, are reduced to a central episode: the Upton Inn sequence. Two minor aspects of the novel are enlarged in the movie: the famous eating scene between Tom and Mrs. Waters and the fox-hunting episode. These **sequences** are included because two of Fielding's favourite sources of metaphors throughout the novel are drawn from eating and hunting. In effect, Osborne uses these scattered **metaphors** as raw material, or filmic "equivalents," in Bazin's sense.

Literal adaptations are usually restricted to plays. As we have seen, the two basic modes of drama—action and dialogue—are also found in films. The major problem with stage adaptations is in the handling of space and time rather than language. If the film adapter were to leave the camera at long shot and restrict the editing to scene shifts only, the result would be similar to the original. But we've seen that few filmmakers would be willing merely to record a play, nor indeed should they, for in doing so they would lose much of the excitement of the original and contribute none of the advantages of the adapting medium, particularly its greater freedom in treating space and time.

Movies can add many dimensions to a play, especially through the use of **close-ups** and edited juxtapositions. Because these techniques aren't found in the theatre, even "literal" adaptations are not strictly literal; they're simply more subtle in their modifications. Stage dialogue is often retained in film adaptations, but its effect is different on the audience. In live theatre, the meaning of the language is determined by the fact that the characters are on the same stage at the same time, reacting to the same words. In a movie, time and space are fragmented by the individual shots. Furthermore, because even a literary film is primarily visual and only secondarily verbal, nearly all the dialogue is modified by the images. The differences between loose, faithful, and literal adaptations, then, are essentially matters of degree. In each case, the cinematic form inevitably alters the content of the literary original.

GENRE AND MYTH

A genre film is a specific type of movie—a war picture, a gangster film, science fiction, and so on. There are literally hundreds of them, especially in the United States and Japan, where virtually all fiction movies can be classified according to genre. Genres are distinguished by a characteristic set of conventions in style, subject matter, and values. Genre is also a convenient way of focusing and organizing the story materials.

2–18. *It Happened One Night* **(U.S.A., 1934),** *with Clark Gable and Claudette Colbert, written by Robert Riskin, directed by Frank Capra.*
Genres can be classified according to subject matter, style, period, national origin, and a variety of other criteria. In the 1930s, a new American genre was born: screwball comedy. Its heyday was roughly 1934–1945. Essentially love stories, these films feature zany but glamorous lovers, often from different social classes. More realistic than the slapstick of the silent era, screwball comedy is also more collaborative, requiring the sophisticated blending of talents of writers, actors, and directors. The snappy dialogue crackles with wit and speed. Sappy, sentimental speeches are often meant to deceive. The narrative premises are absurdly improbable, and the plots, which are intricate and filled with preposterous twists and turns, tend to snowball out of control. *(Columbia Pictures)*

Many genre films are directed at a specific audience. Coming-of-age films are generally aimed at teenagers. Action-adventure genres tend to focus on all-male activities. Women are usually relegated to an incidental function, or they provide "romantic interest." The American **women's picture** and Japanese mother films focus on domestic life. In these female-oriented genres, men are conventionalized in a similar manner—usually as breadwinners, sexual objects, or "the other man."

André Bazin once referred to the western as "a form in search of a content." The same could be said of all genre films. A genre is a loose set of expectations, then, not a divine injunction; that is, each example of a given story type is related to its predecessors, but not in ironclad bondage. Some genre films are good; others are terrible. It's not the genre that determines artistic excellence, but how well the artist exploits the conventions of its form.

The major shortcoming of genre pictures is that they're easy to imitate and have been debased by stale mechanical repetition. Genre conventions are mere clichés unless they're united with significant innovations in style or subject matter. But this is true of all the arts, not just movies. As Aristotle noted in *The Poetics*, gen-

2–19. *M. Butterfly* (Canada/U.S.A., 1993), *with Jeremy Irons and John Lone (kneeling), directed by David Cronenberg.*

In Cronenberg's adaptation of the hit play by the Chinese-American playwright David Henry Hwang, it is clear to the audience from very early on that the female imper-sonator (Lone) with whom the French diplomat (Irons) has an affair is actually a male. Some critics felt that it was a mistake of direction or casting to make Lone's char-acter so obviously male, arguing that it sim-ply makes the diplomat look like a fool. Others likened the film to Cronenberg's horror films, in which lonely people often become trapped in their own subjective fantasies, and argued that the adaptation becomes a moving depiction of a man who blinds himself to what everybody else sees. *(Geffen Pictures)*

res are qualitatively neutral: The conventions of classical tragedy are basically the same whether they're used by a genius or a forgotten hack. Certain genres enjoy more cultural prestige because they have attracted the most gifted artists. Genres that haven't are widely regarded as innately inartistic, but in many cases their déclassé status is due to neglect rather than intrinsic hopelessness. For example, the earliest film critics considered slapstick comedy an infantile genre—until such important comic artists as Chaplin and Keaton entered the field. Today, no critic would malign the genre, for it boasts a considerable number of masterpieces.

The most critically admired genre films strike a balance between the form's preestablished conventions and the artist's unique contributions. The artists of ancient Greece drew on a common body of mythology, and no one thought it strange when dramatists and poets returned to these tales again and again. Incompetent artists merely repeat. Serious artists reinterpret. By exploiting the broad outlines of a well-known tale or story type, the storyteller can play off its main features, creating provocative tensions between the genre's conventions and the artist's inventions, between the familiar and the original, the general and the particular. Myths embody the common ideals and aspirations of a civilization, and by returning to these communal tales the artist becomes, in a sense, a psychic explorer, bridging the chasm between the known and the unknown. The stylized conventions and **archetypal** story patterns of genres encourage viewers to partici-pate ritualistically in the basic beliefs, fears, and anxieties of their age.

2–20. *Rocky* (U.S.A., 1976), *with Sylvester Stallone, directed by John Avildsen.*
One of the most popular U.S. story patterns is the Horatio Alger myth—the inspiring tale of a social nobody who, through hard work and perseverance, and against all odds, manages to pull himself up by his bootstraps and achieve extraordinary success. *(United Artists)*

Filmmakers are attracted to genres because they automatically synthesize a vast amount of cultural information, freeing the filmmaker to explore more personal concerns. A nongeneric movie must be more self-contained. The artist is forced to communicate virtually all the major ideas and emotions within the work itself—a task that preempts a lot of screen time. On the other hand, the genre artist never starts from scratch. He or she can build on the accomplishments of predecessors, enriching their ideas or calling them into question, depending on his or her inclinations.

The most enduring genres tend to adapt to changing social conditions. Most of them begin as naive allegories of Good versus Evil. Over the years they become more complex in both form and thematic range. Finally they veer into an ironic mode, mocking many of the genre's original values and conventions. Some critics claim that this evolution is inevitable and doesn't necessarily represent an aesthetic improvement.

Film critics and scholars classify genre movies into four main cycles:

1. *Primitive.* This phase is usually naive, though powerful in its emotional impact, in part because of the novelty of the form. Many of the conventions of the genre are established in this phase.

2. *Classical.* This intermediate stage embodies such classical ideals as balance, richness, and poise. The genre's values are assured and widely shared by the audience.

3. *Revisionist.* The genre is generally more symbolic, ambiguous, less certain in its values. This phase tends to be stylistically complex, appealing more to the intellect than to the emotions. Often the genre's preestablished conventions are exploited as ironic foils to question or undermine popular beliefs.

2-21. *On the Town* (U.S.A., 1949), *with (clockwise, from one o'clock) Gene Kelly, Vera-Ellen, Anne Miller, Betty Garrett, Frank Sinatra, and Jules Munshin, directed by Kelly and Stanely Donen.* Musicals were among the most popular genres throughout the big-studio era, appealing to men as well as women, to young audiences as well as adults. Most musicals heighten the artificiality of their narrative structures. For example, in this movie, everything comes in threes—three dashing sailor heroes and three spirited working-girl heroines. *(MGM)*

4. *Parodic.* This phase of a genre's development is an outright mockery of its conventions, reducing them to howling clichés and presenting them in a comic manner.

For example, the western's primitive phase is exemplified by Edwin S. Porter's *The Great Train Robbery* (1903), the first western ever made, and an enormously popular movie with the public. It was imitated and embellished on for decades. The western's classical phase could be typified by many of the works of John Ford, especially *Stagecoach* (1939), one of the few westerns of that era to win wide critical approval as well as box-office success **(1–8)**. *High Noon* (1952) was one of the first revisionist westerns, ironically questioning many of the populist values of the genre's classical phase **(5–13)**. Throughout the following two decades, most westerns remained in this skeptical mode, including such major works as *The Wild Bunch* (1969) and *McCabe and Mrs. Miller* (1971). Some critics pointed to Mel Brooks's parodic *Blazing Saddles* (1973) as the genre's death blow, for many of its conventions are mercilessly lampooned. However, genres have a way of springing back to life after being allowed to rest for a few years. For example, Clint Eastwood's popular *Pale Rider* (1985) is unabashedly classical. Many cultural theorists insist that questions of individual value in a genre's evolution are largely matters of taste and fashion, not the intrinsic merit of the phase per se.

Some of the most suggestive critical studies have explored the relationship of a genre to the society that nurtured it. This sociopsychic approach was pioneered by the French literary critic Hippolyte Taine in the nineteenth cen-

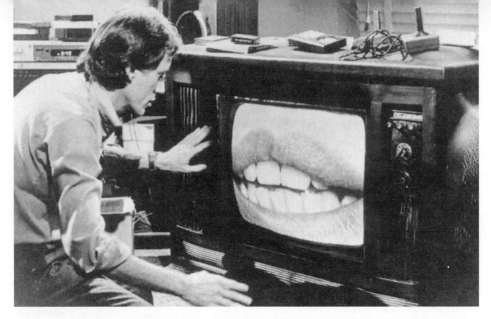

2-22. *Videodrome* (Canada, 1981), *with James Woods, directed by David Cronenberg.*
Genre films often deal with anxieties generated by cultural change. The horror film has always drawn on fears of sexuality and death, but Cronenberg's "body horror" films combine these fears with contemporary concerns about the impact of technology on the body. In this film, Max Renn (Woods), the owner of an independent Canadian television station, is first fascinated by video images of sex and violence received by satellite from an unknown source, and then finds that his body has developed a video slot for tapes which can be used by a sinister corporation to program his actions.   *(Copyright © 1981 by Universal City Studios, Inc. Courtesy of Universal Studios Publishing Rights. All Rights Reserved.)*

tury. Taine claimed that the social and intellectual anxieties of a given era and nation will find expression in its art. The implicit function of an artist is to harmonize and reconcile cultural clashes of value. He believed that art must be analyzed for both its overt and covert meaning, that beneath its explicit content there exists a vast reservoir of latent social and psychic information **(2–25)**.

This approach tends to work best with popular genres, which reflect the shared values and fears of a large audience. Such genres might be regarded as contemporary myths, lending philosophical meaning to the facts of everyday life. As social conditions change, genres often change with them, challenging some traditional customs and beliefs, reaffirming others. Gangster films, for example, are often covert critiques of American capitalism. They are often vehicles for exploring rebellion myths and are especially popular during periods of social breakdown. The protagonists—usually played by small men—are likened to ruthless businessmen, their climb to power a sardonic parody of the Horatio Alger myth. During the Jazz Age, gangster films like *Underworld* (1927) dealt with the violence and glamour of the Prohibition era in an essentially apolitical manner. During the harshest years of the Depression in the early 1930s, the genre became subversively ideological. Movies like *Little Caesar* (1930) reflected the country's shaken confidence in authority and traditional social institutions. In the final years of the Depression, gangster films like *Dead*

2–23. *E.T.: The Extra-Terrestrial* **(U.S.A., 1982),** *with Henry Thomas and E.T., directed by Steven Spielberg.*
All narratives can be interpreted on a symbolic level. There is a principle of universality that can be inferred no matter how unique or strange a given story may be. In this scene from Spielberg's masterpiece, E.T. and his friend Eliot must say goodbye. But E.T. will live forever inside Eliot's mind. Symbolically, the boy will soon outgrow his childhood world of imaginary best friends, scary-looking creatures, and the vast Unknown. But he will never forget the beauty and innocence of that world. Nor will we. *(Universal Studios)*

End (1937) were pleas for liberal reform, arguing that crime is the result of broken homes, lack of opportunity, and slum living. Gangsters of all periods tend to suffer from an inability to relate to women, but during the 1940s movies like *White Heat* (1949) featured protagonists who were outright sexual neurotics. In the 1950s, partly as a result of the highly publicized Kefauver Senate Crime Investigations, gangster movies like *The Phenix City Story* (1955) took the form of confidential exposés of syndicate crime. Francis Ford Coppola's *The Godfather* (1972) and *The Godfather, Part II* (1974) are a virtual recapitulation of the history of the genre, spanning three generations of characters and reflecting the weary cynicism of a nation still numbed by the Vietnam War and the Watergate conspiracy. As Sergio Leone's fablelike title suggests, *Once Upon a Time in America* (1984) is frankly mythic, treating the traditional rise-and-fall structure of the genre in an almost ritualistic manner. Quentin Tarantino's *Pulp Fiction* (1994) is a witty send-up of the genre, parodying many of its conventions.

The ideas of Sigmund Freud and Carl Jung have also influenced many genre theorists. Like Taine, both psychologists believed that art is a reflection of underlying structures of meaning, that it satisfies certain subconscious needs in both the artist and audience. For Freud, art was a form of daydreaming and wish fulfillment, vicariously resolving urgent impulses and desires that can't be satisfied in reality. Pornographic films are perhaps the most obvious

2–24. *Sweet Hours* **(Spain, 1982),** *with Inaki Aierra and Assumpta Serna, directed by Carlos Saura.*
Almost all civilizations have myths dealing with the rebellion of son against father, resulting in son and mother reunited in exclusive love. Sigmund Freud, the father of psychoanalysis, identified one such variant as the Oedipus complex (named for the Greek mythical hero), which he believed was the paradigm of prepubescent human sexuality. Its feminine form is known as the Electra complex, a name also derived from Greek myth. In most cases, this narrative motif is submerged beneath the surface details of a story, or sufficiently disguised to appeal primarily to the subconscious. Saura's *Sweet Hours* plays with this motif in an overt manner. The movie deals with the love affair between a filmmaker (Aierra) and an actress (Serna) who is playing his mother in an autobiographical film he is making about his childhood.   *(New Yorker Films)*

example of how anxieties can be assuaged in this surrogate manner, and in fact Freud believed that most neuroses were sexually based. He thought that art was a by-product of neurosis, although essentially a socially beneficial one. Like neurosis, art is characterized by a repetition compulsion, the need to go over the same stories and rituals to reenact and temporarily resolve certain psychic conflicts **(2–24)**.

Jung began his career as a disciple of Freud but eventually broke away, believing that Freud's theories lacked a communal dimension. Jung was fascinated by myths, fairy tales, and folklore, which he believed contained **symbols** and story patterns that were universal to all individuals in all cultures and periods. According to Jung, unconscious complexes consist of archetypal symbols that are as deeply rooted and as inexplicable as instincts. He called this submerged reservoir of symbols the *collective unconscious*, which he thought had a primordial foundation, traceable to primitive times. Many of these archetypal patterns are bipolar and embody the basic concepts of religion, art, and soci-

2–25. *Pinocchio* **(U.S.A., 1940),** *by Walt Disney.*

The French cultural anthropologist Claude Lévi-Strauss noted that myths have no author, no origin, no core axis—they allow "free play" in a variety of artistic forms. Disney's work draws heavily from fairy tales, myths, and folklore, which are profuse in archetypal elements. *Pinocchio* is a good example of how these elements can be emphasized rather than submerged beneath a surface realism. Early in the film, the boy/puppet Pinocchio is told that to be a "real boy," he must show that he is "brave, truthful, and unselfish." The three principal episodes of the movie represent ritualistic trials, testing the youth's moral fortitude. He dismally fails the first two, but redeems himself in the concluding whale episode, where he does indeed demonstrate courage, honesty, and unselfishness (pictured). Other archetypal elements include a monster (Monstro, the whale), magical transformations, a father's search for his lost son, supernatural creatures like a talking cricket (Jiminy Cricket, Pinocchio's "conscience"), a son's search for his imprisoned father, an anthropomorphized portrayal of nature, and a fairy godmother who rescues the improvident young hero when he fails to act responsibly. Like most of Disney's works, the values in *Pinocchio* are traditional and conservative, an affirmation of the sanctity of the family unit, the importance of a Higher Power in guiding our destinies, and the need to play by society's rules.   *(Walt Disney Productions)*

---

ety: god–devil, active–passive, male–female, static–dynamic, and so on. Jung believed that the artist consciously or unconsciously draws on these archetypes as raw material, which must then be rendered into the generic forms favoured by a given culture. For Jung, every work of art (and especially generic art) is an infinitesimal exploration of universal experience—an instinctive groping toward an ancient wisdom. He also believed that popular culture offers the most unobstructed view of archetypes and myths, whereas elite culture tends to submerge them beneath a complex surface detail.

TONE

A movie's tone refers to its manner of presentation, the general atmosphere that a filmmaker creates through his or her attitude toward the story. Tone can strongly affect our responses to a given set of values. Tone can also be elusive in movies, especially in those works in which it deliberately shifts from scene to scene.

In movies like David Lynch's *Blue Velvet,* for example, we can never be sure of what to make of the events, because Lynch's tone is sometimes mocking, other times bizarre, and occasionally terrifying. In one scene, an innocent high school girl (Laura Dern) recounts to her boyfriend (Kyle MacLachlan) a dream she had about a perfect world. With her blonde hair radiating with halo lighting, she seems almost angelic. In the background we hear organ music emanating from a church. The music and lighting subtly mock her naiveté as a form of stupidity.

A film's tone can be orchestrated in a number of ways. Acting styles strongly affect our response to a given scene. In Idrissa Ouedraogo's *Tilai* (2–26), for example, the tone is objective, matter-of-fact. The acting style by the largely nonprofessional cast is scrupulously realistic. They don't exaggerate the desperation of their situation with heightened emotional fervour. In Guy Maddin's *Careful* (10–15), an exaggerated silent-movie acting style sets the bizarre comic tone.

Genre also helps determine a film's tone. **Epic** films are generally presented with a dignified, larger-than-life importance, as in *Lawrence of Arabia* (4–3) or *The Searchers* (11–15). The best thrillers are usually tough, mean, and hard-boiled, like *The Big Combo* (3–11) and *The Maltese Falcon* (11–1). In comedies, the tone is generally flip, playful, and even silly.

2–26.   *Tilai* **(Burkina Faso, 1990),** *with Rasmane Ouedraogo (holding water jug) and Ina Cisse (collapsed), directed by Idrissa Ouedraogo.*
Winner of the Special Jury Prize at the Cannes Film Festival, *Tilai* is the story of a love triangle that tears a family apart in a remote African village. The tone is dedramatized, simple, and ultimately tragic. The film is complemented by a spare and poignant score by the great jazz musician Abdullah Ibrahim.   *(New Yorker Films)*

A voice-over narrator can be useful for setting a tone that's different from an objective presentation of a scene, creating a double perspective on the events. Voice-overs can be ironic, as in *Sunset Boulevard* (7–26); sympathetic, as in *Dances With Wolves*; paranoid, as in *Taxi Driver* (8–3); or cynical as in *A Clockwork Orange*, which is narrated by a thug.

Music is a common way to establish a movie's tone. A music track consisting primarily of rock 'n' roll will be very different in tone from a picture that's accompanied by Mozart or Ray Charles. In Spike Lee's *Jungle Fever*, the Italian-American scenes are accompanied by the ballads of Frank Sinatra; the African-American scenes are underscored by gospel and soul music.

Without taking a film's tone into account, a mechanistic analysis of its ideological values can be misleading. For example, Howard Hawks's *Bringing Up Baby* might be interpreted as a **leftist** critique of a decadent society. Set in the final years of the Great Depression, the movie deals with the desperate schemes of an idle society woman (Katharine Hepburn) in luring a dedicated scientist (Cary Grant) away from his work—to join her in amorous frolic. This is hardly a goal that would be applauded by most leftists, who tend to disapprove of frivolous play.

2-27. *J. A. Martin, photographe* (Canada, 1977), *with Monique Mercure and Marcel Sabourin, directed by Jean Beaudin.*
The tone of this film takes its cue from the formal portraits produced by J. A. Martin, a nineteenth-century photographer. It is gentle and slowly paced in its depiction of the quiet determination with which Rose-Aimée insists on accompanying her husband on his annual business trip and their joint discovery of the limitations of the gender and social codes of the time. Small gestures become powerful and moving, and the relevance of the film to contemporary relationships emerges despite, but also because of, the film's emotional restraint. Mercure won the Best Actress award at the 1978 Cannes festival for her performance. *(National Film Board of Canada)*

But the movie's tone says otherwise. In the first place, the Grant character is engaged to be married to a prim, sexless associate who is utterly devoid of humour. She regards their work as all-important—even to the exclusion of taking a honeymoon or eventually having children. She is the Work Ethic incarnate. Enter the Hepburn character—flighty, beautiful, and rich. Once she discovers that Grant is about to be married, she determines that only she must have him and she contrives a series of ruses to lure him away from his fiancée. Hepburn's character is exciting and exasperating—but fun. Grant is forced to shed his stodgy demeanour merely to keep up with her desperate antics. She proves to be his salvation, and they are united at the film's conclusion. Clearly, they are made for each other.

In short, the charm of Hawks's **screwball comedy** lies precisely in what critic Robin Wood described as "the lure of irresponsibility." The middle-class work ethic is portrayed as joyless—as dry as the fossil bones that Grant and his fiancée have devoted their lives to.

Is the film devoid of ideology? Certainly not. During the 1930s there were many American movies that dealt with the style and glamour of the rich, who were often portrayed as eccentric and good-hearted. Hawks's film is very much in this tradition. The hardships of the Depression are not even alluded to in the movie, and the film's settings—expensive nightclubs, swanky apartments, gracious country homes—are precisely what audiences of that era craved in order to forget about the Depression.

But the movie is not overtly political. The emphasis is on the charisma of the leading players and the madcap adventures they pursue. The luxurious lifestyle of the heroine enhances her appeal, and the fact that she doesn't have a job (nor seem to want one) is simply not relevant. *Bringing Up Baby* is a comedy and a love story, not a social critique.

A story can be many things. To a **producer** it's a **property** that has a box-office value. To a writer it's a screenplay. To a film star it's a vehicle. To a director it's an artistic medium. To a genre critic it's a classifiable narrative form. To a sociologist it's an index of public sentiment. To a psychologist it's an instinctive exploration of hidden fears or communal ideas. To a moviegoer it can be all of these, and more.

➤ **Colour Plate 1.** *The Age of Innocence* (U.S.A., 1993), *with Michelle Pfeiffer and Daniel Day-Lewis, directed by Martin Scorsese.* Based on the great American novel by Edith Wharton, this movie explores a forbidden love among New York's upper crust in the 1870s. The film's colours–reflecting the conservative values of the society itself–are tastefully subdued, correct, almost repressed. *(Columbia Pictures)*

➤ **Colour Plate 2.** *When Night is Falling* (**Canada, 1994**), *with Rachael Crawford (left) and Pascale Bussières, directed by Patricia Rozema.*
The life of a professor of mythology at a theological college is turned upside-down when she becomes attracted to a performer in a fantastic circus, where myths come to life. The warm colours of this close-up emphasize the moment that she realizes her true feelings. *(Patricia Rozema/Caroline Benjo)*

➤ **Colour Plate 3.** *Married to the Mob* **(U.S.A., 1988),** *with Michelle Pfeiffer and Matthew Modine, directed by Jonathan Demme.*
Demme's likable Mafia comedy is a cartoon version of organized crime. Like all good cartoons, the colours are gaudy and deliciously trashy. Even in this photo, you can tell that Modine is an outsider. *(Orion Pictures)*

➤ **Colour Plate 4.** *The Godfather* **(U.S.A., 1972),** *with Marlon Brando (red rose), directed by Francis Ford Coppola.* In films dealing with sombre subjects, colour is generally suppressed or smothered in darkness.

(Paramount Pictures)

➤ **Colour Plate 5.** *Lulu* **(Canada, 1996),** *with Kim Lieu and Michael Rhoades, directed by Srinivas Krishna.*
The lack of light and the dominant browns of the apartment, in which Steven/Lucky (Rhoades) and Khuyen/Lulu (Lieu) live, emphasize their feelings of entrapment despite their need for a refuge from the threatening reality of the world outside.   *(Alliance Communications)*

➤ **Colour Plate 6.** *The Road Warrior* **(Australia, 1982),** *with Vernon Welles, directed by George Miller.*
Black is often the colour of villainy. In this movie, the villainy is wittily undercut by such campy touches as the off-the-shoulder feathers and a red-tinged Mohawk mane.
(Warner Bros.)

➤ **Colour Plate 7.** *Who Framed Roger Rabbit* **(U.S.A., 1988),** *with Bob Hoskins and friend, directed by Robert Zemeckis, animation directed by Richard Williams.*
This film combines the washed-out browns of the 1940s Los Angeles setting with the pop colours of the world of "Toons." *(Touchstone Pictures/Amblin Entertainment)*

➤ **Colour Plate 8.** *Dark Victory* **(U.S.A., 1939),** *with Bette Davis and George Brent, directed by Edmund Goulding.*
"Tell me the truth now. Do you think this suit is *too* blue?" *(Warner Bros./Turner Entertainment)*

➤ **Colour Plate 9.** *Radio Days* **(U.S.A., 1987),** *with Mia Farrow (centre) and Danny Aiello,*
directed by Woody Allen.
This nostalgic re-creation of radio's golden age–the late 1930s and early 40s–is heightened by
the amber filters and warm glowing colours of most of the scenes.   *(Orion Pictures)*

➤ **Colour Plate 10.** *Le Vent du Wyoming* **("A Wind from Wyoming," Canada, 1994),** *with Sarah-Jeanne*
Salvy (left), Léo Munger (centre), and France Castel, directed by André Forcier.
Forcier uses filters and colour to give each location in this "magic realist" film a specific symbolic
atmosphere. In the womb-like motel bar, a woman confronts her mother surrounded by customers,
some of whom are wax dummies.   *(TRANSFILM/EGM Productions/Eiffel Productions)*

▶ **Colour Plate 11.** *Edward Scissorhands* **(U.S.A., 1990),** *with Johnny Depp, directed by Tim Burton.*
Burton is one of the foremost expressionists of the contemporary cinema, a conjuror of magical worlds
of colour and light, and myth and imagination. His worlds are created in the sealed-off confines of the
studio, far removed from the contaminations of prosaic reality. *(Twentieth Century–Fox)*

▶ **Colour Plate 12.** *Crash* **(Canada, 1996),** *with James Spader and Deborah Unger, directed by David Cronenberg.*
Much of Cronenberg's bizarre fable was shot on location in Toronto. The colour scheme is dominated
by the contrast between flesh and the glossy surface of metal and plastic, with the natural world
relegated to the strips of grass beside urban highways. *(Alliance Communications)*

➤ **Colour Plate 13.** *The Little Mermaid* **(U.S.A., 1989),** *directed by John Musker and Ron Clements.*
From the very beginning in the 1930s, the Disney organization was in the forefront in
developing colour as an expressive emotional language in animation. Disney is still in the
vanguard: Note the subtle violets in this photo, the sinister yet slightly campy blacks, and
the playful squiggle of pink to the left–a pure abstract expressionist whimsy. *(Walt Disney Pictures)*

➤ **Colour Plate 14.** *Pulp Fiction* **(U.S.A.**
1994), *with John Travolta, written and directed by*
Quentin Tarantino.
A bizarre nightclub. The servers impersonate
famous movie stars of the past. A junkie/
hitman (Travolta) does a weird dance with a
zonked-out gangster's moll. Each seems to be
in a different mental zone, gyrating to a private
beat. A red filter drenches the scene in a hell-
ish hue, as though a pop Dante had photographed the dancers, coiling and twisting
like demonic zombies. *(Miramax Films)*

> **Colour Plate 15.** *Jerusalem* **(Sweden, 1997),** *written and directed by Bille August.*
As spring arrives in a small Swedish village, the young people celebrate by stomping their feet in a joyous and carefree dance. The bluish tinge of the lower half of the image suggests the lingering chill of winter, while the upper portion is warmed by the sun's pale yellow rays.   *(First Look Pictures)*

> **Colour Plate 16.** *The Sweet Hereafter* **(Canada, 1997),** *with Sarah Polley and Tom McCamus,*
directed by Atom Egoyan.
The colourful but deserted fairground behind the couple gives this early moment in the film a sense of carefree normality that will soon be shattered not only by the bus accident, but by the gradual revelation that this is an incestuous relationship.   *(Ego Film Arts/Johnnie Eisen)*

FURTHER READING

BROOKS, PETER, *Reading for the Plot: Design and Intention in Narrative* (New York: Knopf, 1984). Primarily about literature.

CHATMAN, SEYMOUR, *Story and Discourse* (Ithaca, N.Y.: Cornell University Press, 1978). Well written, clear, and useful, covering literature as well as film.

FELL, JOHN L., *Film and the Narrative Tradition* (Berkeley: University of California Press, 1974). Historical influences on early film narrative, covering stage melodramas, comic strips, dime novels, and other forms of pop culture.

FIELD, SYD, *The Screenwriter's Workbook* (New York: Dell, 1984). A practical handbook, emphasizing the classical paradigm.

GRANT, BARRY KEITH, ed., *Film Genre Reader II* (Austin: University of Texas Press, 1995). A collection of important critical discussions of genre.

MARTIN, WALLACE, *Recent Theories of Narrative* (Ithaca, N.Y.: Cornell University Press, 1986). Lucid and helpful, primarily about literature.

MOEWS, DANIEL, *Keaton: The Silent Features Close Up* (Berkeley: University of California Press, 1977). An excellent critical study, especially strong on Keaton's plots.

NASH, CHRISTOPHER, ed., *Narrative in Culture* (London and New York: Routledge, 1990). Multidisciplinary essays.

SCHATZ, THOMAS, *Hollywood Genres: Formulas, Filmmaking, and the Studio System* (New York: Random House, 1981). Thoughtful discussions of major genres.

THOMPSON, KRISTIN, *Storytelling in the New Hollywood: Understanding Classical Narrative Technique* (Cambridge, Mass.: Harvard University Press, 1999). Close reading of films from the 1980s and 1990s.

PHOTOGRAPHY | 3

Ego Film Arts/Johnny Eisen

*A photograph is by no means a complete and whole
reflection of reality: the photographic picture
represents only one or another selection
from the sum of physical attributes
of the object photographed.*

—VLADIMIR NILSEN

SUMMARY

The cinematographer: the film director's main visual collaborator. The shots: apparent distance of the camera from the subject. The angles: looking up, down, or at eye level. Lighting styles: high key, low key, high contrast. The symbolism of light and darkness. Colour symbolism. How lenses distort the subject matter: telephoto, wide-angle, and standard lenses. Filtered reality: more distortions. Special effects and the optical printer.

THE CINEMATOGRAPHER

Cinema is a collaborative enterprise, the result of the combined efforts of many artists, technicians, and businesspeople. Because the contributions of these individuals vary from film to film, it's hard to determine who's responsible for what in a movie. As we have seen, many critics argue that the director is generally the dominant artist in the best movies. The principal collaborators—actors, writers, **cinematographers**—perform according to the director's unifying sensibility. But many films are stamped by the personalities of others—a prestigious **star,** for example, or a skillful editor who manages to make sense out of a director's botched **footage.**

Cinematographers sometimes chuckle sardonically when a director's visual style is praised by critics. Some directors don't even bother looking through the **viewfinder** and leave such matters as composition, **angles**, and **lenses** up to the cinematographer. When directors ignore these important formal elements, they throw away some of their most expressive pictorial opportunities and function more like stage directors, who are concerned with dramatic rather than visual values—that is, with the **script** and the acting rather than the photographic quality of the image itself.

On the other hand, a few cinematographers have been praised for their artistry when in fact the effectiveness of a film's images is largely due to the director's pictorial skills. Hitchcock provided individual **frame** drawings for most of the **shots** in his films, a technique called **storyboarding.** His cinematographers framed up according to Hitchcock's precise sketches. Hence, when Hitchcock claimed that he never looked through the viewfinder, he meant that he assumed his cinematographer had followed instructions.

It is impossible to make sweeping statements about the role of the cinematographer, for it varies widely from film to film and from director to director. In actual practice, virtually all cinematographers agree that the style of the photography should be geared to the **story,** theme, and mood of the film. William Daniels had a prestigious reputation as a glamour photographer at MGM and for many years was known as "Greta Garbo's cameraman." Yet Daniels also shot Erich von Stroheim's harshly realistic *Greed* (**4–7**), and the cinematographer won an Academy Award for his work in Jules Dassin's *Naked City*, which is virtually a semidocumentary.

3-1. Twentieth Century-Fox publicity photo of Marilyn Monroe (1953). Cinematographers often comment that the camera "likes" certain individuals and "doesn't like" others, even though these others might be good-looking people in real life. Highly photogenic performers like Marilyn Monroe are rarely uncomfortable in front of the camera. Indeed, they often play to it, ensnaring our attention. Photographer Richard Avedon said of Marilyn, "She understood photography, and she also understood what makes a great photograph—not the technique, but the content. She was more comfortable in front of the camera than away from it." *(Twentieth Century-Fox)*

During the big-**studio** era, most cinematographers believed that the aesthetic elements of a film should be maximized—beautiful pictures with beautiful people was the goal. Today such views are considered rigid and doctrinaire. Sometimes images are even coarsened if such a technique is considered appropriate to the dramatic materials. For example, Vilmos Zsigmond, who photographed *Deliverance,* didn't want the rugged forest setting to appear too pretty because beautiful visuals would contradict the Darwinian theme of the film. He wanted to capture what Tennyson described as "nature red in tooth and claw." Accordingly, Zsigmond shot on overcast days as much as possible to eliminate the bright blue skies. He also avoided reflections in the water because they tend to make nature look cheerful and inviting. "You don't make beautiful compositions just for the sake of making compositions," cinematographer Laszlo Kovacs has insisted. Content always determines form; form should be the embodiment of content.

3–2.   *The Emigrants* (Sweden, 1972), *with Liv Ullmann and Max von Sydow, photographed and directed by Jan Troell.*
If we were to view a scene similar to this in real life, we would probably concentrate most of our attention on the people in the wagon. But there are considerable differences between reality and cinematic realism. Realism is an artistic style. In selecting materials from the chaotic sprawl of reality, the realist filmmaker necessarily eliminates some details and emphasizes others into a structured hierarchy of visual significance. For example, the stone wall in the foreground of this shot occupies more space than the humans. Visually, this dominance suggests that the rocks are more important than the people. The unyielding stone wall symbolizes divisiveness and exclusion—ideas that are appropriate to the dramatic context. If the wall were irrelevant to the theme, Troell would have eliminated it and selected other details from the copiousness of reality—details that would be more pertinent to the dramatic context.   *(Warner Bros.)*

"Many times, what you don't see is much more effective than what you do see," Gordon Willis has noted. Willis is arguably the most respected of all American cinematographers, a specialist in **low-key** lighting styles. He photographed all three of Francis Ford Coppola's *Godfather* films—which many traditionalists considered too dark. But Willis was aiming for poetry, not **realism**. Most of the interior scenes were very dark, to suggest an atmosphere of evil and secrecy.

Willis's preference for low levels of light has been enormously influential in contemporary cinema. Unfortunately, many filmmakers today regard low-key lighting as intrinsically more "serious" and "artistic," whatever the subject matter. These needlessly dark movies are often impenetrably obscure when shown on the television screen in VCR format. Conscientious filmmakers often supervise the transfer from film to video because each medium requires different lighting intensities. Generally, low-key images must be lightened for video.

Many filmmakers understand the technology of cinematography very well. Others are totally ignorant of such matters and require impossible results. Astonishingly, these artists often manage to deliver. Cinematographers have to be extraordinarily hearty, flexible, and resourceful. Daniels, for example, was required to work in 56°C heat for the Death Valley sequences of *Greed*. Often

3–3.   *Women on the Verge of a Nervous Breakdown* (Spain, 1988), *with Carmen Maura, directed by Pedro Almodóvar.*
What's wrong with this photo? For one thing, the character is not centred in the composition. The image is asymmetrical, apparently off balance because the "empty" space on the right takes up over half the viewing area. Visual artists often use "negative space" such as this to create a vacuum in the image, a sense of something missing, something left unsaid. In this case, the pregnant protagonist (Maura) has just been dumped by her lover. He is an unworthy swine, but inexplicably, perversely, she still loves him. His abandonment has left a painful empty place in her life.   *(Orion Pictures)*

camera operators must work underwater; in deep, dark, narrow pits; high overhead on precarious ledges; and in almost every kind of dangerous situation.

There are some great movies that are photographed competently, but
without distinction. Realist directors are especially likely to prefer an unobtrusive style. Many of the works of Buñuel, for example, can only be described as
"professional" in their cinematography. Buñuel was rarely interested in formal
beauty—except occasionally to mock it. Rollie Totheroh, who photographed
most of Chaplin's works, merely set up his camera and let Chaplin the actor
take over. Photographically speaking, there are few memorable shots in his
films. What makes the images compelling is the genius of Chaplin's acting. This
photographic austerity—some would consider it poverty—is especially apparent in those rare scenes when Chaplin is off camera.

But there are far more films in which the only interesting or artistic
quality is the cinematography. For every great work like Fritz Lang's *You Only
Live Once*, Leon Shamroy had to photograph four or five bombs of the ilk of
Snow White and the Three Stooges. Lee Garmes photographed several of von Sternberg's visually opulent films, but he also was required to shoot undistinguished
films like *My Friend Irma Goes West*.

3–4. *Speaking Parts* **(Canada, 1989),** *with Gabrielle Rose, directed by Atom Egoyan.*
Cameras are an increasingly visible part of everyday reality, and are frequently seen on our
movie screens. More often than not these cameras are video cameras—surveillance cameras
or camcorders. Egoyan's films explore the impact on our lives of this new image technology.
In this film, a couple make love long-distance by means of a tele-conferencing link, and Clara
(Rose) communes with her dead brother in a video mausoleum where funeral urns have
been replaced by video monitors.   *(Ego Film Arts/Johnny Eisen)*

THE SHOTS

The different cinematic shots are defined by the amount of subject matter that's included within the frame of the screen. In actual practice, however, shot designations vary considerably. A **medium shot** for one director might be considered a **close-up** by another. Furthermore, the longer the shot, the less precise are the designations. In general, shots are determined on the basis of how much of the human figure is in view. The shot is not necessarily defined by the distance between the camera and the object photographed, for in some instances certain lenses distort distances. For example, a **telephoto lens** can produce a close-up on the screen, yet the camera in such shots is generally quite distant from the subject matter.

Although there are many different kinds of shots in the cinema, most of them are subsumed under the six basic categories: **(1)** the **extreme long shot, (2)** the **long shot, (3)** the **full shot, (4)** the medium shot, **(5)** the close-up, and **(6)** the **extreme close-up.** The **deep-focus shot** is usually a variation of the long or extreme long shot.

The extreme long shot is taken from a great distance, sometimes almost half a kilometre away. It's almost always an exterior shot and shows much of the locale. Extreme long shots also serve as spatial frames of reference for the closer shots and for this reason are sometimes called **establishing shots.** If people are included in extreme long shots, they usually appear as mere specks on the screen. The most effective use of these shots is often found in **epic** films, where locale plays an important role: westerns, war films, samurai films, and historical movies. Not surprisingly, the greatest masters of the extreme long shot are those directors associated with epic **genres:** D. W. Griffith, Sergei Eisenstein, John Ford, Akira Kurosawa, and Steven Spielberg.

The long shot is perhaps the most complex in the cinema, and the term itself one of the most imprecise. Usually, long-shot ranges correspond approximately to the distance between the audience and the stage in live theatre **(3–6).** The closest range within this category is the full shot, which just barely includes the human body in full, with the head near the top of the frame and the feet near the bottom. Charles Chaplin and other slapstick comedians favoured the full shot because it was best suited to the art of pantomime yet was close enough to capture at least gross facial expressions.

The medium shot contains a figure from the knees or waist up **(3–5).** A functional shot, it's useful for shooting exposition scenes, for carrying movement, and for dialogue. There are several variations of the medium shot. The **two shot** contains two figures from the waist up. The **three shot** contains three figures; beyond three, the shot tends to become a full shot, unless the other figures are in the background. The over-the-shoulder shot usually contains two figures, one with part of his or her back to the camera, the other facing the camera.

3–5. *Before Sunrise* (U.S.A., 1995), *with Julie Delpy and Ethan Hawke, written and directed by Richard Linklater.*
Above all, the medium shot is the shot of the couple, romantic or otherwise. Generally, two shots have a split focus rather than a single dominant: The bifurcated composition usually emphasizes equality, two people sharing the same intimate space. The medium two-shot reigns supreme in such genres as romantic comedies, love stories, and buddy films.
(Castle Rock Entertainment)

The close-up shows very little if any locale and concentrates on a relatively small object—the human face, for example. Because the close-up magnifies the size of an object, it tends to elevate the importance of things, often suggesting a **symbolic** significance. The extreme close-up is a variation of this shot. Thus, instead of a face, the extreme close-up might show only a person's eyes or mouth.

The deep-focus shot is usually a long shot, consisting of a number of focal distances and photographed in depth **(5–18).** Sometimes called a wide-angle shot because it requires a **wide-angle lens** to photograph, this type of shot captures objects at close, medium, and long ranges simultaneously, all of them in sharp focus. The objects in a deep-focus shot are carefully arranged in a succession of planes. By using this layering technique, the director can guide the viewer's eye from one distance to another. Generally, the eye travels from a close range to a medium to a long.

3–6. *Mary Shelley's Frankenstein* **(U.S.A., 1994),** *with Robert De Niro (under wraps) and Kenneth Branagh, directed by Branagh.*
At its most distant range, the long shot encompasses roughly the same amount of space as the staging area of a large theatre. Setting can dominate characters unless they're located near the foreground. Lighting a long shot is usually costly, time-consuming, and labour-intensive. The laboratory in this movie had to be moody and scary, yet still sufficiently clear to enable us to see back into the "depth" of the set. Note how the lighting in this shot is layered, punctuated with patches of gloom and accusatory shafts of light from above.   *(TriStar Pictures)*

THE ANGLES

The angle from which an object is photographed can often serve as an authorial commentary on the subject matter. If the angle is slight, it can serve as a subtle form of emotional colouration. If the angle is extreme, it can represent the major meaning of an image. The angle is determined by where the camera is placed, not the subject photographed. A picture of a person photographed from a **high angle** actually suggests an opposite interpretation from an image of the same person photographed from a **low angle**. The subject matter can be identical in the two images, yet the information we derive from both clearly shows that the form is the content, the content the form.

Filmmakers in the realistic tradition tend to avoid extreme angles. Most of their scenes are photographed from eye level, roughly one and a half to two metres off the ground—approximately the way an actual observer might view a scene. Usually these directors attempt to capture the clearest view of an object. **Eye-level shots** are seldom intrinsically dramatic, because they tend to be the norm. Virtually all directors use some eye-level shots, particularly in routine expository scenes.

Formalist directors are not always concerned with the clearest image of an object, but with the image that best captures an object's expressive essence. Extreme angles involve distortions. Yet many filmmakers feel that by distorting the surface realism of an object, a greater truth is achieved—a symbolic truth. Both realist and formalist directors know that the viewer tends to identify with the camera's lens (3–7). The realist wishes to make the audience forget that there's a camera at all. The formalist is constantly calling attention to it.

There are five basic angles in the cinema: (1) the **bird's-eye view,** (2) the high angle, (3) the eye-level shot, (4) the low angle, and (5) the **oblique angle.** As in the case of shot designations, there are many intermediate kinds of angles. For example, there can be a considerable difference between a low and extreme-low

---

3–7. *Bonnie and Clyde* (U.S.A., 1967), *with Faye Dunaway and Warren Beatty, directed by Arthur Penn.*

High angles tend to suggest entrapment, powerlessness, or assailability. The higher the angle, the more it tends to imply fatality. The camera's angle can be inferred from the background of a shot: High angles usually show the ground or floor; low angles the sky or ceiling. Because we tend to associate light with safety, high-key lighting is generally nonthreatening and reassuring. But not always. We have been socially conditioned to believe that danger lurks in darkness, so when a traumatic assault takes place in broad daylight, as in this scene, the effect is doubly scary because it's so unexpected.   *(Warner Bros.)*

3-8.   *Au revoir les enfants* *("Goodbye, Children,"* **France, 1987),** *with Gaspard Manesse,*
directed by Louis Malle.
Movie children are generally photographed from high angles, forcing us to look down on the
adorable little tykes. Malle is not so sentimental. His semiautobiographical protagonist (pictured) is presented objectively, mostly from neutral angles. Though the boy is usually dominated from above by the adults in the story, thanks to the predominantly eye-level camera,
we view him as an equal, not an inferior.   *(Orion Pictures)*

angle—although usually, of course, such differences tend to be matters of
degree. Generally speaking, the more extreme the angle, the more distracting
and conspicuous it is in terms of the subject matter being photographed.

The bird's-eye view is perhaps the most disorienting angle of all, for it
involves photographing a scene from directly overhead. Because we seldom
view events from this perspective, the subject matter of such shots might initially seem unrecognizable and abstract, like the kaleidoscopic arrangements of
choreographer Busby Berkeley (**5–2**). For this reason, filmmakers tend to avoid
this type of camera **setup.** In certain contexts, however, this angle can be highly
expressive. In effect, bird's-eye shots permit us to hover above a scene like all-
powerful gods. The people photographed seem antlike and insignificant.
Directors whose themes revolve around the idea of fate—Hitchcock and Fritz
Lang, for example—tend to favour high angles.

Ordinary high-angle shots are not so extreme, and therefore not so
disorienting. The camera is placed on a **crane,** or some natural high promon-

tory, but the sense of audience omnipotence is not overwhelming. High angles give a viewer a sense of a general overview, but not necessarily one implying destiny or fate. High angles reduce the height of the objects photographed and usually include the ground or floor as background. Movement is slowed down: This angle tends to be ineffective for conveying a sense of speed, useful for suggesting tediousness. The importance of setting or environment is increased: The locale often seems to swallow people. High angles reduce the importance of a subject. A person seems harmless and insignificant photographed from above. This angle is also effective for conveying a character's self-contempt.

Some filmmakers avoid angles because they are too manipulative and judgmental. In the movies of the Japanese master Yasujiro Ozu, the camera is usually placed just over a metre from the floor—as if an observer were viewing the events while seated Japanese style (4–6). Ozu treated his characters as equals; his approach discourages us from viewing them either condescendingly or sentimentally. For the most part, they are ordinary people, neither very virtuous nor very corrupt. But Ozu lets them reveal themselves. He believed that value judgments are implied through the use of angles, and he kept his camera neutral and dispassionate. Eye-level shots permit us to make up our own minds about what kind of people are being presented.

3-9. *Nosferatu* **(Germany, 1922),** *with Max Schreck, cinematography by Fritz Arno Wagner, directed by F. W. Murnau.*
When an extreme low angle is combined with a perspective-distorting wide-angle lens, a character can seem threatening, for he or she looms above the camera—and us—like a towering giant.   *(Janus Films)*

Low angles have the opposite effect of high. They increase height and thus are useful for suggesting verticality. More practically, they increase a short actor's height. Motion is speeded up, and in scenes of violence especially, low angles capture a sense of confusion. Environment is usually minimized in low angles, and often the sky or a ceiling is the only background. Psychologically, low angles heighten the importance of a subject. The figure looms threateningly over the spectator, who is made to feel insecure and dominated. A person photographed from below inspires fear, awe, and respect. For this reason, low angles are often used in propaganda films or in scenes depicting heroism.

An oblique angle involves a lateral tilt of the camera. When the image is projected, the horizon is skewed. A man photographed at an oblique angle will look as though he's about to fall to one side. This angle is sometimes used for **point-of-view shots**—to suggest the imbalance of a drunk, for example. Psychologically, oblique angles suggest tension, transition, and impending movement. The natural horizontal and vertical lines of a scene are converted into unstable diagonals. Oblique angles are not used often, for they can disorient a viewer. In scenes depicting violence, however, they can be effective in capturing precisely this sense of visual anxiety (**3–10**).

3-10. *Shallow Grave* (Britain, 1994), *with Kerry Fox, Ewan McGregor, and Christopher Eccleston, directed by Danny Boyle.*
Oblique angles, sometimes known as "Dutch tilt" shots, produce a sense of irresolution, of visual anxiety. The scene's normal horizontal and vertical lines are tilted into tense, unresolved diagonals. Such shots are generally employed in thrillers, especially in scenes such as this that are meant to throw the spectator off balance with a shocking revelation. *(Gramercy Pictures)*

LIGHT AND DARK

Generally speaking, the cinematographer (who is also known as the director of photography, or DP) is responsible for arranging and controlling the lighting of a film and the quality of the photography. Usually the cinematographer executes the specific or general instructions of the director. The illumination of most movies is seldom a casual matter, for lights can be used with pinpoint accuracy. Through the use of spotlights, which are highly selective in their **focus** and intensity, a director can guide the viewer's eyes to any area of the photographed image. Motion-picture lighting is seldom static, for even the slightest movement of the camera or the subject can cause the lighting to shift. Movies take so long to complete, in part because of the enormous complexities involved in lighting each new shot. The cinematographer must make allowances for every movement within a continuous **take.** Each different colour, shape, and texture reflects or absorbs differing amounts of light. If an image is photographed in depth, an even greater complication is involved, for the lighting must also be in depth. Furthermore, cinematographers don't have at their disposal most of the darkroom techniques of a still photographer: variable paper, dodging, airbrushing, choice of development, enlarger filters, etc. In a colour film, the subtle effects of lights and darks are often obscured, for colour tends to obliterate shadings and flatten images: Depth is negated.

There are a number of different styles of lighting. Usually designated as a lighting key, the style is geared to the theme and mood of a film, as well as its genre. Comedies and musicals, for example, tend to be lit in **high key,** with bright, even illumination and few conspicuous shadows. Tragedies and melodramas are usually lit in **high contrast,** with harsh shafts of lights and dramatic streaks of blackness **(3–12).** Mysteries and thrillers are generally in low key, with diffused shadows and atmospheric pools of light **(3–11).** Each lighting key is only an approximation, and some images consist of a combination of lighting styles—a low-key background with a few high-contrast elements in the foreground, for example. Movies shot in studios are generally more stylized and theatrical, whereas location photography tends to use available illumination, with a more natural style of lighting.

Lights and darks have had symbolic connotations since the dawn of humanity. The Bible is filled with light–dark symbolism. Rembrandt and Caravaggio used light–dark contrasts for psychological purposes as well. In general, artists have used darkness to suggest fear, evil, the unknown. Light usually suggests security, virtue, truth, joy. Because of these conventional symbolic associations, some filmmakers deliberately reverse light–dark expectations **(3–7).** Hitchcock's movies attempt to jolt the viewers by exposing their shallow sense of security. He staged many of his most violent scenes in the glaring light.

Lighting can also be used to subvert subject matter. Paul Brickman's *Risky Business* is a coming-of-age comedy, and like most examples of its genre, the adolescent hero (Tom Cruise) triumphs over the System and its hypocritical morality. But in this movie, the naive hero learns to play the game and becomes a winner by being even more hypocritical than the upholders of the System. Most of the film is shot in low-key lighting—unusual for any comedy—which

3–11. *The Big Combo* (U.S.A., 1955), *with Jean Wallace and Cornell Wilde, directed by Joseph H. Lewis.*
Film noir (literally, "black cinema") is a style defined primarily in terms of light—or the lack of it. This style typified a variety of American genres in the 1940s and early 1950s. Noir is a world of night and shadows. Its milieu is almost exclusively urban. The style is profuse in images of dark streets, cigarette smoke swirling in dimly lit cocktail lounges, and symbols of fragility, such as window panes, sheer clothing, glasses, and mirrors. Motifs of entrapment abound: alleys, tunnels, subways, elevators, and train cars. The tone of film noir is fatalistic and paranoid. It's suffused with pessimism, emphasizing the darker aspects of the human condition. *(Allied Artists)*

darkens the tone of the comic scenes. By the conclusion of the film, we're not entirely sure if the hero's "success" is ironic or straight. The movie would probably have been funnier if it had been shot in the usual high key, but the low-key photography makes it a more serious comedy—ironic and paradoxical.

Lighting can be used realistically or expressionistically. The realist tends to favour **available lighting**, at least in exterior scenes. Even out of doors, however, most filmmakers use some lamps and reflectors, either to augment the natural light or, on bright days, to soften the harsh contrasts produced by the sun. With the aid of special lenses and more light-sensitive film stocks, some directors have managed to dispense with artificial lighting completely. Available lighting tends to produce a documentary look in the film image, a hard-edged quality and an absence of smooth modelling. For interior shots, realists tend to prefer images with an obvious light source—a window or a lamp. Or they often use a diffused kind of lighting with no artificial, strong contrasts. In short, the realist doesn't use conspicuous lighting unless its source is dictated by the context.

Formalists use light less literally. They are guided by its symbolic implications and will often stress these qualities by deliberately distorting natural

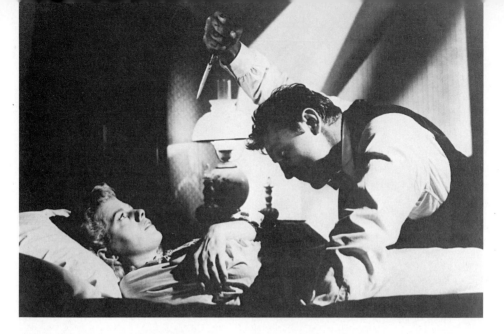

3–12. ***The Night of the Hunter*** (U.S.A., 1955), *with Shelley Winters and Robert Mitchum, directed by Charles Laughton.*
High-contrast lighting is boldly theatrical, infusing the photographed materials with a sense of visual anguish. This style of lighting is typical of such genres as crime films, melodramas, thrillers, and mysteries. The lack of light in such movies symbolizes the unknown, deceptive surfaces, evil itself. Photographed by Stanley Cortez, one of the great cinematographers of the big-studio era, this film's visual flamboyance is indebted to the extreme stylization of the German expressionist movement. *(United Artists)*

---

light patterns. A face lighted from below almost always appears sinister, even if the actor assumes a totally neutral expression. Similarly, an obstruction placed in front of a light source can assume frightening implications, for it tends to threaten our sense of safety. On the other hand, in some contexts, especially in exterior shots, a silhouette effect can be soft and romantic.

Lighting a face obviously from above produces a certain angelic quality, known as the halo effect. "Spiritual" lighting of this type tends to border on the cliché, however. **Backlighting,** which is a kind of semisilhouetting, is soft and ethereal. Love scenes are often photographed with a halo effect around the heads of the lovers to give them a romantic aura. Backlighting is especially evocative when used to highlight blonde hair.

Through the use of spotlights, an image can be composed of violent contrasts of lights and darks. The surface of such images seems disfigured, torn up. The formalist director uses such severe contrasts for psychological and thematic purposes.

By deliberately permitting too much light to enter the aperture of the camera, a filmmaker can overexpose an image—producing a blanching flood of light over the entire surface of the picture. **Overexposure** has been most effectively used in nightmare and fantasy sequences. Sometimes this technique can suggest a kind of horrible glaring publicity, a sense of emotional exaggeration.

a   b

3-13. *Leatherface: The Texas Chainsaw Massacre III* **(U.S.A., 1990),** *with R. A. Mihailoff, directed by Jeff Burr.*
Many would argue that low-key lighting **(a)** is more frightening than frontal lighting **(b).** Horrific as Leatherface's features are, at least we know what we have to deal with, whereas the faceless killer **(a)** conjures unspeakable unseen terrors.   *(New Line Cinema)*

COLOUR

Colour in film didn't become commercially widespread until the 1940s. There were many experiments in colour before this period, however. Some of Méliès's movies, for example, were painted by hand in assembly-line fashion, with each painter responsible for colouring a minute area of the filmstrip. The original version of *The Birth of a Nation* (1915) was printed on various tinted stocks to suggest different moods: The burning of Atlanta was tinted red, the night scenes blue, the exterior love scenes pale yellow. Many silent filmmakers used this tinting technique to suggest different moods.

Sophisticated film colour was developed in the 1930s, but for many years a major problem was its tendency to prettify everything. If colour enhanced a sense of beauty—in a musical or a historical extravaganza—the effects were often appropriate. Thus, the best feature films of the early years of colour were usually those with artificial or exotic settings. Realistic dramas were thought to be unsuitable vehicles for colour. The earliest colour processes tended also to emphasize garishness, and often special consultants had to be called in to harmonize the colour schemes of costumes, makeup, and decor.

Furthermore, each colour process tended to specialize in a certain base hue—red, blue, or yellow, usually—whereas other colours of the spectrum were somewhat distorted. It was well into the 1950s before these problems were resolved. Compared with the subtle colour perceptions of the human eye, however, and despite the apparent precision of most present-day colour processing, cinematic colour is still a relatively crude approximation.

The most famous colour films tend to be **expressionistic**. Michelangelo Antonioni's attitude is fairly typical: "It is necessary to intervene in a colour film, to take away the usual reality and replace it with the reality of the moment." In *Red Desert* (photographed by Carlo Di Palma), Antonioni spray-painted natural locales to emphasize internal, psychological states. Industrial wastes, river pollution, marshes, and large stretches of terrain were painted grey to suggest the ugliness of contemporary industrial society and the heroine's drab, wasted existence. Whenever red appears in the movie, it suggests sexual passion. Yet the red—like the loveless sexuality—is an ineffective cover-up of the pervasive grey.

Colour tends to be a subconscious element in film. It's strongly emotional in its appeal, expressive and atmospheric rather than conspicuous or intellectual. Psychologists have discovered that most people actively attempt to interpret the lines of a composition, but they tend to accept colour passively, permitting it to suggest moods rather than objects. Lines are associated with nouns; colour with adjectives. Line is sometimes thought to be masculine; colour feminine. Both lines and colours suggest meanings, then, but in somewhat different ways.

Since earliest times, visual artists have used colour for symbolic purposes. Colour symbolism is probably culturally acquired, though its implications are surprisingly similar in otherwise differing societies. In general, cool colours (blue, green, violet) tend to suggest tranquility, aloofness, and serenity. Cool colours also have a tendency to recede in an image. Warm colours (red, yellow, orange) suggest aggressiveness, violence, and stimulation. They tend to come forward in most images.

3-14. *The Color Purple* (U.S.A., 1985), *with Whoopi Goldberg, directed by Steven Spielberg.*
Spielberg often places his characters in front of a single light source like a bright window, thus creating a tender silhouette—a technique called backlighting.   *(Warner Bros.)*

Some filmmakers deliberately exploit colour's natural tendency to garishness. Fellini's *Juliet of the Spirits* features many bizarre costumes and settings to suggest the tawdry but fascinating glamour of the world of show business. Bob Fosse's *Cabaret* is set in Germany and shows the early rise of the Nazi party. The colours are somewhat neurotic, with emphasis on such 1930s favourites as plum, acid green, purple, and florid combinations, like gold, black, and pink.

Black-and-white photography in a colour film is sometimes used for symbolic purposes. Some filmmakers alternate whole episodes in black and white with entire sequences in colour. The problem with this technique is its facile symbolism. The jolting black-and-white sequences are too obviously "significant" in the most arty sense. A more effective variation is simply not to use too much colour, to let black and white predominate. In De Sica's *The Garden of the Finzi-Continis,* which is set in Fascist Italy, the early portions of the movie are richly resplendent in shimmering golds, reds, and almost every shade of green. As political repression becomes more brutal, these colours almost imperceptibly begin to wash out, until near the end of the film the images are dominated by whites, blacks, and blue-greys.

In the colour photo section, we can see that film colour functions in a variety of ways. In *When Night Is Falling* (**Colour Plate 2**), a circus performer's colourful costumes suggest both the love and the risk she brings into the life of a teacher at a theological college. In stories dealing with the darker side of the human condition, filmmakers generally avoid bright colours, which are incongruously cheerful. The gangsters of *The Godfather* (**Colour Plate 4**) are smothered in darkness and shadows—a symbol of the unspeakable evil of their world.

3–15. *Eraserhead* (U.S.A., 1978), *with Jack Nance, directed by David Lynch.*
Ordinarily the halo effect created by backlighting is romantic, but here it suggests an electrifying shriek. The effect is wholly appropriate, given the character's unique hair style and the murderous insects that swarm ferociously in this "dream of dark and troubling things," as Lynch referred to his audacious cult classic.   *(Libra Films)*

3–16. *From Here to Eternity* (U.S.A., 1953), *with Montgomery Clift and Burt Lancaster, directed by Fred Zinnemann.*

The expert cinematographers of the big-studio era were adept in revealing a surprising amount of detail even in scenes that take place at night, as in this photo. The preponderance of shadow in this shot clearly establishes the nighttime milieu, but note how an offscreen street lamp conveniently manages to illuminate the characters' facial expressions and body language. (They're both very drunk, sitting in the middle of a dirt road.) Sometimes studio-era directors of photography preferred to use the day-for-night filter, which gives the illusion of an evening setting even though the scene was originally photographed in daylight. *(Columbia Pictures)*

The futuristic film *The Road Warrior* (**Colour Plate 6**) is whimsical in its use of colour, combining incongruous elements like studded black leather, shoulder pads, bare midriff, and fluffy feathers for a soupçon of elegance. Expressionistic fantasy-oriented movies like *Edward Scissorhands* (**Colour Plate 11**) are usually electric in bright pop colours—the colours of the imagination, not reality.

In the 1980s, new computer technology was developed that allowed black-and-white movies to be "colourized"—a process that provoked a howl of protest from most film artists and critics. The colourized versions of some genres, like period films, musicals, and other forms of light entertainment, are not damaged too seriously by this process, but the technique is a disaster in carefully photographed black-and-white films, like *Citizen Kane,* with its **film noir** lighting style and brilliant deep-focus photography.

3–17. *Crime and Punishment* **(U.S.A., 1935),** *with Peter Lorre, cinematography by Lucien Ballard, directed by Josef von Sternberg.*
Sternberg was a master of atmospheric lighting effects and closely supervised the photography of his films. His stories are unfolded primarily in terms of light and shade, rather than conventional dramatic means. "Every light has a point where it is brightest, and a point toward which it wanders to lose itself completely," he explained. "The journey of rays from that central core to the outposts of blackness is the adventure and drama of light." Note how the closed form of the mise en scène and the light encircling the protagonist (Lorre) produce an accusatory effect, a sense of entrapment.   *(Paramount Pictures)*

Colourization also throws off the compositional balance of some shots, creating new **dominants.** In the shot from *Dark Victory* **(Colour Plate 8),** for example, the dominant is Brent's blue suit, which is irrelevant to the dramatic context. In the original black-and-white version, Davis is the dominant, her dark outfit contrasting with the white fireplace that frames her figure. Distracting visual dominants undercut the dramatic impact of such scenes. We keep thinking Brent's suit *must* be important. It is, but only to the computer.

3–18. *Starman* **(U.S.A., 1984),** *with Karen Allen and Jeff Bridges, directed by John Carpenter.* Many of the earlier portions of this sci-fi film are photographed in a plain, functional style. After the earthling protagonist (Allen) falls in love with an appealing and hunky alien (Bridges), the photographic style becomes more romantic. The city's lights are etherealized by the shimmering, soft-focus photography. The halo effect around the lovers' heads reinforces the air of enchantment. The gently falling snowflakes conspire to enhance the magical moment. These aren't just lovers, these are soulmates.   *(Columbia Pictures)*

LENSES, FILTERS, STOCKS, OPTICALS, AND GAUGES

Because the camera's lens is a crude mechanism when compared with the human eye, some of the most striking effects in a movie image can be achieved through the distortions of the photographic process itself. Particularly with regard to size and distance, the camera lens doesn't make mental adjustments but records things literally. For example, whatever is placed closest to the camera's lens will appear larger than an object at a greater distance. Hence, a coffee cup can totally obliterate a human being if the cup is in front of the lens and the human is standing at long-shot range.

Realist filmmakers tend to use normal, or standard, lenses to produce a minimum of distortion. These lenses photograph subjects more or less as they are perceived by the human eye. Formalist filmmakers often prefer lenses and **filters** that intensify given qualities and suppress others. Cloud formations, for example, can be exaggerated threateningly or softly diffused, depending on what kind of lens or filter is used. Different shapes, colours, and lighting intensities can be radically altered through the use of specific optical modifiers. There are literally dozens of different lenses, but most of them are subsumed under three major categories: those in the standard (nondistorted) range, the telephoto lenses, and the wide angles.

The telephoto lens is often used to get close-ups of objects from extreme distances. For example, no cinematographer is likely to want to get close enough to a lion to photograph a close-up with a standard lens. In cases such as these, the telephoto is used, thus guaranteeing the safety of the cinematographer while still producing the necessary close-up. Telephotos also allow cinematographers to work discreetly. In crowded city locations, for example, passersby are likely to stare at a movie camera. The telephoto permits the cinematographer to remain hidden—in a truck, for example—while he or she shoots close shots through the windshield or back window of the truck. In effect, the lens works like a telescope, and because of its long focal length, it is sometimes called a long lens.

Telephoto lenses produce a number of side effects that are sometimes exploited by directors for symbolic use. Most long lenses are in sharp focus on one distance plane only. Objects placed before or beyond that distance blur, go out of focus—an expressive technique, especially to the formalist filmmaker **(3–19).** The longer the lens, the more sensitive it is to distances; in the case of extremely long lenses, objects placed a mere few centimetres away from the selected focal plane can be out of focus. This deliberate blurring of planes in the background, foreground, or both can produce striking photographic and atmospheric effects.

The focal distance of long lenses can usually be adjusted while one is actually shooting, and thus, the director is able to neutralize planes and guide the viewer's eye to various distances in a sequence—a technique called **rack focusing,** or selective focusing. In *The Graduate,* director Mike Nichols used a slight focus shift instead of a cut when he wanted the viewer to look first at the young heroine, who then blurs out of focus, then at her mother, who is standing in a doorway nearby. The focus-shifting technique suggests a cause–effect relationship and parallels the heroine's sudden realization that her boyfriend's secret mistress is her own mother. In *The French Connection,* William Friedkin used selective focus in a sequence showing a criminal under surveillance. He remains in sharp focus while the city crowds of his environment are an undifferentiated blur. At strategic moments in the sequence, Friedkin shifted the focus plane from the criminal to the dogged detective who is tailing him in the crowd.

Long lenses also flatten images, decreasing the sense of distance between depth planes. Two people standing metres apart might look much closer when photographed with a telephoto lens. With very long lenses, distance planes are so compressed that the image can resemble a flat surface of abstract patterns. When anything moves toward or away from the camera in such shots, the mobile object doesn't seem to be moving at all. In *Marathon Man,* the hero (Dustin Hoffman) runs desperately toward the camera, but because of the flattening of the long lens, he seems almost to be running in place rather than moving toward his destination.

3–19. Four degrees of separation.

The lens of each of these four shots provides a subtle commentary on the relationship of the characters to their settings.

3–19a. *Trois couleurs Bleu* (*"Three Colours: Blue,"* France/Poland, 1993), *with Juliette Binoche, directed by Krzyzstof Kieslowski.*
Kieslowski's image is photographed with an extreme telephoto lens that focuses on the Binoche character at the near exclusion of her setting, which is blurred to a hazy remoteness. The background softness romanticizes the image, providing a dreamy environment to set off the delicate beauty of the actress's features and to enhance the character's private moment of insight.
(Miramax Films)

3–19b. *Trop belle pour toi* (*"Too Beautiful for You,"* France, 1989), *with Carole Bouquet and Gérard Depardieu, directed by Bertrand Blier.*
Moderate telephoto lenses are often used to enhance the lyrical potential of an image. Although not so extreme a telephoto as **(a)**, Blier's lens converts the reflections on the cars' rooftops into rhapsodic brushstrokes of light, heightening the erotic ecstasy of the characters. *(Orion Pictures)*

The wide-angle lenses, also called short lenses, have short focal lengths and wide angles of view. These are the lenses used in deep-focus shots, for they preserve a sharpness of focus on virtually all distance planes. The distortions involved in short lenses are both linear and spatial. The wider the angle, the more lines and shapes tend to warp, especially at the edges of the image. Distances between various depth planes are also exaggerated with these lenses: Two people standing very close to each other can appear metres apart in a wide-angle image. Orson Welles's films are filled with wide-angle shots. In *The Trial,* for example, he used such lenses to emphasize the vast, vacuous distance between people. In close-up ranges, wide-angle lenses tend to make huge bulbs of people's noses and slanting, sinister slits of their eyes. Welles used several such shots in *Touch of Evil.*

Movement toward or away from the camera is exaggerated when photographed with a short lens. Two or three ordinary steps can seem like inhumanly lengthy strides—an effective technique when a director wants to emphasize

3–19c. *King of the Hill* (U.S.A., 1993), with Jesse Bradford (left) and Jeroen Krabbé, directed by Steven Soderbergh.

A ne'er-do-well father (Krabbé) has just told his young son that he'll have to stay home alone for several weeks while the father tries to hustle a living on the road. The boy's anxiety and fear are intensified by his sharp focus, the father's remoteness by his somewhat blurred presentation. If Soderbergh wanted to emphasize the father's feelings, the boy would be in soft focus and the father in sharp. If the director wanted to stress the equality of their emotions, he would have used a wide-angle lens, which would render both characters in sharp focus. *(Gramercy Pictures)*

3–19d. *Schindler's List* (U.S.A., 1993), with Liam Neeson (outstretched arms), directed by Steven Spielberg.

Wide-angle lenses are used whenever deep-focus photography is called for. Objects close to the lens as well as those in the "depth" of the background are in equal focus, reinforcing the interconnectedness of the visual planes. Deep-focus photography tends to be objective, matter-of-fact, unromantic. The foreground is not necessarily more important than the mid- or background. This movie deals with a German industrialist (Neeson) who saved the lives of hundreds of Jews during the Nazi Holocaust. Because deep focus allows for

the repetition of visual motifs into infinity, Spielberg is able to suggest that Jews all over Europe were being herded in a similar manner, but they were not as lucky as the "Schindler Jews." *(Universal Pictures)*

---

a character's strength, dominance, or ruthlessness. The fish-eye lens is the most extreme wide-angle modifier; it creates such severe distortions that the lateral portions of the screen seem reflected in a sphere, as though we were looking through a crystal ball.

Lenses and filters can be used for purely cosmetic purposes—to make an actor or actress taller, slimmer, younger, or older. Josef von Sternberg sometimes covered his lens with a translucent silk stocking to give his images a gauzy, romantic aura. A few glamour actresses beyond a certain age even had clauses in their contracts stipulating that only beautifying **soft-focus** lenses could be used for their close-ups. These optical modifiers eliminate small facial wrinkles and skin blemishes.

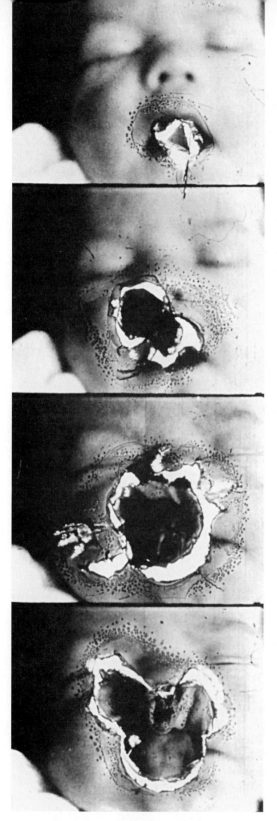

3–20. Dog Star Man (U.S.A., 1959–1964), *directed by Stan Brakhage.*
Avant-garde filmmakers are often anti-illusionist—they attempt to break down the realism of an image by calling attention to its artificiality and its material properties. A movie image is printed on a strip of celluloid, which can be manipulated, even violated. In this sequence, a baby emerges from the mouth of another baby. Brakhage is playing with the idea of what's "behind" a film image.
(Anthology Film Archives)

There are even more filters than there are lenses. Some trap light and refract it in such a way as to produce a diamond-like sparkle in the image. Many filters are used to suppress or heighten certain colours. Colour filters can be especially striking in exterior scenes. Robert Altman's *McCabe and Mrs. Miller* (photographed by Vilmos Zsigmond) used green and blue filters for many of the exterior scenes, yellow and orange for interiors. These filters emphasized the bitter cold of the winter setting and the communal warmth of the rooms inside the primitive buildings.

Though there are a number of different kinds of film **stocks**, most of them fall within the two basic categories: fast and slow. **Fast stock** is highly sensitive to light and in some cases can register images with no illumination except what's available on location, even in nighttime sequences. **Slow stock** is relatively insensitive to light and requires as much as ten times more illumination than fast stocks. Traditionally, slow stocks are capable of capturing colours with precision, without washing them out.

Fast stocks were commonly associated with documentary movies, for with their great sensitivity to light, these stocks can reproduce images of events while they're actually occurring. The documentarist is able to photograph people and places without having to set up cumbersome lights. Because of this light sensitivity, fast stocks produce a grainy image in which lines tend to be fuzzy and colours tend to wash out. In a black-and-white film, lights and darks contrast sharply and many variations of grey can be lost **(3–22)**.

3–21.   **Filmstrips of the four principal gauges used in movies, expressed in millimetres wide.**

Photographic quality depends in part on the gauge of the film used to photograph and project the images. **(1)** Suitable for projecting in an average-sized room, 8 mm and Super 8 mm are primarily for home use. **(2)** The gauge ordinarily used in schools and museums is 16 mm; if projected in extremely large halls, 16 mm images tend to grow fuzzy and the colour tends to fade. **(3)** The standard gauge for the vast majority of movie theatres is 35 mm. **(4)** For epic subjects requiring a huge screen, 70 mm is generally used; the images retain their linear sharpness and colour saturation even in enormous theatres.

Ordinarily, technical considerations such as these would have no place in a book of this sort, but the choice of stock can produce considerable psychological and aesthetic differences in a movie. Since the early 1960s, many fiction filmmakers have switched to fast stocks to give their images a documentary sense of urgency.

The **optical printer** is an elaborate machine that produces many special effects in the cinema. It includes a camera and projector precisely aligned, and it permits the operator to rephotograph all or a portion of an existing frame of a film. **Double exposure,** or the superimposition of two images, is one of the most important of these effects, for it permits the director to portray two levels of reality simultaneously. For this reason, the technique is often used in fantasy and dream sequences, as well as in scenes dealing with the supernatural. The optical printer can also produce **multiple exposures,** or the superimposition of many images simultaneously. Multiple exposures are useful for suggesting

---

3–22. *A tout prendre ("The Way It Goes,"* **Canada, 1963),** *with Claude Jutra and Victor Désy, directed by Jutra.*
Small-budget independent films often have grainy images as a result of using fast stocks that allow filming with available light. Many, like Jutra's pioneering Canadian feature film, were also originally shot on 16 mm and "blown up" to 35 mm for commercial distribution. The effect often evokes the authenticity of documentary realism and has frequently been imitated by filmmakers with much larger budgets.   *(The Claude Jutra Estate)*

3-23. *Pas de deux* **(Canada, 1968),** *directed by Norman McLaren.*
The optical printer is an invaluable piece of equipment, particularly to the formalist film-maker, because, among other things, it allows the superimposition of two or more realities within a unified space. This film uses a technique called chronophotography, in which the movements of two dancers are staggered and overlayed by the optical printer to produce a stroboscopic effect: As the dancers move, they leave a ghostly imprint on the screen. *(National Film Board of Canada)*

mood, time lapses, and any sense of mixture—of time, places, objects, events. The optical printer can combine one actor with moving images of others in a different time and place.

In this chapter, we've been concerned with visual images largely as they relate to the art and technology of cinematography. But the camera must have materials to photograph—objects, people, settings. Through the manipulation of these materials, the director is able to convey a multitude of ideas and emotions spatially. This arrangement of objects in space is referred to as a director's **mise en scène**—the subject of the following chapter.

FURTHER READING

ALTON, JOHN, *Painting with Light* (New York: Macmillan, 1962).

CLARKE, CHARLES, *Professional Cinematography* (Hollywood: American Society of Cinematographers, 1964). A practical manual.

COE, BRIAN, *The History of Movie Photography* (London: Ash & Grant, 1981).

EYMAN, SCOTT, *Five American Cinematographers* (Metuchen, N.J. & London: Scarecrow Press, 1987). Interviews with Karl Struss, Joseph Ruttenberg, James Wong Howe, Linwood Dunn, and William Clothier.

FIELDING, RAYMOND, *The Techniques of Special Effects Cinematography* (New York: Hastings House, 1965).

FINCH, CHRISTOPHER, *Special Effects: Creating Movie Magic* (New York: Abbeville, 1984). Lavishly illustrated.

MASCELLI, JOSEPH, *The Five C's of Cinematography* (Hollywood: Cine/Graphics, 1965). A practical manual.

ROVIN, JEFF, *Movie Special Effects* (San Diego, Cal.: A. S. Barnes, 1977).

SCHAEFER, DENNIS, and LARRY SALVATO, eds., *Masters of Light* (Berkeley: Univ. of California Press, 1984). Excellent collection of interviews with contemporary cinematographers.

YOUNG, FREDDIE, *The Work of the Motion Picture Cameraman* (New York: Hastings House, 1972). Technical emphasis.

MISE EN SCÈNE 4

Warner Bros.

One must compose images as the old masters did their canvases, with the same preoccupation with effect and expression.

—MARCEL CARNÉ

SUMMARY

Mise en scène: How the visual materials are staged, framed, and photographed. The frame's aspect ratio: dimensions of the screen's height and width. Film, TV, video. Functions of the frame: excluding the irrelevant, pinpointing the particular, symbolizing other enclosures. The symbolic implications of the geography of the frame: top, bottom, centre, and edges. What's off-frame and why. How images are structured: composition and design. Where we look first: the dominant. The territorial imperative: How space can be used to communicate ideas about power. Staging positions vis-à-vis the camera and what they suggest. How much room for movement: tight and loose framing. Proxemic patterns and how they define the relationships between people. Camera proxemics and the shots. Open and closed forms: windows or proscenium-framed images? The fifteen elements of a mise en scène analysis.

Mise en scène was originally a French theatrical term, meaning "placing on stage." The phrase refers to the arrangement of all the visual elements of a theatrical production within a given playing area—the stage. This area can be defined by the proscenium arch, which encloses the stage in a kind of picture frame; or the acting area can be more fluid, extending even into the auditorium. No matter what the confines of the stage may be, its mise en scène is always in three dimensions. Objects and people are arranged in actual space, which has depth as well as height and width. This space is also a continuation of the same space that the audience occupies, no matter how much a theatre director tries to suggest a separate "world" on the stage.

In movies, mise en scène is somewhat more complicated, a blend of the visual conventions of the live theatre with those of the plastic arts. Like the stage director, the filmmaker arranges objects and people within a given three-dimensional space. But once this arrangement is photographed, it's converted into a two-dimensional image of the real thing. The space in the "world" of the movie is not the same as that occupied by the audience. Only the image exists in the same physical area, like a picture in an art gallery. Mise en scène in the movies resembles the art of painting in that an image of formal patterns and shapes is presented on a flat surface and is enclosed within a **frame.** But because of its theatrical heritage, cinematic mise en scène is also a fluid choreographing of visual elements that correspond to a dramatic idea, or complex of ideas.

THE FRAME

Each movie image is enclosed by the frame of the screen, which defines the world of the film, separating it from the actual world of the darkened auditorium. Unlike the painter or still photographer, the filmmaker doesn't conceive of the framed compositions as self-sufficient statements. Like drama, film is a tem-

4–1. *Manhattan* **(U.S.A., 1979),** *with Woody Allen and Diane Keaton, directed by Allen.*
Mise en scène is a complex analytical term, encompassing four distinct formal elements:
(1) the staging of the action, **(2)** the physical setting and decor, **(3)** the manner in which
these materials are framed, and **(4)** the manner in which they are photographed. The art of
mise en scène is indissolubly linked with the art of cinematography. In this shot, for example, the story content is simple: The characters are conversing, getting to know each other,
becoming attracted. Gordon Willis's tender, low-key lighting, combined with the beauty of
the setting—the sculpture garden of the Museum of Modern Art—provides the scene with
an intensely romantic atmosphere. *(United Artists)*

poral as well as spatial art, and consequently the visuals are constantly in flux. The
compositions are broken down, redefined, and reassembled before our eyes. A
single-frame image from a movie, then, is necessarily an artificially frozen
moment that was never intended to be yanked from its context in time and
motion. For critical purposes, it's sometimes necessary to analyze a still frame in
isolation, but the viewer ought to make due allowances for the dramatic context.

The frame functions as the basis of composition in a movie image.
Unlike the painter or still photographer, however, the filmmaker fits not the
frame to the composition, but the compositions to a single-sized frame. The ratio
of the frame's horizontal and vertical dimensions—known as the **aspect ratio**—
remains constant throughout the movie. Screens come in a variety of aspect
ratios, especially since the introduction of **widescreen** in the early 1950s. Prior to
this time, most movies were shot in a 1.33:1 aspect ratio, though even in the silent
era filmmakers were constantly experimenting with different-sized screens **(4–4).**

4–2. *Notorious* **(U.S.A., 1946),** *with Ingrid Bergman, Claude Rains, and Leopoldine Konstantine, directed by Alfred Hitchcock.*
Hitchcock always regarded himself as a formalist, calculating his effects with an extraordinary degree of precision. He believed that an unmanipulated reality is filled with irrelevancies: "I do not follow the geography of a set, I follow the geography of the screen," he said. The space around actors must be orchestrated from shot to shot. "I think only of that white screen that has to be filled up the way you fill up a canvas. That's why I draw rough setups for the cameraman." Here, the mise en scène is a perfect analogue of the heroine's sense of entrapment, without violating the civilized veneer demanded by the dramatic context. The dialogue in such instances can be perfectly neutral, for the psychological tensions are conveyed by the placement of the camera and the way the characters are arranged in space. *(RKO)*

Today, most movies are projected in one of two aspect ratios: the 1.85:1 (standard) and the 2.35:1 (widescreen). Some films originally photographed in widescreen are cropped down to a conventional aspect ratio after their initial commercial release. This appalling practice is commonplace in movies that are reduced from 35 mm to 16 mm, the standard **gauge** used in most noncommercial exhibitions like those at colleges and museums. The more imaginatively the widescreen is used, the more a movie is likely to suffer when its aspect ratio is violated in this manner. Generally, at least a third of the image is hacked away by lopping off the edges of the frame. This kind of cropping can result in many visual absurdities: A speaker at the edge of the frame might be totally absent in the "revised" composition, or an actor might react in horror at something that never even comes into view. When shown on television—which has an aspect ratio of approximately 1.33:1—some of the greatest widescreen films can actually seem clumsy and poorly composed.

In the traditional visual arts, frame dimensions are governed by the nature of the subject matter. Thus, a painting of a skyscraper is likely to be vertical in shape and would be framed accordingly. A vast panoramic scene would probably be more horizontal in its dimensions. But in movies the frame ratio is imposed from without and isn't necessarily governed by the nature of the materials being photographed. This is not to say that all film images are therefore inorganic, however, for in this regard the filmmaker can be likened to a sonneteer, who chooses a rigid form precisely because of the technical challenges it presents. Much of the enjoyment we derive in reading a sonnet results from the tension between the content and the form, which consists of fourteen intricately rhymed lines. When technique and subject matter are fused in this way, aesthetic pleasure is heightened. The same principle can be applied to framing in film.

The constant size of the movie frame is especially hard to overcome in vertical compositions. A sense of height must be conveyed in spite of the dominantly horizontal shape of the screen. One method of overcoming the problem is through **masking.** In his 1916 masterpiece, *Intolerance,* D. W. Griffith blocked out portions of his images through the use of black masks, which in effect connected the darkened portions of the screen with the darkness of the auditorium. To emphasize the steep fall of a soldier from a wall, the sides of the image were masked out. To stress the vast horizon of a location, Griffith masked out the lower third of the image—thus creating a widescreen effect. Many kinds of masks are used in this movie, including diagonal, circular, and oval shapes. Some years later, the Soviet director Eisenstein urged the adoption of a square screen, on which masked images could be projected in whatever shape was appropriate to the subject matter.

In the silent-movie era, the **iris** (a circular or oval mask that can open up or close in on a subject) was rather overused. In the hands of a master, however, the iris can be a powerful dramatic statement. In *The Wild Child,* François Truffaut used an iris to suggest the intense concentration of a young boy: The surrounding blackness is a metaphor of how the youngster "blocks out" his social environment while focusing on an object immediately in front of him.

As an aesthetic device, the frame performs in several ways. The sensitive director is just as concerned with what's left out of the frame as with what's included. The frame selects and delimits the subject, editing out all irrelevancies and presenting us with only a "piece" of reality. The materials included within a **shot** are unified by the frame, which in effect imposes an order on them—the order that art carves out of the chaos of reality. The frame is thus essentially an isolating device, a technique that permits the director to confer special attention on what might be overlooked in a wider context.

The movie frame can function as a metaphor for other types of enclosures. Some directors use the frame voyeuristically. In many of the films of Hitchcock, for example, the frame is likened to a window through which the audience may satisfy its impulse to pry into the intimate details of the characters' lives. In fact, *Psycho* and *Rear Window* use this peeping technique literally. Other directors use the frame in a less snooping manner. In Jean Renoir's *The Golden Coach,* for instance, the frame suggests the proscenium arch of the live theatre, and appropriately so, since the controlling symbol of the movie centres on the idea of life as a stage.

4-3. *Lawrence of Arabia* (Britain, 1962), *with Omar Sharif and Peter O'Toole, directed by David Lean.*

The widescreen aspect ratio provides some big problems when transferred to a video format. There are several solutions, but all of them have drawbacks. The crudest solution is simply to slice off the edges of the film image and concentrate on the middle, the assumption being that the centre is where the dominant focus is likely to be. This shot would just barely contain the faces of the two characters and nothing past the centre of their heads—an uncomfortably tight squeeze. A second solution is called "pan and scan" in which a TV camera scans the scene, panning to one or the other character as each speaks—like watching a tennis match on rough seas. A similar approach is to re-edit the scene by cutting to each character, thus isolating them into their own separate space cubicles. But the essence of the shot demands that we see both characters at the same time—the drama lies in the subtle interactions of the characters. This interaction would be lost by editing. A fourth solution is called "letterbox-ing"—simply to include the entire movie image and block out the top and bottom of the TV screen. Many people object to this method, complaining that nearly half the screen is thus left empty, making an already small screen smaller.   *(Columbia Pictures)*

Certain areas within the frame can suggest symbolic ideas. By placing an object or actor within a particular section of the frame, the filmmaker can radically alter his or her comment on that object or character. Placement within the frame is another instance of how form is actually content. Each of the major sections of the frame—centre, top, bottom, and edges—can be exploited for such symbolic and metaphoric purposes.

The central portions of the screen are generally reserved for the most important visual elements. This area is instinctively regarded by most people as the intrinsic centre of interest. When we take a snapshot of a friend, we generally centre his or her figure within the confines of the **viewfinder**. Since childhood, we have been taught that a drawing must be balanced, with the middle serving as the focal point. The centre, then, is a kind of norm: We *expect* dominant visual elements to be placed there. Precisely because of this expectation, objects placed in the centre tend to be visually undramatic. Central dominance is generally favoured when the subject matter is intrinsically compelling. **Realist** filmmakers prefer central dominance because formally it's the most unobtrusive kind of framing. The viewer is allowed to concentrate on the subject matter without being distracted by visual elements that seem off centre. However, even **formalists** use the middle of the screen for dominance in routine expository shots.

4-4. *Napoleon* (France, 1927), *directed by Abel Gance.*
Napoleon is the most famous widescreen experiment of the silent era. Its triptych sequences—
such as the French army's march into Italy (pictured)—were shot in what Gance called "Poly-
vision." The process involved the coordination of three cameras so as to photograph a 160°
panorama—three times wider than the conventional aspect ratio. *(Universal Pictures)*

a

b

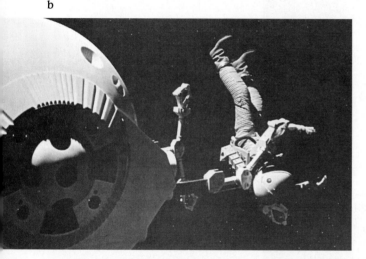

4–5. *2001: A Space Odyssey* **(U.S.A./ Britain, 1968),** *directed by Stanley Kubrick.* The widescreen is particularly suited to capturing the vastness of a locale. If this image were cropped to a conventional aspect ratio **(b)** much of the feel of the infinity of space would be sacrificed. We tend to scan an image from left to right, and therefore, in Kubrick's composition **(a),** the astronaut seems to be in danger of slipping off into the endlessness of space. If the composition is turned upside down, however **(c),** the astronaut seems to be coming home into the safety of the spacecraft.   *(MGM)*

c

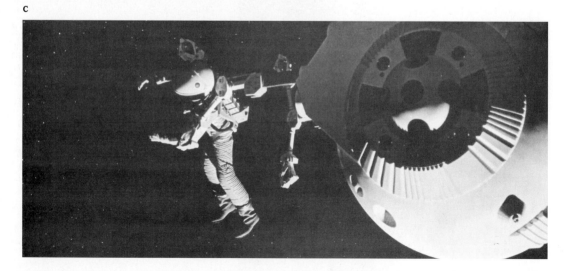

The area near the top of the frame can suggest ideas dealing with power, authority, and aspiration. A person placed here seems to control all the visual elements below, and for this reason, authority figures are often photographed in this manner. In images suggesting spirituality, often the top of the frame is exploited to convey a godlike splendour. This grandeur can also apply to objects—a palace, the top of a mountain. If an unattractive character is placed near the top of the screen, he or she can seem threatening and dangerous, superior to the other figures within the frame. However, these generalizations are true only when the other figures are approximately the same size or smaller than the dominating figure.

The top of the frame is not always used in this symbolic manner. In some instances, this is simply the most sensible area to place an object. In a **medium shot** of a figure, for example, the person's head is logically going to be near the top of the screen, but obviously this kind of framing isn't meant to be symbolic. It's merely reasonable, since that's where we'd *expect* the head to appear in medium shots. Indeed, mise en scène is essentially an art of the **long** and **extreme long shot**, for when the subject matter is detailed in a closer shot, the director has fewer choices concerning the distribution of visual elements.

The areas near the bottom of the frame tend to suggest opposite meanings from the top: subservience, vulnerability, and powerlessness. Objects and figures placed in these positions seem to be in danger of slipping out of the frame entirely. For this reason, these areas are often exploited symbolically to suggest danger. When there are two or more figures in the frame and they are approximately the same size, the figure nearer the bottom of the screen tends to be dominated by those above.

The left and right edges of the frame tend to suggest insignificance, because these are the areas farthest removed from the centre of the screen. Objects and figures placed near the edges are literally close to the darkness outside the frame. Many directors use this darkness to suggest those symbolic ideas traditionally associated with the lack of light—the unknown, the unseen, and the fearful. In some instances, the blackness outside the frame can symbolize oblivion or even death. In movies about people who want to remain anonymous and unnoticed, the director sometimes deliberately places them off centre, near the "insignificant" edges of the screen.

Finally, there are some instances when a director places the most important visual elements completely off frame. Especially when a character is associated with darkness, mystery, or death, this technique can be highly effective, for the audience is most fearful of what it can't see. In the early portions of Fritz Lang's *M,* for example, the psychotic child-killer is never seen directly. We can only sense his presence, for he lurks in the darkness outside the light of the frame. Occasionally, we catch a glimpse of his shadow streaking across the set, and we're aware of his presence by the eerie tune he whistles when he's emotionally excited or upset.

There are two other off-frame areas that can be exploited for symbolic purposes: the space behind the set and the space in front of the camera. By not

4-6. *Tokyo Story* **(Japan, 1953),** *directed by Yasujiro Ozu.*
Ozu's mise en scène is usually formal, its compositional weights balanced with exquisite delicacy. Note how the diagonal thrust of the tree branches (in an image otherwise composed of stately verticals and horizontals) counteracts the weight of the three figures on the right. The scene is staged within a proscenium-like enclosure—a frame within a frame—reinforcing its ceremonial dignity. Ozu exploits these formal compositions as ironic foils to the human materials: The intense emotions of the characters are often at odds with the decorum prescribed by such social rituals.   *(New Yorker Films)*

showing us what is happening behind a closed door, the filmmaker can provoke the viewer's curiosity, creating an unsettling effect, for we tend to fill in such vacuums with vivid imaginings. The final shot from Hitchcock's *Notorious* is a good example. The hero helps the groggy heroine past a group of Nazi agents to a waiting vehicle. The rather sympathetic villain (Claude Rains) escorts the two, hoping his colleagues won't become suspicious. In a **deep-focus long shot,** we see the three principals in the foreground while the Nazi agents remain near the open door of the house in the upper background—watching, wondering. The hero maliciously locks the villain out of the car, then drives out of frame, leaving the villain stranded without an explanation. His colleagues call out his name, and he is forced to return to the house, dreading the worst.

4-7. *Greed* **(U.S.A., 1924),** *with Gibson Gowland and Jean Hersholt (right), directed by Erich von Stroheim.*
Highly symmetrical designs are generally used when a director wishes to stress stability and harmony. In this photo, for example, the carefully balanced weights of the design reinforce these (temporary) qualities. The visual elements are neatly juxtaposed in units of twos, with the two beer-filled glasses forming the focal point. The main figures balance each other, as do the two converging brick walls, the two pairs of curtains, the two windows, the two people in each window, the shape of the picture above the men, and the shape of the resting dog below them.   *(MGM)*

He climbs the stairs and reenters the house with the suspicious agents, who then close the door behind them. Hitchcock never does show us what happens behind the door.

The area in front of the camera can also create unsettling effects of this sort. In John Huston's *The Maltese Falcon,* for example, we witness a murder without ever seeing the killer. The victim is photographed in a medium shot as a gun enters the frame just in front of the camera. Not until the end of the movie do we discover the identity of the off-frame killer.

4–8. *Midnight Express* (U.S.A., 1978), *with Brad Davis (hands raised), directed by Alan Parker.*

All the compositional elements of this shot contribute to a sense of entrapment. The protagonist is totally surrounded, not only by the ring of soldiers who have their guns poised for a kill, but also by an outer ring of compositional weights—the airplane above, the stairs and railing to the left, the bench and huddled bystanders at the lower portions of the frame, and the three gunmen sealing off the right. The high angle and the gridlike lines of the concrete runway reinforce the sense of entrapment. The image might almost be entitled NO EXIT. *(Columbia Pictures)*

COMPOSITION AND DESIGN

Although the photographable materials of movies exist in three dimensions, one of the primary problems facing the filmmaker is much like that confronting the painter: the arrangement of shapes, colours, lines, and textures on a flat rectangular surface. In the **classical cinema**, this arrangement is generally held in some kind of balance, or harmonious equilibrium. The desire for balance is analogous to people balancing on their feet, and indeed to most manufactured structures, which are balanced on the surface of the earth. Instinctively, we assume that balance is the norm in most human enterprises.

In movies, however, there are some important exceptions to this rule. When a visual artist wishes to stress a *lack* of equilibrium, many of the standard

4-9. *Family Viewing* **(Canada, 1986),** *with David Hemblen and Gabrielle Rose, directed by Atom Egoyan.*

Egoyan's films deal with the impact of modern communications technology on human relations. Interweaving film and video images, as well as sequences made in a television studio, this film explores the image and reality of modern family life. At the root of the problem is the father, Stan (Hemblen), who is unable to make love to his wife (Rose) without the aid of a video camera and a telephone sex worker. The placement of the telephone in this shot provides a wry comment on Stan's impotence when the expected call fails to come through on time.   *(Ego Film Arts/Johnny Eisen)*

conventions of classical composition are deliberately violated. In movies, the dramatic context is usually the determining factor in composition. What is superficially a bad composition might actually be highly effective, depending on its psychological context. Many films are concerned with neurotic characters or events that are out of joint. In such cases, the director might well ignore the conventions of classical composition. Instead of centring a character in the image, his or her spiritual maladjustment can be conveyed symbolically by photographing the subject at the edge of the frame. In this manner, the filmmaker throws off the visual balance and presents us with an image that's psychologically more appropriate to the dramatic context.

There are no set rules about these matters. A classical filmmaker like Buster Keaton used mostly balanced compositions. Filmmakers outside the classical tradition tend to favour compositions that are asymmetrical or off centre. In movies a variety of techniques can be used to convey the same ideas and emotions. Some filmmakers favour visual methods, others favour dialogue, still others **editing** or acting **(4–10).**

The human eye automatically attempts to harmonize the formal elements of a composition into a unified whole. The eye can detect as many as seven or eight major elements of a composition simultaneously. In most cases, however, the eye doesn't wander promiscuously over the surface of an image but is guided to specific areas in sequence. The director accomplishes this through the use of a **dominant contrast,** also known as the **dominant.** The dominant is that area of an image that immediately attracts our attention because of a conspicuous and compelling contrast. It stands out in some kind of isolation from the other elements within the image. In black-and-white movies, the dominant contrast is generally achieved through a juxtaposition of lights and darks. For example, if the director wishes the viewer to look first at an actor's hand rather than his face, the lighting of the hand would be harsher than that of the face, which would be lit in a more subdued manner. In colour films, the dominant is often achieved by having one colour stand out from the others. Virtually any formal element can be used as a dominant: a shape, a line, a texture, and so on.

After we take in the dominant, our eye then scans the **subsidiary contrasts** that the artist has arranged to act as counterbalancing devices. Our eyes are seldom at rest with visual compositions, then, even with paintings or still photographs. We look somewhere first, then we look at those areas of diminishing interest. None of this is accidental, for visual artists deliberately structure their images so a specific sequence is followed. In short, movement in film isn't confined only to objects and people that are literally in motion.

In most cases, the visual interest of the dominant corresponds with the dramatic interest of the image. Because films have temporal and dramatic contexts, however, the dominant is often movement itself, and what some aestheticians call **intrinsic interest.** Intrinsic interest simply means that the audience, through the context of a story, knows that an object is more important dramatically than it appears to be visually. Thus, even though a gun might occupy only a small portion of the surface of an image, if we know that the gun is *dramatically* important, it will assume dominance in the picture despite its visual insignificance.

Movement is almost always an automatic dominant contrast, provided that the other elements in the image are stationary. Even a third-rate director can guide the viewer's eyes through the use of motion. For this reason, lazy filmmakers ignore the potential richness of their images and rely solely on movement as a means of capturing the viewer's attention. On the other hand, most directors will vary their dominants, sometimes emphasizing motion, other times using movement as a subsidiary contrast only. The importance of motion

4–10a. *Macbeth* **(U.S.A./Britain, 1971),** *with Francesca Annis and Jon Finch, directed by Roman Polanski.*

Movie images are generally scanned in a structured sequence of eye-stops. The eye is first attracted to a dominant contrast that compels our most immediate attention by virtue of its conspicuousness, and then travels to the subsidiary areas of interest within the frame. In this photo, for example, the eye is initially attracted to the face of Lady Macbeth, which is lit in high contrast and is surrounded by darkness. We then scan the brightly lit "empty" space between her and her husband. The third area of interest is Macbeth's thoughtful face, which is lit in a more subdued manner. The visual interest of this photo corresponds to the dramatic context of the film, for Lady Macbeth is slowly descending into madness and feels spiritually alienated and isolated from her husband.   *(Columbia Pictures)*

4–10b. *Macbeth* **(U.S.A., 1948),** *with Peggy Webber, directed by Orson Welles.* Realists and formalists solve problems in different ways, with different visual techniques. Polanski's presentation of Lady Macbeth's madness is conveyed in a relatively realistic manner, with emphasis on acting and subtle lighting effects. Welles took a more formalistic approach, using physical correlatives to convey interior states, such as the iron fence's knifelike blades, which almost seem to pierce Webber's body. The fence is not particularly realistic or even functional: Welles exploited it primarily as a symbolic analogue of her inner torment. *(Republic Pictures)*

4–11. *Le Déclin de l'empire américain ("The Decline of the American Empire,"* **Canada, 1986),** *with (clockwise from upper left) Louise Portal, Dominique Michel, Dorothée Berryman, and Geneviève Rioux, directed by Denys Arcand.*
A group of women work out, talk, and laugh in a health club while the men in their lives prepare a gourmet meal in an apartment. The circular design in this shot reinforces the air of camaraderie among the women. The shot's design embodies their shared experiences and interconnectedness: literally, a relaxed circle of friends.   *(Cineplex Odeon Films)*

varies with the kind of shot used. Movement tends to be less distracting in the longer shots and highly conspicuous in the closer ranges.

Unless the viewer has time to explore the surface of an image at leisure, visual confusion can result when there are more than eight or nine major compositional elements. If visual confusion is the deliberate intention of an image—as in a battle scene, for example—the director will sometimes overload the composition to produce this effect. In general, the eye struggles to unify various elements into an ordered pattern. For example, even in a complex design, the eye will connect similar shapes, colours, textures, etc. The very repetition of a formal element can suggest the repetition of an experience. These

4-12. *Jules et Jim* **(France, 1961),** *with Henri Serre, Jeanne Moreau, and Oskar Werner, directed by François Truffaut.*
Compositions grouped into units of three, five, and seven tend to suggest dynamic, unstable relationships. Those organized in units of two, four, or six, on the other hand, tend to imply fixed, harmonious relationships. This triangular composition is organically related to the theme of the movie, which deals with the shifting love relationships between the three characters. The woman is almost invariably at the apex of the triangle: She likes it that way.　*(Janus Films)*

connections form a visual rhythm, forcing the eye to leap over the surface of the design to perceive the overall balance. Visual artists often refer to compositional elements as weights. In most cases, especially in classical cinema, the artist distributes these weights harmoniously over the surface of the image. In a totally symmetrical design—almost never found in fiction movies—the visual weights are distributed evenly, with the centre of the composition as the axis point. Because most compositions are asymmetrical, however, the weight of one element is counterpoised with another. A shape, for example, counteracts the weight of a colour. Psychologists and art theorists have discovered that certain portions of a composition are intrinsically weighted. The German art historian Heinrich Wölfflin, for instance, pointed out that we tend to scan pictures from left to right, all other compositional elements being equal. Spectators from non-Western cultures read images differently but, in classical compositions, the image is often more heavily weighted on the left to counteract the intrinsic heaviness of the right.

4–13. *The Graduate* (U.S.A., 1967), *with Anne Bancroft and Dustin Hoffman, directed by Mike Nichols.*

Viewers can be made to feel insecure or isolated when a hostile foreground element (Bancroft) comes between us and a figure we identify with. In this scene, our hero, Benjamin Braddock, college graduate, feels threatened. An older woman, a friend of his parents, tries to seduce him—he thinks. He's not sure. His feelings of entrapment and imminent violation are conveyed not by his words, which are stammering and embarrassed, but by the mise en scène. Blocked off in front by her seminude body, he is also virtually confined at his rear by the window frame—an enclosure within an enclosure (the room) within the enclosure of the movie frame. *(Avco Embassy Pictures)*

The upper part of the composition is heavier than the lower. For this reason, skyscrapers, columns, and obelisks taper upward or they would appear top-heavy. Images seem more balanced when the centre of gravity is kept low, with most of the weights in the lower portions of the screen. A landscape is seldom divided horizontally at the midpoint of a composition, or the sky would appear to oppress the earth. **Epic** filmmakers like Eisenstein and Ford create some of their most disquieting effects with precisely this technique: They let the sky dominate through its intrinsic heaviness. The terrain and its inhabitants seem overwhelmed from above.

Isolated figures and objects tend to be heavier than those in a cluster. Sometimes one object—merely by virtue of its isolation—can balance a whole group of otherwise equal objects. In many movies, the protagonist is shown apart from a hostile group, yet the two seem evenly matched despite the arithmetical differences. This effect is conveyed through the visual weight of the hero in isolation **(5–11).**

Psychological experiments have revealed that certain lines suggest directional movements. Although vertical and horizontal lines seem to be visually at rest, if movement *is* perceived, horizontal lines tend to move from left to right, vertical lines, from bottom to top. Diagonal or oblique lines are more dynamic—that is, in transition. They tend to sweep upward. These psychological phenomena are important to the visual artist, especially the filmmaker, for the dramatic context is not always conducive to an overt expression of emotion **(4–14).** For example, if a director wishes to show a character's inward agitation within a calm context, this quality can be conveyed through the dynamic use of line: An image composed of tense diagonals can suggest the character's inner turmoil, despite the apparent lack of drama in the action. Some of the most expressive cinematic effects can be achieved precisely through this tension between the compositional elements of an image and its dramatic context.

4–14.   *Les Quatre cents coups* **("The 400 Blows,"** France, 1959), *with Jean-Pierre Léaud, directed by François Truffaut.*

Often the context of a scene does not permit a director to express emotions dramatically. Here, the boy's anxiety and tenseness are expressed in purely visual terms. His inward agitation is conveyed by the diagonal lines of the fence. His sense of entrapment is suggested by the tight framing (sides, top, bottom), the shallow focus (rear), and the obstruction of the fence itself (foreground).   *(Janus Films)*

A skeletal structure underlies most visual compositions. Throughout the ages, artists have especially favoured S and X shapes, triangular designs, and circles. These designs are often used simply because they are thought to be inherently beautiful. Visual artists also use certain compositional forms to emphasize symbolic concepts. For example, binary structures emphasize parallelism—virtually any **two shot** will suggest the couple, doubles, shared space **(4–28, 4–35).** Triadic compositions stress the dynamic interplay among three main elements. Circular compositions can suggest security, enclosure, the female principle **(4–11).**

Design is generally fused with a thematic idea, at least in the best movies. In *Jules et Jim,* for example, Truffaut consistently used triangular designs, for the film deals with a trio of characters whose relationships are constantly shifting yet always interrelated. The form of the images in this case is a symbolic representation of the romantic triangle of the dramatic content. These triangular designs dynamize the visuals, keeping them off balance, subject to change **(4–12).** Generally, designs consisting of units of three, five, and seven tend to produce these effects. Designs composed of two, four, or six units seem more stable, and balanced **(4–7).**

SET DESIGN

In the best movies, settings are not merely backdrops for the action, but symbolic extensions of the theme and characterization. Settings can convey an immense amount of information, whether they are specially constructed in a **studio** or filmed on location.

Epic films would be virtually impossible without the extreme long shots of vast expanses of land. Other **genres**, particularly those requiring a degree of stylization or deliberate unreality, have been associated with the studio: musicals, horror films, and many period films. Such genres often stress a kind of magical, sealed-off universe, and images taken from real life tend to clash with these essentially claustrophobic qualities.

However, these are merely generalizations. There are some westerns that have been shot mostly indoors and some musicals that have been photographed in actual locations. If a location is extravagantly beautiful, there's no reason why a romantic musical can't exploit such a setting. The Paris locations of Minnelli's *Gigi* are a good example of how actual locations can enhance a stylized genre. In short, it all depends on how it's done. As the French historian Georges Sadoul pointed out, "The dichotomy between the studio and the street, the antithesis between Lumière and Méliès, are false oppositions when one attempts to find in them the solution to the problems of realism and art. Films completely outside time have been shot out of doors; completely realistic films have been shot in the studio."

In set design, as in other aspects of movies, the terms *realism* and *formalism* are simply convenient critical labels. Most sets tend toward one style or the other, but few are pure examples. For instance, in *The Birth of a Nation*, Griffith proudly proclaims that a number of his **scenes** are historical facsimiles of real places and events—like Ford's Theatre where Lincoln was assassinated, or the signing of the Emancipation Proclamation. These scenes are modelled on actual photographs of the period. Yet Griffith's facsimiles are created in a studio. On the other hand, real locations can be exploited to create a somewhat artificial—formalistic—effect. For example, in shooting *October*, Eisenstein had the Winter Palace at his disposal for several months. Yet the images in the movie are baroque: richly textured and formally complex. Although Eisenstein chose actual locations for their authenticity, they are never just picturesque backgrounds to the action. Each shot is carefully designed. Each exploits the inherent *form* of the setting, contributing significantly to the aesthetic impact of the sequence **(4–21)**. Realistic or formalistic?

Realism is never a simple term. In movies it's used to describe a variety of styles. Some critics use modifiers like "poetic realism," "documentary realism," and "studio realism" to make finer distinctions. The nature of beauty in realism is also a complex issue. Beauty of form is an important component of poetic realism. The early works of Fellini, such as *The Nights of Cabiria*, are handsomely mounted and slightly aestheticized to appeal to our visual sense. Similarly, John Ford shot nine of his westerns in Monument Valley **(1–8, 11–15)** because of its spectacular beauty. Among other things, Ford was a great landscape artist. Many realistic films shot in the studio are also slightly stylized to exploit this "incidental" visual beauty.

In other realistic films, beauty—in this conventional sense—plays a lesser role. A major criterion of aesthetic value in a movie like Pontecorvo's *Battle of Algiers* is its deliberate roughness. The story deals with the struggle for liberation of the Algerian people from their French colonial masters. It was shot entirely in the streets and houses of Algiers. The setting is rarely exploited for its aesthetic beauty. In fact, Pontecorvo's lack of formal organization, his refusal to yield even slightly in matters of "style," is his principal virtue as an artist. The moral power of the materials takes precedence over formal considerations. The setting's beauty is in its truth. In films such as these, style (that is, distortion) is regarded as prettification, a form of insincerity, and therefore ugly. Even outright ugliness can be a criterion of aesthetic beauty. The gaudy sets and decor in *Touch of Evil* are organic to the nature of the materials.

To the unsympathetic, the cult of realism verges on madness. But there's a method to it. For example, John Huston shot *The African Queen* in the tropics because he knew he wouldn't have to worry about a thousand little details, such as how to get the actors to sweat a lot, or how to get their clothes to stick to their bodies. Perhaps the most famous, if not infamous, example of this passion for authenticity is Erich von Stroheim, who detested studio sets. In *Greed*, he insisted that his actors actually live in a seedy boarding house to get the "feel" of the film's low-life setting. He forced them to wear shabby clothing and deprived them of all the amenities that their characters would lack in actuality. Perhaps because of the severe hardships his cast and crew suffered, the movie's authenticity is incontestable.

Spectacle films usually require the most elaborate sets. Historical reconstructions of ancient Rome or Egypt are enormously expensive to build, and they can make or break a film in this genre because spectacle is the major

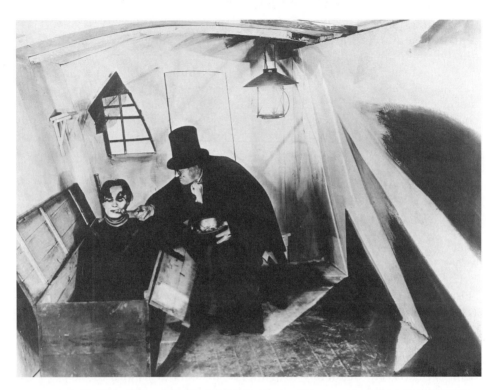

4–15.   *The Cabinet of Dr. Caligari* **(Germany, 1919),** *with Conrad Veidt and Werner Krauss (wearing hat); production design by Hermann Warm, Walter Röhrig, and Walter Reimann; directed by Robert Wiene.*
The German expressionist movement of the post-World War I era emphasized visual design above all. The movement's main contributions were in the live theatre, the graphic arts, and the cinema. The great stage director Max Reinhardt was a seminal influence. In his theory of design, Reinhardt advocated an ideal of "landscapes imbued with soul." The declared aim of most German expressionists was to eliminate nature for a state of absolute abstraction. It is a style steeped in anxiety and terror. The sets are deliberately artificial: flat, obviously painted, with no attempt to preserve the conventions of perspective and scale. They are meant to represent a state of mind, not a place.   *(Museum of Modern Art)*

attraction. Perhaps the most famous sets of this type are found in the Babylonian story of Griffith's *Intolerance.* The unprecedented monumentality of these sets is what skyrocketed Griffith's budget to an all-time high of $1.9 million—an astronomical figure by 1916 standards, hefty even by today's. The banquet scene for Belshazzar's feast alone cost a reputed $250 000 and employed over four thousand extras. The story required the construction of a walled city so vast that for years it remained a standing monument—called "Griffith's Folly" by cynics in the trade. The set extended over a kilometre in length. The court was flanked by enormous colonnades supporting pillars fifteen metres high, each holding up a huge statue of an erect elephant-god. Behind the court were

4–16. Miniature set for *Letter From an Unknown Woman* (U.S.A., 1948), *directed by Max Ophüls.*
Period films often benefit from the slight sense of unreality of studio sets. If a set is needed only for establishing purposes, miniatures are often constructed. These scaled-down sets can be over two metres tall, depending on the amount of detail and realism needed. Note the two studio floodlights behind the houses of this miniature and the flat, two-dimensional apartment dwellings on the horizon in the upper right. *(Universal Pictures)*

---

towers and ramparts, their tops planted with cascading flowers and exotic trees representing Belshazzar's famous Hanging Gardens. The outer walls of the city were sixty metres high, yet were wide enough that two chariots were able to roar past each other on the road that perched on top. Astonishingly, this and other sets in the film were built without architectural plans. As Griffith kept making additional suggestions, his **art director**, Frank "Huck" Wortman, and his crew kept expanding the set from day to day.

Expressionistic sets are usually created in the studio, where the contaminations of reality cannot penetrate. Magic, not realism, is the aim. Méliès is the prototypical example. He was called "the Jules Verne of films" because his feats of prestidigitation astonished the public. The first in a long line of special-effects wizards, Méliès usually painted his sets, often with *trompe-l'oeil* perspectives to suggest depth. He combined live actors with fanciful settings to produce a dreamlike atmosphere. He used **animation**, **miniatures**, and a wide range of optical tricks, charming his audiences with vistas of imaginary realms **(6–3)**.

Expressionistic sets appeal to our sense of the marvellous. The work of Danilo Donati, Italy's best-known designer, is a good example. The extravagant artificiality of the sets and costumes in such movies as Fellini's *Satyricon, Amar-*

cord, and *Casanova* are pure products of the imagination—Fellini's as well as Donati's. The director often provided the designer with preliminary sketches, and the two artists worked closely in determining the visual design of each film. Their conjurations can be moving, as well as witty and beautiful. For example, *Amarcord* is a stylized reminiscence of Fellini's youth in his hometown of Rimini. (The title, from the Romagnan dialect, means "I remember.") But Fellini shot the movie in a studio, not on location. He wanted to capture feelings, not facts. Throughout the film, the townspeople feel stifled by the provincial isolation of their community. They are filled with loneliness and long for something extraordinary to transform their lives. When they hear that a mammoth luxury liner, the Rex, will pass through the ocean waters not far beyond the town's shore, many of these wistful souls decide to row out to sea to greet the ship. Hundreds of them crowd into every available boat and stream away from the beach like fervent pilgrims on a quest. Then they wait. Evening settles, bringing with it a thick fog. Still they wait. In one boat Gradisca, the charming town sexpot, confides to some sympathetic friends of her dissatisfaction with her life. At thirty she is still single, childless, and unfulfilled. Her "heart overflows with love," yet she has never found a "truly dedicated man." In the dark silence, she weeps softly over the prospect of a barren future. Midnight passes, and still the townspeople wait faithfully. Then, when most of the characters are sleeping in their fragile boats, they're awakened by a boy's shout: "It's here!" Like a graceful apparition, the light-bedecked Rex glides past in all its regal grandeur (**4–17**). Nino Rota's rapturous music swells to a crescendo as the townspeople wave and shout joyously. Gradisca's eyes stream with tears of exhilaration and yearning while a blind accordionist asks excitedly, "Tell me what it looks like!" Then, as mysteriously as it appeared, the phantom ship is swallowed by the fog and slips silently off into the night.

During the golden age of the Hollywood studio system, each of the **majors** had a characteristic visual style, determined in large part by the designers at each studio. Some were called production designers, others art directors, a few simply set designers. Their job was to determine the "look" of each film, and they worked closely with **producers** and directors to ensure that the sets, decor, costumes, and photographic style were coordinated to produce a unified effect. For example, MGM specialized in glamour, luxury, and opulent **production values**, and its art director, Cedric Gibbons, virtually stamped each film with "the Metro look." Because all the studios attempted to diversify their products as much as possible, however, their art directors had to be versatile. For instance, RKO's Van Nest Polglase supervised the design of such diverse movies as *King Kong, Top Hat, The Informer*, and *Citizen Kane*. Paramount's Hans Dreier began his career at Germany's famous UFA studio. He was usually at his best creating a sense of mystery and romantic fantasy, as in the films of Josef von Sternberg. Dreier also designed the superb Art Deco sets for Lubitsch's *Trouble in Paradise*. Warner Brothers' art director, Anton Grot, was a specialist in grubby, realistic locales (**4–18**). The studio claimed that its films were "Torn from Today's Headlines!" to quote from its publicity blurbs. Warner Brothers favoured topical genres with an emphasis on working-class life: gangster films,

4–17. *Amarcord* **(Italy, 1974),** *art direction and costumes by Danilo Donati, cinematography by Giuseppe Rotunno, directed by Federico Fellini.*
For Fellini, who began his career as a realist, the studio became a place to create magic—along with his fellow magicians Donati and Rotunno. "To me and other directors like me," Fellini said, "the cinema is a way of interpreting and remaking reality through fantasy and imagination. The use of the studio is an indispensable part of what we are doing." *(New World Pictures)*

urban melodramas, and proletarian musicals. Like his counterparts at other studios, however, Grot could work in a variety of styles and genres. For example, he designed the enchanting sets for *A Midsummer Night's Dream*.

Certain types of locales were in such constant demand that the studios constructed permanent **back-lot sets**, which were used in film after film: a turn-of-the-century street, a European square, an urban slum, and so on. Of course these were suitably altered with new furnishings to make them look different each time they were used. The studio with the largest number of back lots was MGM, although Warner, Paramount, and Twentieth Century–Fox also boasted a considerable number of them. Not all standing sets were located close to the studio. It was cheaper to construct some outside the environs of Los Angeles where real estate values weren't at a premium. If a movie called for a huge realistic set—like the Welsh mining village for *How Green Was My Valley*—it was often built far from the studio **(4–19)**. Similarly, most of the studios owned western frontier towns, ranches, and midwestern-type farms, which were located outside the Los Angeles area.

What matters most in a setting is how it embodies the essence of the story materials and the artistic vision of the filmmaker. As the British designer Robert Mallet-Stevens noted, "A film set, in order to be a good set, must act. Whether realistic or expressionistic, modern or ancient, it must play its part. The set must present the character before he has even appeared. It must indi-

4–18. *Little Caesar* (U.S.A., 1930), *with Edward G. Robinson (standing), art direction by Anton Grot, directed by Mervyn LeRoy.*

Grot was art director at Warner Brothers from 1927 to 1948. Unlike his counterparts Gibbons, Dreier, and Polglase, however, Grot often took an active hand in designing the studio's major films. His earliest work is somewhat in the German expressionist tradition, but he soon became one of the most versatile of artists. He designed films like the gritty and realistic *Little Caesar*, as well as the Busby Berkeley musical *Gold Diggers of 1933*, with its surrealistic, dreamlike sets. *(Warner Brothers)*

cate his social position, his tastes, his habits, his lifestyle, his personality. The sets must be intimately linked with the action."

Settings can also be used to suggest a sense of progression in the characters. For example, in Fellini's *La Strada*, one of his most realistic movies, the protagonist and his simple-minded assistant are shown as reasonably happy, travelling together from town to town with their tacky theatrical act. After he abandons her, he heads for the mountains. Gradually, the landscape changes: Trees are stripped of their foliage, snow and dirty slush cover the ground, the sky is a murky grey. The changing setting is a gauge of the protagonist's spiritual condition: Nature itself seems to grieve after the helpless assistant is left alone to die.

A film can fragment a set into a series of shots, now emphasizing one aspect of a room, later another, depending on the needs of the director in finding appropriate visual analogues for thematic and psychological ideas. In Losey's *The Servant*, a stairway is used as a major thematic symbol. The film deals with a servant's gradual control over his master. Losey uses the stairway as a kind of psychological battlefield where the relative positions of the two men on the stairs give the audience a sense of who's winning the battle. Losey also uses the rails on the stairway to suggest prison bars: The master of the house is often photographed from behind these bars.

Even the furniture of a room can be exploited for psychological and thematic reasons. In one of his classes, Eisenstein once discussed at length the

4-19. *How Green Was My Valley* (U.S.A., 1941), *art direction by Nathan Juran and Richard Day, directed by John Ford.*
The art directors at Twentieth Century–Fox specialized in realistic sets, like this turn-of-the-century Welsh mining village, which covered thirty-five hectares and was built in a California valley. Elaborate sets like these were not dismantled after production, for with suitable alterations they could be converted into other locations. For example, two years after Ford's film, this set was transformed into a Nazi-occupied Norwegian village for *The Moon Is Down.* *(Twentieth Century–Fox)*

significance of a table for a set. The class exercise centred on an adaptation of Balzac's novel *Père Goriot.* The scene is set at a dinner table that Balzac described as circular. But Eisenstein convincingly argued that a round table is wrong cinematically, for it implies equality, with each person linked in a circle. To convey the stratified class structure of the boarding house, Eisenstein suggested the use of a long rectangular table, with the haughty mistress of the house at the head, the favoured tenants close to her sides, and the lowly Goriot alone, near the base of the table.

Such attention to detail often distinguishes a master of film from a mere technician, who settles for only a general effect. The setting of a movie—far more than any play—can even take over as the central interest (**4–20**). In Kubrick's *2001: A Space Odyssey,* the director spends most of his time lovingly photographing the instruments of a spaceship, various space stations, and the enormous expanses of outer space itself. The few people in the movie seem almost incidental and certainly far less interesting than the real centre of concern—the setting. It would be impossible to produce *2001* on stage: The materials of the film are not theatrically convertible. Kubrick's movie is a vivid illustration of André Bazin's observation that the function of the cinema is "to bring to light certain details that the stage would have left untreated."

4–20. *Blade Runner* (U.S.A., 1982), *with Harrison Ford, directed by Ridley Scott.*
A hybrid of science fiction, film noir, detective thriller, bounty-hunter western, and love story, *Blade Runner* is also eclectic in its visual style, a collaborative effort that includes the contributions of art director David Snyder, production designer Lawrence G. Paul, special visual effects designer Douglas Trumbull, and cinematographer Jordan Cronenweth. The story is set in Los Angeles in the year 2019. Nature has gone berserk, deluging the teeming city with an almost constant downpour. Smoke, fog, and steam add to the fumigated congestion. It is a city of dreadful night, punctuated by neon signs in day-glo colours, cheap Orientalized billboards, and a profusion of advertising come-ons. Hunks of long-discarded machinery litter the landscape. The sound track throbs with eerie sounds, echoes, pounding pistons, and the noises of flying vehicles shuttling through the poisonous atmosphere. It is a city choking on its own technology. *(Warner Bros.)*

A systematic analysis of a set involves a consideration of the following characteristics:

1. *Exterior or interior.* If the set is an exterior, how does nature function as a symbolic analogue to the mood, theme, or characterization?
2. *Style.* Is the set realistic and lifelike, or is it stylized and deliberately distorted? Is it in a particular style, such as colonial American, Art Deco, or sleek contemporary?
3. *Studio or location.* If the set is an actual location, why was it chosen? What does it say about the characters?
4. *Period.* What era does the set represent?
5. *Class.* What is the apparent income level of the owners?
6. *Size.* How large is the set? Rich people tend to take up more space than the poor, who are usually crowded in their living area.
7. *Decoration.* How is the set furnished? Are there any status symbols, oddities of taste, etc.?
8. *Symbolic function.* What kind of overall image does the set and its furnishings project?

TERRITORIAL SPACE

So far we have been concerned with the art of mise en scène primarily as it relates to the structuring of patterns on a two-dimensional surface. But since most movie images deal with the illusion of volume and depth, the film director must keep these theatrical considerations in mind while composing the visuals. It's one thing to construct a pleasing arrangement of shapes, lines, colours, and textures; but movie images must also tell a story in time, a story that generally involves human beings and their problems. Unlike notes of music, then, forms in film are not usually pure—they refer specifically to objects in reality.

Directors generally emphasize volume in their images precisely because they wish to avoid an abstract, flat look in their compositions. In most cases, filmmakers compose on three visual planes: the midground, the foreground, and the background. Not only does this technique suggest a sense of depth, it can also radically alter the dominant contrast of an image, serving as a kind of qualifying characteristic, either subtle or conspicuous. For example, a figure is often placed in the midground of a composition. Whatever is placed in the foreground will comment on the figure in some way **(4–14)**. Some foliage, for instance, is likely to suggest a naturalness and blending with the environment. A gauzy curtain in the foreground can suggest mystery, eroticism, and femininity. The cross-hatching of a window frame can suggest self-division. And so on, with as many foreground qualifiers as the director and **cinematographer** can think of. These same principles apply to backgrounds, although objects placed in these areas tend to yield in dominance to mid- and foreground ranges.

One of the most elementary, yet crucial, decisions the film director makes is what shot to use vis-à-vis the materials photographed. That is, how much detail should be included within the frame? How close should the camera get to the subject—which is another way of saying how close should *we* get to the subject, since the viewer's eye tends to identify with the camera's **lens**. These are not minor problems, for the amount of space included within the frame can radically affect our response to the photographed materials. With any given subject, the filmmaker can use a variety of shots, each of which includes or excludes a given amount of surrounding space. But how much space is just right in a shot? What's too much or too little?

Space is a medium of communication, and the way we respond to objects and people within a given area is a constant source of information in life as well as movies. In virtually any social situation, we receive and give off signals relating to our use of space and those people who share it. Most of us aren't particularly conscious of this medium, but we instinctively become alerted whenever we feel that certain social conventions about space are being violated. For example, when people enter a movie theatre, they tend to seat themselves at appropriate intervals from each other. But what's appropriate? And who or what defines it? Why do we feel threatened when someone takes a seat next to us in a nearly empty theatre? After all, the seat isn't ours, and the other person has paid

4-21. *October* (Russia 1928), *directed by Sergei Eisenstein.* Eisenstein is best known for his approach to editing (see Chapter 6) in which contrasting shots collide with each other to create an active response from the spectator. But he also applied the "montage" principle within individual shots, as in this image from his epic celebration of the Russian revolution. The marked contrasts within the shot—between light and dark, high and low, foreground and background—enforce the idea of Lenin as the driving force of the revolution. *(Sovkino)*

for the privilege of sitting wherever he or she wishes. Is it paranoid to feel anxiety in such a situation, or is it a normal instinctive response?

A number of psychologists and anthropologists—including Konrad Lorenz, Robert Sommers, and Edward T. Hall—have explored these and related questions. Their findings are especially revealing in terms of how space is used in cinema. In his study *On Aggression,* for example, Lorenz discusses how most animals—including humans—are territorial. That is, they lay claim to a given area and defend it from outsiders. This territory is a kind of personal haven of safety and is regarded by the organism as an extension of itself. When living creatures are too tightly packed into a given space, the result can be stress, tension, and anxiety. In many cases, when this territorial imperative is violated, the intrusion can provoke aggressive and violent behaviour, and sometimes a battle for dominance ensues over control of the territory.

Territories also have a spatial hierarchy of power. That is, the most dominant organism of a community is literally given more space, whereas the less dominant are crowded together. The amount of space an organism occupies is generally proportional to the degree of control it enjoys within a given territory. These spatial principles can be seen in many human communities as well. A classroom, for example, is usually divided into a teaching area and a student seating area, but the proportion of space allotted to the authority figure is greater than that allotted to each of those being instructed. The spatial structure of virtually any kind of territory used by humans betrays a discernible concept of authority. No matter how egalitarian we like to think we are, most of us conform to these spatial conventions. When a distinguished person enters a crowded room, for example, most people instinctively make room for him or her. In fact, they're giving that person far more room than they themselves occupy.

But what has all this got to do with movies? A great deal, for space is one of the principal mediums of communication in film. The way that people are arranged in space can tell us a lot about their social and psychological relationships. In film, dominant characters are almost always given more space to occupy than others—unless the film deals with the loss of power or the social insignificance of a character. The amount of space taken up by a character in a movie doesn't necessarily relate to that person's actual social dominance, but to his or her dramatic importance. Authoritarian figures like kings generally occupy a larger amount of space than peasants; but if a film is primarily about peasants, they will dominate spatially. In short, dominance is defined contextually in film—not necessarily the way it's perceived in real life.

The movie frame is also a kind of territory, though a temporary one, existing only for the duration of the shot. The way space is shared within the frame is one of the major tools of the **metteur en scène,** who can define, adjust, and redefine human relationships by exploiting spatial conventions. Furthermore, once a relationship has been established, the director can go on to other matters simply by changing the camera **setup.** The film director, in other words, is not confined to a spatial area that is permanent throughout the scene. A master of mise en scène can express shifting psychological and social nuances with a single shot—by exploiting the space between characters, the depth planes within the images, the intrinsically weighted areas of the frame, and the direction the characters are facing vis-à-vis the camera.

An actor can be photographed in any of five basic positions, each conveying different psychological undertones: (1) *full front*—facing the camera; (2) the *quarter turn;* (3) *profile*—looking off frame left or right; (4) the *three-quarter turn;* and (5) *back to camera.* Because the viewer identifies with the camera's lens, the positioning of the actor vis-à-vis the camera will determine many of our reactions. The more we see of the actor's face, the greater our sense of privileged intimacy; the less we see, the more mysterious and inaccessible the actor will seem.

4–22a. *The Blue Angel* **(Germany, 1930),** *with Marlene Dietrich (left foreground), directed by Josef von Sternberg.* (Janus Films)

Density of texture refers to the amount of visual detail in a picture. How much information does the filmmaker pack into the image and why? Most movies are moderately textured, depending on the amount of light thrown on the subject matter. Some images are stark, whereas others are densely textured. The degree of density is often a symbolic analogue of the quality of life in the world of the film. The cheap cabaret setting of *The Blue Angel* is chaotic and packed, swirling in smoke and cluttered with tawdry ornaments. The atmosphere seems almost suffocating. The stark futuristic world of *THX 1138* is sterile and empty.

4–22b. *THX 1138* **(U.S.A., 1971),** *with Robert Duvall and Donald Pleasence, directed by George Lucas.* (Warner Bros.)

4-23a. *La Grande illusion* **(France, 1937),** *with (centre to right) Erich von Stroheim, Pierre Fresnay, and Jean Gabin, directed by Jean Renoir.*

Tight and loose framing derive their symbolic significance from the dramatic context: They're not intrinsically meaningful. In Renoir's World War I masterpiece, for example, the tight frame, in effect, becomes a symbolic prison, a useful technique in films that deal with entrapment, confinement, or literal imprisonment.   *(Janus Films)*

4-23b. *What's Love Got to Do With It* **(U.S.A., 1993),** *with Laurence Fishburne and Angela Bassett, directed by Brian Gibson.*

In this scene, the Fishburne character has just suffered a traumatic shock, and Bassett tries to comfort him by holding him close. The tightly framed shot provides nurturing intimacy: Moving the camera so close to the characters suggests a protective buffer against the hostile outside world. The tight framing doesn't confine, it cocoons the characters.   *(©Touchstone Pictures. All Rights Reserved.)*

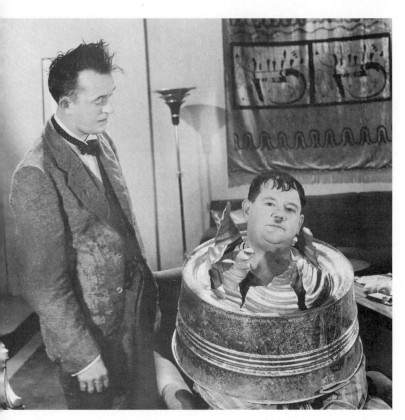

4-24. *Sons of the Desert* (U.S.A., 1933), *with Stan Laurel and Oliver Hardy, directed by William Seiter.* Whenever Stan does something really dumb, which usually results in a loss of dignity for his partner, Ollie turns to the camera—to us— trying to restrain his exaspera- tion, appealing to our sympathy as fellow superior beings. Only we can truly appreciate the pro- found depths of his patience. The dim-witted Stanley, totally puz- zled as usual, is standing in a quarter-turn position, absorbed by other matters entirely, won- dering how he'll defend himself against Ollie's inevitable another- fine-mess accusation. *(MGM)*

The full-front position is the most intimate—the character is looking in our direction, inviting our complicity. In most cases, of course, actors ignore the camera—ignore us—yet our privileged position allows us to observe them when their defences are down, their vulnerabilities exposed. On those rare occasions when a character acknowledges our presence by addressing the camera, the sense of intimacy is vastly increased, for in effect we agree to become his or her chosen confidants. One of the greatest masters of this technique was Oliver Hardy, whose famous slow burn was a direct plea for sympathy and understanding (**4–24**).

The quarter turn is the favoured position of most filmmakers, for it pro- vides a high degree of intimacy but with less emotional involvement than the full-front position. The profile position is more remote. The character seems unaware of being observed, lost in his or her own thoughts (**4–25**). The three- quarter turn is more anonymous. This position is useful for conveying a charac- ter's unfriendly or antisocial feelings, for in effect the character is partially turn- ing his or her back on us, rejecting our interest (**4–26**). When a character has his or her back to the camera, we can only guess what's taking place internally. This position is often used to suggest a character's alienation from the world. It is use- ful in conveying a sense of concealment, mystery. We want to see more (**4–27**).

4-25. *Unforgiven* **(U.S.A., 1993),** *with Clint Eastwood, directed by Eastwood.*
The profile position catches characters unaware as they look off frame left or right. We are allowed unimpeded freedom to stare, to analyze. Less intimate than the full-front or quarter-turn position, the profile view is also less emotionally involving. We view the characters from a detached, neutral perspective.
(Warner Bros.)

4-26. *Night Moves* **(U.S.A., 1975),** *with Gene Hackman (extreme right, in three-quarter-turn position), directed by Arthur Penn.*
The three-quarter-turn position is a virtual rejection of the camera, a refusal to cooperate with our desire to see more. This type of staging tends to make us feel like voyeurs prying into the private affairs of the character, who seems to wish we'd go away. In this shot, Penn's mise en scène embodies a sense of alienation: Each character is imprisoned in his or her own space cubicle. They look buried alive.   *(Warner Bros.)*

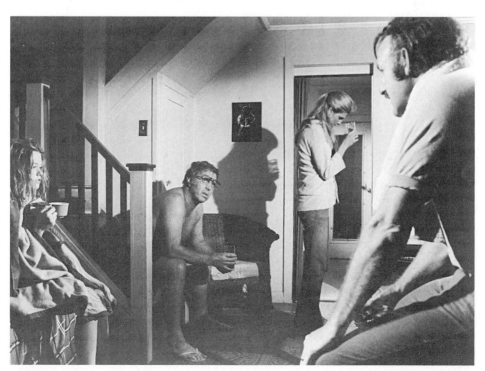

4–27. *Red Desert* **(Italy, 1964),** *with Carlo Chionetti, Monica Vitti, and Richard Harris (back to camera), directed by Michelangelo Antonioni.*
When characters turn their backs to the camera, they seem to reject us outright or to be totally unaware of our existence. We long to see and analyze their facial expressions, but we're not permitted this privilege. The character remains an enigma. Antonioni is one of the supreme masters of mise en scène, expressing complex interrelationships with a minimum of dialogue. The protagonist in this film (Vitti) is just recovering from an emotional break-down. She is still anxious and fearful, even of her husband (Chionetti). In this shot she seems trapped, like a wounded and exhausted animal, between her husband and his business asso-ciate. Note how the violent splashes of red paint on the walls suggest a haemorrhaging effect.
(Rizzoli Film)

The amount of open space within the territory of the frame can be exploited for symbolic purposes. Generally speaking, the closer the shot, the more confined the photographed figures appear to be. Such shots are usually referred to as **tightly framed.** Conversely, the longer, **loosely framed** shots tend to suggest freedom. Prison films often use tightly framed **close-ups** and medium shots because the frame functions as a kind of symbolic prison. In *A Condemned Man Escapes,* for example, Robert Bresson begins the movie with a close-up of the hero's hands, which are bound by a pair of handcuffs. Throughout the film, the prisoner makes elaborate preparations to escape, and Bresson preserves the tight framing to emphasize the sense of claustrophobia that the hero finds unendurable. This spatial tension is not released until the end of the movie when the protagonist disappears into the freedom of the darkness outside the prison walls. His triumphant escape is photographed in a loosely framed long shot—the only one in the film—which also symbolizes his sense of spiritual release. Framing and spatial metaphors of this kind are common in films dealing with the theme of confinement—either literal, as in Renoir's *La Grande illusion* **(4–23a),** or psychological, as in *The Graduate* **(4–13).**

Often a director can suggest ideas of entrapment by exploiting perfectly neutral objects and lines on the set. In such cases, the formal characteristics of these literal objects tend to close in on a figure, at least when viewed on the flat screen. Michelangelo Antonioni is a master of this technique **(4–27).** In *Red Desert,* for example, the heroine (Monica Vitti) describes a mental breakdown suffered by a friend she once knew. The audience suspects she's speaking of her own breakdown, however, for the surface of the image implies constriction: While she talks, she's riveted to one position, her figure framed by the lines of a doorway behind her, suggesting a coffin-like enclosure. When figures are framed within a frame in this manner, a sense of confinement is usually emphasized (see also **4–26).**

Territorial space within a frame can be manipulated with considerable psychological complexity. When a figure leaves the frame, for example, the camera can adjust to this sudden vacuum in the composition by **panning** slightly to make allowances for a new balance of weights. Or the camera can remain stationary, thus suggesting a sense of loss symbolized by the empty space that the character formerly occupied. Hostility and suspicion between two characters can be conveyed by keeping them at the edges of the composition, with a maximum of space between them **(4–28c),** or by having an intrusive character force his or her physical presence into the other character's territory, which is temporarily defined by the confines of the frame.

PROXEMIC PATTERNS

Spatial conventions vary from culture to culture, as anthropologist Edward T. Hall has demonstrated in such studies as *The Hidden Dimension* and *The Silent Language.* Hall discovered that **proxemic patterns**—the relationships of organisms within a given space—can be influenced by external considerations. Noise, danger, and lack of light tend to make people move closer together. Climate is another factor that affects spatial relations: People in northern countries tend to use more space than those in warmer climates. Taking these cultural and contextual considerations into account, Hall subdivides the way people use space into four major proxemic patterns: **(1)** the *intimate,* **(2)** the *personal,* **(3)** the *social,* **(4)** the *public* distances.

4-28a. *Like Water for Chocolate* **(Mexico, 1992),** *with Lumi Cavazos and Marco Leonardi, directed by Alfonso Arau.* (Miramax Films)

4-28b. *I Love Trouble* **(U.S.A., 1994),** *with Julia Roberts and Nick Nolte, directed by Charles Shyer.* (©Ann Hall, Inc. All Rights Reserved.)

4-28c. *Zabriskie Point* **(U.S.A., 1970),** *with Rod Taylor and Daria Halprin, directed by Michelangelo Antonioni.* (MGM)

Although each of these photos portrays a conversation between a man and a woman, each is staged at a different proxemic range, suggesting totally different undertones. The intimate proxemics of *Like Water for Chocolate* is charged with erotic energy: The characters are literally flesh to flesh. In *I Love Trouble* the characters are flirting with each other, but at a more discreet personal proxemic range, with each character respecting the other's space. The characters of *Zabriskie Point* are more wary, the social proxemic range between them implying considerable suspicion and reserve: Psychologically, there's a vast distance between them. Each of these shots contains similar subject matter, but the real content of each is defined by its form—in this case, the proxemic ranges between the actors.

Intimate distances range from skin contact to about half a metre away. This is the distance of physical involvement—of love, comfort, and tenderness between individuals. With strangers, such distances would be regarded as intrusive—most people would react with suspicion and hostility if their space were invaded by someone they didn't know very well. In many cultures, maintaining an intimate distance in public is considered bad taste.

The personal distance ranges roughly from half a metre to about a metre away. Individuals can touch if necessary, since they are literally an arm's-length apart. These distances tend to be reserved for friends and acquaintances rather than lovers or members of a family. Personal distances preserve the privacy between individuals, yet these ranges don't necessarily suggest exclusion, as intimate distances almost always do.

Social distances range from one to about four metres away. These are the distances usually reserved for impersonal business and casual social gatherings. It's a friendly range in most cases, yet somewhat more formal than the personal distance. Ordinarily, social distances are necessary when there are more than three members of a group. In some cases, it would be considered rude for two individuals to preserve an intimate or personal distance within a social situation. Such behaviour might be interpreted as standoffish.

Public distances extend from four to eight metres and more away. This range tends to be formal and rather detached. Displays of emotion are considered bad form at these distances. Important public figures are generally seen in the public range, and because a considerable amount of space is involved, people generally must exaggerate their gestures and raise their voices to be understood clearly.

Most people adjust to proxemic patterns instinctively. We don't usually say to ourselves, "This person is invading my intimate space" when a stranger happens to stand half a metre away from us. However, unless we're in a combative mood, we involuntarily tend to step away in such circumstances. Obviously, social context is also a determining factor in proxemic patterns. In a crowded subway car, for example, virtually everyone is in an intimate range, yet we generally preserve a public attitude by not speaking to the person whose body is literally pressed against our own.

Proxemic patterns are perfectly obvious to anyone who has bothered to observe the way people obey certain spatial conventions in actual life. But in movies, these patterns are also related to the shots and their distance ranges. Although shots are not always defined by the literal space between the camera and the object photographed, in terms of psychological effect, shots tend to suggest physical distances.

Usually filmmakers have a number of options concerning what kind of shot to use to convey the action of a scene. What determines their choice—though usually instinctively rather than consciously—is the emotional impact of the different proxemic ranges. Each proxemic pattern has an approximate camera equivalent. The intimate distances, for example, can be likened to the close and **extreme close shot** ranges. The personal distance is approximately a medium close range. The social distances correspond to the medium and **full shot** ranges. And the public distances are roughly within the long and extreme

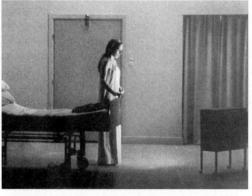
a

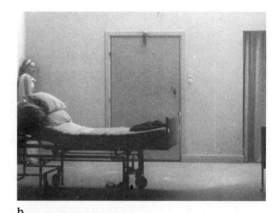
b

c

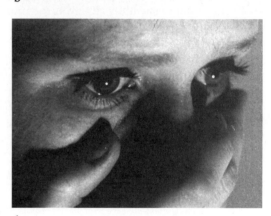
d

4–29. *Persona* (Sweden, 1966), *with Liv Ullmann, directed by Ingmar Bergman.*
Throughout this scene, which contains no dialogue, Bergman uses space to communicate his ideas—space within the frame and the space implied between the camera (us) and the subject. The character is in a hospital room watching the news on television **(a)**. Suddenly, she sees a horrifying scene of a Buddhist monk setting himself on fire to protest against the war in Vietnam. She retreats to the corner of the room, to the very edge of the frame **(b)**. Bergman then cuts to a closer shot **(c)**, intensifying our emotional involvement. The full horror of her reaction is conveyed by the extreme close-up **(d)**, bringing us into an intimate proximity with her.   *(United Artists)*

long shot ranges. Because our eyes identify with the camera's lens, in effect we are placed within these ranges vis-à-vis the subject matter. When we are offered a close-up of a character, for example, in a sense we feel that we're in an intimate relationship with that character. In some instances, this technique can bind us to the character, forcing us to care about him or her and to identify with his or her problems. If the character is a villain, the close-up can produce an emotional revulsion in us; in effect, a threatening character seems to be invading our space.

4–30a. *The Gold Rush* (U.S.A., 1925), *with Charles Chaplin and Georgia Hale, directed by Chaplin.*

Both these scenes involve a fear of rejection by a woman Charlie holds in awe. The scene from *The Gold Rush* is predominantly comical. The tramp has belted his baggy pants with a piece of rope, but he doesn't realize it is also a dog's leash, and while dancing with the saloon girl, Charlie is yanked to the floor by the jittery dog at the other end of the rope. Because the camera remains relatively distant from the action, we tend to be more objective and detached and to laugh at his futile attempts to preserve his dignity. On the other hand, the famous final shot from *City Lights* isn't funny at all and produces a powerful emotional effect. Because the camera is in close, *we* get close to the situation. The proxemic distance between the camera and the subject forces us to identify more with his feelings, which we can't ignore at this range.   *(rbc Films)*

4–30b. *City Lights* (U.S.A., 1931), *with Charles Chaplin, directed by Chaplin.*

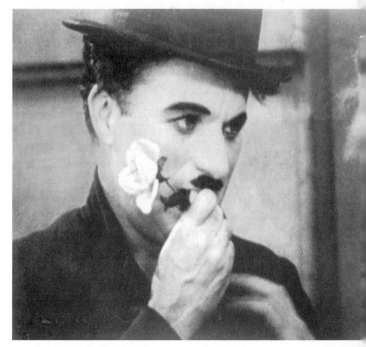

In general, the greater the distance between the camera and the subject, the more emotionally neutral we remain. Public proxemic ranges tend to encourage a certain detachment. Conversely, the closer we are to a character, the more we feel that we're in proximity with him or her and hence the greater our emotional involvement. "Long shot for comedy, close-up for tragedy" was one of Chaplin's most famous pronouncements. The proxemic principles are sound, for when we are close to an action—a person slipping on a banana peel, for example—it's seldom funny, because we are concerned for the person's safety. If we see the same event from a greater distance, however, it often strikes us as comical. Chaplin used close-ups sparingly for this very reason. As long as Charlie remains in long shots, we tend to be amused by his antics and absurd predicaments. In scenes of greater emotional impact, however, Chaplin resorted to closer shots, and their effect is often devastating on the audience. We suddenly realize that the situation we've been laughing at is no longer funny.

Perhaps the most famous instance of the power of Chaplin's close-ups is found at the conclusion of *City Lights*. Charlie has fallen in love with an impoverished flower vendor who is blind. She believes him to be an eccentric millionaire, and out of vanity he allows her to continue in this delusion. By engaging in a series of monumental labours—love has reduced him to work— he manages to scrape together enough money for her to receive an operation that will restore her sight. But he is dragged off to jail before she can thank him properly for the money. The final scene takes place several months later. The young woman can now see and owns her own modest flower shop. Charlie is released from prison, and dishevelled and dispirited, he meanders past her shop window. She sees him gazing at her wistfully and jokes to an assistant that she's apparently made a new conquest. Out of pity she goes out to the street and offers him a flower and a small coin. Instantly she recognizes his touch. Hardly able to believe her eyes, she can only stammer, "You?" In a series of alternating close-ups, their embarrassment is unbearably prolonged **(4–30b)**. Clearly he is not the idol of her romantic fantasies, and he is painfully aware of her disappointment. Finally he stares at her with an expression of shocking emotional nakedness. The film ends on this image of sublime vulnerability.

The choice of a shot is generally determined by practical considerations. Usually the director selects the shot that most clearly conveys the dramatic action of a scene. If there is a conflict between the effect of certain proxemic ranges and the clarity needed to convey what's going on, most filmmakers will opt for clarity and gain their emotional impact through some other means. But there are many times when shot choice isn't necessarily determined by functional considerations.

OPEN AND CLOSED FORMS

The concepts of **open** and **closed forms** are generally used by art historians and critics, but these terms can also be useful in film analysis. Like most theoretical constructs, they are best used in a relative rather than absolute sense. There are no movies that are completely open or completely closed in form, only those that tend toward these polarities. Like other critical terms, these should be applied only when they are relevant and helpful in understanding what actually exists in a movie. If the concepts don't seem relevant, they should be discarded and replaced with something that is. Criticism is the handmaiden of art, not vice versa.

Open and closed forms are two distinct attitudes about reality. Each has its own stylistic and technical characteristics. The two terms are loosely related to the concepts of realism and formalism as they have been defined in these chapters. In general, realist filmmakers tend to use open forms, whereas formalists lean toward closed. Open forms tend to be stylistically recessive, whereas closed forms are generally self-conscious and conspicuous.

In terms of visual design, open form emphasizes informal, unobtrusive compositions. Often such images seem to have no discernible structure and suggest a random form of organization. Objects and figures seem to have been found rather than deliberately arranged (**4–31**). Closed form emphasizes a more stylized design. Although such images can suggest a superficial realism,

---

4-31. *The Garden of the Finzi-Continis* **(Italy, 1970),** *with Dominique Sanda (centre), directed by Vittorio De Sica.*
Realist directors are more likely to prefer open forms, which tend to suggest fragments of a larger external reality. Design and composition are generally informal. Influenced by the aesthetic of the documentary, open-form images seem to have been discovered rather than arranged. Excessive balance and calculated symmetry are avoided in favour of an intimate and spontaneous effect. Still photos in open form are seldom picturesque or obviously artful. Instead, they suggest a frozen instant of truth—a snapshot wrested from the fluctuations of time.   *(Cinema 5)*

seldom do they have that accidental, discovered look that typifies open forms. Objects and figures are more precisely placed within the frame, and the balance of weights is elaborately worked out.

Open forms stress apparently simple techniques, because with these unselfconscious methods the filmmaker is able to emphasize the immediate, the familiar, the intimate aspects of reality. Sometimes such images are photographed in only partially controlled situations, and these **aleatory** conditions can produce a sense of spontaneity and directness that would be difficult to capture in a rigidly controlled context **(4–32).** Closed forms are more likely to emphasize the unfamiliar. The images are rich in textural contrasts and compelling visual effects. Because the mise en scène is more precisely controlled and stylized, there is often a deliberate artificiality in these images—a sense of visual improbability, of being one remove from reality. Closed forms also tend to be more densely saturated with visual information; richness of form takes precedence over considerations of surface realism. If a conflict should arise, formal beauty is sacrificed for truth in open forms; in closed forms, on the other hand, literal truth is sacrificed for beauty.

4–32.   *Eldorado* **(Canada, 1995),** *with Pascale Bussières, directed by Charles Binamé.*
Open forms make us aware that reality extends beyond the film's frame. In *Eldorado,* the images are often filmed with a handheld camera to suggest the instability of the lives of the six young Montrealers whose stories intersect in its loosely constructed narrative. The rooftop setting of this shot captures both the exhilaration and the precarious balance of a character who wanders aimlessly through the city.   *(Alliance Communications)*

Compositions in open and closed forms exploit the frame differently. In open-form images, the frame tends to be de-emphasized. It suggests a window, a temporary masking, and implies that more important information lies outside the edges of the composition. Space is continuous in these shots, and to emphasize its continuity outside the frame, directors often favour panning their camera across the locale. The shot seems inadequate, too narrow in its confines to contain the copiousness of the subject matter. Like many of the paintings of Edgar Degas (who usually favoured open forms), objects and even figures are arbitrarily cut off by the frame to reinforce the continuity of the subject matter beyond the formal edges of the composition. In closed forms, the shot represents a miniature proscenium arch, with all the necessary information carefully structured within the confines of the frame. Space seems enclosed and self-contained rather than continuous. Elements outside the frame are irrelevant, at least in terms of the formal properties of the individual shot, which is isolated from its context in space and time (**4–33**).

For these reasons, still photos taken from movies that are predominantly in open form are not usually very pretty. There is nothing intrinsically striking or eye-catching about them. Books about movies tend to favour photos in closed form because they are usually more obviously beautiful, more "composed." The beauty of an open-form image, on the other hand, is more elusive. It can be likened to a snapshot that miraculously preserves some candid, rare expression, a kind of haphazard instant of truth. Open form also tends to value a certain visual ambiguity. Often the charm of such images lies precisely in their impenetrability—a mysterious half-smile on the face of a character, an evocative shadow that casts a strange pattern across the set.

In open-form movies, the dramatic action generally leads the camera. In such movies as *Faces* and *Husbands,* for example, John Cassavetes emphasized the fluidity of the camera as it dutifully follows the actors wherever they wish to go, seemingly placed at their disposal. Such films suggest that chance plays an important role in determining visual effects. Needless to say, it's not what actually happens on a set that's important, but what *seems* to be happening on the screen. In fact, many of the simplest effects in an open-form movie are achieved after much painstaking labour and manipulation.

In closed-form films, on the other hand, the camera often anticipates the dramatic action. Objects and actors are visually blocked out within the confines of a predetermined camera setup. **Anticipatory setups** tend to imply fatality or determinism, for in effect the camera seems to know what will happen even before it occurs. In the films of Fritz Lang, for example, the camera often seems to be waiting in an empty room: The door opens, the characters enter, and the action then begins. In some of Hitchcock's movies, a character is seen at the edge of the composition, and the camera seems to be placed in a disadvantageous position, too far removed from where the action is apparently going to occur. But then the character decides to return to that area where the camera has been waiting. When such setups are used, the audience also tends to anticipate actions. Instinctively, we expect something or someone to fill in the visual vacuum of the shot. Philosophically, open forms tend to suggest freedom of

4–33. *Another Country* **(Britain, 1984),** *with Rupert Everett (centre doorway), directed by Marek Kanievska.*
In closed form, the frame is a self-sufficient miniature universe with all the formal elements held in careful balance. Though there may be more information outside the frame, for the duration of any given shot this information is visually irrelevant. Closed forms are often used in scenes dealing with entrapment or confinement, such as this shot in which the protagonist is about to be disciplined by his boarding school superiors.   *(Orion Classics)*

choice, a multiplicity of options open to the characters. Closed forms, conversely, tend to imply destiny and the futility of the will: The characters don't seem to make the important decisions, the camera does—and in advance.

Open and closed forms are most effective in movies where these techniques are appropriate to the subject matter. A prison film using mostly open forms is not likely to be emotionally convincing. Most movies use both open and closed forms, depending on the specific dramatic context. Renoir's *La Grande illusion,* for example, uses closed forms for the prison camp scenes and open forms after two of the prisoners escape.

Like most cinematic techniques, open and closed forms have certain limitations as well as advantages. When used to excess, open forms can seem sloppy and naïve, like an artless home movie. Too often, open forms can seem uncontrolled, unfocused, and even visually ugly. Occasionally, these techniques are so blandly unobtrusive that the visuals are boring. On the other hand, closed forms can seem arty and pretentious. The images are so unspontaneous

a

4–34. *Full Metal Jacket* **(Britain/U.S.A., 1987),** *directed by Stanley Kubrick.*
Even within a single scene, filmmakers will switch from open to closed forms, depending on the feelings or ideas that are being stressed in each individual shot. For example, both of these shots take place during a battle scene in the Vietnamese city of Hue. In **(a)**, the characters are under fire, and the wounded soldier's head is not even in the frame. The form is appropriately open. The frame functions as a temporary masking device that's too narrow in its scope to include all the relevant information. Often the frame seems to cut figures off in an arbitrary manner in open form, suggesting that the action is continued off screen, like newsreel footage that was fortuitously photographed by a camera operator who was unable to superimpose an artistic form on the runaway materials. In **(b)**, the form is closed, as four soldiers rush to their wounded comrade, providing a protective buffer from the outside world. Open and closed forms aren't intrinsically meaningful, then, but derive their significance from the dramatic context. In some cases, closed forms can suggest entrapment **(4–33)**; in other cases, such as **(b)**, closed form implies security and camaraderie. *(Warner Bros.)*

b

4–35.   *The Krays (Britain, 1990), with Gary Kemp (front left) and Martin Kemp (front right), directed by Peter Medak.*
One of the filmmaker's principal concerns is to find formal equivalents for the feelings and ideas outlined in the script. This movie is based on the real-life twins (one gay, one straight) who dominated London's organized crime world in the 1960s. Medak cast actual brothers as the Kray twins, and as often as possible, he doubled his mise en scène with visual parallels, suggesting a mirror reflection.   *(Miramax Films)*

that their visual elements look computer-programmed. Many viewers are turned off by the stagy flamboyance of some closed-form films. At their worst, these movies can seem decadently overwrought—all icing and no cake.

A systematic mise en scène analysis of any given shot includes the following fifteen elements:

1. *Dominant.* Where is our eye attracted first? Why?
2. *Lighting key.* **High key**? **Low key**? **High contrast**? Some combination of these?
3. *Shot and camera proxemics.* What type of shot? How far away is the camera from the action?
4. *Angle.* Are we (and the camera) looking up at or down on the subject? Or is the camera neutral (eye level)?
5. *Colour values.* What is the dominant colour? Are there contrasting foils? Is there colour symbolism?
6. *Lens/filter/stock.* How do these distort or comment on the photographed materials?

7. *Subsidiary contrasts.* What are the main eye-stops after taking in the dominant?

8. *Density.* How much visual information is packed into the image? Is the texture stark, moderate, or highly detailed?

9. *Composition.* How is the two-dimensional space segmented and organized? What is the underlying design?

10. *Form.* Open or closed? Does the image suggest a window that arbitrarily isolates a fragment of the scene? Or a proscenium arch, in which the visual elements are carefully arranged and held in balance?

11. *Framing.* Tight or loose? Do the characters have no room to move around, or can they move freely without impediments?

12. *Depth.* On how many planes is the image composed? Does the background or foreground comment in any way on the midground?

13. *Character placement.* What part of the framed space do the characters occupy? Centre? Top? Bottom? Edges? Why?

14. *Staging positions.* Which way do the characters look vis-à-vis the camera?

15. *Character proxemics.* How much space is there between the characters?

These visual principles, with appropriate modifications, can be applied to any image analysis. Of course, while we're actually watching a movie, most of us don't have the time or inclination to explore all fifteen elements of mise en scène in each shot. Nonetheless, by applying these principles to a still photo, we can train our eyes to "read" a movie image with more critical sophistication.

For example, the image from *M* (**4–36**) is a good instance of how form (mise en scène) is actually content. The shot takes place near the end of the movie. A psychotic child-killer (Lorre) has been hunted down by the members of the underworld. These "normal" criminals have taken him to an abandoned warehouse where they intend to prosecute and execute the psychopath for his heinous crimes and in doing so take the police heat off themselves. In this scene, the killer is confronted by a witness (centre) who holds an incriminating piece of evidence—a balloon. The components of the shot include the following:

1. *Dominant.* The balloon, the brightest object in the frame. When the photo is turned upside down and converted to a pattern of abstract shapes, its dominance is more readily discernible.

2. *Lighting key.* Murky low key, with high-contrast spotlights on the balloon and the four main figures.

3. *Shot and camera proxemics.* The shot is slightly more distant than a full shot. The camera proxemic range is social, perhaps about three metres from the dominant.

4. *Angle.* Slightly high, suggesting an air of fatality.

5. *Colour values.* The movie is in black and white.

6. *Lens/filter/stock.* A standard lens is used, with no apparent filter. Standard slow stock.

7. *Subsidiary contrasts.* The figures of the killer, the witness, and the two criminals in the upper left.

4–36. *M (Germany, 1931), with Peter Lorre (extreme right), directed by Fritz Lang.*   (Janus Films)

8. *Density.* The shot has a high degree of density, especially considering the low-key lighting. Such details as the texture of the brick walls, the creases in the clothing, and the expressive faces of the actors are highlighted.

9. *Composition.* The image is divided into three general areas—left, centre, and right—suggesting instability and tension.

10. *Form.* Definitely closed: The frame suggests a constricting cell, with no exit for the prisoner.

11. *Framing.* Tight: The killer is trapped in the same territory with his threatening accusers.

12. *Depth.* The image is composed on three depth planes: the two figures in the foreground, the two figures on the stairs in the midground, and the brick wall of the background.

13. *Character placement.* The accusers and balloon tower above the killer, sealing off any avenue of escape, while he cowers below at the extreme right edge, almost falling into the symbolic blackness outside the frame.

14. *Staging position.* The accusers stand in a quarter-turn position, implying a greater intimacy with us than the main character, who is in the profile position, totally unaware of anything but his own terror.

15. *Character proxemics.* Proxemics are personal between the foreground characters, the killer's immediate problem; and intimate between the men on the stairs, who function as a double threat. The range between the two pairs is social.

A filmmaker has literally hundreds of different ways to convey meanings. Like the painter or still photographer, the movie director can emphasize visual dominants. In a scene portraying violence, for example, he or she can use diagonal and zigzagging lines, aggressive colours, close-ups, extreme angles, harsh lighting contrasts, unbalanced compositions, large shapes, and so on. Unlike most other visual artists, the filmmaker can also suggest violence through movement, either of the subject itself, the camera, or both. The film artist can suggest violence through editing, by having one shot collide with another in a kaleidoscopic explosion of different perspectives. Furthermore, through the use of the soundtrack, violence can be conveyed by loud or rapid dialogue, harsh sound effects, or strident music. Precisely because there are so many ways to convey a given effect, the filmmaker will vary the emphasis, sometimes stressing image, sometimes movement, other times sound. Occasionally, especially in climactic scenes, all three are used at the same time.

FURTHER READING

ARNHEIM, RUDOLF, *Art and Visual Perception: A Psychology of the Creative Eye* (Berkeley: University of California Press, 1954). Primarily about paintings and drawings.

———, *Towards a Psychology of Art* (Berkeley: University of California Press, 1966). A theoretical discussion emphasizing a gestalt approach.

BORDWELL, DAVID, JANET STAIGER, and KRISTIN THOMPSON, *The Classical Hollywood Cinema: Film Style and Mode of Production to 1960* (New York: Columbia University Press, 1985). Scholarly study.

DONDIS, DONIS A., *A Primer of Visual Literacy* (Cambridge, Mass., and London, England: The M.I.T. Press, 1974). Primarily on design and composition.

FREEBURG, VICTOR O., *Pictoral Beauty on the Screen* (New York: Macmillan, 1923). A discussion of the conventions of classical composition.

HALL, EDWARD T., *The Hidden Dimension* (Garden City, N.Y.: Doubleday, 1969). How humans and other animals use space.

NILSEN, VLADIMIR, *The Cinema as a Graphic Art* (New York: Hill and Wang, 1959). How reality is shaped by form, with major emphasis on classical composition.

RUESCH, JURGEN, and WELDON KEES, *Nonverbal Communication* (Berkeley: University of California Press, 1966).

SOMMERS, ROBERT, *Personal Space* (Englewood Cliffs, N.J.: Prentice-Hall, 1969). How individuals use and abuse space.

MOVEMENT 5

Warner Bros.

The opening of a door, a hand, or an eye can bring about a climax as thrilling as a crash of locomotives on the screen.
—RICHARD DYER MACCANN

SUMMARY

How movement can "mean." Different types of movement: realistic, pantomime, mime. Dance and choreography: the art of motion. The psychology of movement: lateral motions, left or right, up or down, toward or away from the camera? Movement in relation to the shots and angles. Movement and film genres: slapstick comedies, action films, dance movies, animation, and musicals. Movement as metaphor: kinetic symbolism. The moving camera: kineticizing space. Dolly shots versus editing: the implications of each. Stasis versus dynamism: tripods or tracks? The mercurial instability of the handheld camera. Lyricism: cranes and other flying forms. Faux movement: zoom shots. Mechanical distortions of motion: animation, fast motion, slow motion, reverse motion, and freeze frames.

"Movies," "motion pictures," "moving pictures"—all these phrases suggest the central importance of motion in the art of film. Cinema derives from the Greek word for "movement," as do the words *kinetic, kinesthesia,* and *choreography*—terms usually associated with the art of dance. Yet oddly enough, filmgoers and critics give surprisingly little consideration to movement per se as a medium of communication, as a language system. Like the image itself, motion is usually thought of in terms of gross subject matter. We tend to remember "what happens" only in a general sense. If we were to describe a sequence from a ballet in such vague terms, our discussion would certainly strike the sophisticated dance enthusiast as naïve. Yet cinematic sequences—which can be choreographed with just as much or even greater complexity—are seldom appreciated for their **kinetic** richness and beauty.

KINETICS

Like images, motion can be literal and concrete or highly stylized and **lyrical.** In the kinetic arts—pantomime, ballet, modern dance—we find a wide variety of movements, ranging from the realistic to the formally abstract. This stylistic spectrum can also be seen in movies. For example, a naturalistic actor like Spencer Tracy used only realistic movements, the same sort that could be observed in actual life. Tracy moves so simply in his films that he hardly seems to be acting. Pantomimists are more stylized in their movements. Chaplin, for example, tended to use motion more balletically, more symbolically. A swaggering gait and a twirling cane symbolized Charlie's (usually fleeting) arrogance and conceit.

Even more stylized are the movements of performers in a musical. In this **genre,** characters express their most intense emotions through song and dance. A dance number is seldom meant to be taken literally: It's a stylized **convention** that we accept as a symbolic expression of certain feelings and ideas. In *Singin' in*

5-1. *Singin' in the Rain* (U.S.A., 1952), *with Gene Kelly, choreography by Kelly, directed by Kelly and Stanley Donen.*
Kelly worked in a broad range of dancing styles—tap, ballroom, modern, and ballet. He was usually at his best in muscular, gymnastic styles, with an emphasis on virile trajectories and bravura leaps. But he was also charming in nonchalant styles, to which he usually added a characteristic swagger. He often incorporated lengthy ballet sequences in his films, generally a dream sequence or a fantasy. Above all, Kelly's dancing is sexy, with an emphasis on pelvic movements, tensed loins, twisting torsos, and erotic, close-to-the-floor gyrations. *(MGM)*

the Rain, for example, Gene Kelly does an elaborate dance routine in a downpour **(5–1).** He twirls around lampposts, splashes through puddles like a happy idiot, and leaps ecstatically through pelting rain—literally nothing can dampen the exhilaration of his love. A wide gamut of emotions is expressed in this sequence, with each kinetic variation symbolizing the character's feelings about his girl. She can make him feel dreamy, childlike, erotically stimulated, brave and forthright, dopey and moonstruck, and finally wild with joy. In some kinds of action genres, physical contests are stylized in a similar manner. Samurai and kung-fu films, for example, often feature elaborately choreographed sequences.

Ballet and mime are even more abstract and stylized. A great mime artist like Marcel Marceau was not so much concerned with expressing literal ideas (which is more properly the province of pantomime) as the *essence* of an idea, stripped of superfluities. A twisted torso can suggest an ancient tree, bent elbows its crooked branches, fluttering fingers the rippling of its leaves. In ballet, movements can be so stylized that we can't always assign a discernible content to them, though the narrative context generally provides us with at least a vague sense of what the movements are supposed to represent. On this level of abstraction, however, movements acquire self-justifying characteristics. They are lyrical; that is, we respond to them more for their own beauty than for their function as symbolic expressions of ideas.

This concern with kinetic beauty for its own sake can be seen in certain schools of modern dance. Many of the choreographies of Merce Cunningham and Erick Hawkins, for example, aren't meant to symbolize anything of a narrative nature. Abstract motion is presented for its own sake, somewhat in the same manner that pure colours, shapes, and lines are offered for their own sakes in nonrepresentational painting. In movies, nonrepresentational movements are most often found in **avant-garde** films, which seldom tell stories.

In dance, movements are defined by the space that encloses the choreography—a three-dimensional stage. In film, the **frame** performs a similar function. However, with each **setup** change, the cinematic "stage" is redefined. The intrinsic meanings associated with various portions of the frame are closely related to the significance of certain kinds of movements. For example, with vertical movements, an upward motion seems soaring and free because it conforms to the eye's natural tendency to move upward over a composition. Movements in this direction often suggest aspiration, joy, power, and authority—those ideas associated with the superior portions of the frame. Downward movements suggest opposite ideas: grief, death, insignificance, depression, weakness, and so on.

Because the Western eye tends to read a picture from left to right, physical movement in this direction seems psychologically natural, whereas movement from the right to left often seems inexplicably tense and uncomfortable. The sensitive filmmaker exploits these psychological phenomena to reinforce the dramatic ideas. Frequently the protagonists of a movie travel toward the right of the screen, whereas the villains move toward the left. In John Huston's *The Red Badge of Courage,* the hero moves from right to left when he runs away from a battle in fear. Later, when he courageously joins an infantry charge, his movements are from left to right.

Movement can be directed toward or away from the camera. Because we identify with the camera's **lens**, the effect of such movements is somewhat like a character moving toward or away from us. If the character is a villain, walking toward the camera can seem aggressive, hostile, and threatening, for in effect he or she is invading our space. If the character is attractive, movement toward the camera seems friendly, inviting, sometimes seductive. In either case, movement toward the audience is generally strong and assertive, suggesting confidence on the part of the moving character **(5–29)**.

Movement away from the camera tends to imply opposite meanings. Intensity is decreased and the character seems to grow remote as he or she withdraws from us. Audiences feel safer when villains move away in this manner, for they thereby increase the protective distance between us and them. In some contexts, such movements can seem weak, fearful, and suspicious. Most movies end with a withdrawal of some sort, either of the camera from the locale or of the characters from the camera.

There are considerable psychological differences between lateral movements on the screen and depth movements—that is, movements toward or away from the camera. A script might simply call for a character to move from one place to another, but *how* the director chooses to photograph this move-

5-2. *Dames* (U.S.A., 1934), *choreographed by Busby Berkeley, directed by Ray Enright.*
Berkeley liberated the camera from the tyranny of the proscenium arch. He often photographed his dancers from unusual angles, like this bird's-eye shot. His style was the most abstract of all American choreographers. He sometimes didn't even bother to use dancers, preferring a uniform contingent of comely maidens who are used as camera material, like bits of glass in a shifting kaleidoscope of formal patterns. *(Warner Bros.)*

ment will determine much of its psychological implications. Generally speaking, if the character moves from one side of the screen to the other, he or she will seem determined and efficient, a person of action. Unless the camera is at **extreme long shot** range, these movements are necessarily photographed in brief **takes**—shots lasting only a few seconds. Lateral movements tend to emphasize speed and efficiency, so they are often used in action movies.

On the other hand, when a character moves in or out of the depth of a scene, the effect is often one of slowness. Unless the camera is at close range or an extreme **wide-angle lens** is used, movements toward or away from the camera take longer to photograph than lateral movements. With a **telephoto lens,** such movements can seem hopelessly dragged out. Furthermore, when depth movement is photographed in an uninterrupted lengthy take, the audience tends to anticipate the conclusion of the movement, thus intensifying the sense of tedium while we wait for the character to arrive at his or her destination. Especially when a character's physical goal is apparent—the length of a long corridor, for example—audiences generally grow restless if they are forced to view the entire movement **(5–4).**

Most **classical** filmmakers would photograph the action in several different setups, thus compressing the time and space from the inception of the movement to its conclusion. Classical filmmakers also tend to stage movement diagonally, to create a more dynamic trajectory of motion.

The distance and **angle** from which movement is photographed determine much of its meaning. In general, the longer and higher the **shot**, the

5-3.   *Zero Patience* (Canada, 1993), *with Charles Azulay, David Gale, and Howard Rosenstein, directed by John Greyson.*
The energy and spectacle of classic Hollywood musicals drew their audiences into an utopian world where they could forget their everyday problems. *Zero Patience* is a musical about AIDS. Greyson's witty and provocative film uses musical conventions to draw attention to the myths about AIDS and the cultural attitudes that lie behind them. Sir Richard Burton, a Victorian explorer now unaccountably working in a Toronto museum, investigates the life of the so-called Patient Zero, a French-Canadian flight attendant who supposedly brought the epidemic to North America. The film also depicts the suffering of an AIDS victim, a former friend of Zero, but its use of fantasy and artifice allows it to place the individual experience in its historical and cultural context.   *(John Greyson)*

slower the movement tends to appear. If movement is recorded from close and low angles, it seems more intense, speeded-up. A director can photograph the same subject—a running man, for example—in two different setups and produce opposite meanings. If the man is photographed in an extreme long shot from a **high angle**, he will seem ineffectual and impotent. If he's photographed from a **low angle** in a **medium shot,** he will seem a dynamo of energy. Although the subject matter in each setup is absolutely identical, the true content of each shot is its form.

Even film critics (who should know better) are often ignorant of these perceptual differences, thinking of movement only in terms of story and gross physical action. The result has been a good deal of naïve theorizing on what is "intrinsically cinematic." The more movement is perceived as extravagant in real life, they argue, the more "filmic" it becomes. **Epic** events and exterior

5-4. *L'Avventura* **(Italy, 1960),** *with Monica Vitti, directed by Michelangelo Antonioni.*
Psychological films often use movements in and out of the depth of an image, especially to create a sense of tediousness and exhaustion. Shots of this sort require anticipatory setups that reinforce these qualities, for we see the destination of a character's movement long before it's completed. Here, the heroine's search for her lover in the corridors of a hotel suggests the futility of her love affair. The endless succession of doors, fixtures, and hallways implies, among other things, the repetition of the frustration she is now experiencing. Much of the meaning of shots such as these lies in their duration: Space is used to suggest time. Needless to say, Antonioni's movies are among the slowest paced of the contemporary cinema: Long after the viewer has had time to absorb the visual information of a shot, it continues on the screen. When this film was originally shown at the Cannes Film Festival, an audience of hostile critics kept shouting "Cut! Cut!" at the screen. The shots were so lengthy and the pace so slow that viewers assumed the director was inept at editing. But like many of Antonioni's works, *L'Avventura* is about spiritual erosion, and the movie's slow rhythm is organically related to this theme. *(Janus Films)*

5–5.   *Farewell My Concubine* (Hong Kong/China, 1993), *with Leslie Cheung, Zhang Fengyi, and Gong Li, directed by Chen Kaige.*
Montage sequences are created by the optical printer to suggest a sense of multiple actions, superimposed onto one image. (In Europe, montage usually refers to the art of editing.) Generally, montage sequences such as this condense time, suggesting the passing of months and even years into a few seconds of screen time.   *(Miramax Films)*

locations are presumed to be fundamentally more suited to the medium than intimate, restricted, or interior subjects. Such views are based on a misunderstanding of movement in film. True, one can use the terms *epic* and *psychological* in describing the general emphasis of a movie. Even on this general level, however, arguments about intrinsically cinematic subjects are usually crude. No sensible person would claim that Tolstoy's *War and Peace* is intrinsically more novelistic than Dostoyevsky's *Crime and Punishment,* although we may refer to one as an epic and the other as a psychological novel. In a similar vein, only a naïve viewer would claim that Michelangelo's Sistine Chapel frescoes are intrinsically more visual than a Vermeer painting of a domestic scene. It is different, yes, but not necessarily better or worse, and certainly not through any intrinsic quality. In short, there are some good and bad epic works of art, and some good and bad psychological works. It's the treatment that counts, not the material per se.

Movement in film is a subtle issue, for it's necessarily dependent on the kind of shot used. The cinematic **close-up** can convey as much movement as the most sweeping vistas in an extreme long shot. In fact, in terms of the area covered on the screen's surface, there is actually more movement in a close-up showing tears running down a person's face than there is in an extreme long shot of a parachutist drifting twenty metres **(5–6).**

5–6a. *The Stunt Man* (U.S.A., 1980), *directed by Richard Rush.* *(Twentieth Century-Fox)*

5–6b. *L'Enfant sauvage* (*"The Wild Child,"* **France, 1969**), *with Jean-Pierre Cargol, directed by François Truffaut.* *(United Artists)*

Unlike movement in dance or the live theatre, cinematic movement is always relative. Only gross movements are likely to be perceived in an extreme long shot, whereas the flicker of an eye can rivet our attention in a close-up. In these photos, for example, the path of the boy's tear covers more screen space than the pilot's fall from the sky.

Epic and psychological movies use movement in different ways, with emphasis on different shots. Epic movies usually depend on the longer shots for their effects, whereas psychological films tend to use the closer shots. Epics are concerned with a sense of sweep and breadth, psychological movies with depth and detail. Epics often emphasize events, psychological films the implications of events. One stresses action, the other reaction.

Two filmmakers can approach the same story and produce totally different results. *Hamlet* is a good example. Laurence Olivier's film version of this play is essentially an epic, with emphasis on the longer shots. Franco Zeffirelli's version is primarily a psychological study, dominated by close and medium shots. Olivier's movie emphasizes setting. There are many **long shots,** especially of the brooding castle of Elsinore. Much is made of Hamlet's interaction with this moody locale. We are informed at the beginning of the film that the story is about "a man who could not make up his mind." The long shots are used to emphasize this interpretation visually. Most of them are **loosely framed,** suggesting that Hamlet (played by Olivier) has considerable freedom of movement, freedom to act. But he refuses to use this freedom, preferring to sulk in dark corners, paralyzed with indecision. When he does move, the motion is generally recorded from long distances, thus reinforcing the impotence of the protagonist in relationship to his environment.

Zeffirelli's *Hamlet* (with Mel Gibson) is usually photographed in **tightly framed** close and medium shots. Unlike Olivier's indecisive Hamlet, Gibson's is impulsive and rash, a man who often acts before he thinks. Imprisoned by the confining close shots, the tortured hero virtually spills off the edges of the frame into oblivion. The unstable **handheld** camera can barely keep up with him as he lunges hyperkinetically from place to place. If the same movements were photographed from a long-shot range, of course, the character would seem to move more normally **(5–7)**.

5–7. *Hamlet* **(U.S.A./Britain/Italy, 1990),** *with Glenn Close and Mel Gibson, directed by Franco Zeffirelli.*
When the camera is close to the action, as in this photo, even small gestures seem magnified and highly kinetic. Gibson's portrayal of Shakespeare's tragic hero is volatile, exploding with energy—a far cry from the contemplative and indecisive Hamlet made famous in Laurence Olivier's 1948 film version of the play.   *(Icon Distribution, Inc.)*

In live theatre, these two interpretations would have to be achieved through other means. Although the drama is in part a visual medium, the "frame" size (the confines of the set or the proscenium arch) remains the same for the duration of the play. Live theatre, in short, is restricted to "long shots," where such distortions of movement are virtually impossible.

If there is a great deal of movement in the closer shots, its effect on the screen will be exaggerated. For this reason, filmmakers tend to use these ranges for relatively static scenes. The animation of two people talking and gesturing, for example, has enough movement to prevent most medium shots from appearing static.

Close-ups are even more subtle in their recording of movement. Robert Bresson and Carl Dreyer often highlighted subtle movements by photographing an expressive face in close-up. In fact, these two filmmakers referred to the human face as a spiritual "landscape." In Dreyer's *Passion of Joan of Arc,* for instance, one of the most powerful scenes is a close shot of Joan as a tear slowly trickles down her face. Expanded thousands of times by the close-up, the path of the tear represents a cataclysmic movement on the screen, far more powerful than the inane cavalry charges and clashing armies of routine epic films.

Hackneyed techniques are almost invariably the sign of a second-rate filmmaker. Certain emotions and ideas—like joy, love, hatred—are so prevalent in the cinema that serious artists are constantly searching for new methods of presentation, methods that confer uniqueness to the commonplace, that trans-

5–8.   *Volcano* (U.S.A., 1997), *directed by Mick Jackson.*
Movement in film is closely related to mise en scène. The top of the image is often associated with power and control, the bottom with vulnerability. In this special-effects shot, the fiery lava erupts from the top of the frame, spilling down to Wilshire Boulevard in Los Angeles. The outclassed firefighters and their trucks are kept low—impotent before the volcano's overwhelming force.   *(Twentieth Century-Fox)*

5–9. *Deux secondes* (Canada, 1998), *with Charlotte Laurier, directed by Manon Briand.*
A downhill bike racer (Laurier) hesitates for two seconds at the beginning of a race and loses her place on the team. Briand uses fast motion, slow motion and freeze frames to suggest the character's experience of the relativity of time as she adjusts to her new life as a bicycle courier in Montreal. *(France Filme)*

---

form the familiar into something fresh and unexpected. For example, death scenes are common in movies. But because of their frequency, they are often presented tritely. Of course, death remains a universal concern, one that can still move audiences if handled with any degree of originality and imagination.

One method of avoiding staleness is to convey emotions through kinetic symbolism. Like the choreographer, the filmmaker can exploit the meanings inherent in certain types of movements. Even so-called abstract motions tend to suggest ideas and feelings. Some movements strike us as soft and yielding, for example, whereas others seem harsh and aggressive. Curved and swaying motions are generally graceful and feminine. Those that are straight and direct strike us as intense, stimulating, and powerful. Furthermore, unlike the choreographer, the filmmaker can exploit these symbolic movements even without having people perform them.

If a dancer were to convey a sense of grief at the loss of a loved one, his or her movements would probably be implosive, withdrawn, with an emphasis on slow, solemn, downward movements. A film director might use this same kinetic principle but in a totally different physical context. For instance, in Walter Lang's *The King and I*, we realize that the seriously ailing king (Yul Brynner) has died when we see a close-up of his hand slowly slipping toward the bottom of the frame, disappearing finally off the lower edge into darkness.

In Eisenstein's *Old and New* (also known as *The General Line*), a valuable stud bull dies, and its death has disastrous consequences for the agricultural commune that has purchased the animal. These consequences are expressed through

5–10. *Frantic* (U.S.A., 1988), *with Harrison Ford, directed by Roman Polanski.*
Filmmakers often exploit "negative space" to anticipate action that has not yet occurred. In this photo, for example, the camera seems to be waiting for something to fill in the empty space on the right. The unsuspecting protagonist does not know that he will soon be threatened by a careening auto that will almost run him down. But we have already been forewarned of the impending action by Polanski's framing. Anticipatory setups like these are especially common in thrillers. They are a kind of warning to the viewer to be prepared: Art as well as nature abhors a vacuum. *(Warner Bros.)*

two parallel shots emphasizing the same kinetic symbolism. First Eisenstein shows us an **extreme close-up** of the dying bull's eye as it slowly closes. The mournful lowering of the eyelid is magnified many times by the closeness of the shot. Eisenstein then cuts to a shot of the sun lowering on the horizon, its streaming shafts of light slowly retracting as the sun sinks below the earth's rim. Trivial as a bull's death might seem, to the hardworking members of the commune it suggests an almost cosmic significance. Their hopes for a better future die with the animal.

Of course, context is everything in movies. The kind of symbolism in *Old and New* would probably seem pretentious and arty in a more realistic movie. However, the same kinetic *principle* can be used in almost any kind of context. In Norman Jewison's *In the Heat of the Night,* for example, a police officer (Sidney Poitier) must inform a woman (Lee Grant) that her husband has been brutally murdered. When she hears the news, the woman shields her body with her arms in a kind of shrivelling, implosive gesture. In effect, she withdraws into herself, her body withering as the news sinks in. She will not permit even the sympathetic officer to touch or comfort her in any way.

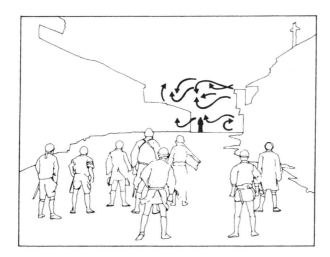

5–11. *Yojimbo* **(Japan, 1961),** *directed by Akira Kurosawa.*
Kurosawa's movies are rich in symbolic kinetic techniques. He often creates dramatic tensions by juxtaposing static visual elements with a small but dynamic whirlpool of motion. In this scene, for example, the greatly outnumbered protagonist (Toshiro Mifune) prepares to do battle with a group of vicious hoodlums. In static visual terms, the samurai hero seems trapped by the enclosing walls and the human wall of thugs that block off his space. But surrounding the protagonist is a furious whipping wind (the dominant contrast of the shot), which symbolizes his fury and physical power. *(Janus Films)*

5-12. ***The French Connection*** (U.S.A., 1971), *directed by William Friedkin.*
Expansive outward movements and sunburst effects are generally associated with explosive emotions, like joy or terror. In this shot, however, the symbolism is more complex. The scene occurs at the climax of a furious chase sequence in which the protagonist (Gene Hackman, with gun) finally triumphs over a vicious killer by shooting him—just as he seems on the verge of eluding the dogged police officer once again. This kinetic outburst on the screen symbolizes not only the bullet exploding in the victim's body, but a joyous climax for the protagonist after his humiliating and dangerous pursuit. The kinetic "ecstasy of death" also releases the dramatic tension that has built up in the audience during the chase sequence: In effect, we are seduced into sharing the protagonist's joy in the kill. *(Twentieth Century–Fox)*

In Charles Vidor's *Ladies in Retirement,* these same kinetic principles are used in a totally different context. An impoverished housekeeper (Ida Lupino) has asked her aging employer for financial assistance to prevent the housekeeper's two retarded sisters from being put away in an asylum. The employer, a vain, selfish woman who acquired her wealth as the mistress of a rich man, refuses to help her employee. As a last resort, the desperate housekeeper decides to kill the old woman and use her isolated cottage as a refuge for the good-naturedly dotty sisters. The murder scene itself is conveyed through kinetic symbolism. We see the overdressed dowager playing a ditty at her piano. The housekeeper, who plans to strangle the woman from behind, slowly creeps up while she is singing. But instead of showing us the actual strangulation,

a

b

5-13. *High Noon* **(U.S.A., 1952),** *with Gary Cooper, directed by Fred Zinnemann.* The closer and tighter the shot, the more motion dominates. In longer, more loosely framed shots, movement tends to recede in importance, usually in direct proportion to the distance of the kinetic action from the camera. Even the slightest alterations in framing can affect our reactions. The two fight sequences portrayed here, for example, imply subtle differences. The closer, more tightly framed shot **(a)** suggests more danger and desperation because the antagonist (Lloyd Bridges) almost manages to pull the protagonist off screen right. In the somewhat longer, looser shot **(b),** the protagonist's control over his adversary is reinforced by the amount of space allowed for the hero's movements. By allowing more space and distance, the director is able to present the fight scene with a greater degree of stylization and objectivity. The control of the visual elements within the frame becomes a spatial metaphor for the protagonist's control over his antagonist. *(United Artists)*

Vidor cuts to a medium close shot of the floor, where, one by one, the dowager's pearls drop to the floor. Suddenly a whole clump of pearls splatters near the old lady's now motionless feet. The symbolism of the dropping pearls is appropriate to the context, for they embody not only the woman's superfluous wealth, but her vanity and selfishness as well. Each falling pearl suggests an elegantly encrusted drop of blood: Drop by drop, her life ebbs away, until the remaining strands of pearls crash to the floor and the wretched creature is dead. By conveying the murder through this kinetic symbolism, Vidor prevents us from witnessing the brutal event, which probably would have lost the audience's sympathy for the housekeeper.

In each of these instances, the filmmakers—Lang, Eisenstein, Jewison, and Vidor—were faced with a similar problem: how to present a death scene with freshness and originality. Each director solved the problem by exploiting similar movements: a slow, contracting, downward motion—the same kind of movement that a dancer would use literally on a stage.

Kinetic symbolism can be used to suggest other ideas and emotions as well. For example, ecstasy and joy are often expressed by expansive motions, fear by a variety of tentative or trembling movements. Eroticism can be conveyed through the use of undulating motions. In Kurosawa's *Rashomon*, for example, the provocative sexuality of a woman is suggested by the sinuous motions of her silk veil—a movement so graceful and tantalizing that the protagonist (Toshiro Mifune) is unable to resist her erotic allure. Since most Japanese viewers regard overt sexuality in the cinema as tasteless—even kissing is rare in their movies—sexual ideas are often expressed through these symbolic methods.

Every art form has its rebels, and cinema is no exception. Because movement is almost universally regarded as basic to film art, a number of directors have experimented with the idea of stasis. In effect, these filmmakers are deliberately working against the nature of their medium, stripping it of all but the most essential motions. Such filmmakers as Bresson, Ozu, and Dreyer have been described as **minimalists** because their kinetic techniques are so austere and restrained. When virtually nothing seems to be moving in an image, even the slightest motion can take on enormous significance. In many cases, this stasis is exploited for symbolic purposes: Lack of motion can suggest spiritual or psychological paralysis, as in the movies of Antonioni, for example.

THE MOVING CAMERA

Before the 1920s, filmmakers tended to confine movements to the subject photographed. There were relatively few who moved their cameras during a shot, and then usually to keep a moving figure within the frame. In the 1920s such German filmmakers as F. W. Murnau and E. A. Dupont moved the camera within the shot not only for physical reasons but for psychological and thematic reasons as well. The German experiments permitted subsequent filmmakers to use the mobile camera to communicate subtleties previously

5–14. *Forrest Gump* **(U.S.A., 1994),** *with Tom Hanks, directed by Robert Zemeckis.* Reverse dolly shots such as this are more unsettling than conventional travelling shots. When we dolly into a scene, we can usually see where we're headed, to a geographical goal of some sort. But when the camera moves in reverse, sweeping backwards as it keeps the running protagonist in frame, we have no sense of a final destination, just the urgent, desperate need to flee.

(Paramount Pictures)

considered impossible. True, **editing**—that is, moving the camera *between* shots—is faster, cheaper, and less distracting, but cutting is also abrupt, disconnected, and unpredictable compared to the fluid lyricism of a moving camera.

A major problem of the moving camera involves time. Films that use this technique extensively tend to seem slow-moving, since moving in or out of a scene is more time-consuming than a straight cut. A director must decide whether moving the camera is worth the film time involved, and whether the movement warrants the additional technical and budgetary complications. If a filmmaker decides to move the camera, he or she must then decide how. Should it be mounted on a vehicle or simply moved around the axis of a stationary tripod? Each major type of camera movement implies different meanings, some obvious, others subtle. There are seven basic moving camera shots: **(1) pans, (2) tilts, (3) crane shots, (4) dolly shots, (5) zoom shots, (6) handheld shots,** and **(7) aerial shots.**

Panning shots—those movements of the camera that scan a scene horizontally—are taken from a stationary axis point, with the camera mounted on a tripod. Such shots are time-consuming because the camera's movement must ordinarily be smooth and slow to permit the images to be recorded clearly. Pans are also unnatural in a sense, for when the human eye pans a scene, it jumps from one point to another, skipping over the intervals between points. The most common use of a pan is to keep the subject within frame. If a person moves from one position to another, the camera moves horizontally to keep the person in the centre of the composition. Pans in extreme long shots are especially effective in epic films where an audience can experience the vastness of a locale. But pans can be just as effective at medium and close ranges. The so-called **reaction shot,** for instance, is a movement of the camera away from the central attraction—usually a speaker—to capture the reaction of an onlooker or listener. In such cases, the pan is an effective way of preserving the cause–effect relationship between the two subjects and of emphasizing the solidarity and connectedness of people.

The **swish pan** (also known as a "flash pan" and a "zip pan") is a variation of this technique and is often used for transitions between shots—as a substitute cut. The swish pan involves a whirling of the camera at a speed so rapid that only blurred images are recorded. Although they actually take more time than cuts, swish pans connect one scene to another with a greater sense of simultaneity than cuts can suggest. For this reason, flash pans are often used to connect events at different locales that might otherwise appear remote from each other.

Pan shots tend to emphasize the unity of space and the connectedness of people and objects within that space. Precisely because we expect a panning shot to emphasize the literal contiguity of people sharing the same space, these shots can surprise us when their realistic integrity is violated. In Robert Benton's *Places in the Heart,* for example, the final shot of the movie connects the world of the living with the dead. The film is a celebration of the simple Christian values that bind a small Texas community together during the troubled times of the 1930s depression. The final shot takes place in a church. The camera begins to pan the congregation in a long sweeping motion down each row of pews. Interspersed among the surviving characters are several that we know to be dead, including a murderer and his victim, worshipping side by side. Though the rest of the movie is realistically presented, this final shot leaps to a symbolic level, suggesting that the unified spirit of the community includes all its members, deceased as well as living.

Tilt shots are vertical movements of the camera around a stationary horizontal axis. Many of the principles that apply to pans also apply to tilts: They can be used to keep subjects within frame, to emphasize spatial and psychological interrelationships, to suggest simultaneity, and to emphasize cause–effect relationships. Tilts, like pans, can also be used subjectively in **point-of-view shots:** The camera can simulate a character's looking up or down a scene, for instance. Since a tilt is a change in angle, it is often used to suggest a psychological shift within a character. When an eye-level camera tilts downward, for example, the person photographed suddenly appears more vulnerable.

Dolly shots, sometimes called trucking or tracking shots, are taken from a moving vehicle (dolly). The vehicle literally moves in, out, or alongside a moving figure or object while the action is being photographed. Tracks are sometimes laid on the set to permit the vehicle to move smoothly—hence the term *tracking shot.* If these shots involve long distances, the tracks have to be laid or withdrawn while the camera is moving in or out. Today, any vehicular movement of the camera can be referred to as a dolly shot. The camera can be mounted on a car, a train, even a bicycle.

5–15. *Rope* (U.S.A., 1948), *with James Stewart (left), Farley Granger (right), and John Dall (second from right), directed by Alfred Hitchcock.*
An incorrigible experimenter in form, Hitchcock shot this film in a single uninterrupted take, the camera and characters choreographed so the size of the images could be varied from close-ups to long shots. During shooting, whenever the camera had to be reloaded (every ten minutes), he devised ways to mask the cut between shots, such as having a character's back momentarily darken the screen and continuing the "uninterrupted" scene when the character moves away from the lens. The film is one of the few examples of a literal adherence to the unities of time, place, and action.   *(Warner Bros.)*

Tracking is a useful technique in point-of-view shots to capture a sense of movement in or out of a scene. If a filmmaker wants to emphasize the *destination* of a character's movement, the director is more likely to use a straight cut between the initiation of the movement and its conclusion. If the experience of the movement itself is important, the director is more likely to dolly. Thus, if a character is searching for something, the time-consuming point-of-view dolly helps to elongate the suspense of the search. Similarly, the **pull-back dolly** is an effective technique for surprising the character (and audience) with a revelation **(5–14, 5–18)**. By moving back, the camera reveals something startling, something previously off frame.

5–16. Production photo from the set of *Broken Arrow* (U.S.A., 1996), *with Christian Slater, director John Woo (in white shirt), and John Travolta.*
Action and adventure films are among the most kinetic of genres, stressing physical movement above all other qualities. Action films also tend to be violent, fast-paced, and steeped in machismo values. The genre is dominated by Americans, though it has attracted such international talent as Hong Kong's John Woo. Asian films in general tend to be slow-paced, but action films made in the East (and especially Hong Kong) are often frenzied, with one brawl spilling over into the next, driving toward an orgiastic explosion of violence at the climax. Woo's American movies have been somewhat less frantic, though still energetically and stylishly directed. *(Twentieth Century-Fox)*

A common function of travelling shots is to provide an ironic contrast with dialogue. In Jack Clayton's *The Pumpkin Eater,* a distraught wife (Anne Bancroft) returns to an ex-husband's house, where she has an adulterous liaison with him. As the two lie in bed, she asks him if he had been upset over their divorce and whether or not he missed her. He assures her that he wasn't upset, but while their voices continue on the soundtrack, the camera belies his words by slowly dollying through his living room, revealing pictures and mementos of the ex-wife. The shot is a kind of direct communication between the director and audience, bypassing the characters. These techniques are deliberate authorial intrusions. They are favoured by filmmakers who view their characters with skepticism or irony—Lubitsch and Hitchcock, for example.

One of the most common uses of dolly shots is to emphasize psychological rather than literal revelations. By slowly tracking in on a character, the filmmaker is getting close to something crucial. The movement acts as a signal to the audience, suggesting, in effect, that we are about to witness something important. A cut to a close-up would tend to emphasize the rapidity of the discovery, but slow dolly shots suggest a more gradual revelation. For example, in

5-17. *An American in Paris* (U.S.A., 1951), *with Gene Kelly (centre), choreographed by Kelly, directed by Vincente Minnelli.*
In some respects, film choreography can be more complex than stage choreography, which is always viewed from a stationary position. In movies, however, the camera can be choreographed as well as the dancers. Kelly's choreography often features lyrical crane shots in which the camera's swirling motions are dreamily counterpointed by the motions of the dancer—a virtual pas de deux, with the camera/viewer serving as surrogate partner.   *(MGM)*

Clive Donner's *The Caretaker* (also known as *The Guest*), this technique is used several times. Based on Harold Pinter's play, the movie concerns two brothers and an old tramp who tries to set one brother against the other. The dialogue, as is often the case in a Pinter **script**, is evasive and not very helpful in providing an understanding of the characters. The brothers are different in most respects. Mick (Alan Bates) is materialistic and aggressive. Aston (Robert Shaw) is gentle and withdrawn. Each brother has a crucial speech in which the camera slowly tracks from a long range to a close-up. Neither of the speeches is really very informative, at least not on a literal level. However, the juxtaposition of the dialogue with the implications of the dolly shot helps the audience to feel that it has finally "arrived" at an understanding of each character.

5-18. *Gone With the Wind* **(U.S.A., 1939),** *with Vivien Leigh (left, in front of boiling cauldron), directed by Victor Fleming.*
The pull-back dolly or crane shot begins with a close view of a subject, then withdraws to reveal the larger context. The contrast between the close and distant views can be funny, shocking, or sadly ironic. In this famous scene, the camera begins with a close shot of the heroine (Leigh), then slowly pulls back, revealing the wounded bodies of hundreds of soldiers, and stopping finally at a distant long-shot range, in front of a high flagpole, the tattered Confederate flag blowing in the wind like a shredded remnant.   *(MGM)*

A stationary camera tends to convey a sense of stability and order, unless there is a great deal of movement within the frame. The moving camera—by its very instability—can create ideas of vitality, flux, and sometimes disorder. Orson Welles exploited the mobile camera to suggest the leading character's dynamic energy in *Othello* **(12–27)**. Early in the movie, the confident Moor is often photographed in travelling shots. In the ramparts scene, he and Iago walk with military briskness as the camera moves with them at an equally energetic pace. When Iago tells him of his suspicions, the camera slows down, then comes to a halt. Once Othello's mind has been poisoned, he is photographed mostly from stationary setups. Not only has his confident energy drained away, but a spiritual paralysis invades his soul. In the final shots of the

5-19. *Goodfellas* (U.S.A., 1990), *with Lorraine Bracco and Ray Liotta, directed by Martin Scorsese.*
Scorsese is an unsurpassed master of the moving camera. He often uses this technique even in conventional dialogue scenes and close shots. These spontaneous eruptions destabilize the visual materials, infusing the action with a surge of energy, almost a kinetic high.   *(Warner Bros.)*

movie, he barely moves, even within the still frame. This paralysis motif is completed when Othello kills himself.

When the camera literally follows a character, the audience assumes that it will discover something along the way. A journey, after all, usually has a destination. But travelling shots are often symbolic rather than literal. In Federico Fellini's *8½*, for example, the moving camera is used to suggest a variety of thematic ideas. The protagonist, Guido (Marcello Mastroianni), is a film director who's trying to put together a movie near a bizarre health spa. Everywhere he turns, he's confronted by memories, fantasies, and realities more fantastic than anything he can imagine. But he is paralyzed by indecision. What, if anything, from all this copious flux will he select for his movie? He can't use it all, for it won't fit together—the materials are too sprawling. Throughout the film, the camera wanders restlessly, prowling over the fantastic locale, compulsively hoarding images of faces, textures, and shapes. All are absorbed by Guido, but he is unable to detach them from their contexts to form a meaningful artistic structure.

5-20. *Strictly Ballroom* (Australia, 1992), *with Tara Morice and Paul Mercurio, directed by Baz Lurhmann.*

"Dance is the activity where the sexual connection is most explicit," Michael Malone has pointed out, "which is why movies use it to symbolize sex and why skillful dancing is an invariable movie clue to erotic sophistication, a prerequisite for the lover." See Michael Malone, *Heroes of Eros: Male Sexuality in the Movies* (New York: E. P. Dutton, 1979). *(Miramax Films)*

The film's travelling shots function on several levels. They are used to suggest Guido's increasingly desperate search for a theme, a story, or a cinematic structure of some kind. They are also analogues of Guido's passive receptivity. He is like a walking recording machine, seeking out and storing image upon image for their own sakes. The travelling shots, in conjunction with the movement of people, processions, and traffic, are also analogues for the unbroken flow of experiences that comprises Guido's reality—a reality he finally refuses to simplify for the sake of producing a tidy little movie. But where Guido fails, Fellini succeeds triumphantly. The final sequence of the film (which takes place in Guido's imagination) emphasizes the continuity and coherence of *all* his experiences. The characters from his life—including those of Guido's past and fantasies—join hands and dance joyously around a circus ring, a ritual celebration of the limitlessness of the artistic imagination. The ring is a visual symbol of Fellini's conception of life's infinite flow, which has no beginning or end.

5-21. *Born on the Fourth of July* **(U.S.A., 1989),** *with Tom Cruise, directed by Oliver Stone.* In film, as in other arts, subject matter usually determines technique. This scene portrays an antiwar protest rally during the Vietnam War era. The scene is deliberately shot in a ragged manner, with shaky handheld shots, fragmentary editing, and open-form asymmetrical compositions that look like newsreel footage captured in the midst of the chaos. A stable, aesthetically balanced shot would be more beautiful, but such a composition would be completely at odds with the essence of the subject matter.   *(Universal City Studios)*

A number of film theorists have discussed the unique capacity of cinema to convert space into time and time into space. The amount of time it takes to photograph a concrete object can be the main purpose of a shot, especially a travelling shot. The acknowledged master of these types of dolly shots was Max Ophüls. In such movies as *Letter From an Unknown Woman* and *The Earrings of Madame De . . . ,* the heroines throw themselves into imprudent but glorious love affairs. The camera tracks relentlessly as the women become more and more irrevocably involved with their lovers. As critic Andrew Sarris pointed out, Ophüls uses his dolly shots as metaphors of time's cruel prodigality. His world is one of tragic flux and instability in which love is destined to run its eventually bitter course. These lengthy tracking shots preserve the continuity of time by preserving the continuity of space. There is no time for pause and reflection "between shots" in these films. This symbolic technique can be overlooked by the casual viewer because the dolly shots are to some degree functional: They follow characters in their daily round of activities. But a stationary camera would be just as functional (not to mention less expensive), for the characters could move toward or away from a fixed setup.

5-22. *The Killing Fields* (U.S.A., 1984), *with Haing S. Ngor (carrying child), cinematography by Chris Menges, directed by Roland Joffé.*
When the handheld camera is used to photograph confusing or agitated events, these traits are intensified by the instability of the camera. In this movie, for example, one of the scariest sequences is the panic-stricken evacuation of Phnom Penh, the Cambodian capital, just as the barbaric Khmer Rouge guerrillas are about to enter the city. People stream in and out of the frame, scurrying to escape. The camera races with them, sweeping first in one direction, then another. Nothing is stable.
(Warner Bros.)

Handheld shots are generally less lyrical, more noticeable than vehicular shots. Handheld cameras, which are usually mounted with a harness on the **cinematographer**'s shoulder, were perfected in the 1950s to allow camera operators to move in or out of scenes with greater flexibility and speed. Originally used by documentarists to permit them to shoot in nearly every kind of location, these cameras were quickly adopted by many fiction film directors as well. Handheld shots are often jumpy and ragged. The camera's rocking is hard to ignore, for the screen exaggerates these movements, especially if the shots are taken from close ranges. For this reason, filmmakers often use the handheld camera for point-of-view shots. In Mike Nichols's *The Graduate,* for example, a handheld shot is used to simulate the hero's attempts to manoeuvre through a crowded room of people. However, most cinematographers can manipulate a lightweight camera as steadily as a dolly if the situation requires.

Crane shots are essentially airborne dolly shots. A crane is a kind of mechanical arm, often more than six metres in length. In many respects, it resembles the cranes used by the telephone company to repair lines. It can lift a cinematographer and camera in or out of a scene. It can move in virtually any direction: up, down, diagonally, in, out, or any combination of these. Because of this flexibility, a crane shot can suggest a number of complex ideas. It can move from high, long distances to low, close ones, as it does in Hitchcock's *Notorious,* where the camera sweeps from an extreme high-angle long shot of a ballroom to an extreme close-up of the hand of the heroine (Ingrid Bergman) clasping a small key.

5-23. *Circle of Friends* (Ireland, 1994), *with Minnie Driver and Chris O'Donnell, directed by Pat O'Connor.*
Movement is not always an automatic dominant. In this scene, for example, unimportant characters dance in and out of the frame, occasionally obscuring our view of the two central characters, who are not moving much as they dance and talk. Note how O'Connor shoots the scene with a telephoto lens, with the romantic couple in focus and the other dancers blurred into an undulating sea of irrelevance. What matters for these two is here and now in each other's arms. The rest of the world seems very far away. *(Savoy Pictures)*

Zoom lenses don't usually involve the actual movement of the camera, but on the screen their effect is very much like an extremely fast tracking or crane shot. The zoom is a combination of lenses, which are continuously variable, permitting the camera to change from close wide-angle distances to extreme telephoto positions (and vice versa) almost simultaneously. The effect of the zoom is a breathtaking sense of being plunged into a scene, or an equally jolting sense of being plucked out of it. Zoom shots are used instead of dolly or crane shots for a number of reasons. They can zip in or out of a scene much faster than any vehicle. From the point of view of economy, they are cheaper than dolly or crane shots since no vehicle is necessary. In crowded locations, zoom lenses can be useful for photographing from long distances, away from the curious eyes of passersby.

There are certain psychological differences between zoom shots and those involving an actual moving camera. Dolly and crane shots tend to give the viewer a sense of entering into or withdrawing from a set: Furniture and people seem to stream by the sides of the screen, as the camera penetrates a

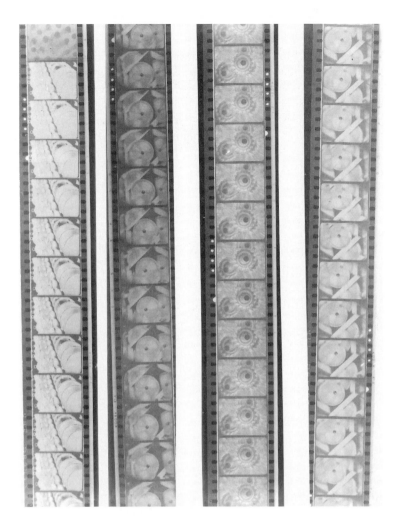

5-24. *Ballet Mécanique* **(France, 1924),** *directed by Fernand Léger.*
Best known for his cubist paintings, Léger was also an avant-garde filmmaker. One of the first to explore abstraction in the cinema, he created many striking kinetic effects by animating and choreographing ordinary objects like crockery, dishes, and machine gears. *(Museum of Modern Art)*

three-dimensional space. Zoom lenses foreshorten people and flatten space. The edges of the image simply disappear on all sides. The effect is one of sudden magnification. Instead of feeling as though we are entering a scene, we feel as though a small portion of it has been thrust toward us. In shots of brief duration, these differences are not significant, but in lengthier shots, the psychological differences can be pronounced.

Aerial shots, usually taken from a helicopter, are really variations of the crane shot. Like a crane, the helicopter can move in virtually any direction. When a crane is impractical—usually on exterior locations—an aerial shot can duplicate the effect. The helicopter shot can be much more extravagant, of course, and for this reason is occasionally used to suggest a swooping sense of freedom. In *Jules et Jim,* an aerial shot conveys Jim's lyrical exhilaration when, after many years, he plans to visit his friend Jules and his wife in Germany. In *Apocalypse Now,* Francis Ford Coppola used aerial shots to produce a godlike sense of inexorability, as swirling American helicopters annihilate a Vietnamese village. The sequence is a kinetic tour de force, suffusing the action with a sense of exhilaration—and horror. Virtually every shot in this brilliantly edited sequence contains a forward rush, a sense of being swept up by events that are out of control.

MECHANICAL DISTORTIONS OF MOVEMENT

Movement in film is not a literal phenomenon but an optical illusion. Present-day cameras record movement at twenty-four frames per second (fps). That is, in each second, twenty-four separate still pictures are photographed. When the film is shown in a projector at the same speed, these still photographs are mixed instantaneously by the human eye, giving the illusion of movement. This phenomenon is called the *persistence of vision.* By simply manipulating the timing mechanism of the camera and/or projector, a filmmaker can distort movement on the screen. Even at the turn of the century, Méliès was experimenting with various kinds of trick photography, and although most of these experiments were just clever stunts, subsequent directors have used these discoveries with artistic results. There are five basic distortions of this kind: **(1) animation, (2) fast motion, (3) slow motion, (4) reverse motion,** and **(5) freeze frames.**

There are two fundamental differences between animation and live-action movies. In animation sequences, each frame is photographed separately, rather than continuously at the rate of twenty-four frames per second. Another difference is that animation, as the word implies, doesn't ordinarily involve the photographing of subjects that move by themselves. The subjects photographed are generally drawings or static objects. Thus, in an animated movie, thousands of frames are separately photographed. Each frame differs from its neighbour only to an infinitesimal degree. When a sequence of these frames is projected at twenty-four fps, the illusion is that the drawings or objects are moving, and hence, are "animated."

The common denominator of both animated and live-action film procedures is the use of the camera, the photographic process. Many of the features of Walt Disney, for instance, are as dramatic as ordinary fiction films. In fact, a number of parents have considered Disney's *Bambi* too frightening and violent for children. On the other hand, some of the brilliant animated films of the Canadian Norman McLaren and the Yugoslavian Zagreb School are virtually abstract expressionist paintings on celluloid **(5–26).**

A popular misconception about animated movies is that they are intended primarily for the entertainment of children—perhaps because the

5–25.   *Beauty and the Beast* (U.S.A., 1991), *directed by Gary Trousdale and Kirk Wise.*
Beginning with the "Silly Symphonies" of the early 1930s, the field of animation was dominated for many years by Disney, whose movies were ostensibly aimed at children. Disney's great feature-length films—*Snow White and the Seven Dwarfs, Fantasia, Pinocchio, Bambi, Dumbo,* and *Beauty and the Beast*—are classics of the cinema and appeal to adults as well. See also Christopher Finch, *The Art of Walt Disney* (New York: Abrams, 1973).   *(©Walt Disney Productions)*

field was dominated for so many years by Disney. In actuality, the gamut of sophistication in the genre is as broad as in live-action fiction films. The works of Disney and the puppet films of the Czech Jiri Trnka appeal to both children and adults. A few of these films are as sophisticated as the drawings of Paul Klee. There are even some X-rated animated films, most notably Ralph Bakshi's *Fritz the Cat* and *Heavy Traffic.*

Another popular misconception about animated movies is that they are simpler than live-action films. The contrary is more often the case. For every second of screen time, twenty-four separate drawings usually have to be photographed. Thus, in an average ninety-minute feature, over 129 600 drawings are necessary. Furthermore, some animators use transparent plastic sheets (called **cels**), which they layer over each other to give the illusion of depth to their drawings. Some single frames consist of as many as three or four layers of cels. Most animated films are short precisely because of the overwhelming difficulty of producing all the necessary drawings for a longer movie. Feature-length animated movies are usually produced in assembly-line fashion, with dozens of artists drawing thousands of separate frames.

5-26.   *Blinkity Blank* **(Canada, 1955),** directed by Norman McLaren.
Whereas animation in the Disney tradition combines fantasy with lifelike drawings, many of McLaren's animated films feature purely abstract patterns created without a camera. In this ingenious six-minute film, the designs were scratched directly on the celluloid and accompanied by both instrumental music and sounds "drawn" on the soundtrack.   *(National Film Board of Canada)*

Technically, animated films can be as complex as live-action movies. The same techniques can be used in both forms: travelling shots, zooms, angles, various lenses, editing, **dissolves,** etc. The only difference is that animators *draw* these elements into their images. Furthermore, animators can also use most of the techniques of the painter: different kinds of paints, pens, pencils, pastels, washes, acrylics, and so on.

Some filmmakers have even combined the techniques of live action with animation. In *Neighbours,* for example, McLaren used a technique called **pixillation**, which involves photographing live actors frame by frame, a method sometimes called **stop-motion photography**. When the sequence is projected on the screen, the actors move in abrupt, jerky motions, suggesting a primitive cartoon figure. Other filmmakers have combined animation and theatrical film techniques within the same frame. This mixture is accomplished with the aid of the **optical printer.** Two film strips are superimposed—one consisting of animated frames, the other of photographs of actual people and things. **Mattes**

5-27. *King Kong* (U.S.A., 1933), *with Fay Wray, special effects by Willis H. O'Brien, directed by Merian C. Cooper and Ernest B. Schoedsack.*
O'Brien was a specialist in model animation, which uses stop-motion photography on minia-ture models with malleable parts. When animated, these models become giant prehistoric creatures. Actually, a variety of special effects were used in the film, including matte and process shots and composite shots produced by the optical printer. In this "realistic" shot, for example, a live-action print was fused with an animated print using a forty-five-centimetre model of Kong. There were six miniature models in all, plus a six-metre bust of Kong's head and shoulders and a two and a half metre-long mechanized hairy hand, which could lift the screaming Miss Wray up, down, and away.   *(RKO)*

are used to block out areas of the real scene where the animated drawings will appear in the finished print.

One of the most successful instances of combining live action with ani-mation is *Who Framed Roger Rabbit,* directed by Robert Zemeckis. Richard Williams was the director of animation for the project, which involved over 320 animators. Nearly two million drawings were made for the movie. Some single frames were so complex that they required two dozen drawings. The integra-tion of real details with cartoon characters is startling. A cartoon rabbit drinks from a real coffee cup, which rattles. Cartoon characters throw real shadows on the set. They bump into live people, knocking them down (see **Colour Plate 7**).

5-28. *Tom Jones* (Britain, 1963), *with George Cooper, Albert Finney, and Joyce Redman, directed by Tony Richardson.*
Richardson uses fast motion in this movie when he wishes to emphasize the machinelike behaviour of the characters—especially of the randy hero (Finney) whose sex drive often overpowers his judgment. In the famous Upton Inn mixup (pictured), Tom is rudely interrupted in his nocturnal amours by the hot-tempered Mr. Fitzpatrick. The sequence is shot in fast motion to heighten the comedy: The drunken Fitzpatrick flails at our besieged hero as his terrified paramour screams for her life, thus waking all the inhabitants of the inn, including Sophie Western, the only woman Tom truly loves. *(The Samuel Goldwyn Company)*

Fast motion is achieved by having events photographed at a slower rate than twenty-four fps. Ordinarily, the subject photographed moves at a normal pace. When the sequence is projected at twenty-four fps, the effect is one of acceleration. This technique is sometimes used to intensify the natural speed of a scene—one showing galloping horses, for example, or cars speeding past the camera. Early silent comedies were photographed before the standardization of cameras and projectors at twenty-four fps, and therefore their sense of speed is exaggerated at present-day projector speeds. Even at sixteen or twenty fps, however, some of these early directors used fast motion for comic effects. Without the use of acceleration, the comedies of Mack Sennett would lose much of their loony vitality.

According to the French aesthetician Henri Bergson, when people act mechanically rather than flexibly, comedy is the result. People, unlike machines, can think, feel, and act reasonably. A person's intelligence is measured by his or her ability to be flexible. When behaviour becomes machinelike

5–29. *Chariots of Fire* (Britain, 1981), *with Ben Cross, directed by Hugh Hudson.*
Slow motion is often used in movies about athletic events. The technique can prolong the balletic grace of an athlete's movements. In other cases, like this re-creation of a 1924 Olympic track event, the slow motion heightens the agonized strain in every muscle of an athlete's body as he hurtles himself against the finishing tape. *(Warner Bros.)*

and inflexible, we find it laughable. One aspect of machinelike behaviour is speed: When a person's movements are speeded up on film, he or she seems inhuman, ridiculous. Dignity is difficult in fast motion, for acceleration robs us of our humanity. The Upton Inn mixup in Richardson's *Tom Jones* is funny precisely because the fast motion captures the machinelike predictability of all the characters: Tom flies from Mrs. Waters' bed, Mr. Fitzpatrick flies off the handle, Squire Western screams for his daughter, and the servants scream for their lives **(5–28).**

Slow-motion sequences are achieved by photographing events at a faster rate than twenty-four fps and projecting the film strip at the standard speed. Slow motion tends to ritualize and solemnize movement. Even the most commonplace actions take on a choreographic gracefulness in slow motion. Where speed tends to be the natural rhythm of comedy, slow, dignified movements tend to be associated with tragedy. In *The Pawnbroker,* Sidney Lumet used slow motion in a **flashback** sequence, showing the protagonist as a young man on an idyllic country outing with his family. The scenes are lyrical and otherworldly—too perfect to last.

When violent scenes are photographed in slow motion, the effect is paradoxically beautiful. In *The Wild Bunch,* Peckinpah used slow motion to photograph the grisliest scenes of horror—flesh tearing, blood spattering, horses toppling, an almost endless variety. By aestheticizing these scenes of ugliness,

5-30. *Hair* (U.S.A., 1979), *choreography by Twyla Tharp, directed by Milos Forman.*
Slow motion etherealizes movement, lending it a dreamy, otherworldly grace. Throughout this musical, slow motion is used in the dance numbers to emphasize the individuality rather than the uniformity of the dancers. Twyla Tharp's choreography is organic to the story, which deals with the freewheeling lifestyle of some 1960s hippies. The dance numbers are loose and spontaneous, with each dancer doing his or her own thing—like jiggling links in a chain. *(United Artists)*

Peckinpah demonstrates why the men are so addicted to a life of violence when it seems so profitless. Violence becomes almost an aesthetic credo, somewhat as it's portrayed in the fiction of Hemingway. Slow-motion violence became virtually a trademark in the works of Peckinpah; but after the late 1960s, other directors reduced it to a cinematic cliché.

Reverse motion simply involves photographing an action with the film running reversed. When projected on the screen, the events run backward. Since Méliès's time, reverse motion has not progressed much beyond the gag stage. In *The Knack*, Richard Lester used reverse motion as a comic choreographic retake for a quick laugh when an egg "returns" to its shell. One of the most expressive uses of reverse motion—combined with slow motion—is in Jean Cocteau's *Orpheus*. The protagonist has taken a journey into Hell to regain his lost wife. He makes a serious blunder while there and expresses a wish to return to his original point of decision to correct his mistake. Magically, he is whisked into the past before our eyes, as the previous sequence unfurls backwards in slow motion—to the physical setting where the fateful decision was made. The reverse motion in this sequence is a good instance of how space can be temporalized and time spatialized in the cinema.

A freeze frame suspends all movement on the screen. A single image is selected and reprinted for as many frames as is necessary to suggest the halting of motion. By interrupting a sequence with a freeze shot, the director calls

5–31. *Viridiana* (Mexico/Spain, 1961), *directed by Luis Buñuel.*
This notorious freeze-frame parody of Leonardo's *Last Supper* is only one example of Buñuel's savage assault on the Church, sentimental liberalism, and middle-class morality. His sardonic wit is often shocking and blasphemous. For example, the context of this freeze frame is a drunken orgy of beggars who pose for a group photo to the accompaniment of Handel's *Messiah*. A woman reeling in boozy stupor "snaps" the picture not with a camera but her genitals. This raucous gesture throws the "disciples" into paroxysms of laughter. Though a nonbeliever, Buñuel was able to infuse a sense of scandal in these sacrilegious jokes. "Thank God I am still an atheist," he once sighed. *(Audio-Brandon Films)*

attention to an image—offering it, as it were, for our delectation. Sometimes, the image is a fleeting moment of poignance that is over in a fraction of a second, as in the final shot of Truffaut's *The 400 Blows*. Directors also use freeze frames for comic purposes. In *Tom Jones,* Richardson freezes the shot of Tom dangling on a noose while the off-screen narrator urbanely explains to the audience why Tom should not hang until his tale is finished.

In other instances, the freeze frame can be used for thematic purposes. The final image of Richardson's *The Loneliness of the Long Distance Runner* is frozen to emphasize the permanence of the protagonist's status at the end of the picture. Freeze frames are ideal metaphors for dealing with time, for in effect the frozen image permits no change. Near the end of *True Grit*, for example, Henry Hathaway froze a shot of the protagonist (John Wayne) and his horse leaping over a fence. By halting the shot at the crest of the leap, Hathaway creates a metaphor of timeless grandeur: The image suggests a heroic equestrian statue, immune from the ravages of time and decay. Of course, the total absence of movement is often associated with death, and Hathaway's freeze frame also implies this idea. Perhaps a more explicit metaphor of death can be seen in the conclusion of George Roy Hill's *Butch Cassidy and the Sundance Kid,* where the two heroes (Paul Newman and Robert Redford) are "frozen" just before they are shot to death. Like Hathaway's freeze frame, Hill's suggests an ultimate triumph over death.

Most of the aforementioned mechanical distortions were discovered by Méliès. For many years after, they were largely ignored by the majority of commercial filmmakers until the late 1950s, when the French **New Wave** directors revived them. Since then, many of these techniques have been used promiscu-ously. Zooms, freeze frames, and slow-motion sequences became almost *de rigueur* in the 1960s. In many cases, they degenerated into clichés—modish flourishes that were tacked on to the materials, regardless of whether the tech-niques were organic to the spirit of the subject.

Movement in film is not simply a matter of "what happens." The direc-tor has dozens of ways to convey motion, and what differentiates a great direc-tor from a merely competent one is not so much a matter of what happens, but *how* things happen—how suggestive and resonant are the movements in a given dramatic context? Or, how effectively does the form of the movement embody its content?

FURTHER READING

BACHER, LUTZ, *The Mobile Mise en Scène* (New York: Arno Press, 1978). Primarily on lengthy takes and camera movements.

DEREN, MAYA, "Cinematography: The Creative Use of Reality," in *The Visual Arts Today,* Gyorgy Kepes, ed. (Middletown, Conn.: Wesleyan University Press, 1960). A discus-sion of dance and documentary in film.

GIANNETTI, LOUIS D., "The Aesthetic of the Mobile Camera," in *Godard and Others: Essays in Film Form* (Cranbury, N.J.: Fairleigh Dickinson University Press, 1975). Symbolism and the moving camera.

HALAS, JOHN, and ROGER MANVELL, *Design in Motion* (New York: Focal Press, 1962). Movement and mise en scène.

HOLLOWAY, RONALD, *Z Is for Zagreb* (San Diego, Cal.: A. S. Barnes, 1972). A discussion of the famous Zagreb animators.

HOLMAN, BRUCE L., *Puppet Animation in the Cinema* (San Diego, Cal.: A. S. Barnes, 1975). Emphasis on Czech and Canadian animators.

JACOBS, LEWIS, et al., "Movement" in *The Movies as Medium,* Lewis Jacobs, ed. (New York: Farrar, Straus & Giroux, 1970). A collection of essays.

KNIGHT, ARTHUR, "The Street Films: Murnau and the Moving Camera," in *The Liveliest Art* (rev. ed.) (New York: Mentor, 1979). The German school of the 1920s.

LINDSAY, VACHEL, *The Art of the Moving Picture* (New York: Liveright, 1970). Reprint of an early classic study.

STEPHENSON, RALPH, *The Animated Film* (San Diego, Cal.: A. S. Barnes, 1973). Historical survey.

EDITING $\Big|$ 6

The Samuel Goldwyn Company

The foundation of film art is editing.

—V. I. Pudovkin

SUMMARY

Real time versus reel time: the problem of continuity. Cutting to continuity: condensing unobtrusively. D. W. Griffith and the development of a universal cutting style. The invisible manipulation of classical cutting: editing for emphasis and nuance. The problem of time. Subjective editing: thematic montage and the Soviet school. Pudovkin and Eisenstein: two early masters of thematic cutting. The famous Odessa Steps sequence of *Battleship Potemkin*. The countertradition: the realism of André Bazin. How editing lies. When not to cut and why. Real time and space and how to preserve them. The realist arsenal: sound, deep focus, sequence shots, widescreen.

So far, we have been concerned with cinematic communication as it relates to the single **shot**, the basic unit of construction in movies. Except for travelling shots and **lengthy takes**, however, shots in film tend to acquire meaning when they are juxtaposed with other shots and structured into an **edited** sequence. Physically, editing is simply joining one strip of film (shot) with another. Shots are joined into scenes. On the most mechanical level, editing eliminates unnecessary time and space. Through the association of ideas, editing connects one shot with another, one scene with another, and so on. Simple as this may now seem, the convention of editing represents what critic Terry Ramsaye referred to as the "syntax" of cinema, its grammatical language. Like linguistic syntax, the syntax of editing must be learned. We don't possess it innately.

CONTINUITY

In the earliest years of cinema, the late 1890s, movies were brief, consisting of short events photographed in **long shot** in a single **take**. The duration of the shot and the event were equal. Soon filmmakers began to tell stories—simple ones it's true, but requiring more than a single shot. Scholars have traced the development of narrative to filmmakers in France, Great Britain, and the United States.

By the early twentieth century, filmmakers had already devised a functional style of editing we now call **cutting to continuity**. This type of cutting is a technique used in most fiction films even today, if only for exposition scenes. Essentially, this style of editing is a kind of shorthand, consisting of time-honoured **conventions**. Continuity cutting tries to preserve the fluidity of an event without literally showing all of it.

For example, a continuous shot of a woman leaving work and going home might take forty-five minutes. Cutting to continuity condenses the action into five brief shots, each of which leads by association to the next. (**1**) She enters a corridor as she closes the door to her office. (**2**) She leaves the office building. (**3**) She enters and starts her car. (**4**) She drives her car along a highway. (**5**) Her car turns into her driveway at home. The entire forty-five minute

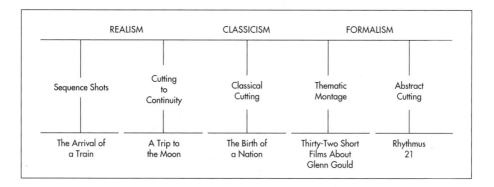

6-1. Editing styles can be classified according to how intrusive or interpretive the cutting is. The least manipulative style is found in a sequence shot, which contains no editing. Cutting to continuity merely condenses the time and space of a completed action. Classical cutting interprets an action by emphasizing certain details over others. Thematic montage argues a thesis—the shots are connected in a relatively subjective manner. Abstract cutting is a purely formalistic style of editing, totally divorced from any recognizable subject matter.

action might take ten seconds of screen time, yet nothing essential is left out. It's unobtrusive condensation.

To keep the action logical and continuous, there must be no confusing breaks in an edited sequence of this sort. Often, all the movement is carried out in the same direction on the screen to avoid confusion. For example, if the woman moves from right to left in one shot and her movements are from left to right in the other shots, we might think that she is returning to her office. Cause-effect relationships must be clearly set forth. If the woman slams on her brakes, the director is generally obliged to offer us a shot of what prompted the driver to stop so suddenly.

The continuity of actual space and time is fragmented as smoothly as possible in this type of editing. Unless the audience has a clear sense of a continuous action, an editing transition can be disorienting. Hence, the term **jump cut**, which means an editing transition that's confusing in terms of space and time. To make their transitions smooth, filmmakers generally use **establishing shots** at the beginning of their stories or at the beginning of any new scene within the narrative.

Once the location is established, filmmakers can cut to closer shots of the action. If the events require a considerable number of cuts, the filmmaker might cut back to a **reestablishing shot**—a return to the opening long shot. In this way, the viewer is reminded of the spatial context of the closer shots. "Between" these various shots, time and space can be expanded or contracted with considerable subtlety.

6-2. *L 'Arrivée d'un train ("The Arrival of a Train,"* **France, 1895),** *directed by Louis and Auguste Lumière.*
The Lumière brothers might be regarded as the godfathers of the documentary movement. Their brief *actualités* (as they called them) are primitive documentaries shot for the most part in single takes. *(Museum of Modern Art)*

By 1908, when the American genius D. W. Griffith entered the field of filmmaking, the industry had already learned how to tell stories thanks to the technique of cutting to continuity. But the stories were simple and crude compared with those in more sophisticated narrative mediums such as literature and drama. Nonetheless, movie storytellers already knew that by breaking up an action into different shots, the event could be contracted or expanded, depending on the number of shots. In other words, the shot, not the scene, was the basic unit of film construction.

Movies before Griffith were usually photographed in stationary **long shot**—roughly the position of a close observer in the live theatre. But with the breakup of shots into both exterior and interior locations, the spectator is, in effect, at both places at once. Furthermore, because film time doesn't depend

6–3. *La Voyage dans la lune* ("*A Trip to the Moon*," France, 1902), *directed by Georges Méliès.*
Around 1900, in America, England, and France, filmmakers began to tell stories. Méliès was one of the first to devise the style of cutting to continuity. The narrative segments are connected by a fade—the diminishing of the light at the conclusion of a scene. The next scene then fades in, often in a different location and at a different time, though usually with the same characters. Méliès advertised these films as stories in "arranged scenes."   *(Museum of Modern Art)*

on the duration of the literal event, filmmakers of this era introduced a more subjective time, one that's determined by the duration of the shots (and the elapsed time implied between them), not by the actual occurrence.

D. W. GRIFFITH AND CLASSICAL CUTTING

The basic elements of editing syntax were already in place when Griffith entered the field, but it was he more than any other individual who moulded these elements into a language of power and subtlety. Film scholars have called this language **classical cutting**. Griffith has been called the Father of Film because he consolidated and expanded many of the techniques invented by his predecessors and was the first to go beyond gimmickry into the realm of art. By 1915, the year of his masterpiece *The Birth of a Nation* (**6–4**), classical cutting was already an editing style of great sophistication and expressiveness. Griffith had seized on the principle of the association of ideas in the concept of editing and expanded it in a variety of ways.

Classical cutting involved editing for dramatic intensity and emotional emphasis rather than for purely physical reasons. Through the use of the **close-up** within the scene, Griffith managed to achieve a dramatic impact that was

6-4. *The Birth of a Nation* **(U.S.A., 1915),** *directed by D. W. Griffith.*
Griffith's greatest gift to the cinema was classical cutting—a style of editing that still charac-
terizes most of the fiction films around the world. Classical cutting allows filmmakers to
inflect their narratives, to add nuances and emphasis. It also subjectivizes time. For example,
in this famous last-minute rescue finale, Griffith cross-cuts to four different groups. Despite
the sense of speed suggested by the brevity of the shots, the sequence actually expands time.
Griffith used 255 separate shots for about twenty minutes of screen time.   *(Museum of Modern Art)*

unprecedented. Close-ups had been used earlier, but Griffith was the first to
use them for psychological rather than physical reasons alone. Audiences were
now permitted to see the smallest details of an actor's face. No longer were performers required to flail their arms and tear their hair. The slightest arch of an
eyebrow could convey a multitude of subtleties.

By splitting the action into a series of fragmentary shots, Griffith
achieved not only a greater sense of detail, but a far greater degree of control
over his audience's reactions. In carefully selecting and juxtaposing long,
medium, and close shots, he constantly shifted the spectator's point of view
within a scene—expanding here, excluding there, emphasizing, consolidating,
connecting, contrasting, paralleling, and so on. The possibilities were far ranging. The space and time continuum of the real scene was radically altered. It
was replaced by a subjective continuity—the association of ideas implicit in the
connected shots.

6-5. *Thirty-Two Short Films About Glenn Gould* (Canada, 1994), *with Colm Feore, directed by François Girard.*

This movie combines elements from documentary filmmaking, fiction films, and the avant-garde. Its editing style is radically subjective. The movie features documentary footage of the late Glenn Gould, a controversial and eccentric Canadian pianist considered to be one of the great musicians of the twentieth century. There are also many re-created scenes with the brilliant Colm Feore playing the quirky and obsessive artist. The movie's structure is not a straightforward narrative, but a series of fragments, loosely based on the thirty-two-part "Goldberg Variations" of Johann Sebastian Bach—one of Gould's most celebrated virtuoso performances. The film is structured around ideas rather than a linear story, and for this reason, thematic montage is its style of editing. *(The Samuel Goldwyn Company)*

In its most refined form, classical cutting presents a series of psychologically connected shots—shots that aren't necessarily separated by real time and space. For example, if four characters are seated in a room, a director might cut from one speaker to a second with a dialogue exchange, then cut to a **reaction shot** of one of the listeners, then to a **two shot** of the original speakers, and finally to a close-up of the fourth person. The sequence of shots represents a kind of psychological cause–effect pattern. In other words, the breakup of shots is justified on the basis of dramatic rather than literal necessity. The scene could be photographed just as functionally in a single shot, with the camera at long shot range. This type of **setup** is known as a **master shot** or a **sequence shot**. Classical cutting is more nuanced and more intrusive. It breaks down the unity of space, analyzes its components, and refocuses our attention to a series of details. The action is mental and emotional rather than literal (**6–7**).

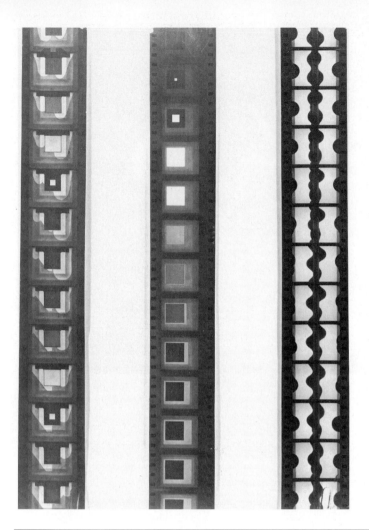

6–6. *Rhythmus 21* (Germany, 1921), *directed by Hans Richter.* In the avant-garde cinema, subject matter is often suppressed or exploited primarily as abstract data. The continuity between shots has nothing to do with a story but is determined by purely subjective or formal considerations. Along with many other European abstract artists of his generation, Richter was a champion of the "absolute film," which consists solely of nonrepresentational forms and designs. *(Museum of Modern Art)*

During the golden years of the American **studio** system—roughly the 1930s and 1940s—directors were often urged (or forced) to adopt the master shot technique of shooting. An entire scene was filmed in long shot without cuts; this take contained all the dramatic variables and hence served as the basic or "master" shot for the scene. The action was then repeated a number of times, with the camera photographing medium shots and close-ups of the principles in the scene. When all this footage was gathered together, the editor had a number of choices in constructing a story continuity. Often disagreements arose over the proper sequence of shots. Usually the studio director was permitted a **first cut**—that is, the sequence of shots representing his or her interpretation of the materials. Under this system, the studios usually had the right to a **final cut**. Many directors disliked master shot techniques precisely because, with so much footage available, a **producer** could construct a radically different continuity.

Master shots are still used by many directors. Without a master, editors often complain of inadequate footage—that the available shots won't cut

6–7. *Fat City* **(U.S.A., 1972),** *directed by John Huston.*
Classical cutting involves editing for dramatic emphasis, to highlight details that might otherwise be overlooked. In Huston's fight scene, for example, the entire boxing match could have been presented in a single setup **(a)**, though such a presentation would probably strike us as unexciting. Instead, Huston breaks up his shots according to the psychological actions and reactions within the fighter protagonist (Stacy Keach, **b**), his manager (Nicholas Colosanto, **c**), and two friends in the auditorium (Jeff Bridges and Candy Clark, **d**). *(Columbia Pictures)*

smoothly. In complex battle scenes, most directors are likely to shoot many **cover shots**—that is, general shots that can be used to reestablish a sequence if the other shots won't cut. In *The Birth of a Nation*, Griffith used multiple cameras to photograph many of the battle scenes, a technique also used by Kurosawa in some sequences of *The Seven Samurai*.

Griffith and other **classical** filmmakers developed a variety of editing conventions that they thought made the cutting "invisible," or at least didn't call attention to itself. One of these techniques is the eyeline match. We see character A look off frame left. Cut to a shot—from his point of view—of character B. We assume B is to A's left. Cause–effect.

Another convention of classical cutting is matching action. Character A is seated but begins to rise. Cut to another shot of character A concluding the rising action and then moving away. The idea is to keep the action fluid, to mask the cut with a smooth linkage that's not noticed because the motion of the character takes precedence. The continuity of the movement conceals the suture.

The so-called 180° rule is still observed by filmmakers, though even during the big-studio era there was nothing sacred about it. (For example, John Ford loved violating the 180° rule. He loved violating almost any rule.) This convention involves **mise en scène** as well as editing. The purpose is to stabilize the space of the playing area so the spectator isn't confused or disoriented. An imaginary "axis of action" line is drawn through the middle of a scene, viewed from the **bird's-eye** angle **(6–8)**. Character A is on the left, character B is on the right. If the director wanted a two shot, he or she would use camera 1. If we then go to a close-up of A (camera 2), the camera must stay on the same side of the 180° line to keep the same background—a continuity aid for the spectator. Similarly, a close-up of character B (camera 3) would be shot on the same side of the axis of action.

In **reverse-angle-shot** exchanges—common for dialogue sequences— the director takes care to fix the placement of the characters from shot to shot.

6–8.   Bird's-eye view of 180° rule.

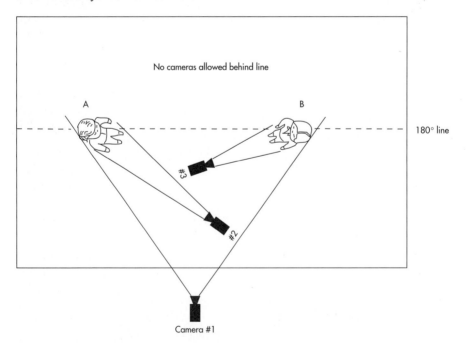

If character A is on the left and character B is on the right in the first shot, they must remain that way in the reverse angle taken from over the shoulder of character B. Usually the reverse angle is not literally 180° opposite, but we agree to accept it as such.

Even today, filmmakers rarely take the camera behind the imaginary axis line, unless their deliberate intention is to confuse the spectator. During fight scenes and other types of chaotic clashes, the filmmaker often wants the spectator to feel threatened, disoriented, anxious. This can be accomplished by violating the 180° rule.

Griffith also perfected the conventions of the chase—still very much with us. Many of his movies ended with a chase and last-minute rescue sequence. Most of them feature **parallel editing**—the alternation of shots of one scene with another at a different location **(6–9)**. By **cross-cutting** back and forth between the two (or three or four) scenes, Griffith conveyed the idea of simultaneous time. For example, near the end of *The Birth of a Nation*, Griffith cross-cuts between four groups. In juxtaposing shots from these separate scenes, he manages to intensify the suspense by reducing the duration of the shots as the sequence reaches its climax. The sequence itself lasts twenty minutes of film time, but the psychological effect of the cross-cutting (the shots average about five seconds each) suggests speed and tension. Generally speaking,

6–9. *The Hunt for Red October* (U.S.A., 1990), *with Alec Baldwin, directed by John McTiernan.* Suspense thrillers often feature cat-and-mouse stalking scenes between the hunter and the hunted, and the tension is heightened by cutting back and forth between them. Usually they occupy the same space only when the sequence is peaking to a climax—when the protagonist must confront the antagonist for control of their mutually shared space. *(Paramount Pictures)*

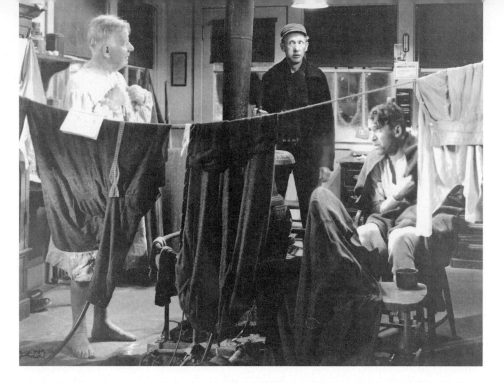

6–10. *It's a Wonderful Life* (U.S.A., 1946), *with James Stewart, directed by Frank Capra.*
Capra was a master of classical editing. His cutting style was fast, light, and seamless. But he never displayed his editing virtuosity for its own sake. Like every other technique, editing is subordinated to the needs of the characters in action—the cardinal commandment of classical cutting. In this and other scenes, Capra included a "reactive character" who guides the viewer's response to the action. This character represents a kind of norm, the way an average person would respond to a given situation. In this scene, for example, Capra's charming fantasy takes a whimsical turn. The forlorn hero (Stewart) listens to his guardian angel (Henry Travers, left) explain why he isn't a very *distinguished* angel (he has yet to earn his wings). A casual bystander (Tom Fadden, centre) happens to overhear and is totally spooked by their conversation. Capra is able to punctuate the comedy of the scene by cutting to this character's response whenever the angel says something weird. *(RKO)*

the greater the number of cuts within a scene, the greater its sense of speed. To avoid the risk of monotony during this sequence, Griffith changed his setups many times. There are **extreme long**, long, medium, and close shots, varied **angles**, lighting contrasts, even a moving camera (it was mounted on a truck).

If the continuity of a sequence is reasonably logical, the fragmentation of space presents no great difficulties. But the problem of time is more complex. Its treatment in film is more subjective than the treatment of space. Movies can compress years into two hours of projection time. They can also stretch a split second into many minutes. Most films condense time. There are only a handful that attempt to make screen time conform to real time: Agnès Varda's *Cleo From Five to Seven* and Fred Zinnemann's *High Noon* are perhaps the bestknown examples. Both deal with about two hours of time—also the approximate length of the films. Even these movies cheat by compressing time in the expository opening sequences and expanding it in the climactic scenes. In actual practice, time exists in a kind of limbo: As long as the audience is absorbed by the screen action, time is what the film says it is. The problem, then, is to absorb the viewer.

On the most mechanical level, screen time is determined by the physical length of the filmstrip containing the shot. This length is governed generally by the complexity of the image subject matter. Usually, longer shots are more densely saturated with visual information than close-ups and need to be held longer on the screen. Raymond Spottiswoode, an early film theorist, claimed that a cut must be made at the peak of the "content curve"—that is, the point in a shot at which the audience has been able to assimilate most of its information. Cutting after the peak of the content curve produces boredom and a sense of dragging time. Cutting before the peak doesn't give the audience time to assimilate the visual action. An image with a complex mise en scène requires more time to assimilate than a simple one. Once an image has been established, however, a return to it during the sequence can be considerably shorter, because it works as a reminder.

But the sensitive treatment of time in editing is largely an instinctive matter that defies mechanical rules. Most great directors have edited their own films, or at least worked in close collaboration with their editors, so crucial is this art to the success of films. The best-edited sequences are determined by mood as well as subject matter. Griffith, for example, generally edited love scenes in long **lyrical** takes, with relatively few setups. His chase and battle scenes were composed of brief shots, jammed together. Paradoxically, the love scenes actually compress real time, whereas the rapidly cut sequences elongate it.

There are no fixed rules concerning rhythm in films. Some editors cut according to musical rhythms. The march of soldiers, for example, could be edited to the beat of a military tune, as can be seen in several marching sequences in King Vidor's *The Big Parade*. This technique is also common with American **avant-garde** filmmakers, who feature rock music soundtracks or cut according to a mathematical or structural formula. In some cases, a director will cut before the peak of the content curve, especially in highly suspenseful sequences. In a number of movies, Hitchcock teases the audience by not providing enough time to assimilate all the meanings of a shot. Violent scenes are conventionally cut in a highly fragmented manner. On the other hand, Antonioni usually cuts long after the content curve has peaked. In *La Notte*, for example, the rhythm is languorous and even monotonous: The director attempts to create a sense of weariness in the audience, paralleling that of the characters. Antonioni's characters are usually tired people—in every sense of the term.

Tact is another editing principle that's difficult to generalize about, because it too depends on content. None of us likes to have the obvious pointed out to us, whether in real life or while watching a movie. Like personal tact, directorial tact is a matter of restraint, taste, and respect for the intelligence of others. Hack directors often present us with emotionally gratuitous shots, falling over themselves to make sure we haven't missed the point. In many TV dramatic series, for example, the main characters gather together at the conclusion, at

6–11. *The Deer Hunter* (U.S.A., 1978), *directed by Michael Cimino.*
Editing is an art as well as a craft. Like all art, it often defies mechanical formulations, taking on a life of its own. For example, when sneak preview audiences were asked for their reactions to this three-hour-long movie, most viewers responded enthusiastically but felt that the hour-long wedding sequence at the opening could have been cut down. In terms of its plot, nothing much "happens" in this sequence. Its purpose is primarily lyrical—a loving celebration of the social rituals that bind the community together. The story content of the sequence could be condensed to a few minutes of screen time—which is exactly what its makers did. When the shortened version was shown to audiences, reactions were negative. Cimino and his editor, Peter Zinner, restored the cut footage. The long wedding sequence is necessary not for its story content so much as for its experiential value. It provides the movie with a sense of balance. The community solidarity of the sequence is what the characters fight for in the subsequent battle footage of the film. *(Universal Pictures)*

---

which time they revel in an orgy of self-congratulation. The smugness of these scenes is offensive in long shot, insufferable when individualized in a series of cloying close-ups. Such edited sequences lack tact. They're pushy.

Griffith's most radical experiments in editing are found in his 1916 masterpiece, *Intolerance*. This movie was the first fiction film to explore the idea of **thematic montage**. Both the film and the technique exerted an enormous influence on movie directors of the 1920s, especially in the Soviet Union. Thematic montage stresses the association of ideas, irrespective of the continuity of time and space.

Intolerance is unified by the theme of people's inhumanity to other people. Rather than tell one story, Griffith **intercut** four. One takes place in ancient Babylon. The second deals with the crucifixion of Jesus. The third concerns the massacre of the Huguenots by the Catholic royalists in sixteenth-century France. The last story takes place in America in 1916 and deals with a battle between labour and management.

6–12. *The Fourth Man* (Holland, 1984), *with Jeroen Krabbé, directed by Paul Verhoeven.*
Editing can shift the action from reality to fantasy in an instant. Often such shifts are accompanied by a cue—eerie music, for example, or a rippling image that suggests a different level of consciousness. At other times, the shift is undetectable, a deliberate attempt to disorient the viewer. The novelist hero of this movie often intermingles reality with fantasy. In this scene, he is trying to shave while suffering from a colossal hangover. His roommate is practising his music, making the shaky hero even shakier. In exasperation, he walks over to the roommate and strangles him. A moment later, we see the hero shaving again and the roommate still practising his music. The strangulation took place only in the hero's vivid imagination. Because it is presented with no transitional cue, we too confuse reality with fantasy—the theme of the film. *(International Spectrafilm Distribution)*

The four stories are developed not separately but in parallel fashion. Scenes of one time period are intercut with scenes of another. At the conclusion of the movie, Griffith features suspenseful chase sequences in the first and last stories; a brutal scene of slaughter in the French story; and a slow, tragic climax in the killing of Jesus. The concluding sequence contains literally hundreds of shots, juxtaposing images that are separated by great spans of time and distance. All these different time periods and locations are unified by the central theme of intolerance. The continuity is no longer physical, or even psychological, but conceptual—that is, thematic.

Intolerance was not a commercial success, but its influence was immense. The filmmakers of the Soviet Union were dazzled by Griffith's movie and based their own theories of **montage** on his practices in this film. A great many directors have profited from Griffith's experiments in the subjective treatment of time. In *The Pawnbroker*, for example, Sidney Lumet exploits the art of editing to produce a series of parallels that are thematically rather than chronologically related. He uses a kind of subliminal editing, in which some shots are held on the screen for only a fraction of a second. The central character is a middle-aged Jew who survived a Nazi concentration camp twenty-five years earlier; all his loved ones, however, were killed there. He tries to repress the memories of these earlier experiences, but they force their way into his consciousness. Lumet suggests this psychological process by intercutting a few frames of the memory shots during a scene that is occurring in the present. A present-tense

6-13. *Flashdance* (U.S.A., 1983), *with Jennifer Beals, directed by Adrian Lyne.*
Editing is often used to deceive—to conceal rather than reveal. For example, the dance numbers in this film were performed by a double, a professional dancer whose identity is cunningly concealed by the artful lighting and the discreetly distanced camera. The dance shots were intercut with closer shots of Jennifer Beals, wearing the same costume and moving to the same music. With the musical number providing the continuity, these intercut shots create the illusion of a continuous movement, with Beals featured throughout. These editing techniques are also commonly used in such scenes as sword fights, dangerous stunts, and many other activities requiring specialized skills. *(Paramount Pictures)*

event detonates the protagonist's memory of something similar from his past. As past contends with present, the flickering memory shots endure longer, until a **flashback** sequence eventually becomes dominant, and the present is momentarily suspended. With only a few exceptions, however, it was not until the 1960s that such unorthodox editing practices became widespread. Griffith seldom cut before the peak of the content curve, and most of his successors patterned themselves on his model.

Filmmakers can interrupt the present with shots not only of the past but of the future as well. In Sydney Pollack's *They Shoot Horses, Don't They?* short **flash-forwards** of a courtroom scene are interspersed throughout the present-tense story. The flash-forwards suggest predestination: Like the dance contest of the story proper, the future is rigged, and personal effort is equated with self-deception. Flash-forwards are also used in Alain Resnais's *La Guerre est finie* and Joseph Losey's *The Go-Between.*

Griffith also restructured time and place through the use of fantasy inserts. In *Intolerance*, for example, a young woman on the verge of murdering her unfaithful boyfriend imagines a scene where she is apprehended by the police. Flashbacks, flash-forwards, and cutaways to fantasies allow filmmakers to develop ideas thematically rather than chronologically, freeing them to explore the subjective nature of time. The very flexibility of time in movies makes the theme of temporality an ideal subject for the medium.

Like Faulkner, Proust, and other novelists, filmmakers have succeeded in cracking the tyranny of mechanically measured time. One of the most complex instances of the restructuring of time is found in Stanley Donen's *Two for the Road.* The story deals with the development and gradual disintegration of a love relationship. It unfolds in a series of mixed flashbacks; that is, the flashbacks are not in chronological sequence, nor are they completed in any one scene. Rather, they are jumbled and fragmented, somewhat in the manner of a Faulkner novel. To complicate matters, most of the flashbacks take place on the road, during various trips the couple has taken in the past. If each of the time periods of the film were designated with the letters A, B, C, D, and E, its temporal structure might be charted as follows: E (present), A (most distant past), B, C, D, B, A, E, C, D, B ... ending with E. The audience gradually learns to identify each time period through various **continuity** clues: the heroine's hairstyles, the modes of transportation, the particular crisis during each trip, and so on.

From its crude beginnings, Griffith expanded the art of editing to include a wide variety of functions: locale changes, time lapses, shot variety, emphasis of psychological and physical details, overviews, symbolic inserts, parallels and contrasts, associations, point-of-view shifts, simultaneity, and repetition of **motifs**.

Griffith's method of editing was also more economical. Related shots could be bunched together in the shooting schedule, regardless of their positions (or "time" and "place") in the finished film. Especially in later years, in the era of high-salaried **stars**, directors could shoot all the star sequences in a brief period and out of cinematic continuity. Less expensive details (extreme long shots, minor actors, close-ups of objects, etc.) could be shot at a more convenient time. Later, the shots would be arranged in their proper sequence on the editor's cutting bench.

SOVIET MONTAGE AND THE FORMALIST TRADITION

Griffith was a practical artist, concerned with communicating ideas and emotions in the most effective manner possible. In the 1920s, the Soviet filmmakers expanded his associational principles and established the theoretical premises for thematic editing, or montage as they called it (from the French *monter,* "to assemble"). V. I. Pudovkin wrote the first important theoretical treatises on what he called constructive editing. Most of his statements are explanations of Griffith's practices, but he differed with the American (whom he praised lavishly) on several points. Griffith's use of the close-up, Pudovkin claimed, is too limited. The close-up is used simply as a clarification of the long shot, which carries most of the meaning, and in effect the close-up is merely an interruption, offering no meanings of its own. Pudovkin insisted that each shot should make a new point. Through the juxtaposition of shots, new meanings can be created. The meanings, then, are in the juxtapositions, not in one shot alone.

6-14. *Evita* (U.S.A., 1996), *with Madonna, directed by Alan Parker.*
Musicals are often edited in a radically formalist style, without having to observe the cutting conventions of ordinary dramatic movies. In Evita, Andrew Lloyd Webber's music provides the continuity for most of the sequences while the edited images fast-forward the story. Sometimes many months are compressed in these montage sequences, even though the musical number takes up only a few minutes of screen time. *(Cinergi Pictures Entertainment)*

Filmmakers in the Soviet Union were strongly influenced by the psychological theories of Pavlov, whose experiments in the association of ideas served as a basis for the editing experiments of Lev Kuleshov, Pudovkin's mentor. Kuleshov believed that ideas in cinema are created by linking together fragmentary details to produce a unified action. These details can be totally unrelated in real life. For example, he linked together a shot of Moscow's Red Square with a shot of Washington's White House, close-ups of two men climbing stairs with another close-up of two hands shaking. Projected as a continuous scene, the linked shots suggest that the two men are in the same place at the same time.

Kuleshov conducted another famous experiment that provided a theoretical foundation for the use of nonprofessional actors in movies. Kuleshov and many of his colleagues believed that traditional acting skills were quite unnecessary in the cinema. First he shot a close-up of a bowl of soup. Then he joined the close-up of the actor with a shot of a coffin containing a female corpse. Finally, he linked the actor's neutral expression with a shot of a little girl playing. When these combinations were shown to audiences, they exclaimed at the actor's expressiveness in portraying hunger, deep sorrow, and paternal pride. In each case, the meaning was conveyed by juxtaposing two shots, not by one alone. Actors can be used as raw material, as objects juxtaposed with other objects. The emotion is produced not by the actor's performance, but by associations brought about by the juxtapositions. In a sense, the

6–15. *Lifeboat* **(U.S.A., 1944),** *with Tallulah Bankhead (centre), directed by Alfred Hitchcock.* Hitchcock was one of Pudovkin's most articulate champions. "Cinema is form," Hitchcock insisted. "The screen ought to speak its own language, freshly coined, and it can't do that unless it treats an acted scene as a piece of raw material which must be broken up, taken to bits, before it can be woven into an expressive visual pattern." He referred to the piecing together of fragmentary shots as "pure cinema," like individual notes of music that combine to produce a melody. In this movie, he confined himself entirely to nine characters adrift at sea in a small boat. In other words, this photo contains the raw material for every shot in the film. Formalists insist that the artistry lies not in the materials per se, but in the way they are taken apart and reconstructed expressively.   *(Twentieth Century-Fox)*

viewer creates the emotional meanings, once the appropriate objects have been linked together by the filmmaker.

For Kuleshov and Pudovkin, a sequence was not filmed, it was constructed. Using far more close-ups than Griffith, Pudovkin built a scene from many separate shots, all juxtaposed for a unified effect. The environment of the scene is the source of the images. Long shots are rare. Instead, a barrage of close-ups (often of objects) provides the audience with the necessary associations to link together the meaning. These juxtapositions can suggest emotional and psychological states, even abstract ideas.

The Soviet theorists of this generation were criticized on several counts. This technique detracts from a scene's sense of **realism**, some critics complained, for the continuity of actual time and place is totally restructured. But Pudovkin and the other Soviet **formalists** claimed that realism captured in long shot is *too* near reality: It's theatrical rather than cinematic. Movies must capture the essence, not merely the surface, of reality, which is filled with irrelevancies. Only by juxtaposing close-ups of objects, textures, symbols, and other selected details can a filmmaker convey *expressively* the idea underlying the undifferentiated jumble of real life.

Some critics also believe that this manipulative style of editing guides the spectator too much—the choices are already made. The audience must sit back passively and accept the inevitable linking of associations presented on the screen. Political considerations are involved here, for the Soviets tended to link film with propaganda. Propaganda, no matter how artistic, doesn't usually involve free and balanced evaluations.

Like many Soviet formalists, Sergei Eisenstein was interested in exploring general principles that could be applied to a variety of apparently different forms of creative activity. He believed that these artistic principles were organically related to the basic nature of all human activity, and ultimately to the nature of the universe itself. Only the barest outline of his complex theories can be offered here. Like the ancient Greek philosopher Heraclitus, Eisenstein believed that the essence of existence is constant change. He believed that nature's eternal fluctuation is **dialectical**—the result of the conflict and synthesis of opposites. What appears to be stationary or unified in nature is only temporary, for all phenomena are in various states of becoming. Only energy is permanent, and energy is constantly in a state of transition to other forms. Every opposite contains the seed of its own destruction in time, Eisenstein believed, and this conflict of opposites is the mother of motion and change.

The function of all artists is to capture this dynamic collision of opposites, to incorporate dialectical conflicts not only in the subject matter of art but in its techniques and forms as well. Conflict is universal in all the arts, according to Eisenstein, and therefore all art aspires to motion. Potentially, at least, cinema is the most comprehensive of the arts because it can incorporate the visual conflicts of painting and photography, the **kinetic** conflicts of dance, the tonal conflicts of music, the verbal conflicts of language, and the character and action conflicts of fiction and drama.

Eisenstein placed special emphasis on the art of editing. Like Kuleshov and Pudovkin, he believed that montage was the foundation of film art. He agreed with them that each shot of a sequence ought to be incomplete, contributory rather than self-contained. However, Eisenstein criticized the concept of linked shots for being mechanical and inorganic. He believed that editing ought to be dialectical: The conflict of two shots (thesis and antithesis) produces a wholly new idea (synthesis). Thus, in film terms, the conflict between shot A and shot B is not AB (Kuleshov and Pudovkin), but a qualitatively new factor—C (Eisenstein). Transitions between shots should not be flowing, as Pudovkin suggested, but sharp, jolting, even violent. For Eisenstein, editing produces harsh collisions, not subtle linkages. A smooth transition, he claimed, was an opportunity lost.

Editing for Eisenstein was an almost mystical process. He likened it to the growth of organic cells. If each shot represents a developing cell, the cinematic cut is like the rupturing of the cell when it splits into two. Editing is done at the point that a shot "bursts"—that is, when its tensions have reached their maximum expansion. The rhythm of editing in a movie should be like the explosions of an internal combustion engine, Eisenstein claimed. A master of dynamic rhythms, his films are almost mesmerizing in this respect: Shots of contrasting volumes, durations, shapes, designs, and lighting intensities collide against each other like objects in a torrential river plunging toward their inevitable destination.

The differences between Pudovkin and Eisenstein may seem academic. In actual practice, however, the two approaches produced sharply contrasting results. Pudovkin's movies are essentially in the classical mould. The shots tend to be additive and are directed toward an overall emotional effect, which is guided by the story. In Eisenstein's movies, the jolting images represent a series of essentially intellectual thrusts and parries, directed toward an ideological argument. The directors' narrative structures also differed. Pudovkin's stories didn't differ much from the kind Griffith used. On the other hand, Eisenstein's stories were much more loosely structured, usually a series of documentary-like episodes used as convenient vehicles for exploring ideas.

When Pudovkin wanted to express an emotion, he conveyed it in terms of physical images—objective correlatives—taken from the actual locale. Thus, the sense of anguished drudgery is conveyed through a series of shots showing details of a cart mired in the mud; close-ups of the wheel, the mud, hands coaxing the wheel, straining faces, the muscles of an arm pulling the wheel, and so on. Eisenstein, on the other hand, wanted film to be totally free of literal continuity and context. Pudovkin's correlatives, he felt, were too restricted by realism.

Eisenstein wanted movies to be as flexible as literature, especially to make figurative comparisons without respect to time and place. Movies should include images that are thematically or metaphorically relevant, Eisenstein claimed, regardless of whether they can be found in the locale or not. Even in his first feature, *Strike* (1925), Eisenstein intercut shots of workmen being machine-gunned with images of oxen being slaughtered. The oxen are not literally on location, but are intercut purely for metaphorical purposes. A famous sequence from *Battleship Potemkin* links three shots of stone lions: one asleep, a second aroused and on the verge of rising, and a third on its feet and ready to pounce. Eisenstein considered the sequence an embodiment of a metaphor: "The very stones roar."

Ingenious as these metaphorical comparisons can be, the major problem with this kind of editing is its tendency to be obvious—or impenetrably obscure. Eisenstein saw no difficulty in overcoming the space and time differences between film and literature. But the two mediums use metaphors in different ways. We have no difficulty in understanding what's meant by the comparison "he's timid as a sheep," or even the more abstract metaphor, "whorish time undoes us all." Both statements exist outside of time and place. The simile isn't set in a pasture, nor is the metaphor set in a brothel. Such comparisons are not meant to be understood literally, of course. In movies, figurative devices of this kind are more difficult. Editing can produce a number of figurative comparisons, but they don't work in quite the same way that they do in literature. Eisenstein's theories of collision montage have been explored primarily in the avant-garde cinema and in TV commercials. Most fiction filmmakers have found them too intrusive and heavy-handed.

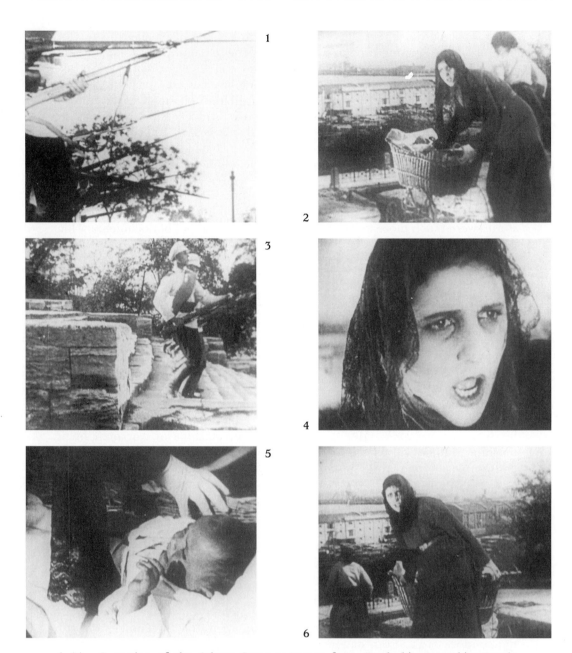

6-16.   A portion of the Odessa Steps sequence from *Battleship Potemkin* **(Russia, 1925),** *directed by Sergei Eisenstein.*

This sequence, based on an actual massacre during the failed revolution of 1905, is the one most often used to demonstrate the possibilities of montage editing. Its full impact can be experienced only by viewing the sequence in its entirety with a musical accompaniment, either the original music composed by Edmund Meisel or music taken from Dmitri Shostakovich's *Symphony No. 11*, inspired by the same events. This brief extract gives some idea of the graphic conflicts between and within shots.   *(Audio-Brandon Films)*

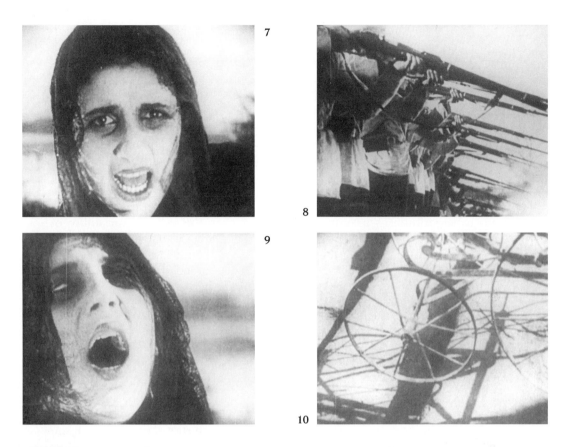

ANDRÉ BAZIN AND THE TRADITION OF REALISM

André Bazin was not a filmmaker, but he was influential as both a critic and theorist. For a number of years, he was the editor of the influential French journal *Cahiers du cinéma*, in which he set forth an aesthetic of film that was in sharp opposition to such formalists as Pudovkin and Eisenstein. Bazin was untainted by dogmatism. Although he emphasized the realistic nature of the cinema, he was generous in his praise of movies that exploited editing effectively. Throughout his writings, however, Bazin maintained that montage was merely one of many techniques a director could use in making movies. Furthermore, he believed that in many cases, editing could acually destroy the effectiveness of a scene (**6–17** and **6–19**).

Bazin's realist aesthetic was based on his belief that photography, television, and cinema, unlike the traditional arts, produce images of reality automatically, with a minimum of human interference. This technological objectivity connects the moving image with the observable physical world. A novelist or a painter must represent reality by re-presenting it in another medium— through language and colour pigments. The filmmaker's image, on the other hand, is essentially an objective recording of what actually exists. No other art, Bazin felt, can be as comprehensive in the presentation of the physical world. No other art can be as realistic, in the most elementary sense of that word.

Bazin's aesthetic had a moral as well as technological bias. He was influenced by the philosophical movement called Personalism. This school of thought emphasized the individualistic and pluralistic nature of truth. Just as most Personalists agreed that there are many truths, Bazin felt that in the cinema there are many ways of portraying the real. The essence of reality, he believed, lies in its ambiguity. To capture this ambiguity, the filmmaker must be modest and self-effacing, a patient observer willing to follow where reality leads. The film artists that Bazin admired most—Flaherty, Renoir, and De Sica, for example—are those whose movies reflect a sense of wonder before the ambiguous mysteries of reality.

Bazin believed that the distortions involved in using formalist techniques—especially thematic editing—often violate the complexities of reality. Montage superimposes a simplistic ideology over the infinite variability of actual life. Formalists tend to be too egocentric and manipulative, he felt. They are concerned with imposing their narrow view of reality, rather than allowing reality to exist in its awesome complexity. He was one of the first to point out that such great filmmakers as Charles Chaplin, Kenji Mizoguchi, and Friedrich Wilhelm Murnau preserved the ambiguities of reality by minimizing editing.

Bazin even viewed classical cutting as potentially corrupting. Classical cutting breaks down a unified scene into a certain number of closer shots that correspond implicitly to a mental process. But the technique encourages us to follow the shot sequence without our being conscious of its arbitrariness. "The editor who cuts for us makes in our stead the choice which we would make in real life," Bazin pointed out. "Without thinking, we accept his analysis because it conforms to the laws of attention, but we are deprived of a privilege." He believed that classical cutting subjectivizes an event because each shot represents what the filmmaker thinks is important, not necessarily what we would think.

One of Bazin's favourite directors, the American William Wyler, reduced editing to a minimum in many of his films, substituting the use of **deep-focus** photography and lengthy takes. "His perfect clarity contributes enormously to the spectator's reassurance and leaves to him the means to observe, to choose, and form an opinion," Bazin said of Wyler's austere cutting style. In such movies as *The Little Foxes, The Best Years of Our Lives,* and *The Heiress,* Wyler achieved an unparalleled neutrality and transparency. It would be naive to confuse this neutrality with an absence of art, Bazin insisted, for all of Wyler's effort tends to hide itself.

Unlike some of his followers, Bazin did not advocate a simple-minded theory of realism. He was perfectly aware, for example, that cinema—like all art—involves a certain amount of selectivity, organization, and interpretation. In short, a certain amount of distortion. He also recognized that the values of the filmmaker will inevitably influence the manner in which reality is perceived. These distortions are not only inevitable, but in most cases desirable. For Bazin, the best films were those in which the artist's personal vision is held in delicate balance with the objective nature of the medium. Certain aspects of reality must be sacrificed for the sake of artistic coherence, then, but Bazin felt that abstraction and artifice ought to be kept to a minimum. The materials should be allowed to speak for themselves. Bazinian realism is not mere newsreel objectiv-

6-17. *Goin' Down the Road* (Canada, 1970), *with Doug McGrath (left) and Paul Bradley, directed by Don Shebib.*
After Joey (Bradley) and Pete (McGrath) arrive in Toronto from Nova Scotia, their efforts to find well-paying jobs are thwarted by their lack of skills. Shebib films many of the sequences in long takes, giving the film a sense of authenticity, as if it were a direct cinema documentary (see Chapter 9). As Bazin would have appreciated, the pressures on their relationship are vividly conveyed by keeping the two men and their surroundings in the same frame.   *(Evdon Films)*

ity—even if there were such a thing. He believed that reality must be heightened somewhat in the cinema, that the director must reveal the poetic implications of ordinary people, events, and places. By poeticizing the commonplace, the cinema is neither a totally objective recording of the physical world nor a symbolic abstraction of it. Rather, the cinema occupies a unique middle position between the sprawl of raw life and the artificially re-created worlds of the traditional arts.

Bazin wrote many articles overtly or implicitly criticizing the art of editing, or at least pointing out its limitations. If the essence of a scene is based on the idea of division, separation, or isolation, montage can be an effective technique in conveying these ideas. But if the essence of a scene demands the simultaneous presence of two or more related elements, the filmmaker ought to preserve the continuity of real time and space **(6–17)**. He or she can do this by including all the dramatic variables within the same **frame**—that is, by exploiting the resources of the long shot, the lengthy take, deep focus, and **widescreen**. The filmmaker can also preserve actual time and space by **panning**, **craning**, **tilting**, or **tracking** rather than cutting to individual shots.

6–18a. *Le Chagrin et la pitié ("The Sorrow and the Pity,"* **France/Switzerland/W. Germany, 1970),** *directed by Marcel Ophüls.*

Even in the world of documentary films, editing styles can range from ultra-realistic to ultra-formalistic. Like most cinéma-vérité documentarists, Marcel Ophüls keeps editing to an absolute minimum. Implicit in the art of editing is artifice—that is, the manipulation of formal elements to produce a seductive aesthetic effect. Many documentarists believe that an edited analysis of a scene shapes and aestheticizes it—compromising its authenticity. A selected sequence of shots, however factually based, extrapolates one person's truth from an event and, in so doing, infuses it with an ideology. An unedited presentation, on the other hand, preserves a multiplicity of truths.   *(Cinema 5)*

6–18b. *Baraka* **(U.S.A., 1992),** *directed by Ron Fricke.*

The editing style of *Baraka* is subjective and self-consciously personal. The film was shot in twenty-four countries over a period of five years. Circling round the globe three times with his 70 mm cameras, director Fricke and his collaborators created a torrent of exotic images, ranging from spiritual rituals to images of war, aggression, and competition. He also contrasts ethereal landscapes like this with devastated wastelands polluted by humans. The movie provides a kaleidoscopic explosion of artfully juxtaposed images—more like a stream-of-consciousness poem than a conventional documentary.

(Magidson Films)

Most documentaries fall between these two extremes, as filmmaker Albert Maysles has pointed out. "We can see two kinds of truth here. One is the raw material, which is the footage, the kind of truth that you get in literature in the diary form—it's immediate, no one has tampered with it. Then there's the other kind of truth that comes in extracting and juxtaposing the raw material into a more meaningful and coherent storytelling form which finally can be said to be more than just raw data. In a way, the interests of the people in shooting and the people in editing (even if it's the same individual) are in conflict with one another, because the raw material doesn't want to be shaped. It wants to maintain its truthfulness. One discipline says that if you begin to put it into another form, you're going to lose some of the veracity. The other discipline says if you don't let me put this into a form, no one is going to see it and the elements of truth in the raw material will never reach the audience with any impact, with any artistry, or whatever. So there are these things which are in conflict with one another and the thing is to put it all together, deriving the best from both. It comes almost to an argument of content and form, and you can't do one without the other."

6–19. *Safety Last* (U.S.A., 1923), *with Harold Lloyd, directed by Fred Newmeyer and Sam Taylor.*
In direct opposition to Pudovkin, Bazin believed that when the essence of a scene lies in the simultaneous presence of two or more elements, editing is ruled out. Such scenes gain their emotional impact through the unity of space, not through the juxtaposition of separate shots. In this famous sequence, for example, Lloyd's comedy of thrills is made more comic and more thrilling by the scene's realistic presentation: the dangling hero and the street below are kept in the same frame. Actually, the distance between the two is exaggerated by the cunning placement of the camera, and there was always at least a platform about three stories below him—"but who wants to fall three stories?" Lloyd asked.   *(Museum of Modern Art)*

John Huston's *The African Queen* contains a shot illustrating Bazin's principle. In attempting to take their boat downriver to a large lake, the two protagonists (Humphrey Bogart and Katharine Hepburn) get sidetracked on a tributary of the main river. The tributary dwindles down to a stream and finally trickles into a tangle of reeds and mud, where the dilapidated boat gets hopelessly mired. The exhausted travellers resign themselves to a slow death in the suffocating reeds, and eventually fall asleep on the floor of the boat. The camera then moves upward, over the reeds, where—just a few hundred metres away—the lake is. The bitter irony of the scene is conveyed by the continuous movement of the camera, which preserves the physical proximity of the boat, the intervening reeds, and the lake. If Huston had cut to three separate shots, we wouldn't understand these spatial interrelationships, and therefore the irony would be sacrificed.

Bazin pointed out that in the evolution of movies, virtually every technical innovation pushed the medium closer to a realistic ideal: in the late 1920s, sound; in the 1930s and 1940s, colour and deep-focus photography; in the 1950s, widescreen. In short, it is usually technology rather than critics and theorists that alters technique. For example, when *The Jazz Singer* ushered in the talkie revolution in 1927, sound eclipsed virtually every advance made in the art of editing since Griffith's day. With the coming of sound, films *had* to be more realistically edited, whether their directors wished them so or not. Microphones were placed on the set itself, and sound had to be recorded while the scene was being photographed. Usually the microphones were hidden—in a vase of flowers, a wall sconce, etc. Thus, in the earliest sound movies, not only was the camera restricted, but the actors were as well. If they strayed too far from the microphone, the dialogue couldn't be recorded properly.

The effects on editing of these early talkies were disastrous. **Synchronized sound** anchored the images, so whole scenes were played with no cuts—a return to the "primitive" sequence shot. Most of the dramatic values were aural. Even commonplace sequences held a fascination for audiences. If someone entered a room, the camera recorded the fact, whether it was dramatically important or not, and millions of spectators thrilled to the sound of the door opening and slamming shut. Critics and filmmakers despaired: The days of the recorded stage play had apparently returned. Later these problems were solved by the invention of the **blimp**, a soundproof camera housing that permits the camera to move with relative ease, and by the practice of **dubbing** sound after the shooting is completed (see Chapter 7).

But sound also provided some distinct advantages. In fact, Bazin believed that it represented a giant leap in the evolution toward a totally realistic medium. Spoken dialogue and sound effects heightened the sense of reality. Acting styles became more sophisticated as a result of sound. No longer did performers have to exaggerate visually to compensate for the absence of voices. Talkies also permitted filmmakers to tell their stories more economically, without the intrusive titles that interspersed the visuals of silent movies. Tedious expository scenes could also be dispensed with. A few lines of dialogue easily conveyed what an audience needed to know about the premise of the story.

The use of deep-focus photography also exerted a modifying influence on editing practices. Prior to the 1930s, most cameras photographed interiors on one focal plane at a time. These cameras could capture a sharp image of an object from virtually any distance, but unless an enormous number of extra lights were set up, other elements of the picture that weren't at the same distance from the camera remained blurred, out of **focus**. One justification for editing, then, was purely technical: clarity of image.

The aesthetic qualities of deep-focus photography permitted composition in depth: Whole scenes could be shot in one setup, with no sacrifice of detail, for every distance appeared with equal clarity on the screen. Deep focus tends to be most effective when it adheres to the real time–space continuum. For this reason, the technique is sometimes thought to be more theatrical than cinematic, for the effects are achieved primarily through a spatially unified mise en scène rather than a fragmented juxtaposition of shots.

Bazin liked the objectivity and tact of deep focus. Details within a shot can be presented more democratically, as it were, without the special attention that a close-up inevitably confers. Thus, realist critics like Bazin felt that audiences would be more creative—less passive—in understanding the relationships between people and things. Unified space also preserves the ambiguity of life. Audiences aren't led to an inevitable conclusion but are forced to evaluate, sort out, and eliminate "irrelevancies" on their own.

6–20. *Utamaro and His Five Women* **(Japan, 1955),** *directed by Kenji Mizoguchi.* Bazin and his disciples were enthusiastic champions of the films of Mizoguchi. The Japanese master favoured the use of lengthy takes rather than editing. He generally cut within a continuous take only when there was a sharp psychological shift within the scene. Used sparingly in this way, the cut acquires a greater dramatic impact than can be found in most conventionally edited movies. *(New Yorker Films)*

In 1945, immediately following World War II, a movement called **neorealism** sprang up in Italy and gradually influenced directors all over the world. Spearheaded by Roberto Rossellini and Vittorio De Sica, two of Bazin's favourite filmmakers, neorealism de-emphasized editing. The directors favoured deep-focus photography, long shots, lengthy takes, and an austere restraint in the use of close-ups. Rossellini's *Paisan* features a sequence shot that was much admired by realistic critics. An American GI talks to a Sicilian young woman about his family, his life, and his dreams. Neither character understands the other's language, but they try to communicate in spite of this considerable obstacle. By refusing to condense time through the use of separate shots, Rossellini emphasizes the awkward pauses and hesitations between the two characters. Through its preservation of real time, the lengthy take forces us to experience the increasing, then relaxing, tensions that exist between them. An interruption of time through the use of a cut would have dissipated these tensions.

When asked why he de-emphasized editing, Rossellini replied: "Things are there, why manipulate them?" This statement might well serve as Bazin's theoretical credo. He deeply admired Rossellini's openness to multiple interpretations, his refusal to diminish reality by making it serve an a priori thesis. "Neorealism by definition rejects analysis, whether political, moral, psychological, logical, or social, of the characters and their actions," Bazin pointed out. "It looks on reality as a whole, not incomprehensible, certainly, but inescapably one."

6–21. *Clerks* **(U.S.A., 1994),** *with Brian O'Halloran and Jeff Anderson; written, edited, and directed by Kevin Smith.*
Sometimes economics dictates style, as with this witty low-budget feature. Everyone worked for free. Smith shot the movie in the same convenience store he worked at (for $5 an hour) during the day. He also used lengthy takes in a number of scenes. The actors were required to memorize pages of dialogue (often very funny) so that the entire sequence could be shot without a cut. Why? Because Smith didn't need to worry about such costly decisions as where to put the camera with each new cut or how to light each new shot or whether he could afford to rent editing equipment to cut the sequence properly. Lengthy takes require one setup: The lights and camera usually remain stationary for the duration of the scene. The movie's final cost: a piddling $27 575. He charged it. It went on to win awards at the Sundance and Cannes film festivals. *(Miramax Films)*

Sequence shots tend to produce (often unconsciously) a sense of mounting anxiety in the viewer. We expect setups to change during a scene. When they don't, we often grow restless, hardly conscious of what's producing our uneasiness. Jim Jarmusch's bizarre comedy *Stranger Than Paradise* uses sequence shots throughout **(6–22)**. The camera inexorably waits at a predetermined location. The young characters enter the scene and play out their tawdry, comic lives, complete with boring stretches of silence, glazed expressions of torpor, and random tics. Finally, they leave. Or they just sit there. The camera sits with them. **Fade** out. Very weird.

Like many technological innovations, widescreen provoked a wail of protest from many critics and directors. The new screen shape would destroy the close-ups, many feared, especially of the human face. There simply was too much space to fill, even in long shots, others complained. Audiences would never be able to assimilate all the action, for they wouldn't know where to look. It was suitable only for horizontal compositions, some argued, useful for epic films, but too

6-22. *Stranger Than Paradise* (U.S.A., 1984), *directed by Jim Jarmusch.*
Each scene in this movie is a sequence shot—a lengthy take without cuts. Far from being "primitive," the sequence-shot technique produces a sophisticated, wry effect, bizarre and funny. In this scene, the two protagonists (John Lurie and Richard Edson) eat yet another goulash dinner while Lurie berates his stout, outspoken aunt (Cecillia Stark) for still speaking Hungarian after years of living in the United States. The scene's comic rhythms are accented by the staging. The bickering relatives must bend forward to see each other, while the visitor, caught in the crossfire, tries unsuccessfully to stay neutral.   *(Samuel Goldwyn)*

spacious for interior scenes and small subjects. Editing would be further minimized, the formalists complained, for there would be no need to cut to something if everything was already there, arranged in a long horizontal series.

At first, the most effective widescreen films were, in fact, westerns and historical extravaganzas. But before long, directors began to use the new screen with more sensitivity. Like deep-focus photography, scope meant that they had to be more conscious of their mise en scène. More relevant details had to be included within the frame, even at its edges. Films could be more densely saturated and—potentially at least—more effective artistically. Filmmakers discovered that the most expressive parts of a person's face were the eyes and mouth, and consequently close-ups that chopped off the tops and bottoms of actors' faces weren't as disastrous as had been predicted.

Not surprisingly, the realist critics were the first to reconsider the advantages of widescreen. Bazin liked its authenticity and objectivity. Here was yet another step away from the distorting effects of editing, he pointed out. As

6-23.   *The Hidden Fortress* (Japan, 1958), *directed by Akira Kurosawa.*
Most filmmakers bemoaned the advent of widescreen in the 1950s almost as much as they bemoaned sound in the late 1920s. Bazin and other realists embraced the innovation as yet another step away from the distorting effects of montage. Widescreen tends to de-emphasize depth in favour of breadth, but Bazin believed that a horizontal presentation of the visual materials could be more democratic—less distorting even than deep focus, which tends to emphasize visual importance in terms of an object's closeness to the camera's lens.   *(Toho Films)*

with deep focus, widescreen helped to preserve spatial and temporal continuity. Close-ups containing two or more people could now be photographed in one setup without suggesting inequality, as deep focus often did in its variety of depth planes. Nor were the relations between people and things fragmented as they were with edited sequences. Scope was also more realistic because the widescreen enveloped the viewer in a sense of an experience, even with its edges—a cinematic counterpart to the eye's peripheral vision. All the same advantages that had been applied to sound and deep focus were now applied to widescreen: its greater fidelity to real time and space; its detail, complexity, and density; its more objective presentation; its more coherent continuity; its greater ambiguity; and its encouragement of creative audience participation.

Interestingly, several of Bazin's protégés were responsible for a return to more flamboyant editing techniques in the following decades. Throughout the 1950s, Godard, Truffaut, and Chabrol wrote criticism for *Cahiers du cinéma*. By the end of the decade, they turned to making their own movies. The **Nouvelle vague**, or **New Wave** as this movement was called in English, was eclectic in its theory and practice. The members of this group, which was not very tightly knit, were unified by an almost obsessional enthusiasm for film culture, especially

6-24. *The Innocents* **(Britain, 1961),** *with Deborah Kerr, directed by Jack Clayton.*
Throughout most of this psychological thriller (which is based on Henry James's novelette *The Turn of the Screw*), we are not sure if the ghost is "real" or simply the hysterical projection of a repressed governess (Kerr), because we usually see the apparition through her eyes; that is, the camera represents her point of view, which may or may not be reliable. But when an objective camera is used, as in this photo, both the governess and the ghost are included in the same space, with no cutting between separate shots. Hence, we conclude that the spirit figure has an independent existence outside of the governess's imagination.   *(Twentieth Century-Fox)*

American film culture. Unlike that of most previous movements, the range of enthusiasms of these critic/filmmakers was extraordinarily broad: Hitchcock, Renoir, Eisenstein, Hawks, Bergman, Ford, and many more. Although rather dogmatic in their personal tastes, the New Wave critics tended to avoid theoretical dogmatism. They believed that technique was meaningful only in terms of subject matter. In fact, it was the New Wave that popularized the idea that *what* a movie says is inextricably bound up with *how* it's said. Furthermore, editing styles ought to be determined not by fashion, the limitations of technology, or dogmatic pronouncements, but by the essence of the subject matter itself.

FURTHER READING

BARR, CHARLES, "CinemaScope: Before and After," in *Film Theory and Criticism* (3rd ed.), Gerald Mast and Marshall Cohen, eds. (New York: Oxford University Press, 1985). An attack on Eisenstein's editing theories in favour of Bazin, with emphasis on mise en scène and the widescreen.

BAZIN, ANDRÉ, *What Is Cinema?* Hugh Gray, ed. and trans. (Berkeley: University of California Press, vol. I, 1967, vol II, 1971). A collection of essays emphasizing the realistic nature of the film medium.

DMYTRYK, EDWARD, *On Film Editing* (Boston: Focal Press, 1984). A practical handbook by a former editor turned director.

EISENSTEIN, SERGEI, *Film Form* (New York: Harcourt Brace Jovanovich, 1949). One of the classic studies of montage, written in Eisenstein's typically elliptical, difficult style.

GRAHAM, PETER, ed., *The New Wave* (London: Secker & Warburg, 1968). A collection of essays by and about Bazin, Truffaut, Godard, and others.

JACOBS, LEWIS, "Art: Edwin S. Porter and the Editing Principle," "D.W. Griffith: *The Birth of a Nation* and *Intolerance*," in *The Rise of the American Film* (New York: Teachers College Press, 1968). A historical account of the evolution of editing in its early years.

LA VALLEY, ALBERT J., ed., *Focus on Hitchcock* (Englewood Cliffs: N.J.: Prentice-Hall, 1972).

PUDOVKIN, V. I., *Film Technique and Film Acting.* Ivor Montague, ed. and trans. (New York: Grove Press, 1960). See also *Kuleshov on Film*, Ronald Levaco, ed. and trans. (Berkeley: Univeristy of California Press, 1974).

REISZ, KAREL, *The Technique of Film Editing* (New York: Hastings House, 1968). The standard text on the history, practice, and theory of editing.

ROSENBLUM, RALPH, and ROBERT KAREN, *When the Shooting Stops...The Cutting Begins* (New York: Viking, 1970). An insider's account of the art and craft of editing, by the editor of such films as *The Pawnbroker* and *Annie Hall.*

Paramount Pictures

*Cinematic sound is that which does not simply add to,
but multiplies, two or three times,
the effect of the image.*

—AKIRA KUROSAWA

SUMMARY

The talkie revolution. The late 1920s: early problems with sound recording. Microphones versus cameras. Synchronous and nonsynchronous sounds. A new genre: the musical. What talkies did to editing styles and silent film acting. Sound effects: pitch, volume, tempo, and texture. Off-screen sounds. Sound symbolism. The uses of silence. Functions of music: establishing tone, period, ethnicity, and locale. The emotional appeal of music. Music as characterization. Background music. Opera and other musical genres. Spoken language: tone of voice, dialects, vocal emphasis. The ideology of speech. Text versus subtext: What's beneath the language? Monologues, voice-overs, spoken narration: Who's telling this story? Foreign-language movies. What to do about translating: dubbing versus subtitles. Rough language: Is it necessary? Why? When?

There are three classifications of sound in movies: sound effects, music, and spoken language. These can be used independently or in any combination. **Realistic** sounds tend to be **synchronous**; that is, they derive their source from the images and are often recorded simultaneously with them. Many exposition scenes, for example, use synchronized sound (dialogue) with corresponding images **(two shots).** Even **long** and **extreme long shots** are sometimes shot synchronously—to capture the actual noise of traffic in an urban location, for example. **Formalists** tend to use sound **nonsynchronously.** That is, sounds are detached from their sources, often acting in contrast with the image or existing as totally separate sources of meaning.

HISTORICAL BACKGROUND

In 1927, when *The Jazz Singer* ushered in the talkie era **(7–1)**, many critics felt that sound would deal a death blow to the art of movies. But the setbacks were temporary, and today sound is one of the richest sources of meaning in film art. Actually, there never was a silent period, for virtually all movies prior to 1927 were accompanied by some kind of music. In the large city theatres, full orchestras provided atmospheric background to the visuals. In small towns, a piano was often used for the same purpose. In many theatres, the "Mighty Wurlitzer" organ, with its bellowing pipes, was the standard musical accompaniment. Music was played for practical as well as artistic reasons, for these sounds muffled the noises of the patrons who were occasionally rowdy, particularly when entering the theatre.

Most of the early "100-percent talkies" were visually dull. The equipment of the time required the simultaneous recording of sound and image: The camera was restricted to one position, the actors couldn't move far from the microphone, and **editing** was restricted to its most minimal function—primarily scene changes. The major source of meaning was in the sound, especially dialogue. The images tended merely to illustrate the soundtrack. Before

7-1. *The Jazz Singer* (U.S.A., 1927), *with Al Jolson, directed by Alan Crosland.*
There had been a number of experiments in synchronous sound prior to this film, but they failed to create much of a stir with the public. Significantly, Warner Brothers managed to break the sound barrier with a new genre, the musical. Actually, even this movie was mostly silent. Only Jolson's musical numbers and a few snatches of dialogue were in synch sound. See John Springer, *All Talking, All Singing, All Dancing!* (New York: Citadel, 1966). *(Warner Bros.)*

long, adventurous directors began experimenting. The camera was housed in a soundproof **blimp,** thus permitting the camera to move in and out of a scene silently. Soon, several microphones, all on separate channels, were placed on the set. Overhead sound **booms** were devised to follow an actor on a set, so his or her voice was always within range, even when the actor moved around.

Despite these technical advances, formalist directors remained hostile to the use of realistic (synchronous) sound recording. Eisenstein was especially wary of dialogue, and he predicted an onslaught of "highly cultured dramas" that would force the cinema back to its stagy beginnings. Synchronous sound, he believed, would destroy the flexibility of editing and thus kill the very soul of film art. Synchronous sound did, in fact, require a more literal **continuity,** especially in dialogue sequences. Eisenstein's metaphoric cutting, with its leaps in time and space, wouldn't make much sense if realistic sound had to be provided with each image. Indeed, Hitchcock pointed out that the most cinematic sequences are essentially silent. Chase scenes, for example, require only some general sound effects to preserve their continuity.

Most of the talented directors of the early sound era favoured nonsynchronous sound. The Frenchman René Clair believed that sound should be used selectively, not indiscriminately. The ear, he believed, is just as selective as

7–2. *Modern Times* **(U.S.A., 1936),** *with Charles Chaplin, directed by Chaplin.*
Sound shortened the careers of many film artists, especially the great silent clowns, like Keaton, Lloyd, and Harry Langdon, who did not survive long in the new aural medium. Like Laurel and Hardy, Chaplin managed to bridge the transition, but in the process he was forced to give up his tramp character. In *Modern Times,* which was made nine years after the talkie revolution, he put up a gallant but ultimately futile battle against spoken language. It was the last appearance of the tramp. Though the film contains sound effects and a musical score (composed by Chaplin himself), the only spoken dialogue is recited by a Big Brother figure on a television monitor. *(rbc Films)*

the eye, and sound can be edited in the same way images can. Even dialogue sequences needn't be totally synchronous, Clair believed. Conversation can act as a continuity device, freeing the camera to explore contrasting information—a technique especially favoured by ironists like Hitchcock and Ernst Lubitsch.

Clair made several musicals illustrating his theories. In *Le Million,* for example, music and song often replace dialogue. Language is juxtaposed ironically with nonsynchronous images. Many of the scenes were photographed without sound and later **dubbed** when the **montage** sequences were completed. These charming musicals are never immobilized by the stagy confinement that ruined most sound films of this era. The dubbing technique of Clair, though ahead of its time, eventually became a major approach in sound film production.

Several other directors also experimented with sound in these early years. Like Clair, Lubitsch used sound and image nonsynchronously to produce a number of witty and often cynical juxtapositions. The celebrated

7-3. *She Done Him Wrong* (U.S.A., 1933), *with Mae West, directed by Lowell Sherman.* Tone of voice can be far more communicative than words in revealing a person's thoughts. This is why most sophisticated moviegoers prefer written subtitles to dubbing in foreign language movies. Mae West was an expert in conveying sexual innuendos through tone of voice—so much so, in fact, that censors insisted on monitoring her scenes during production for fear that the apparently neutral dialogue in her screenplays would be delivered in a "salacious" manner. America responded enthusiastically to Mae's insolence and snappy wisecracks. In this film she's at her outspoken best: cool, lecherous, cynical. In her opening scene, she saucily proclaims herself to be "one of the finest women who ever walked the streets." *(Paramount Pictures)*

"Beyond the Blue Horizon" sequence from his musical *Monte Carlo* is a good example of his mastery of the new mixed medium. While the spunky heroine (Jeanette MacDonald) sings cheerily of her optimistic expectations, Lubitsch provides us with a display of technical bravura. **Shots** of the speeding train that carries the heroine to her destiny are **intercut** with **close-ups** of the whirring locomotive wheels in rhythmical syncopation with the huffing and the chugging and the tooting of the train. Unable to resist a malicious fillip, Lubitsch even has a chorus of suitably obsequious peasants chime in with the heroine in a triumphant reprise as the train plunges past their fields in the countryside. The sequence is both exhilarating and outrageously funny. Critic Gerald Mast observed, "This visual-aural symphony of music, natural sound, composition, and cutting is as complex and perfect an example of montage-in-sound as Eisenstein's editing devices in *Potemkin* were of montage in silents."

The increased realism brought on by sound inevitably forced acting styles to become more natural, for performers no longer needed to compensate visually for the lack of dialogue. Like stage actors, film players realized that the subtlest nuances of meaning could be conveyed through the voice. The movable camera is a further advantage for screen actors. If they are required to mutter under their breath, for example, they can do so naturally, photographed in close-up. They need not, like the stage actor, mutter in stage whisper—a necessary convention in live theatre.

In silent cinema, directors had to use titles to communicate nonvisual information: dialogue, exposition, abstract ideas, and so on. In some films, these interruptions nearly ruined the delicate rhythm of the visuals. Dreyer's *Passion of Joan of Arc,* for example, has frequent interjections of explanatory titles and dialogue. Other directors avoided titles by dramatizing visually as much as possible. This practice led to many visual clichés. Early in the story, for example, the villain might be identified by showing him kicking a dog; or a heroine could be recognized by the halo-effect lighting around her head, and so forth.

7-4.   *Wings of Desire* (Germany, 1988), *with Bruno Ganz, directed by Wim Wenders.*
Silence can be more powerful than sound in certain cases. In this poetic fantasy about an angel (Ganz) who yearns to become mortal, the protagonist often sits on a statue high above the city of Berlin. The discordant clash of modern life is softened and silenced by the soothing distance.   *(Orion Classics)*

Coming from the world of radio, Orson Welles was an important innovator in the field of sound. In *The Magnificent Ambersons,* he perfected the technique of sound montage, in which the dialogue of one character overlaps with that of another, or several others. The effect is almost musical, for the language is exploited not necessarily for the literal information it may convey, but as pure sound orchestrated in terms of emotional tonalities. One of the most brilliant episodes using this technique is the leave-taking scene at the final Amberson ball. The scene is shot in **deep focus,** with **expressionistic** lighting contrasts

7-5. *The Merry Widow* (U.S.A., 1925), *with Mae Murray and John Gilbert, directed by Erich von Stroheim.*
Talkies wiped out the careers of many silent film stars, including that of John Gilbert, the most popular leading man of the late silent era. Gilbert's voice was said to be too high pitched, though in fact it wasn't. The problem was far more complex. Silent film acting was stylized and visually heightened to compensate for the lack of sound. Even by silent standards, Gilbert was known for his emotional intensity—his gestures romantically exaggerated, his ardour raised to a fever pitch. The increased realism brought on by the advent of talkies made such acting techniques seem comically overwrought.   *(MGM)*

7–6. *A Fish Called Wanda* (Britain/ U.S.A., **1988),** *with John Cleese, directed by Charles Crichton.*

As a graduate of the legendary Monty Python's Flying Circus troupe, John Cleese is, of course, perfectly comfortable with truly tasteless slapstick comedy. But like many British comedians, he is also highly literate, and his dialogue for this movie is fiendishly witty. And of course truly tasteless, too. *(MGM)*

throwing most of the characters into silhouette. The dialogue of one group of characters gently overlaps with that of another, which in turn overlaps with a third group. The effect is hauntingly poetic, despite the relative simplicity of the words themselves. Each person or couple is characterized by a particular sound texture: The young people speak rapidly in a normal to loud volume, a middle-aged couple whispers intimately and slowly. The shouts of various other family members punctuate these dialogue sequences in sudden outbursts. The entire scene seems choreographed, both visually and aurally: Silhouetted figures stream in and out of the **frame** like graceful phantoms, their words floating and undulating in the shadows. The quarrels among the Amberson family are often recorded in a similar manner. Welles's actors don't wait patiently for cues: Accusations and recriminations are hurled simultaneously, as they are in life. The violent words, often irrational and disconnected, spew out in spontaneous eruptions of anger and frustration. As in many family quarrels, everyone shouts, but people only half listen.

Robert Altman used similar sound montage techniques in *M*A*S*H*, *Nashville,* and other movies. Like Welles, Altman often uses language as pure sound, particularly in *McCabe and Mrs. Miller,* in which as many as twenty different soundtracks were **mixed**. In several scenes, speeches are deliberately thrown away and we're able to catch only a fleeting phrase here and there; however, these phrases are sufficient to give us a sense of what's really going on in a scene. More important, they give us a sense of how language and sounds are actually heard in reality—in ambiguous, elliptical wisps that are often incongruous and funny.

SOUND EFFECTS

Although the function of sound effects is primarily atmospheric, they can also be precise sources of meaning in film. The pitch, volume, and tempo of sound effects can strongly affect our responses to any given noise. High-pitched sounds are generally strident and produce a sense of tension in the listener. Especially if these types of noises are prolonged, the shrillness can be totally unnerving. For this reason, high-pitched sounds (including music) are often used in suspense sequences, particularly just before and during the climax. Low-frequency sounds, on the other hand, are heavy, full, and less tense. Often they are used to emphasize the dignity or solemnity of a scene, like the male humming chorus in *The Seven Samurai*. Low-pitched sounds can also suggest anxiety and mystery: Frequently a suspense sequence begins with such sounds, which gradually increase in frequency as the scene moves toward its climax.

Sound volume works in much the same way. Loud sounds tend to be forceful, intense, and threatening, whereas quiet sounds strike us as delicate, hesitant, and often weak. These same principles apply to tempo. The faster the tempo of sound, the greater the tension produced in the listener. In the chase sequence of Friedkin's *The French Connection,* all of these principles are used masterfully. As the chase reaches its climax, the screeching wheels of the pursuing car and the crashing sound of the runaway train grow louder, faster, and higher pitched.

Off-screen sounds bring off-screen space into play: The sound expands the image beyond the confines of the frame. Sound effects can evoke terror in suspense films and thrillers. We tend to fear what we can't see, so directors will sometimes use off-screen sound effects to strike a note of anxiety. The sound of a creaking door in a darkened room can be more fearful than an image of someone stealing through the door. In Lang's *M,* the child murderer is identified by a tune he whistles off screen. During the early portions of the movie, we never see him; we recognize him only by his sinister tune.

In several scenes of Hitchcock's *Psycho,* Bernard Herrmann's score—consisting entirely of strings—suggests shrill bird noises. This **motif** is used as a form of characterization. A shy and appealing young man (Anthony Perkins) is associated with birds early on in the film. He stuffs birds as a hobby, and his own features are intense and rather hawklike. During a brutal murder sequence, the soundtrack throbs with screeching bird music. The audience assumes the murderer is the boy's mother, but birds have been associated with him, not her. One of Hitchcock's recurrent themes is the transference of guilt. In this film, the transfer is rather complex. The youth has dug up his long-dead mother's body and literally stuffed it. Often he dresses himself up in her clothing. Although we think we see the mother killing two victims, we have in fact seen the schizophrenic youth as his other self—his mother. The bird music offers an early clue to this psychological transference.

Because images tend to dominate sounds while we're actually experiencing a movie, many sound effects work on a subconscious level. In *Psycho,* the heroine (Janet Leigh) drives her car through a rainstorm. On the soundtrack, we hear her windshield wiper blades slashing furiously against the downpour. Later, when she is taking a shower in a motel, these sounds are repeated. The source of the water noise is apparent, but the slashing sounds seem to come from nowhere—until a demented killer crashes into the bathroom brandishing a knife.

Sound effects can also serve symbolic functions, which are usually determined by the dramatic context. In Luis Buñuel's *Belle de Jour,* for example, the sounds of jingling bells are associated with the heroine's sexual fantasies. Other symbolic sound effects are more universally understood. In Bergman's *Wild Strawberries,* the protagonist, an elderly professor, has a nightmare. The **surrealistic** sequence is virtually silent except for the insistent sound of a heartbeat—a *memento mori* for the professor, a reminder that his life will soon end.

7–7.   *The Exorcist* (U.S.A., 1973), *directed by William Friedkin.*
Sound in film is generally geared to space: When a severe discrepancy exists, the effect can be disorienting and even frightening. In this movie, the devil has possessed a young girl (Linda Blair, lying on bed). The sounds emanating from her small body echo loudly, creating a cavernous effect, as if the girl's slight figure had been spiritually expanded thousands of times to accommodate the demons that inhabit it.   *(Warner Bros.)*

In reality, there's a considerable difference between hearing and listening. Our minds automatically filter out irrelevant sounds. While talking in a noisy city location, for example, we listen to the speaker, but we barely hear the sounds of traffic. The microphone is not so selective. Most movie soundtracks are cleaned up of such extraneous noises. A sequence might include selected city noises to suggest the urban locale, but once this context is established, outside sounds are diminished and sometimes even eliminated to permit us to hear the conversation clearly.

Since the 1960s, however, a number of directors have retained these noisy soundtracks in the name of greater realism. Influenced by the documentary school of **cinéma vérité**—which tends to avoid simulated or re-created sounds—directors like Jean-Luc Godard even allowed important dialogue scenes to be partly washed out by on-location sounds. In *Masculin–Féminin,* Godard's use of sound is especially bold. His insistence on natural noises—all of them as they were recorded on the set—dismayed many critics, who complained of the "cacophonous din." The movie deals with violence and the lack of privacy, peace, and quiet. Simply by exploiting his soundtrack, Godard avoided the need to comment overtly on these themes—they are naggingly persistent in virtually every scene.

7–8. *Never Cry Wolf* (U.S.A., 1983), *with Charles Martin Smith, directed by Carroll Ballard.* The hero of this movie, based on the actual Canadian author Farley Mowat (Smith), spends much of his time alone in the Arctic to study the behaviour of wolves. Whether we hear the melancholy whine of the wind, the crunch of snow underfoot, or the plaintive howl of distant wolves, the sound effects are masterfully mixed, often producing a haunting, poetic effect. *(©MCMLXXXIII Walt Disney Productions)*

7–9. *Saturday Night Fever* **(U.S.A., 1977),** *with Karen Lynn Gorney and John Travolta, directed by John Badham.*

A film's rhythm is often created through its musical score. In this famous dance musical, director Badham used the pulsating Bee Gees disco tune "Staying Alive" as a basis for both the staging and the editing rhythms. "Every time we shot a shot," Badham explained, "that music would be playing, so that all the movie that is on screen is in exact tempo to that [song]." The film triggered off a disco dance craze that swept the Western world in the late 1970s. *(Paramount Pictures)*

The final scene of a movie is often the most important. Because of its privileged position, it can represent the filmmaker's summing up of the significance of the previous scenes. In Ermanno Olmi's *Il Posto* ("The Job," also known as *The Sound of Trumpets*), the director undercuts the ostensible "happy ending" with an ironic sound effect. The movie deals with a shy working-class youth who struggles diligently to land a lower-level clerking job with a huge, impersonal corporation in Milan. Finally, he is hired. The boy is especially pleased that he has a secure job "for life." Olmi is more ambivalent. The final scene of the film presents a picture of stupefying tedium and entrapment: A close-up of the youth's sensitive face is juxtaposed with the monotonous sound of a mimeograph machine, clacking louder and louder and louder.

Sound effects can also express internal emotions. In Robert Redford's *Ordinary People,* for example, an uptight mother (Mary Tyler Moore) has prepared French toast for her emotionally unstable son. Though it is his favourite breakfast food, the young man is too tense to eat: His ambivalent attitude toward his mother is one of his main problems. Irritated by his "selfish" indif-

7-10. *Apocalypse Now* **(U.S.A., 1979),** *directed by Francis Ford Coppola.*
The sound mixing in Coppola's surrealistic Vietnam epic is masterful, suffused with grotesque ironies. In this sequence, American helicopters hover and swirl like huge mechanized gods, dropping napalm bombs on a jungle village to the accompaniment of Wagner's inexorable "Ride of the Valkyries," which thunders on the sound track. As terrified peasants scurry for shelter, American soldiers prepare to go surfing in the poisonous fumes of battle. *(United Artists)*

ference to her gesture of maternal concern, she swoops up his plate and carries it to the sink, where she stuffs the French toast into the garbage disposal, its grinding roar a symbolic embodiment of her anger and agitation.

Like absolute stasis, absolute silence in a sound film tends to call attention to itself. Any significant stretch of silence creates an eerie vacuum—a sense of something impending, about to burst. Arthur Penn exploited this phenomenon in the conclusion of *Bonnie and Clyde.* The lovers stop on a country road to help a friend (actually an informer) with his truck, which has presumably broken down. Clumsily, he scrambles under the truck. There is a long moment of silence while the two lovers exchange puzzled, then anxious, glances. Suddenly, the sound track roars with the noise of machine guns as the lovers are brutally cut down by policemen hiding in the bushes.

Like the **freeze frame,** silence in a sound film can be used to symbolize death, because we tend to associate sound with the presence of ongoing life. Kurosawa uses this technique effectively in *Ikiru,* after the elderly protagonist has been informed by a doctor that he is dying of cancer. Stupefied by the spectre of death, the old man stumbles out on the street, the soundtrack totally silent. When he's almost run over by a speeding auto, the soundtrack suddenly roars with the noise of city traffic. The protagonist is yanked back into the world of the living.

235

MUSIC

Music is a highly abstract art, tending toward pure form. It's impossible to speak of the "subject matter" of a musical phrase. When merged with lyrics, music acquires a more concrete content because words, of course, have specific references. Both words and music convey meanings, but each in a different manner. With or without lyrics, music can be more specific when juxtaposed with film images. In fact, many musicians have complained that images tend to rob music of its ambiguity by anchoring musical tones to specific ideas and emotions. For example, few moviegoers can listen to Richard Strauss's *Thus Spake Zarathustra* without being reminded of Kubrick's *2001: A Space Odyssey*. Some music lovers have lamented that Ponchielli's elegant "Dance of the Hours" conjures images of ridiculous dancing hippos, one of Disney's most brilliant sequences in *Fantasia*.

Theories about film music are surprisingly varied. Pudovkin and Eisenstein insisted that music must never serve merely as accompaniment: It ought to retain its own integrity. The film critic Paul Rotha claimed that music must even be allowed to dominate the image on occasion. Some filmmakers insist on purely descriptive music—a practice referred to as **mickeymousing** (so called because of Disney's early experiments with music and **animation**). This type of score uses music as a literal equivalent to the image. If a character stealthily tiptoes from a room, for example, each step has a musical note to emphasize the

7–11.   *Do the Right Thing* (U.S.A., 1989), *with Spike Lee and Danny Aiello, written and directed by Lee.*
Set in a predominantly African-American section of Brooklyn, this movie explores the tensions between the black community and the Italian-American proprietor (Aiello) of a pizza restaurant. The two cultures are characterized by their music as well as their lifestyles. The African-American characters listen to soul, gospel, and rap music, whereas the ballads of Frank Sinatra are more typical of the Italian-American characters. Spike Lee, who hails from a musical family himself, is painstakingly precise about his musical scores. *(Universal Pictures)*

suspense. Other directors believe that film music shouldn't be too good or it will detract from the images. Most imaginative directors reject this notion. For them, the music of even the greatest composers can be used in movies.

The list of composers who have worked directly in film is a long and impressive one, including Darius Milhaud, Arthur Honegger, Paul Hindemith, Dmitri Shostakovich, Arnold Schoenberg, Sergei Prokofiev, William Walton, Benjamin Britten, Aaron Copland, Quincy Jones, Duke Ellington, The Modern Jazz Quartet, Virgil Thomson, Kurt Weill, Bob Dylan, George Gershwin, Ralph Vaughan Williams, Richard Rodgers, Cole Porter, Leonard Bernstein, and the Beatles, to mention only a few of the best known.

A filmmaker doesn't need to have technical expertise to use music effectively. As Aaron Copland pointed out, directors must know what they want from music *dramatically:* It's the composer's business to translate these dramatic needs into musical terms. Directors and composers work in a variety of ways. Most composers begin working after they have seen the **rough cut** of a movie— that is, the major footage before the editor has tightened up the slackness between shots. Some composers don't begin until the film has been totally completed except for the music. Directors of musicals, on the other hand, usually work with the composer before shooting begins.

Beginning with the opening credits, music can serve as a kind of overture to suggest the mood or spirit of the film as a whole. John Addison's opening music in *Tom Jones* is a witty, rapidly executed harpsichord piece. The harpsichord itself is associated with the eighteenth century, the period of the film. The occasionally jazzy phrases in the tune suggest a sly twentieth-century overview—a musical equivalent of the blending of centuries found in the movie itself.

Certain kinds of music can suggest locales, classes, or ethnic groups. For example, John Ford's westerns feature simple folk tunes like "Red River Valley" or religious hymns like "Shall We Gather at the River," which are associated with the American frontier of the late nineteenth century. Richly nostalgic, these songs are often played on frontier instruments—a plaintive harmonica or a concertina. Similarly, many Italian movies feature lyrical, highly emotional melodies, reflecting the operatic heritage of that country. The greatest composer of this kind of film music was Nino Rota, who scored virtually all of Fellini's films, as well as such distinguished works as Zeffirelli's *Romeo and Juliet* and Coppola's *Godfather* movies.

Music can be used as foreshadowing, particularly when the dramatic context doesn't permit a director to prepare an audience for an event. Hitchcock, for example, often accompanied an apparently casual sequence with "anxious" music—a warning to the audience to be prepared. Sometimes these musical warnings are false alarms; other times they explode into frightening crescendos. Similarly, when actors are required to assume restrained or neutral expressions, music can suggest their internal—hidden—emotions. Bernard Herrmann's music functions in both ways in *Psycho.*

Modern atonal and dissonant music generally evokes a sense of anxiety in listeners. Often such music seems to have no melodic line and can even

7-12. Audiovisual score from *Alexander Nevsky* (Russia, 1938), *music by Sergei Prokofiev, directed by Sergei Eisenstein.*
The composer need not always subordinate his or her talents to those of the film director. Here, two great Soviet artists aligned their contributions into a totally fused production in which the music corresponds to the movement of the images set in a row. Prokofiev avoided purely "representational" elements (mickeymousing). Instead, the two concentrated sometimes on the images first, other times on the music. The result was what Eisenstein called "vertical montage," where the notes on the staff, moving from left to right, parallel the movements or major lines of the images which, set side by side, also "move" from left to right. Thus, if the lines in a series of images move from lower left to upper right, the notes of music would move in a similar direction on the musical staff. If the lines of a composition were jagged and uneven, the notes of music would also zigzag in a corresponding manner. See Sergei Eisenstein, "Form and Content: Practice," in *Film Sense* (New York: Harvest Books, 1947).

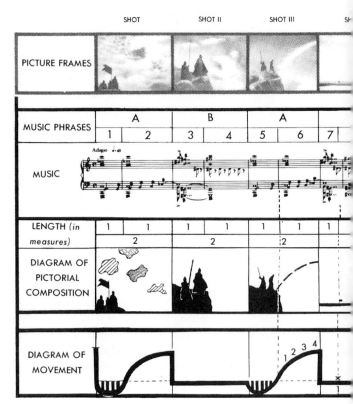

resemble a series of random noises. Giovanni Fusco's music for several of Antonioni's films (*L'Avventura, Red Desert, Eclipse*) produces precisely this sense of neurosis and paranoia. Fusco's music provides a similar function in the movies of Alain Resnais: *Hiroshima mon amour* and *La Guerre est finie.*

Music can also control emotional shifts within a scene. In John Huston's *The Red Badge of Courage,* for example, the protagonist (Audie Murphy), in an irrational outburst of daring, snatches the flag from a dying comrade and charges onto a raging battlefield. To emphasize the youth's surge of patriotism, the scene is accompanied by a spirited rendering of Yankee fighting songs. The charging young soldier stumbles by a wounded Confederate standard-bearer, writhing in pain on the ground, his flag in tatters. The music shifts to an agonizing dirge and gradually transforms into a grotesque distortion of "Dixie." The kinetic excitement of the protagonist's charge might easily have overshadowed the poignancy of the wounded Confederate, but with the aid of the music, the audience as well as the protagonist are suddenly brought to a grim halt.

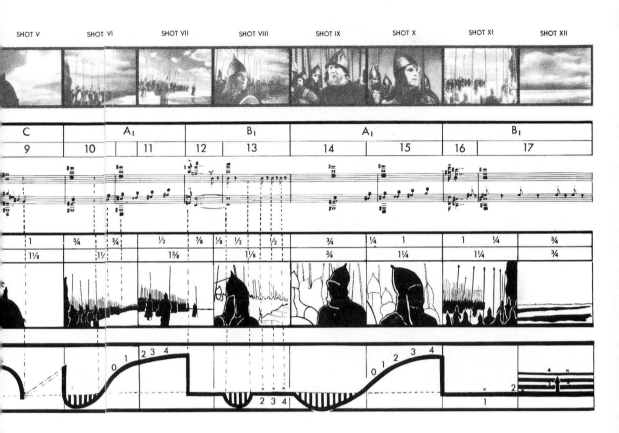

Music can also provide ironic contrast. In many cases, the predominant mood of a scene can be neutralized or even reversed with contrasting music. In *Bonnie and Clyde,* the robbery scenes are often accompanied by spirited banjo music, giving these sequences a jolly sense of fun. In Ermanno Olmi's *The Tree of the Wooden Clogs,* for example, the organ music of Johann Sebastian Bach accompanies many of the scenes, which are virtually documentary re-creations of Italian peasant life around 1900. The music provides these simple episodes with a sense of majesty—celebrating the dignity of labour and the grandeur of the human spirit.

Characterization can be suggested through musical motifs. In Fellini's *La Strada,* the pure, sad simplicity of the heroine (Giulietta Masina) is captured by a melancholy tune she plays on a trumpet. This theme is varied and elaborated on in Nino Rota's delicate score, suggesting that even after her death her spiritual influence is still felt. Bernard Herrmann's score for *Citizen Kane* uses motifs flamboyantly and in a more complex manner (see Chapter 12).

7-13. *Star Wars* (U.S.A., 1977), *with Mark Hamill, Harrison Ford, and Carrie Fisher, directed by George Lucas.*
The enormous popularity of Lucas's original *Star Wars* trilogy revived the tradition of large-scale symphonic accompaniments to heighten the dramatic impact of the scenes. John Williams's score is brassy, powerful, and richly orchestrated, very much in the manner of the lushly romantic and full-bodied scores of Hollywood's golden age. Critic Frank Spotnitz noted that "the score is like a second screenplay, commenting on and enriching the first."   *(Twentieth Century-Fox)*

Characterization can be even more precise when lyrics are added to music. In *The Last Picture Show,* for instance, pop tunes of the 1950s are used in association with specific characters. The bitchy Jacy (Cybill Shepherd) is linked to "Cold, Cold Heart," and her deceived boyfriend Duane (Jeff Bridges) is characterized by "A Fool Such as I." *American Graffiti* uses pop tunes in a similar manner. Two young lovers who have just quarrelled are shown dancing at a sock hop to the tune of "Smoke Gets in Your Eyes." The lyric "yet today my love has flown away" acquires particular poignancy for the girl because the boy has just told her that he intends to date others when he goes off to college. The lovers are reconciled at the end of the movie when he decides not to leave after all. On the soundtrack, "Only You" is appropriately intoned, its syrupy lyrics emphasizing the destiny of love.

7–14. *Mon oncle Antoine* (Canada, 1971), *with Monique Mercure, directed by Claude Jutra.* The arrival of the glamorous wife of a local dignitary in the village store coincides with an explosion at the nearby mine, a comic sound effect that suggests just how conscious she is of her impact on the stunned customers. *(National Film Board of Canada)*

Stanley Kubrick is a bold—and controversial—innovator in the use of film music. In *Dr. Strangelove: or, How I Learned to Stop Worrying and Love the Bomb,* he sardonically juxtaposed Vera Lynn's sentimental World War II tune, "We'll Meet Again," with images of a global nuclear holocaust—a grim reminder that we probably *won't* meet again after World War III. In *2001: A Space Odyssey,* Kubrick juxtaposed images of a twenty-first-century rocket ship gliding through the blueness of space with the sounds of Johann Strauss II's nineteenth-century "Blue Danube Waltz"—an aural foreshadowing of man's obsolete technology in the more advanced technological universe beyond Jupiter. In *A Clockwork Orange,* Kubrick used music as a distancing device, particularly in violent scenes. Musical incongruity undercuts the realism of an otherwise vicious gang fight that takes place to the accompaniment of Rossini's urbane and witty overture to *The Thieving Magpie.* A brutal attack and rape scene is accompanied by a grotesque song-and-dance routine set to the tune of "Singin' in the Rain."

7–15.   *Sleepless in Seattle* (U.S.A., 1993), *with Tom Hanks, written and directed by Nora Ephron.*

Ephron's romantic comedy is a winsome combination of the contemporary with the traditional. This double perspective is best illustrated by the songs on the soundtrack. Many of them are classic tunes of the 1940s, but sung by today's singers—such as "In the Wee Small Hours of the Morning" sung by Carly Simon, or "When I Fall in Love," a sweet duet sung by Celine Dion and Clive Griffin. Other standards: "As Time Goes By" sung by Jimmy Durante, "A Kiss to Build a Dream On" by the incomparable Louis Armstrong, and "Stardust" crooned by the velvet-voiced Nat King Cole. The musical score of the movie became a huge best-selling album (produced by Sony Music).   *(Tri-Star Pictures)*

7–16.   *The Yellow Submarine* (Britain, 1968), *directed by George Dunning.*
Inspired by the Beatles' revolutionary album, *Sergeant Pepper's Lonely Hearts Club Band,* this animated feature captures the youthful spirit of whimsy and charm that typified British pop culture during the 1960s.   *(Apple Films)*

A frequent function of film music is to underline speech, especially dialogue. A common assumption about this kind of music is that it merely acts to prop up bad dialogue or poor acting. The hundreds of mediocre love scenes performed to quivering violins have perhaps prejudiced many viewers against this kind of musical accompaniment. However, some of the most gifted actors have benefited from it. In Olivier's *Hamlet,* the composer William Walton worked out his score with painstaking precision. In the "To be or not to be" soliloquy, the music provides a counterpoint to Olivier's brilliantly modulated delivery, adding yet another dimension to this complex speech.

MUSICALS AND OPERA

One of the most enduring and popular film genres is the musical, whose principal raison d'être is song and dance. Like opera and ballet, the narrative elements of a musical are usually pretexts for the production numbers, but many musicals are exceptionally sophisticated dramatically. Musicals can be divided into the realistic and the formalistic. Realistic musicals are generally backstage stories, in which the production numbers are presented as dramatically plausible. Such musicals usually justify a song or dance with a brief bit of dialogue—"Hey kids, let's rehearse the barn number"—and the barn number is then presented to the audience. A few realistic musicals are virtually dramas with music. In George Cukor's *A Star Is Born,* for example, the narrative events would hold up without the musical numbers, although audiences would thereby be deprived of some of Judy Garland's best scenes—a documentation, as it were, of her character's talent. *New York, New York* (**7–18**) and *Cabaret* are also dramas interspersed with music.

Formalist musicals make no pretense at realism. Characters burst out in song and dance in the middle of a scene without easing into the number with a plausible pretext. This convention must be accepted as an aesthetic premise, otherwise the entire film will strike the viewer as absurd. Everything is heightened and stylized in such works—sets, costumes, acting, etc. Most of Vincente Minnelli's musicals are of this type: *Meet Me in St. Louis, The Band Wagon* (**7–17**), *An American in Paris,* and *Gigi.*

Although musicals have been produced in several countries, the **genre** has been dominated by Americans, perhaps because it's so intimately related to the American **studio** system. In the 1930s, several major studios specialized in a particular type of musical. RKO produced the charming Fred Astaire–Ginger Rogers vehicles such as *Top Hat, Shall We Dance?* and *Carefree,* all directed by Mark Sandrich. Paramount specialized in sophisticated "continental" musicals like Lubitsch's *The Love Parade, One Hour With You,* and *Monte Carlo.* At Warner Brothers, choreographer–director Busby Berkeley delighted audiences with his proletarian show-biz stories like *Gold Diggers of 1933* and *Dames.* Berkeley's stylistic signature is his fondness for abstract geometrical patterns (created with the **optical printer**) and photography of dancers from unconventional **angles** (see **5–2**).

In the 1940s and 1950s, the musical was dominated by MGM, which had the finest musical directors under contract: Kelly, Donen, and Minnelli. Indeed,

7–17. *The Band Wagon* (U.S.A., 1953), *with Fred Astaire, Nanette Fabray, and Jack Buchanan; music by Howard Dietz and Arthur Schwartz; directed by Vincente Minnelli.*

The best movie musicals are generally created directly for the screen and are seldom stage adaptations. This charming "Triplets" number would be difficult to pull off in the live theatre, for the three performers were required to strap false legs and feet onto their knees, their real legs bent behind them as they execute their song and dance. *(MGM)*

7–18. *New York, New York* (U.S.A., 1977), *with Liza Minnelli and Robert De Niro, music by John Kander and Fred Ebb, directed by Martin Scorsese.*

A number of commentators have pointed out that the most enduring genres tend to evolve toward a revisionist phase—mocking many of the genre's original values by subjecting them to skeptical scrutiny. For example, most musicals of the big-studio era were essentially love stories and are concluded with the obligatory boy-wins-girl finale. Such revisionist musicals as *Cabaret* and *New York, New York,* however, end with the lovers going their separate ways, too absorbed by their own careers to submit to love's rituals of self-sacrifice. *(United Artists)*

this prosperous studio had a virtual monopoly on the musical personalities of the day, including Garland, Kelly, Frank Sinatra, Mickey Rooney, Ann Miller, Vera-Ellen, Leslie Caron, Donald O'Connor, Cyd Charisse, Howard Keel, Mario Lanza, Kathryn Grayson, and many others. MGM also lured away Astaire, Pan, and Berkeley, who, along with Michael Kidd, Bob Fosse, Gower Champion, and the ubiquitous Kelly, created most of the choreographies for the studio. Arthur Freed was the **producer** of most of MGM's important musicals, including the majority of Minnelli's films, as well as the stylish works of Donen: *On the Town, Singin' in the Rain* (both codirected by Kelly), and the exquisite *Funny Face.*

The combining of music with drama is a practice extending back at least to ancient Greece, but no other medium excels the expressive range of the cinema. The stage has no equivalent to the musical documentary, like *Woodstock* or *Gimme Shelter.* Movie musicals can take the form of animated fantasies, such as the Disney features *Bambi* and *Dumbo.* Musical biographies like *Amadeus* and *The Buddy Holly Story* are commonplace in film. Examples of great musicals created directly for the screen are *Singin' in the Rain* and *The Band Wagon.* Others are loose adaptations of stage musicals, like *My Fair Lady, Hair,* and *Little Shop of Horrors.*

The cinema is also an ideal operatic medium, as can be seen in Ingmar Bergman's *The Magic Flute* and Joseph Losey's *Don Giovanni* (Mozart's two greatest operas). These movies are more flexible spatially than any stage productions could hope to be, without compromising the music. Only a handful of operatic films approach major stature, perhaps because only a handful of first-rate filmmakers have been attracted to the subgenre. One immense advantage is that movie subtitles are far more convenient than theatrical librettos for explaining the action. With subtitles, the spectator can concentrate on the immediacy of the musical moment rather than having to place it within a larger narrative context. Each opera requires a different approach, some "realistic" **(7–19),** others more stylized **(7–20).** One thing is certain: Pictures of singing heads may be accurate recordings of opera performances, but they aren't real movies.

SPOKEN LANGUAGE

A common misconception, held even by otherwise sophisticated moviegoers, is that language in film cannot be as complex as it is in literature. The fact that Shakespeare has been successfully brought to the screen—with no significant impoverishment in either language or visual beauty—should stand as an obvious contradiction to this notion. Nevertheless, a number of great films are not particularly literary. This is not to say that movies are incapable of literary distinction, but only that some filmmakers wish to emphasize other aspects of their art. Those who dismiss literary movies as uncinematic find themselves in the shaky position of condemning Welles, Bergman, Huston, Richardson, Losey, Wilder, Truffaut, and Woody Allen, to mention only a few directors with literary sensibilities.

In some respects, language in film can be more complex than in literature. In the first place, the words of a movie, like those of live theatre, are spoken,

7-19. *The Magic Flute* **(Sweden, 1974),** *with Josef Kostlinger, music by Wolfgang Amadeus Mozart, directed by Ingmar Bergman.*
In adapting opera to the screen, the filmmaker must adjust the style of presentation to fit the essence of the materials. For example, Mozart's *The Magic Flute* was originally created for a popular, nonsophisticated audience, and its loony storyline is based on fairy tales and the esoteric symbolism of eighteenth-century freemasonry. Bergman decided to stage it "realistically"—that is, as a straightforward presentation in the eighteenth-century manner, complete with all the wires and stage fakery in plain sight, thus creating an air of childlike enchantment. From time to time, Bergman cuts to reaction shots of present-day spectators watching the production from the opera house auditorium.   *(Surrogate Release)*

7-20. *Don Giovanni* **(France, 1979),** *music by Wolfgang Amadeus Mozart, directed by Joseph Losey.*
The story materials of this opera are more coherent, less supernatural, than those of *The Magic Flute,* and Losey accordingly staged the action in real locations in Italy. Instead of concentrating exclusively on images of the singers, Losey often juxtaposes them with their dramatic environments, allowing the sound track to provide the continuity for the fragmentation of the editing.   *(New Yorker Films)*

not written, and the human voice is capable of far more nuances than the cold printed page. The written word is a crude approximation of the connotative richness of spoken language. Thus, to take a simple example of no literary merit, the meaning of the words "I will see him tomorrow" seem obvious enough in written form. But an actor can emphasize one word over the others and thus change the meanings of the sentence completely. Here are a few possibilities:

I will see him tomorrow.	(Implying, not you or anyone else.)
I *will* see him tomorrow.	(Implying, and I don't care if you approve.)
I will *see* him tomorrow.	(Implying, but that's all I'll do.)
I will see *him* tomorrow.	(Implying, but not anyone else.)
I will see him *tomorrow.*	(Implying, not today, or any other time.)

Of course a novelist or poet could emphasize specific words by italicizing them. But unlike actors, writers don't generally underline words in every sentence. On the other hand, actors routinely go through their speeches to see which

---

7–21. *Seven* **(U.S.A., 1995),** *with Morgan Freeman, directed by David Fincher.*
Fincher, a successful director of music videos, uses the possibilities of digital surround sound to enhance the impact of this dark thriller. As the detectives, played by Freeman and Brad Pitt, descend into the nightmare world of a serial killer, the ambient sounds of the many apartment buildings and hotels complement the dark images of the rain-covered city streets. The raw music of groups like Nine Inch Nails and Howard Shore's dissonant score add to the unsettling effect. This almost visceral soundscape contrasts with the highly literate screenplay (written by Andrew Kevin Walker) in which the killer chooses victims who represent the seven deadly sins and leaves clues that allude to the Bible, Dante, Shakespeare, Milton, the Marquis de Sade, and many other classic texts. The older detective (Freeman) is able to follow these clues, but his younger partner is out of his depth and is sucked into the demented logic of the killer. *(New Line Cinema)*

words to stress, which to "throw away," and the ways to best achieve these effects—in each and every sentence. To a gifted actor, the written speech is a mere blueprint, an outline, compared with the complexities of spoken speech. A performer with an excellent voice—a Meryl Streep or a James Earl Jones—could wrench ten or twelve meanings from this simple sentence, let alone a Shakespearean soliloquy.

Written punctuation is likewise a simplified approximation of speech rhythms. The pauses, hesitancies, and rapid slurs of speech can only be partially suggested by punctuation:

> I will . . . see him—tomorrow.
> I will see him—tomorrow!
> I . . . will . . . see him—tomorrow?

7-22.   *Xala* (Senegal, 1975), *directed by Ousmane Sembene.*
Senegal, a former French colony, has a population of only four million, yet it has produced Africa's most important movies, most notably those of Sembene, the continent's best-known filmmaker. *Xala* (which roughly translates as "The Curse of Impotence") is spoken in French and Wolof, the native language of Senegal. The movie is an exposé of the nation's servile ruling class, whose members have eagerly embraced the culture of their white colonial predecessors. (At this lavish wedding reception, for example, several Frenchified Beautiful People wonder what the English translation is for "le weekend.") The cultural commentator Hernandez Arregui has observed, "Culture becomes bilingual not due to the use of two languages but because of the conjuncture of two cultural patterns of thinking. One is national, that of the people, and the other is estranging, that of the classes subordinated to outside forces. The admiration that the upper classes express for the United States or Europe is the highest expression of their subjection."   *(New Yorker Films)*

And so on. But how is one to capture all the meanings that have no punctuation equivalents? Even professional linguists, who have a vast array of diacritical marks to record speech, recognize that these symbols are primitive devices at best, capable of capturing only a fraction of the subtleties of the human voice. An actor like Laurence Olivier built much of his reputation on his genius in capturing little quirks of speech—an irrepressible giggle between words, for example, or a sudden vocal plummeting on one word, a gulp, or a hysterical upsurge in pitch.

The effects of spoken language are often tied to the use of dialects and accents that convey social meanings. Dialects are made up of the distinctive idioms, vocabulary, and pronunciation used by specific groups of speakers. Speech patterns deviating radically from the official dialect are generally regarded as substandard. Because such dialects are spoken by people outside the Establishment, they can be used to subversive effect. For example, the comic art of Richard Pryor is steeped in the jivy idioms of America's black ghettos—best illustrated by his diabolically funny concert films. A number of European filmmakers have also exploited the expressive richness of dialects, most notably Lina Wertmüller (7–24).

A spoken language also involves many variations of accent—the way sounds are pronounced—which is often, but not always, associated with a dialect and which also affects our response to the speakers. In Britain a standard "southern" accent, often called BBC English, was regarded as the correct way of speaking until the 1960s when regional accents gained acceptance, partly because of the success of films set in northern industrial cities and rock groups like the Beatles and Rolling Stones (7–25). Canadian films also incorporate a rich variety of regional and ethnic accents, although characters with such accents rarely occupy positions of power or authority (7–23).

Because language is spoken in movies and plays, these two mediums enjoy an advantage over printed language in that the words of a text can be juxtaposed with the ideas and emotions of a **subtext.** Briefly, a subtext refers to those implicit meanings *behind* the language of a film or play script. For example, the following lines of dialogue might be contained in a script:

> Woman: May I have a cigarette, please?
> Man: Yes, of course. (Lights her cigarette.)
> Woman: Thank you. You're very kind.
> Man: Don't mention it.

As written, these four not very exciting lines seem simple enough and rather neutral emotionally. But, depending on the dramatic context, they can be exploited to suggest other ideas, totally independent of the apparent meaning of the words. If the woman was flirting with the man, for example, she would deliver the lines very differently than an efficient businesswoman. If they detested one another, the lines would take on another significance. If the man were flirting with a hostile female, the lines would be delivered in yet another way, suggesting other meanings. In short, the meaning of the passage is provided by the actors, not the language, which is merely camouflage. (For a more detailed discussion of the concept of a subtext, see Chapter 8.)

7-23. *La Maudite galette* **(Canada, 1972), with Marcel Sabourin, J. Léo Gagnon, and Luce Guilbeault, directed by Denys Arcand.**
The French spoken in Quebec is quite different from the French spoken in France. The difference is at its most extreme in *joual,* a dialect used mainly by the urban working class, with its own vocabulary, idioms, and structures. Although the title of Arcand's comic film noir (virtually impossible to translate into English—"The Damned Dough" has been suggested) uses a colloquial phrase familiar to French audiences, the language spoken by the characters in their heavy Quebec accents would require subtitles if the film were shown in France.   *(Cinak ltée)*

Any script meant to be spoken has a subtext, even one of great literary distinction. A good example from a classic text can be seen in Zeffirelli's *Romeo and Juliet,* in which Mercutio (John McEnery) is played not as the witty *bon vivant* who's intoxicated with his own talk, but as a neurotic young man with a shaky grasp of reality. This interpretation upset some traditionalists, but in the context of the movie, it reinforces the loving bond between Romeo and his best friend and helps justify Romeo's impulsive (and self-destructive) act of revenge later in the film when Mercutio is killed by Tybalt.

Some contemporary filmmakers deliberately neutralize their language, claiming that the subtext is what they're really after. Harold Pinter, the dramatist and screenwriter, is perhaps the most famous example of a contemporary writer who stresses the significance of the subtext. In *The Homecoming,* a scene of extraordinary eroticism is conveyed through dialogue involving the request for a glass of water! Pinter claims that language is often a kind of "cross-talk," a

7-24. *All Screwed Up* (Italy, 1973), *directed by Lina Wertmüller.*
Wertmüller is acutely sensitive to the ideological implications of dialects. Much of her comedy is mined from the earthy idioms of her working-class southerners in contrast with the standard (Tuscan) dialect spoken in the north of Italy. Her characters frequently swear or express themselves in coarse language, which is often very funny. Much of this comedy is lost in translation. The language is sometimes drained of its vitality, reduced to bland respectability. For example, "Piss off!" becomes "Go away," or worse yet, "Please leave me alone." *(New Line Cinema)*

way of concealing fears and anxieties. In some respects, this technique can be even more effective in film, where close-ups can convey the meanings behind words more subtly than an actor on a stage. Pinter's movie scripts are among the most suggestive subtexts of the contemporary cinema: *The Pumpkin Eater, The Servant, Accident, The Go-Between, The Caretaker, The Homecoming, The French Lieutenant's Woman,* and *Betrayal.*

But these are merely some of the advantages of language that film enjoys over literature—advantages shared, in large part, by live theatre. As an art of juxtapositions, movies can also extend the meanings of language by contrasting spoken words with images. The sentence "I will see him tomorrow" acquires still other meanings when the image shows the speaker smiling, for example, or frowning, or looking determined. All sorts of juxtapositions are possible. The

7-25. *The Loneliness of the Long-Distance Runner* (Britain, 1962), *with Tom Courtenay, directed by Tony Richardson.*
Spoken language is steeped in ideology. It's an instant revealer of class, education, and cultural bias. The working-class Nottingham dialect of the protagonist of this film (Courtenay) places him outside the spheres of power and prestige. He's an outsider, a lowly prole, déclassé. *(Audio-Brandon Films)*

sentence could be delivered with a determined emphasis, but an image of a frightened face (or eye, or a twitching mouth) can modify the verbal determination or even cancel it out. The juxtaposed image could be a **reaction shot**—thus emphasizing the effect of the statement on the listener. Or the camera could photograph an important object, implying a connection among the speaker, the words, and the object. If the speaker is photographed in long shot, his or her juxtaposition with the environment could also change the meanings of the words. The same line spoken in close-up would emphasize yet different meanings.

This advantage of simultaneity extends to other sounds. Music and sound effects can modify the meanings of words considerably. The same sentence spoken in an echo chamber will have different connotations from the sentence whispered intimately. If a clap of thunder coincided with the utterance of the sentence, the effect would be different from the chirping of birds or the whining of the wind. Because film is also a mechanical medium, the sentence could be modified by a deliberate distortion in the sound recording. In short, depending on the vocal emphasis, the visual emphasis, and the accompanying soundtrack, this simple sentence could have dozens of different meanings in film, some of them impossible to capture in written form.

Movies contain two types of spoken language: the monologue and dialogue. Monologues are often associated with documentaries, in which an off-screen narrator provides the audience with factual information accompanying

7-26.   *Sunset Boulevard* (U.S.A., 1950), *with Gloria Swanson, directed by Billy Wilder.*
Voice-over monologues are often used to produce ironic contrasts between the past and the present. Almost inevitably, such contrasts suggest a sense of destiny or fate. This film is narrated by a dead man (William Holden). The flashback images show us how he got himself killed: by exploiting the foolishness of a deluded recluse, Norma Desmond (Swanson), who was once a silent film star. Near the end of the movie, she cracks under the strain of his abandonment and shoots him. She now believes that the police and reporters surrounding her are members of a film crew photographing her comeback performance. Holden's final voice-over speech is poetic, uncharacteristically gentle: "So they were turning after all, those cameras. Life, which can be strangely merciful, had taken pity on Norma Desmond. The dream she had clung to so desperately had enfolded her." *(Paramount Pictures)*

the visuals. Most documentary theorists are agreed that the cardinal rule in the use of this technique is to avoid duplicating the information given in the image itself. The commentary should provide what is not apparent on the screen. The audience, in short, is provided with two types of information, one concrete (visuals), the other abstract (narration). Cinéma vérité documentarists have extended this technique to include interviews, a practice pioneered by the

French filmmaker Jean Rouch. Thus, instead of an anonymous narrator, the soundtrack conveys the actual words of the subjects of the documentary—slum dwellers, perhaps, or students. The camera can focus on the speaker or can roam elsewhere, with the soundtrack providing the continuity.

Monologues have also been used in fiction films. This technique is especially useful in condensing events and time. Narrative monologues can be used omnisciently to provide an ironic contrast with the visuals. In Richardson's *Tom Jones,* John Osborne's script features an off-screen narrator who's nearly as witty and urbane as Fielding's, though necessarily less chatty. This narrator sets up the story, provides us with thumbnail sketches of the characters, connects many of the episodes with necessary transitions, and comments philosophically on the escapades of the incorrigible hero.

Off-screen narration tends to give a movie a sense of objectivity and often an air of predestination. Many of the works of Billy Wilder are structured in **flashbacks,** with ironic monologues emphasizing fatality: The main interest is not what happened, but how and why. In *Double Indemnity,* for example, the

7-27.   *The Usual Suspects* (U.S.A., 1995), *with Kevin Pollak, Stephen Baldwin, Benicio Del Toro, Gabriel Byrne, and Kevin Spacey; directed by Bryan Singer.*

Voice-overs are especially effective in presenting us with a contrast between what's said socially and what's thought privately. Almost always, the private voice-over contains the truth, the character's real feelings about a situation. *The Usual Suspects*, a quirky psychological crime thriller, is unusual in that the voice-over narrator is a compulsive liar and manipulator. Almost everything he tells us is a crock. And we fall for his story, at least until the final scene when we discover—surprise—we've been duped.   *(Gramercy Pictures)*

story is narrated by the fatally wounded hero, who admits his guilt at the opening of the film. As Wilder pointed out, "By identifying the criminals right off the bat—and identifying ourselves with them—we can concentrate on what follows: their efforts to escape, the net closing, closing."

The interior monologue is one of the most valuable tools of filmmakers, for with it they can convey what a character is thinking. The interior monologue is frequently used in adaptations of plays and novels. Before Olivier, most film soliloquies were delivered as they are on stage: That is, the camera and microphone record a character literally talking to himself. Olivier's *Hamlet* introduced a more cinematic soliloquy. In the "To be or not to be" speech, several of the lines are not spoken but "thought"—via a **voice-over** soundtrack. Suddenly, at a crucial line, Olivier spews out the words in exasperation. Through the use of the soundtrack, private ruminations and public speech can be combined in interesting ways, with new and often more subtle emphases.

A major difference between stage dialogue and screen dialogue is degree of density. One of the necessary conventions of live theatre is articulation: If something is bothering a character, we can usually assume that he or she will *talk* about the problem. Theatre is a visual as well as an aural medium, but in general the spoken word is dominant: We tend to hear before we see. If information is conveyed visually in the theatre, it must be larger than life, for most of the audience is too far from the stage to perceive visual nuances. The convention of articulation is necessary, therefore, to compensate for this visual

7-28. *Badlands* **(U.S.A., 1973),** *with Sissy Spacek, written and directed by Terrence Malick.*
Not all voice-over narratives are omniscient. This movie is narrated by a bored and dimwitted teenager (Spacek) who talks in *True Romance* clichés and hasn't a glimmer of insight into what wrecked her life.   *(Warner Bros.)*

loss. Like most artistic conventions, stage dialogue is not usually realistic or natural, even in so-called realistic plays. In real life, people don't articulate their ideas and feelings with such precision. In movies, the convention of articulation can be relaxed. Because the close-up can show the most minute detail, verbal comment is often superfluous. This greater spatial flexibility means that film language doesn't have to carry the heavy burden of stage dialogue. In fact, the image conveys most meanings, so dialogue in film can be as spare and realistic as it is in everyday life.

Movie dialogue doesn't have to conform to natural speech. If language is stylized, the director has several options for making it believable. Like Olivier, he or she can emphasize an intimate style of delivery—sometimes even whispering the lines. Welles's Shakespearean films are characterized by a visual flamboyance: The expressionistic stylization of the images in *Othello* complements the artificiality of the language. Generally speaking, if dialogue is nonrealistic, the images must be coexpressive: Sharp contrasts of style between language and visuals can produce jarring and often comic incongruities.

7-29.   *Reservoir Dogs* (U.S.A., 1992), *with Steve Buscemi and Harvey Keitel, written and directed by Quentin Tarantino.*
This stylized gangster film features an almost steady torrent of foul language, as violent as the lives of the characters. In fact, eventually the swearing becomes grotesquely comical, adding to the movie's bizarre tone, which blends violence, cruelty, and pathos with black comedy. In cases like this, sanitized dialogue would be a form of aesthetic dishonesty, totally at odds with the movie's nasty edge of realism.   *(Miramax Films)*

Foreign-language movies are shown either in dubbed versions or in their original language, with written subtitles. Both methods of translation have obvious limitations. Dubbed movies often have a hollow, tinny sound, and in most cases the dubbing is performed by less gifted actors than the originals. Sound and image are difficult to match in dubbed films, especially in the closer ranges where the movements of the actors' lips aren't synchronized with the sounds. Even bilingual actors who do their own dubbing are less nuanced when they're not speaking their native language. For example, Sophia Loren's performance in the English-language version of *Two Women* is very good, but it lacks the vocal expressiveness of her brilliant line-readings in the original Italian. In English, Loren's classy pear-shaped tones are somewhat at odds with her role as an earthy peasant. In a similar vein, actors with highly distinctive voices, like Mae West or John Wayne, sound preposterous when dubbed in German or Japanese. On the other hand, dubbed movies permit the spectator to concentrate on the visuals rather than the subtitles, which are distracting and can absorb much of a viewer's energy. Nobody likes to "read" a movie.

Most experienced filmgoers still prefer subtitles, however, despite their cumbersomeness. In the first place, some spectators are sufficiently conversant in foreign languages to understand most of the dialogue (especially in Europe, where virtually all educated people speak a second language, and in some cases three or four). An actor's tone of voice is often more important than the dialogue per se, and subtitled movies allow us to hear these vocal nuances. In short, subtitles permit us to hear what the original artists said, not what some disinterested technician—however clever—decided we would settle for.

The advantages of sound, then, make it indispensable to the film artist. As René Clair foresaw many years ago, sound permits a director more visual freedom, not less. Because speech can reveal a person's class, region, occupation, prejudices, etc., the director doesn't need to waste time establishing these facts visually. A few lines of dialogue can convey all that's necessary, thus freeing the camera to go on to other matters. There are many instances where sound is the most economical and precise way of conveying information in film.

FURTHER READING

CAMERON, EVAN WILLIAM, et al., eds., *Sound and the Cinema: The Coming of Sound to American Film* (Pleasantville, N.Y.: Redgrave Publishing, 1980). A collection of useful articles.

EVANS, MARK, *Soundtrack: The Music of the Movies* (New York: Hopkinson and Blake, 1975). General history.

EVERSON, WILLIAM, K., *American Silent Film* (New York: Oxford University Press, 1978). Historical study and aesthetic analysis.

GORBMAN, CLAUDIA, *Unheard Melodies: Narrative Film Music* (Bloomington: Indiana University Press, 1987). Theoretical emphasis.

HAGEN, EARL, *Scoring for Films* (New York: Wehman, 1972). Technical emphasis.

McCARTHY, CLIFFORD, *Film Composers in America* (New York: Da Capo, 1972). Survey of major figures.

MORDDEN, ETHAN, *The Hollywood Musical* (New York: St. Martin's Press, 1982). Eccentric, astute, well written.

PRENDERGAST, ROY M., *Film Music* (New York: Norton, 1977). Excellent analysis.

WALKER, ALEXANDER, *The Shattered Silents* (New York: William Morrow, 1979). A well-written history.

WEIS, ELISABETH, and JOHN BELTON, eds., *Film Sound: Theory and Practice* (New York: Columbia University Press, 1985). A collection of scholarly articles.

ACTING | 8

*In the cinema the actor must think
and let his thoughts work upon his face.
The objective nature of the medium will do the rest.
A theatrical performance requires magnification,
a cinema performance requires an inner life.*
—CHARLES DULLIN

SUMMARY

Acting classifications: nonprofessionals, extras, pros, stars. Stage and screen: amplification versus inner truth. Film acting as a directorial language system. Beauty, charm, and sex appeal. The physical requirements of acting: face, voice, body. Expressiveness in film acting. Performances constructed on the editing bench. The star system. The Golden Age of the Hollywood studios. The mythology of the stars. Stars and American popular culture. The down side of stardom. Personality stars versus actor stars. Iconography: the accretion of meaning in a star's persona. Styles of acting: realism and expressionism. National styles. Genre and its requirements. Silent film acting. Star acting: Hollywood romanticism during the big-studio era. British acting traditions. Post–World War II realism. The American Method school of acting. Texts and subtexts. Improvisation. Casting as characterization. Typecasting, casting against type. How casting determines thematic and iconographic meaning.

Film acting is a complex and variable art, which can be broken down into four categories:

1. *Extras.* These actors are used primarily to provide a sense of a crowd—as in "a cast of thousands." Players of this type are used as camera material, like a landscape or a set.

2. *Nonprofessional performers.* These are amateur players who are chosen not because of their acting ability, which can be negligible, but because of their authentic appearance—they *look* right for a given part.

3. *Trained professionals.* These stage and screen performers are capable of playing a variety of roles in a variety of styles. The majority of actors fall into this category.

4. *Stars.* These are famous performers who are widely recognized by the public. Their drawing power is one of the main attractions of a film or stage play. The **star system** was developed and has been dominated by the American cinema, though it's hardly unique to movies. Virtually all the performing arts—opera, dance, live theatre, television, concert music—have exploited the box-office popularity of a charismatic performer.

However a film actor is classified, virtually all performers in this medium concede that their work is shaped by the person who literally and figuratively calls the shots. Even Charlie Chaplin, the most famous movie star of his era, admitted, "Film acting is unquestionably a director's medium." In short, the movie actor is ultimately a tool of the director—another "language system" through which the filmmaker communicates ideas and emotions.

STAGE AND SCREEN ACTING

The differences between stage and screen acting are largely determined by the differences in space and time in each medium. The essential requisites for the stage performer are to be seen and heard clearly. Thus, the ideal theatrical actor must have a flexible, trained voice. Most obviously, his or her voice must be powerful enough to be heard even in a theatre containing thousands of seats. Because language is the major source of meaning in most forms of theatre, the nuances of the dialogue must be conveyed through vocal expressiveness. An actor's voice must be capable of much variety. It's necessary to know which words to stress and how to stress them, how to phrase properly for

8–1. *Narcissus* **(Canada, 1983),** *with Jean-Louis Morin and Sylvie Kinal, directed by Norman McLaren.*

The beauty of the human form provides one of the main pleasures of cinema. Dance also celebrates this beauty: Choreography makes the most of the sensuous appeal of bodies in motion while creating an aesthetic framework that allows us to enjoy this appeal without feeling like voyeurs. McLaren's dance films are among the most sensuous cinematic treatments of physical beauty. In this film, the dancers perform against a black background, and McLaren uses techniques such as slow-motion, dissolves, and optical printing to tell the story of Narcissus (Morin) who rejects both female and male lovers and falls in love with his own reflected image.   *(National Film Board of Canada)*

different types of lines, when to pause and for how long, and how fast or slow a line or speech ought to be delivered. Above all, the stage actor must be *believable*, even when reciting dialogue that's highly stylized and unnatural. Most of the credit for an exciting theatrical production is given to the performers, but much of the burden is also theirs, for when we're bored by a production of a play, we tend to assign the responsibility to the actors.

Physical requirements are less exacting in the theatre than in movies. Most obviously, the stage actor must be seen—even from the back of the auditorium. Thus, it helps to be tall, for small actors tend to get lost on a large stage. It also helps to have large and regular features, although makeup can cover a multitude of deficiencies. For this reason, casting a forty-year-old actor as Romeo is not necessarily a disaster in the theatre, for if the actor is in reasonably good physical shape, his age won't show beyond the first rows of seats. Because of the

---

8-2. *In the Name of the Father* (Ireland/Britain, 1993), *with Daniel Day-Lewis and Emma Thompson, directed by Jim Sheridan.*

Day-Lewis and Thompson are among the top British actors of their generation. Like most British actors, they're extraordinarily versatile. Day-Lewis's range is awesome, from the Cockney tough in *My Beautiful Laundrette* to the fruity upper-class twit in *A Room With a View* to the New Age macho man in *The Last of the Mohicans.* Thompson is equally adaptable, playing double roles in *Dead Again,* the sexy and irrepressible Beatrice in *Much Ado About Nothing,* and the drab housekeeper in *The Remains of the Day.* In *In the Name of the Father,* which is based on an actual event, Day-Lewis plays an Irish hippie who is falsely imprisoned for a horrifying crime, and Thompson plays his attorney.   *(Universal Pictures)*

low visual saturation in the theatre, actors can play roles twenty years beyond their actual age, provided their voices and bodies are flexible enough.

The stage actor's entire body is always in view, and for this reason he or she must be able to control it with some degree of precision. Such obvious activities as sitting, walking, and standing are performed differently on the stage than they are in real life. An actor must usually learn how to dance, how to fence, and how to move naturally in period costumes. An actor must know what to do with his or her hands—when to let them hang and when to use them for expressive gestures. Furthermore, stage actors must know how to adjust their bodies to different characters: A seventeen-year-old girl moves differently from a woman of thirty; an aristocrat moves differently from a clerk of the same age. The body must communicate a wide variety of emotions in pantomime: A happy person even stands differently from one who is dejected, or fearful, or bored.

8-3. *Taxi Driver* **(U.S.A., 1976),** *with Robert De Niro, directed by Martin Scorsese.*
Acting is a demanding art, requiring dedication, discipline, and Spartan endurance. De Niro is famous for his rigorous preparations prior to production, researching his roles exhaustively. Widely regarded as the greatest American actor of his generation, he prefers to bury himself in a role. He rarely exploits his personal charisma and is noticeably uncomfortable during interviews, which he rarely grants. De Niro has always insisted that life should take precedence over art. But his is an art that conceals art. Many of his finest performances have been under the direction of his old friend, Martin Scorsese.   *(Columbia Pictures)*

Theatrical acting preserves real time. What's essential for the stage actor is to sustain an energy level for the duration of a scene. Once the curtain rises, actors are alone on the stage. Mistakes aren't easily corrected, nor can a scene be replayed or cut out. The essential requisite for a performer in the movies is what Antonioni calls "expressiveness." That is, he or she must *look* interesting. No amount of technique will compensate for an unphotogenic face (**8–4**).

Acting in the cinema is almost totally dependent on the filmmaker's approach to the story materials. In general, the more **realistic** the director's techniques, the more necessary it is to rely on the abilities of the players. Such directors tend to favour **long shots,** which keep the performer's entire body within the **frame.** This is the camera distance that corresponds to the proscenium arch of live theatre. The realist also tends to favour **lengthy takes**—thus permitting the actors to sustain performances for relatively long periods without interruption. From the audience's point of view, it's easier to evaluate acting in a realistic movie because we are permitted to see sustained scenes without any apparent directorial interference. The camera remains essentially a recording device.

The more **formalistic** the director, the less likely he or she is to value the actor's contribution. Some of Hitchcock's most stunning cinematic effects were achieved by minimizing the contributions of actors. During the production of *Sabotage,* Hitchcock's leading lady, Sylvia Sidney, burst into tears on the set because she wasn't permitted to act a crucial scene. The episode involved a murder in which the sympathetic heroine kills her brutish husband in revenge for his murder of her young brother. On stage, of course, the heroine's feelings

8-4. *The Whisperers* (Britain, **1966),** *with Edith Evans, directed by Bryan Forbes.*

The cinematic close-up allows the film actor to concentrate totally on the truth of the moment—without the need to worry about projecting to the back row. Gestures and facial expressions can be exquisitely nuanced. Stage actors generally must convey such nuances through words. The Hungarian theorist Béla Balázs believed that the movie close-up can isolate the human face from its surroundings and penetrate the soul: "What appears on the face and in facial expression is a spiritual experience," Balázs observed.   *(United Artists)*

and thoughts would be communicated by the actress's exaggerated facial expressions. But in real life, Hitchcock observed, people's faces don't necessarily reveal what they think or feel. The director preferred to convey these ideas and emotions through **edited** juxtapositions **(8–5).**

The setting for the scene is a dinner table. The heroine looks at her husband, who is eating as usual. Then a **close-up** shows a dish containing meat and vegetables with a knife and fork lying next to it; the wife's hands are seen behind the dish. Hitchcock then cuts to a **medium shot** of the wife thoughtfully slicing some meat. Next, a medium shot of the brother's empty chair. Close-up of the wife's hands with knife and fork. Close-up of a bird cage with canaries—a reminder to the heroine of her dead brother. Close-up of wife's thoughtful face. Close-up of the knife and plate. Suddenly a close-up of the husband's suspicious face: He notices the connection between the knife and her thoughtful expression, for the camera **pans,** rather than cuts, back to the knife. He gets up next to her. Hitchcock quickly cuts to a close-up of her hand reaching for the knife. Cut to an **extreme close-up** of the knife entering his body. Cut to a **two shot** of their faces, his convulsed with pain, hers in fear. When Sylvia Sidney saw the finished product, she was delighted with the results. The entire scene, of course, required very little acting in the conventional sense of the term.

Antonioni has stated that he uses his actors only as part of the composition—"like a tree, a wall, or a cloud." Many of the major themes of his films are conveyed through long shots where the juxtaposition of people and their settings is used to suggest complex psychological and spiritual states. Perhaps more than any other director, Antonioni is sensitive to how meanings change, depending on the **mise en scène.** Similarly, the French director Robert Bresson believed that a screen actor is not an interpretive artist but merely one of the "raw materials" of the mise en scène and the editing. He generally preferred to use nonprofessional actors in his movies because trained actors tend to want to convey emotions and ideas through performance, as in the live theatre. For Bresson, films should be made cinematically rather than theatrically, by "bypassing the will of those who appear in them, using not what they do, but what they *are*."

Generalizing about acting in movies is difficult because directors don't approach every film with the same attitudes. Elia Kazan and Ingmar Bergman, distinguished stage directors as well as filmmakers, varied their techniques considerably, depending on the dramatic needs of the film. Nor is there any "correct" approach to filming a scene. A director like Chaplin might convey a specific idea through acting, whereas Bresson might approach the same idea through editing or mise en scène.

But whether a director is a realist or formalist, the differences between film acting and stage acting remain fundamental. For example, a player in movies is not so restricted by vocal requirements because sound volume is controlled electronically. Marilyn Monroe's small breathy voice wouldn't have projected beyond the first few rows in the theatre, but on film it was perfect for conveying that childlike vulnerability that gave her performances such poetic delicacy. Some film actors are popular precisely because of the offbeat charm of their voices. Because acting in movies is not so dependent on vocal flexibility,

8-5. Sequence from *Sabotage* (Britain, 1936), *with Sylvia Sidney and Oscar Homolka, directed by Alfred Hitchcock.*

Through the art of editing, a director can construct a highly emotional "performance" by juxtaposing shots of actors with shots of objects. In scenes such as these, the actor's contribution tends to be minimal: The effect is achieved through the linking of two or more shots. This associational process is the basis of Pudovkin's theory of constructive editing. *(Gaumont-British)*

d

e

f

j

k

l

p

q

r

v

w

x

8-6. *The Act of the Heart* **(Canada, 1970),** *with Geneviève Bujold, directed by Paul Almond.*
Like many Canadian actors before her, Bujold went to Hollywood and became a star. Before she left, she made three films with Almond, who was then her husband, in which she played young women suffering from religious and sexual fears. The characters, like Bujold, are bilingual, linking their crises to tensions within Quebec culture. In *The Act of the Heart*, Martha (Bujold) falls in love with a priest (played by Donald Sutherland, who also left for Hollywood) and then, suddenly and shockingly, burns herself alive in a final act of the heart, apparently in protest against a world without love.
(Quest Film)

8-7. *The Gold Rush* **(U.S.A., 1925),** *with Charles Chaplin and Mack Swain, directed by Chaplin.*
Actors in every medium (except radio) must be conscious of body language and what it reveals about character. Silent actors were deprived of their voices, so they externalized their feelings and thoughts through gesture, movement, facial expression, and body language—all of which had to be heightened to compensate for their lack of speech. In this shot, for example, Big Jim McKay is puzzled by the scary rumbling and quaking of their cabin. The hung-over Charlie explains—through pantomime—that his queasy stomach is the culprit. *(rbc Films)*

8-8. *Secrets & Lies* **(Britain, 1996),** *with Brenda Blethyn (extreme right), Written and directed by Mike Leigh.*

Mike Leigh prefers to work with many of the same actors from film to film, much like a cinematic repertory company. They rehearse extensively, improvising much of their dialogue and reshaping the script with their insights and discoveries. The result of this artistic collaboration is a performance style of extraordinary intimacy, spontaneity, and humanity. They just don't look or sound like actors—they seem to be real people with real hang-ups. In *Secrets & Lies*, the protagonist (Blethyn) always manages to find the worst possible moment to embarrass or shock her family. Weepy, self-pitying, grotesquely funny, and desperately needy, she manages to repel us even while enlisting our compassion. It is only one of several great performances in the movie. The acting is also a far cry from the pear-shaped tones and precise diction of traditional British acting techniques. With Leigh's actors, you don't notice the technique: just the raw emotions.   *(October Films)*

many performers have succeeded despite their wooden, inexpressive voices: Gary Cooper, John Wayne, Clint Eastwood, Arnold Schwarzenegger.

Even the quality of a movie actor's voice can be controlled mechanically. Music and sound effects can totally change the meaning of a line of dialogue. Through electronic devices, a voice can be made to sound garbled, or booming, or hollow. Indeed, Antonioni claims that language in film is primarily pure sound and only secondarily meaningful as dialogue. Much of the dialogue in a movie is **dubbed,** so a director can re-record a line until it's perfect. Sometimes the director will select one or two words from one recorded take and blend them with the words of another, or even a third or fourth. This kind of synthesizing can be carried even further—by combining one actor's face with another actor's voice **(8–9).**

8-9. *La Strada* (Italy, 1954), *with Richard Basehart and Giulietta Masina, directed by Federico Fellini.*
Virtually all Italian movies are dubbed after the footage has been photographed and sometimes even after it's been edited. Fellini selects his players according to their face, body type, or personality. Like many Italian filmmakers, he often uses foreign actors, even in major roles. The American Richard Basehart spoke his lines in English during this film's production. Once shooting was completed, Fellini hired an Italian actor with the same vocal quality to dub in the character's voice. *(Audio-Brandon Films)*

Similarly, the physical requirements for a film actor are different from those of a stage performer. The movie player doesn't have to be tall, even if he's a leading man type. Alan Ladd, for example, was quite short. His directors simply avoided showing his body in full unless there was no one else in frame to contrast with his height. He played love scenes standing on a box, his body cut off at the waist. **Low-angle shots** also tended to make him seem taller. A film actor's features don't have to be large, only expressive—particularly the eyes and mouth. Nor does a film actor have to be attractive. For example, Humphrey Bogart was not a good-looking man, but the camera "liked" him. That is, his face was uncannily photogenic, opening up to the camera in a way that often surprised his **cinematographers**. Sometimes this contrast between reality and its illusion can be intimidating. Complained Jean Arthur, "It's a strenuous job every day of your life to live up to the way you look on the screen."

An actor who moves clumsily is not necessarily at a disadvantage in film. The director can work around the problem by not using many long shots and by photographing the actor *after* he or she has moved. Complicated movements can be faked by using stunt artists or doubles. These shots are **intercut** with closer shots of the leading actor, and the edited juxtaposition leads the audience to assume that the main performer is involved in all the shots (see **6–13**). Even in close-up, the film performer's physical appearance can be changed through the use of special **lenses, filters,** and lights.

Because the **shot** is the basic building unit in film, the actor doesn't have to sustain a performance for very long—even in realistic movies in which the **takes** can run to two or three minutes. In a highly fragmented film—in which shots can last for less than a second—one can scarcely refer to the performer's contribution as acting at all: He or she simply *is*.

The shooting schedule of a movie is determined by economic considerations. Thus, the shooting of various sequences isn't always artistically logical. An actor may be required to perform the climactic scene first and **low-keyed** exposition shots later. The screen actor, then, doesn't "build" emotionally as the stage actor must. The film player must be capable of an intense degree of concentration—turning emotions on and off for very short periods of time. Most of the time the player must seem totally natural, as if he or she weren't acting at all. "You do it just like in reality," Henry Fonda explained. Certainly the film player is almost always at the mercy of the director, who later constructs the various shots into a coherent performance. Some directors have tricked actors into a performance, asking for one quality to get another.

8-10. *The Night of the Shooting Stars* (Italy, 1982), *directed by Paolo and Vittorio Taviani.* Realism in movies can be far more "real" than stage realism, for a theatrical actor's skill and discipline are always apparent to the audience. Film realism is often more convincing precisely because of the player's lack of technical skill. The nonprofessional players of this movie are artless and sincere, totally devoid of actorish mannerisms, and hence totally believable as ordinary peasants trying to survive during the harsh times of World War II.   *(United Artists)*

8-11. *Jagged Edge* (U.S.A., 1985), *with Jeff Bridges and Glenn Close, directed by Richard Marquand.*
Glenn Close is one of today's most versatile actresses, equally at home on the stage, TV, and movies. She has performed in musicals, Shakespeare **(5-7),** comedies, dramas, and thrillers (shown here). She can be maternal (*The World According to Garp*), girlish (*The Natural*), bitchy (*Reversal of Fortune*), sexy (*Dangerous Liaisons*), or demented (*Fatal Attraction*) with total believability.   *(Columbia Pictures)*

Because acting in the cinema is confined to short segments of time and space, the film player doesn't need a long rehearsal period to establish a sense of ease with other actors, the set, or costumes. Many directors keep rehearsals to a minimum so as not to dissipate the spontaneity of the players, their sense of discovery and surprise. Unlike the stage player, the film actor doesn't have to create an intimate rapport with other performers: Sometimes they haven't even met until they arrive on the set or on location. Actors occasionally don't know their lines: This is remedied by having a prompter on the set, or by writing the lines on a blackboard off frame where the actor can read them.

A film actor is expected to play even the most intimate scenes with dozens of technicians on the set, working or observing. The actor must seem totally at ease, even though the lights are unbearably hot and his or her running makeup must be corrected between shots. Because the camera distorts, actors are required to perform some scenes unnaturally. In an embrace, for example, lovers can't really look at each other in the eyes or they will appear cross-eyed on the screen. In **point-of-view shots,** actors must direct their lines at the camera rather than at another player. Much of the time the performer has no idea what he or she is doing, or where a shot might appear in the finished film, if indeed it appears at all, for many an actor's performance has been left on the cutting-room floor. In short, the discontinuity of time and space in the cinema places the performer almost totally in the hands of the director.

THE AMERICAN STAR SYSTEM

The star system has been the backbone of the American film industry since the second decade of the twentieth century. Stars are the creation of the public, its reigning favourites. Their influence in the fields of fashion, values, and public behaviour has been enormous. "The social history of a nation can be written in terms of its film stars," British critic Raymond Durgnat has observed. Stars confer instant consequence to any film they appear in. Their fees have staggered the public. In the 1910s, Charles Chaplin and Canadian-born Mary Pickford were the highest paid employees in the world. Contemporary stars such as Whoopie Goldberg and Kevin Costner command salaries of many millions of dollars per film, so popular are these box-office giants. Some stars had careers that spanned five decades: Bette Davis and John Wayne, to name just two. Alexander Walker, among others, has pointed out that stars are the direct or indirect reflection of the needs, drives, and anxieties of American society: They are the food of dreams, allowing us to live out our deepest fantasies and obsessions. Like the ancient gods and goddesses, stars have been adored, envied, and venerated as mythic icons.

Prior to 1910, actors' names were almost never included in movie credits because producers feared the players would then demand higher salaries. But the public named their favourites anyway. Mary Pickford, for example, was first known by her character's name, "Little Mary." From the beginning, the public often fused a star's artistic **persona** with his or her private personality. In Pickford's case, as with many others, the two were radically dissimilar. She specialized in playing waggish juveniles—the bouncy, high-spirited, and sentimental young heroines of such popular hits as *Rebecca of Sunnybrook Farm* (1917) and *Pollyanna* (1920), in which her blonde curls were her trademark. In actuality, Pickford was clever and sophisticated and the most powerful woman in the American film industry of the silent era. "My career was planned," she insisted, "there was never anything accidental about it." By the time she was five, she was performing in live theatre. She began working with Griffith in 1909 and made seventy-five short films with him at Biograph before leaving the **studio** in 1912. Soon she was earning $40 000 per picture. By 1914 she was pulling in $150 000. She was neck-and-neck with Chaplin in the star salaries sweepstakes, and she collected from $300 000 to $500 000 per film between the years 1917 and 1919. In 1919 she helped form United Artists, with Chaplin, Griffith, and Douglas Fairbanks (her husband) as partners. As an independent **producer**, she grossed as much as $1.2 million per film. Reputedly she was the business brains behind United Artists. She also directed many of her own films, although never with official credit.

8–12. *Deux actrices ("Two Can Play,"* **Canada, 1993),** *with Pascale Bussières and Pascale Paroissien, directed by Micheline Lanctôt.*
The Hollywood star system and the publicity surrounding it have always exploited the powerful effects of identification that movies can create. Audiences tend to confuse actors with the roles they play, and stars have often fallen because they cannot live up to the image they have created. Lanctôt had appeared in numerous films before her debut as a director in 1980 with *L'Homme à tout faire* ("The Handyman"). She is also a film teacher, and *Deux actrices* was made with her students. She appears in it as a director working with two actresses who come to identify with the characters that they play in the film within the film.   *(Stopfilm Inc./Antoine Saito, photographer)*

Unless the public is receptive to a given screen personality, audiences can be remarkably resistant to someone else's notion of a star. For example, producer Samuel Goldwyn ballyhooed his Russian import, Anna Sten, without stinting on costs. But audiences stayed away from her movies in droves. "God makes the stars," the chastened Goldwyn finally concluded. "It's up to the producers to find them."

Throughout the silent era, stars grew giddy with their wealth and power. Intoxicated by the opulence of Hollywood's royalty, the public was eager to learn more of its favourites. Fan (short for fanatic) magazines sprang up by the dozens, and the burgeoning studios churned out a steady stream of publicity to feed this insatiable curiosity. Paramount's rival queens, Gloria Swanson and Pola Negri, vied with each other in the extravagance of their lifestyles. Both of them married many times, and each managed to snare at least one petty nobleman among her stable of rapt admirers. "I have gone through a long apprenticeship," Swanson said. "I have gone through enough of being nobody. I have decided that when I am a star I will be every inch and every moment the star. Everyone from the studio gateman to the highest executive will know it." The mythology of stardom often incorporated this rags-to-riches **motif**. The humble origins of many stars encouraged the public to believe that anyone—even ordinary people—could be "discovered" and make it to Hollywood, where all their dreams would come true.

The so-called golden age of the star system—roughly the 1930s and 1940s—coincided with the supremacy of the Hollywood studio system. Most of the stars during this period were under exclusive contract to the five major production companies: MGM, Warner Brothers, Paramount, Twentieth Century–Fox, and RKO—known in the trade as the Big Five, or the **majors.** Throughout this period, the majors produced approximately 90 percent of the fiction films in America. They also ruled the international market: Between the two world wars, American movies dominated 80 percent of the world's screens and were more popular with foreign audiences than all but a few natively produced movies.

After the talkie revolution, the majors turned to live theatre for new stars. Such important newcomers as James Cagney, Bette Davis, Edward G. Robinson, Cary Grant, Mae West, and Katharine Hepburn became popular in part because of their distinctive manner of speaking—the "personality voices," as they were known in the trade. In their first years under studio contract, they were given maximum exposure. For example, Clark Gable appeared in four-

8–13. *Ace Ventura: When Nature Calls* (U.S.A., 1995), *with Jim Carrey, directed by Steve Oedekerk.*

There are few actors as creatively audacious as Jim Carrey. His face is a mercurial rubber mask, shifting and contorting without shame to get a laugh. The body too is spastically disjointed, a frenzied explosion of tics and twitches. It can collapse like a burst paper bag or swell up like a menacing storm cloud. Unlike Robin Williams, to whom he's sometimes compared, Carrey is no improviser. "He stays up all night and goes to the set strung out on creativity," said Brian Grazer, producer of *Liar Liar*, "but he always knows exactly what he's going to do in a scene—it's all plotted out in his mind."   *(Morgan Creek Productions)*

teen movies in 1930, his first year at MGM. Each of his roles represented a different type, and the studio kept varying them until one clicked with the public. After a particularly popular performance, a star was usually locked into the same type of role—often under protest. Because the demand for stars was the most predictable economic variable in the business of filmmaking, the studios used their stars as a guarantee of box-office success. In short, stars provided some measure of stability in a traditionally volatile industry. To this day, stars are referred to as "bankable" commodities—that is, insurance for large profits to investors.

The majors viewed their stars as valuable investments, and the build-up techniques developed by the studios involved much time, money, and energy. Promising neophytes served an apprenticeship as "starlets," a term reserved for females, although male newcomers were subjected to the same treatment. They were often assigned a new name, were taught how to talk, walk, and wear costumes. Frequently their social schedules were arranged by the studio's publicity department to ensure maximum press exposure. Suitable "romances" were concocted to fuel the columns of the four hundred or more reporters and columnists who covered the Hollywood beat during the studio era. A few zealous souls even agreed to marry a studio-selected spouse if such an alliance would further their careers.

Though stars were often exploited by the studios, there were some compensations. As a player's box-office power increased, so did his or her demands. Top stars had their names above the title of the film, and they often had **script** approval stipulated in their contracts. Some of them also insisted on director, producer, and costar approval. Glamorous stars boasted their own camera operators, who knew how to conceal physical defects and enhance virtues. Many of them demanded their own clothes designers, hair stylists, and lavish dressing rooms. The biggest stars had movies especially tailored for them, thus guaranteeing maximum camera exposure.

And of course, they were paid enormous sums of money. In 1939, for example, there were over fifty stars who earned more than $100 000 a year. But the studios got much more. Mae West rescued Paramount from bankruptcy in the early 1930s. Later in the decade, Shirley Temple made over $20 million for Twentieth Century–Fox. Furthermore, although there were a few important exceptions, movies without stars generally failed at the box office. Serious stars used money and power to further their art, not just to gratify their vanity. Bette Davis was considered "difficult" during her stormy tenure at Warners because she insisted on better scripts, more varied roles, more sensitive directors, and stronger costars.

Top stars attracted the loyalty of both men and women, although as sociologist Leo Handel pointed out, 65 percent of the fans preferred stars of their own gender. The studios received up to 32 million fan letters per year, 85 percent of them from young females. Major stars received about three thousand letters per week, and the volume of their mail was regarded as an accurate barometer of their popularity. The studios spent as much as $2 million a year processing these letters, most of which asked for autographed photos. Box-office appeal was also gauged by the number of fan clubs devoted to a star. The stars with the greatest number of fan clubs were Gable, Jean Harlow, and Joan Crawford—all of them under contract to MGM, "The Home of the Stars." Gable alone had seventy clubs, which partly accounted for his supremacy as the top male star of the 1930s.

The mythology of stardom usually emphasizes the glamour of movie stars, lifting them above the mundane concerns of ordinary mortals. Critic Parker Tyler observed that stars fulfill an ancient need, almost religious in nature: "Somehow their wealth, fame, and beauty, their apparently unlimited field of worldly pleasure—these conditions tinge them with the supernatural, render them immune to the bitterness of ordinary frustrations." Of course, this mythology also involves the tragic victims of stardom, like Marilyn Monroe and James Dean. The fact that many stars have died young—at the height of their physical beauty—only enhances their romantic image of immutable perfection (8–14).

The realities behind the myths are considerably less romantic. For every actor who manages to scale the peaks of stardom, there are hundreds of thousands who fail, their hard work wasted, their sacrifices scoffed at, their dreams shattered. Maureen Stapleton has won important acting awards for her distinguished work in films, television, and the stage, but she has spoken eloquently of the hardships actors must endure in a world that often regards them as fortunate simpletons:

> I believe in the toughness of actors. I have a feeling of genuine pride in actors as my people. . . . We're called egomaniacs; we're thought of as children. Actors are supposed to be irresponsible, stupid, unaware, and a kind of joke. They're accused of having big egos. Well, the actor's ego is no different in size because he's an *actor.* A writer or a painter or a musician can go off into a corner and lick his wounds, but an actor stands out in front of the crowd and takes it. . . . Actors spend years and years being treated like dirt. They're constantly in a state of debasement, making the rounds of casting directors and having to look happy and great. I made the rounds for years, but I wasn't good at it. But then *nobody* is. You need a very strong stomach. You need a sense of the business as a whole, so that you don't get lacerated every time somebody tells you you're lousy. You need strength, and no matter how strong you get, you always need to get stronger. (Quoted in *The Player: A Profile of an Art*)

Stars must pay a high price for their wealth and fame. They must get used to being treated like commodities with a price tag. Even at the beginning of the star system, they were reduced to simplified types: virgins, vamps, swashbucklers, flappers, and so on. Over the years, a vast repertory of types evolved: the Latin lover, the he-man, the heiress, the good–bad girl, the cynical reporter, the career girl, and many others. Of course, all great stars are unique even though they might fall under a well-known category. For example, the cheap blonde has long been one of America's favourite types, but such important stars as Mae West, Jean Harlow, and Marilyn Monroe are highly distinctive as

8-14. Publicity photo of Marilyn Monroe in *The Seven Year Itch* (U.S.A., 1955), *directed by Billy Wilder.*

Marilyn Monroe has become a symbol of the personal tragedy that can befall a star. She was born (out of wedlock) to an emotionally unstable mother who spent most of her life in mental asylums. As a child, Norma Jean Baker was raised in a series of orphanages and foster homes. Even then—especially then—she dreamed of becoming a famous Hollywood star. She was raped at the age of eight, married to her first husband at sixteen. She used sex (like many before her) as a means to an end—stardom. In the late 1940s she had a few bit roles, mostly as sexy dumb blondes. Not until John Huston's *The Asphalt Jungle* (1950) did she create much of a stir. In that same year, Joseph Mankiewicz cast her in *All About Eve,* as "a graduate of the Copacabana School of Dramatic Art," as George Sanders drily deadpans in the film. (Sanders claimed he knew Marilyn would one day become a star "because she desperately needed to be one.") After Twentieth Century–Fox signed her to a contract, the studio didn't know what to do with her. She appeared in a series of third-rate studio projects, but despite their mediocrity, the public clamoured for more Marilyn. She rightly blamed Fox for mismanaging her career: "Only the public can make a star. It's the studios who try to make a system of it," she bitterly complained. At the peak of her popularity, she left Hollywood in disgust, to study at the Actors Studio. When she returned, she demanded more money and better roles—and got both. Joshua Logan, who directed her in *Bus Stop* (1956), said she was "as near genius as any actress I ever knew." Supremely photogenic, she gave herself entirely to the camera, allowing it to probe her deepest vulnerabilities. Laurence Olivier, her costar and director in *The Prince and the Showgirl* (1957), marvelled at her cunning way of fusing guilelessness with carnality—the mind and soul of a little girl wrapped in the body of a prostitute. Throughout her years as a top star, her private life was a shambles. "She was an unfortunate doped-up woman most of the time," biographer Maurice Zolotow observed. Her failed marriages and love affairs were constantly in the headlines, and increasingly she turned to drugs and alcohol for solace. She was notorious for her irresponsibility, often not bothering to show up on set for days at a time, thus incurring enormous cost overruns. Because of her addiction to drugs and alcohol, even when she did show up she scarcely knew who—much less where—she was. She was found dead in 1962, from an overdose of barbiturates and alcohol. *(Twentieth Century–Fox)*

individuals. A successful type was always imitated. In the mid-1920s, for example, the Swedish import Greta Garbo created a sophisticated and complex type, the *femme fatale*. Garbo inspired many imitations, including such important stars as Marlene Dietrich and Carole Lombard, who were first touted as "Garbo types," only with a sense of humour. In the 1950s, Sidney Poitier became the first black star to attract a wide following outside of his own race. In later years a number of other black performers attained stardom in part because Poitier had established the precedent. He was one of the great originals and hence worthy of imitation.

At about the turn of the last century, George Bernard Shaw wrote a famous essay comparing the two foremost stage stars of the day—Eleonora Duse and Sarah Bernhardt. Shaw's comparison is a useful springboard for a discussion of the different kinds of film stars. Bernhardt, Shaw wrote, was a bravura personality, and she managed to tailor each different role to fit this personality. This is what her fans both expected and desired. Her personal charm was larger than life, yet undeniably captivating. Her performances were filled with brilliant effects that had come to be associated with her personality over the years. Duse, on the other hand, possessed a quieter talent, less dazzling in its initial impact. She was totally different with each role, and her own personality never seemed to intrude on the playwright's character. Hers was an invisible art: Her impersonations were so totally believable that the viewer was likely to forget they *were* impersonations. In effect, Shaw was pointing out the major distinctions between a **personality star** and an **actor star.**

Personality stars commonly refuse all parts that go against their type, especially if they're leading men or leading ladies. Performers like Goldie Hawn would never play cruel or psychopathic roles, for example, because such parts would conflict with their sympathetic image. If a star is locked into his or her type, any significant departure can result in box-office disaster. For example, when Pickford tried to abandon her little-girl roles in the 1920s, her public stayed at home: They wanted to see Little Mary or nothing. She retired in disgust at the age of forty, just when most players are at the peak of their powers.

On the other hand, many stars prefer to remain in the same mould, playing variations on the same character type. John Wayne was the most popular star in film history. From 1949 to 1976 he was absent from the top ten only three times. "I play John Wayne in every part regardless of the character, and I've been doing okay, haven't I?" he once asked. In the public mind, he was the archetypal westerner, a man of action—and violence—rather than words. His **iconography** is steeped in a distrust of sophistication and intellectuality. His name is virtually synonymous with masculinity—though his persona suggests more of the warrior than the lover. As he grew older, he also grew more human, developing his considerable talents as a comedian by mocking his own macho image. Wayne was fully aware of the enormous influence a star can wield in transmitting values, and in many of his films he embodied a **right-wing** ideology that made him a hero to conservative Americans (see **11–15).**

Film theorist Richard Dyer has pointed out that stars are signifying entities. Any sensitive analysis of a film with a star in its cast must take into account

8-15. *The Silence of the Lambs* (U.S.A., 1991), *with Anthony Hopkins, directed by Jonathan Demme.*
Character actors are the unsung heroes of the profession, often relegated to secondary roles because of their lack of glamour and star power. Like most British-trained actors, Anthony Hopkins is extraordinarily versatile, equally at home playing Shakespeare, romantic contemporary roles, offbeat character parts, and in a variety of styles and dialects. He did not attract much popular attention until his electrifying performance as the twisted genius, Dr. Hannibal "The Cannibal" Lecter, in this film.
(Orion Pictures)

that star's iconographical significance. Stars like John Wayne and Jane Fonda embody complex political associations simply by demonstrating the lifestyle of their politics and displaying those political beliefs as an aspect of their personas on and off screen. In the contemporary media, image-making has become an important part of politics, but even stars who have no overt political affiliation—Demi Moore, for example—can have a tremendous impact in transmitting values. Dyer also demonstrates how a star's iconography is always developing, incorporating elements from the star's actual life as well as previous roles. For example, Moore's career to date can be divided into five phases:

1. *Pre-stardom.* Unlike Jane Fonda, whose entry into the film industry was facilitated by Henry Fonda's prestige, Moore had a difficult childhood and had to overcome many problems before she became well known. After working as a model, she began her career as a television actor,

appearing as a regular in the soap opera *General Hospital*. She left when she was cast as Michael Caine's daughter in *Blame It On Rio* (1984). Her "white trash" family background and her struggle for recognition became part of her persona after she became a star.

2. *Brat pack.* In her first important roles, Moore became known as a member of a group of young actors often referred to as the "brat pack" because of their rebellious attitudes and rejection of Hollywood codes of glamour. Other members of the pack included Emilio Estevez, with whom Moore had a much-publicized affair, and Rob Lowe, with whom she appeared in *St Elmo's Fire* (1985) and *About Last Night* (1986). At this time, Moore's struggles with drug and alcohol addiction received a good deal of media attention.

3. *Breakthrough.* Moore's image changed following her marriage to television and movie star Bruce Willis in 1987 in an elaborate ceremony presided over by pop singer Little Richard. She became an established star herself when she played the part of a woman haunted by her dead lover in *Ghost* (1990). In this film, she appeared with a mass of brunette hair that gave her an angelic and seductive appeal. Her subsequent roles in *A Few Good Men* (1992) and *Indecent Proposal* (1993) confirmed her star ranking, but some critics felt that her success depended on her ability to manage her image, reportedly including plastic surgery, rather than her acting talents. Her talent for controversial publicity was demonstrated when she posed naked and pregnant for the cover of *Vanity Fair* in 1991 and then wearing only body paint the following year.

4. *Blockbusters.* Her success in the early 1990s made Moore one of the most sought-after Hollywood actors, and she was cast in several high-budget films in which her salary was a major component of the production budget. She received $12.5 million for starring in *Striptease* (1996), in which her role as a "sexy mother" closely paralleled her off-screen persona. Like the pop singer Madonna, her persona combined aspects of the strong and independent modern woman with a sexual display that seemed to conform to older stereotypes. In *Disclosure* (1996) she appeared as an aggressive business woman who sexually harasses one of her male colleagues.

5. *Production.* Moore was able to remain a "bankable" star despite the failure of many of her films, most disastrously *The Scarlet Letter* (1995) and *Striptease*. In 1997 she again created controversy with her role in *G.I. Jane,* in which she appeared as the first female participant in the gruelling U.S. Navy SEAL training program. The most discussed sequence was one in which she shaved off her famous hair, which had impeded her in the physical exercises. This film was also a relative failure at the box office, and Moore has recently worked mainly as a producer. Her separation from Willis in 1998 was seen in the tabloids as further evidence that her star career was on hold, but she still remains a high-profile figure in the media.

The top box-office attractions tend to be personality stars. They stay on top by being themselves, by not trying to impersonate anyone. Gable insisted that all he did in front of the camera was "act natural." Similarly, Marilyn Monroe was always at her best when she played roles that exploited her indecisiveness, her vulnerability, and her pathetic eagerness to please.

On the other hand, there have been many stars who refuse to be typecast and who attempt the widest array of roles possible. Such actor stars as Davis, Hepburn, Brando, and De Niro have sometimes undertaken unpleasant character roles rather than conventional leads to expand their range, for variety and breadth have traditionally been the yardsticks by which great acting is measured.

Many stars fall somewhere between the two extremes, veering toward personality in some films, toward impersonation in others. Such gifted performers as James Stewart, Cary Grant, and Audrey Hepburn played wider variations of certain types of roles. Nonetheless, we couldn't imagine a star like Hepburn playing a woman of weak character or a coarse or stupid woman, so firmly entrenched was her image as an elegant and rather aristocratic female. Similarly, most people know what's meant by "the Clint Eastwood type."

The distinction between a professional actor and a star is not based on technical skill, but on mass popularity. By definition, a star must have enormous personal magnetism, a riveting quality that commands our attention. Few public personalities have inspired such deep and widespread affection as the great movie stars. Some are loved because they embody such traditional Ameri-

8–16. *To Die For* (U.S.A., 1995), *with Nicole Kidman, directed by Gus Van Sant.* There are many talented and even brilliant performers who never achieve film stardom because they lack "a face that opens up to the camera," to quote from a frequent observation of cinematographers. Good bone structure helps, but it's not enough. Beautiful features and a commanding presence are also useful. But mostly, an "open" face implies a lack of self-consciousness, a willingness to let the camera capture the most intimate nuances of emotion and thought. A face like this. *(Columbia Pictures)*

can values as plain speaking, integrity, and idealism: Gary Cooper and Tom Hanks are examples of this type. Others are identified with anti-establishment images and include such celebrated loners as Bogie, Clint Eastwood, and Jack Nicholson. Players such as Cary Grant and Carole Lombard are so captivating in their charm that they're fun to watch in almost anything. And of course many of them are spectacularly good-looking: Names like Michelle Pfeiffer and Tom Cruise are virtually synonymous with godlike beauty.

Sophisticated filmmakers exploit the public's affection for its stars by creating ambiguous tensions between a role as written, as acted, and as directed. "Whenever the hero isn't portrayed by a star the whole picture suffers," Hitchcock observed. "Audiences are far less concerned about the predicament of a character who's played by someone they don't know." When a star rather than a conventional actor plays a role, much of the characterization is automatically fixed by the casting; but what the director and star then choose to add to the written role is what constitutes its *full* dramatic meaning. Some directors have capitalized on the star system with great artistic effectiveness, particularly studio-era filmmakers (8–17).

8-17. *Vertigo* (U.S.A., 1958), *with James Stewart and Kim Novak, directed by Alfred Hitchcock.* Perhaps Hitchcock's greatest genius was how he managed to outwit the system while still succeeding brilliantly at the box office. For example, Hitchcock knew that a star in the leading role virtually guaranteed the commercial success of his pictures. But he liked to push his stars to the dark side—to explore neurotic, even psychotic undercurrents that often subverted the star's established iconography. Everyone loved Jimmy Stewart as the stammering, decent, all-American idealist, best typified by *It's a Wonderful Life* (6–10). In this movie, Stewart's character is obsessed with a romantic idealization of a mysterious woman (Novak). He's convinced himself that he's desperately in love—ironically, with a woman who doesn't exist. Within the generic format of a detective thriller, Hitchcock is able to explore the obsessions, self-delusions, and desperate need that many people call love.   *(Universal Pictures)*

Perhaps the ultimate glory for a star is to become an icon in American popular mythology. Like the gods and goddesses of ancient times, some stars are so universally known that one name alone is enough to evoke an entire complex of symbolic associations—"Marilyn," for example. Unlike the conventional actor (however gifted), the star automatically suggests ideas and emotions that are deeply embedded in his or her persona. These undertones are determined not only by the star's previous roles, but often by his or her actual personality as well. Naturally, over the course of many years, this symbolic information can begin to drain from public consciousness, but the iconography of a great star like Gary Cooper becomes part of a shared experience. As the French critic Edgar Morin has pointed out, when Cooper played a character, he automatically "gary-cooperized" it, infusing himself into the role and the role into himself. Because audiences felt a deep sense of identification with Coop and the values he symbolized, in a sense they were celebrating themselves—or at least their spiritual selves. The great originals are cultural **archetypes,** and their box-office popularity is an index of their success in synthesizing the aspirations of an era. As a number of cultural studies have shown, the iconography of a star can involve communal myths and symbols of considerable complexity and emotional richness.

STYLES OF ACTING

Acting styles differ radically, depending on period, **genre,** tone, national origins, and directorial emphasis. Such considerations are the principal means by which acting styles are classified. Even within a given category, however, generalizations are, at best, a loose set of expectations, not Holy Writ. For example, the realist–formalist dialectic that has been used as a classification aid throughout this book can also be applied to the art of acting, but there are many variations and subdivisions. These terms are also subject to different interpretations from period to period. Lillian Gish was regarded as a great realistic actress in the silent era, but by today's standards, her performances look rather ethereal. In a parallel vein, the playing style of Klaus Kinski in such movies as *Aguirre, the Wrath of God* is stylized, but compared to an extreme form of **expressionistic** acting, such as that of Conrad Veidt in *The Cabinet of Dr. Caligari,* Kinski is relatively realistic (**4–15, 8–18).** It's a matter of degree.

Classifying acting styles according to national origins is also likely to be misleading, at least for those countries that have evolved a wide spectrum of styles, such as Japan, the United States, and Italy. For example, the Italians (and other Mediterranean peoples) are said to be theatrical by national temperament, acting out their feelings with animation, as opposed to the reserved deportment of the Swedes and other Northern Europeans. But within the Italian cinema alone, these generalizations are subject to considerable modification. Southern Italian characters tend to be acted in a manner that conforms to the volatile Latin stereotype, as can be seen in the movies of Lina Wertmüller **(8–19).** Northern Italians, on the other hand, are usually played with more restraint and far less spontaneity, as the works of Antonioni demonstrate.

8-18. *Aguirre, the Wrath of God* **(Germany, 1972),** *with Klaus Kinski, directed by Werner Herzog.*

Expressionistic acting is generally associated with the German cinema—a cinema of directors, rarely actors. Stripped of individualizing details, this style of acting stresses a symbolic concept rather than a believable three-dimensional character. It is presentational rather than representational, a style of extremes rather than norms. Psychological complexity is replaced by a stylized thematic essence. For example, Kinski's portrayal of a Spanish conquistador is conceived in terms of a treacherous serpent. His Dantean features a frozen mask of ferocity, Aguirre can suddenly twist and coil like a cobra poised for a strike. *(New Yorker Films)*

Genre and directorial emphasis also influence acting styles significantly. For example, in such stylized genres as the samurai film, Toshiro Mifune is bold, strutting, and larger than life, as in Kurosawa's *Yojimbo.* In a realistic contemporary story like *High and Low* (also directed by Kurosawa), Mifune's performance is all nuance and sobriety.

The *art* of silent acting encompasses a period of only some fifteen years or so, for though movies were being produced as early as 1895, most historians regard Griffith's *The Birth of a Nation* (1915) as the first indisputable masterpiece of the silent cinema. The changeover to sound was virtually universal by 1930. Within this brief span, however, a wide variety of playing styles evolved, ranging from the detailed, underplayed realism of Gibson Gowland in *Greed,* to the grand, ponderous style of such tragedians as Emil Jannings in *The Last Command.* The great silent clowns like Chaplin, Keaton, Harold Lloyd, Harry Lang-

8–19. *The Seduction of Mimi* (Italy, 1972), *with Giancarlo Giannini and Elena Fiore, directed by Lina Wertmüller.*
Farcical acting is one of the most difficult and misunderstood styles of performance. It requires an intense comic exaggeration and can easily become tiresome and mechanical if the farceur is not able to preserve the humanity of the character. Here, Giannini plays a typical ethnic stereotype—a sleazy, heavy-lidded lothario who, in an act of sexual revenge, embarks on a campaign to seduce the unlovely wife of the man who has cuckolded him.   *(New Line Cinema)*

don, and Laurel and Hardy also developed highly personal styles that bear only a superficial resemblance to each other.

A popular misconception about the silent cinema is that all movies were photographed and projected at "silent speed"—sixteen frames per second (fps). In fact, silent speed was highly variable, subject to easy manipulation because cameras were hand-cranked. Even within a single film, not every scene was necessarily photographed at the same speed. Generally speaking, comic scenes were undercranked to emphasize speed, whereas dramatic scenes were overcranked to slow down the action, usually twenty or twenty-two fps. Because most present-day projectors feature only two speeds—sixteen silent and twenty-four sound—the original rhythms of the performances are violated. This is why players in silent dramas can appear jerky and slightly ludicrous. In comedies, this distortion can enhance the humour, which is why the performances of the silent clowns have retained much of their original charm.

The most popular and critically admired player of the silent cinema was Chaplin. The wide variety of comic skills he developed in his early years of vaudeville made him the most versatile of the clowns. In the area of pantomime, no one approached his inventiveness. Critics waxed eloquent on his balletic grace, and even the brilliant dancer Nijinsky proclaimed Chaplin his equal. His ability to blend comedy with pathos was unique. George Bernard Shaw, the greatest living playwright of this era, described Chaplin as "the only genius developed in motion pictures." After viewing Chaplin's powerful—and very funny—performance in *City Lights*, the fastidious critic Alexander Woolcott, who otherwise loathed movies, said, "I would be prepared to defend the proposition that this darling of the mob is the foremost living artist."

Greta Garbo perfected a romantic style of acting that had its roots in the silent cinema and held sway throughout the 1930s. Critics have sometimes referred to this mode of performance as star acting. "What, when drunk, one sees in other women, one sees in Garbo sober," said the British critic Kenneth Tynan. Almost invariably, MGM cast her as a woman with a mysterious past: mistress, courtesan, the "other woman"—the essence of the Eternal Female. Her face, in addition to being stunningly beautiful, could unite conflicting emotions, withholding and yielding simultaneously, like a succession of waves rippling across her features. Tall and slender, she moved gracefully, her collapsed shoulders suggesting the exhaustion of a wounded butterfly. She could also project a provocative bisexuality, as in *Queen Christina*, where her resolute strides and masculine attire provide a foil to her exquisite femininity.

The love goddess par excellence, Garbo was most famous for her love scenes, which epitomized her romantic style. She is often self-absorbed in these scenes, musing on a private irony that can even exclude the lover. Frequently she looks away from him, allowing the camera—and us—to savour the poignancy of her conflict. She rarely expresses her feelings in words, for her art thrives on silence, on the unspeakable. Her love scenes are sometimes played in literal solitude, with objects serving as erotic fetishes. The way she touches a bouquet of flowers, a bedpost, a telephone—these allude to the missing lover, recalling a multitude of painful pleasures. She is often enraptured by her surroundings, "like Eve on the morning of creation," to use Tynan's memorable phrase. But she is also oppressed by the knowledge that such ecstasy cannot last; she arms herself against her fate with irony and stoicism. Garbo's performances are striking examples of how great acting can salvage bad scripts, and even bad direction. "Subtract Garbo from most of her movies and you are left with nothing," one critic noted.

The most important British film actors are also those most prominent in live theatre. Virtually every medium-sized British city has a resident drama company, where actors can learn their craft by playing a variety of roles from the classic repertory, especially the works of Shakespeare. As players improve, they rise through the ranks, attempting more complex roles. The best of them migrate to the larger cities, where the most prestigious theatre companies are found. The discipline that most British actors have acquired in this repertory system has made them the most versatile of players. The finest of them are regularly employed in the theatres of London, which is also adjacent to the centres of film production in Britain. This centralization allows them to move from live theatre to film to television with a minimum of inconvenience.

British acting traditions tend to favour a mastery of externals, based on close observation. Virtually all players are trained in diction, movement, makeup, dialects, fencing, dancing, body control, and ensemble acting. For example, Laurence Olivier always built his characters from the outside in. He moulded his features like a sculptor or painter. "I do not search the character for parts that are already in me," he explained, "but go out and find the personality I feel the author created." Like most British actors of his generation, Olivier had a keen memory for details: "I hear remarks in the street or in a shop and I retain them. You must constantly observe: a walk, a limp, a run; how a head inclines to one side when listening; the twitch of an eyebrow; the hand that picks the nose when it thinks no one is looking; the moustache puller; the eyes that never look at you; the nose that sniffs long after the cold has gone."

Makeup for Olivier was magical. He loved hiding his real features behind beards, false complexions, fake noses, and wigs. "If you're wise," he warned, "you always take off the part with your makeup." He also prided himself on his ability to mimic dialects: "I always go to endless trouble to learn American accents, even for small television parts. If it's north Michigan, it's bloody well got to be north Michigan."

8-20. *The Rocky Horror Picture Show* **(Britain, 1975),** *with Tim Curry and Richard O'Brien, directed by Jim Sharman.*

A film's tone dictates its acting style. Tone is determined primarily by genre, dialogue, and the director's attitude toward the dramatic materials. The original audiences of *The Rocky Horror Picture Show* were put off by its perversely campy wit and its spirit of mockery. The straight world and its values are mercilessly assaulted by the movie's garish theatricality. The film has long been a cult favourite, grossing over $70 million on the midnight movie circuit of college towns and large cities. Most cult movies appeal to our subversive instincts, our desire to see conventional morality trashed.   *(Twentieth Century-Fox)*

Olivier kept his body in peak condition. Even as an old man, he continued running and lifting weights. When illness curbed these forms of exercises, he took to swimming. At the age of seventy-eight, he was still swimming eight hundred metres almost every morning. "To be fit should be one of the actor's first priorities," he insisted. "To exercise daily is of utmost importance. The body is an instrument which must be finely tuned and played as often as possible. The actor should be able to control it from the tip of his head to his little toe" (quotes are from *Laurence Olivier on Acting*).

The post–World War II era tended to emphasize realistic styles of acting. In the early 1950s, a new interior style of acting, known as "the Method," or "the System," was introduced to American movie audiences. It was commonly associated with director Elia Kazan. Kazan's *On the Waterfront* was a huge success and a virtual showcase for this style of performance (**8–25**). It has since become the dominant style of acting in American cinema as well as live theatre. **The Method** was an offshoot of a system of training actors and rehearsing that had been developed by Constantin Stanislavsky at the Moscow Art Theatre. Stanislavsky's ideas were widely adopted in New York theatre circles, especially by the Actors Studio in New York, which received much publicity during the 1950s because it had developed such well-known graduates as Marlon Brando, James Dean, Julie Harris, Paul Newman, and many others.

Kazan cofounded and taught at the Actors Studio until 1954, when he asked his former mentor, Lee Strasberg, to take over the organization. Within a short period, Strasberg became the most celebrated acting teacher in the United States, and his former students were—and still are—among the most famous performers in the world.

The central credo of Stanislavsky's system was, "You must live the part every moment you are playing it." He rejected the tradition of acting that emphasized externals. He believed that truth in acting can only be achieved by exploring a character's inner spirit, which must be fused with the actor's own emotions. One of the most important techniques he developed is *emotional recall,* in which an actor delves into his or her own past to discover feelings that are analogous to those of the character. "In every part you do," Julie Harris explained, "there is some connection you can make with your own background or with some feeling you've had at one time or another." Stanislavsky's techniques were strongly psychoanalytical: By exploring their own subconscious, actors could trigger *real* emotions, which are recalled in every performance and transferred to the characters they are playing. He also devised techniques for helping actors focus their concentration on the "world" of the play—its concrete details and textures. In some form or another, these techniques are probably as old as the acting profession itself, but Stanislavsky was the first to systematize them with exercises and methods of analysis (hence the terms *the System* and *the Method*). Nor did he claim that inner truth and emotional sincerity are sufficient unto themselves. He insisted that actors need to master the externals as well, particularly for classic plays, which require a somewhat stylized manner of speaking, moving, and wearing costumes.

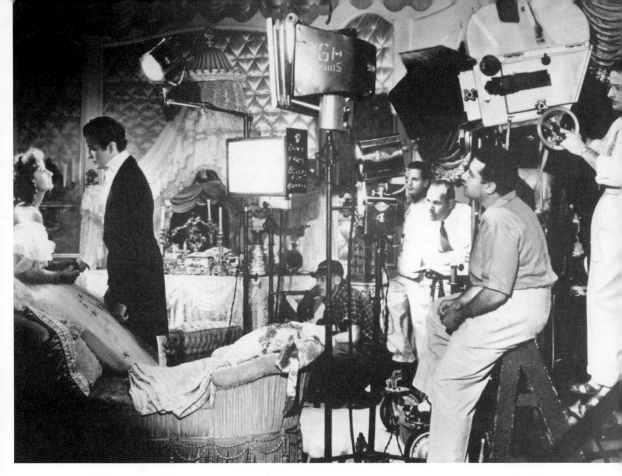

8–21. **Production photo of a scene in progress from** *Camille* **(U.S.A., 1937),** *with Greta Garbo and Robert Taylor (left), directed by George Cukor (sitting on stepladder, right).*
At the extreme right of this photo is William Daniels, who photographed most of Garbo's movies. One of the most difficult disciplines of screen acting is concentration. Garbo insisted on a closed set for her scenes—no one was permitted to watch unless he or she was absolutely essential. If someone dared to sneak on the set, Garbo would stop the scene and refuse to go on until the interloper was ejected. Prima-donna airs? Probably not. It's awfully hard to concentrate on the emotional truth of a scene if dozens of strangers are standing by, gawking. *Camille* is probably Garbo's greatest performance—ironic, passionate, and ethereal. *(MGM)*

Stanislavsky was famous for his lengthy rehearsal periods, in which players were encouraged to improvise with their roles to discover the resonances of the text—the **subtext,** which is analogous to Freud's concept of the subconscious. Kazan and other Method-oriented directors used this concept in directing movies: "The film director knows that beneath the surface of his screenplay there is a subtext, a calendar of intentions and feelings and inner events. What appears to be happening, he soon learns, is rarely what is happening. The subtext is one of the film director's most valuable tools. It is what he directs." Spoken dialogue is secondary for Method players. To capture a character's "inner events," actors sometimes "throw away" their lines, choke on them, or even

8–22a. *Yankee Doodle Dandy* (U.S.A., 1942), *with James Cagney, directed by Michael Curtiz.*
Acting styles are determined in part by a player's energy level. High-voltage performers like Cagney usually project out to the audience, commanding our attention with a bravura style. Much of our pleasure in a Cagney performance is watching him "struttin' his stuff." He was a highly kinetic performer, expressing his character's emotions through movement. His dancing is exhilarating—cocky, sexy, and funny. Even in dramatic roles, he is seldom at rest—edgy, punctuating the air with his hand gestures, prancing on the balls of his feet. "Never settle back on your heels," was his credo. "Never relax. If you relax, the audience relaxes." Other high-energy performers include Harold Lloyd, Katharine Hepburn, Bette Davis, Gene Kelly, George C. Scott, Barbra Streisand, James Woods, Joe Pesci, and Richard Dreyfuss. *(Warner Bros.)*

8–22b. *Le Dernier Métro* (*"The Last Metro,"* **France, 1980),** *with Catherine Deneuve and Gérard Depardieu, directed by François Truffaut.*
Low-key performers like Deneuve are sometimes said to work "small" or "close to the lens." Rather than projecting out to the audience, these performers allow the camera to tune *in* on their behaviour, which is seldom exaggerated for dramatic effect. Eyewitness accounts of Deneuve's acting usually stress how little she seems to be working. The subtleties are apparent only at very close range. Other players in this mode include Harry Langdon, Spencer Tracy, Henry Fonda, Marilyn Monroe, Montgomery Clift, Kevin Costner, Jack Nicholson, and Winona Ryder. Of course dramatic context is all important in determining an actor's energy level. *(United Artists)*

8-23. *Jerry Maguire* **(U.S.A., 1996),** *with Tom Cruise and Cuba Gooding Jr., written and directed by Cameron Crowe.*

Most of the great stars, especially personality stars, become their own genres. That is, their films are tailored to highlight those qualities that made them stars in the first place. These traits are recycled and repackaged to give the public what it wants, and thereby make lots of money. Most of Tom Cruise's movies follow a similar generic pattern: He begins as a brash, confident youth, a bit cocky and full of himself. A great-looking guy, of course. But he's not as smart as he thinks he is, and is humbled by a conspicuous error in judgment. With the help of a supportive young woman who loves him, however, he sees the error of his ways and goes on to even greater success—only now without the swagger. To his credit, Cruise has expanded his range considerably in such offbeat parts as those in *The Color of Money*, *Born on the Fourth of July*, and *Interview With the Vampire.*   *(TriStar Pictures)*

mumble. Throughout the 1950s, Method actors like Brando and Dean were ridiculed by some critics for mumbling their lines.

Stanislavsky disapproved of the star system and individual virtuosity. In his own productions, he insisted on ensemble playing, with genuine interactions among the actor/characters. Players were encouraged to analyze all the specifics of a scene: What does the character really *want?* What has happened prior to the immediate moment? What time of day is it? And so on. When presented with a role utterly foreign to their experience, actors were urged to research the part so it would be understood in their guts as well as their minds. Method actors are famous for their ability to bring out the emotional intensity of their characters. Method-oriented directors generally believe that a player must have a character's experience within him or her, and they go to considerable lengths to learn about the personal lives of their players in order to use such details for characterization.

In the 1960s, the French **New Wave** directors—especially Godard and Truffaut—popularized the technique of improvisation while their players were on camera. The resultant increase in realism was highly praised by critics. Of course there was nothing new in the technique itself. Actors often improvised in the silent cinema, and it was the foundation of silent comedy. For example, Chaplin, Keaton, and Laurel and Hardy needed to know only the premise of a given scene. The comic details were improvised and later refined in the editing stage. The cumbersome technology of sound put an end to most of these practices. Method-trained actors use improvisation primarily as an exploratory

8-24. *Little Dorrit* **(Britain, 1988),** *with Alec Guinness, based on the novel by Charles Dickens, adapted and directed by Christine Edzard.*
Above all, British actors have perfected the art of reciting highly stylized dialogue—the language of Shakespeare, Dickens, and Shaw—without violating the believability of their characters. Because of their great literary heritage, British performers are almost universally considered unsurpassed masters of period styles of acting.   *(Cannon Films)*

rehearsal technique, but their performances are usually set when the camera begins to roll.

Godard and Truffaut, to capture a greater sense of discovery and surprise, would occasionally instruct their players to make up their dialogue while a scene was actually being photographed. The flexible technology introduced by **cinéma vérité** allowed these directors to capture an unprecedented degree of spontaneity. In Truffaut's *The 400 Blows,* for example, the youthful protagonist (Jean-Pierre Léaud) is interviewed by a prison psychologist about his family life and sexual habits. Drawing heavily on his own experience, Léaud (who wasn't informed of the questions in advance) answers them with disarming frankness. Truffaut's camera is able to capture the boy's hesitations, his embarrassment, and his charming macho bravado. Canadian director Don Owen made great use of improvisation in *Nobody Waved Good-bye* and created a powerful effect at the end of the film by not informing one of the actors of a major plot development (see **10–5**).

8-25. *On the Waterfront* **(U.S.A., 1954),** *with Marlon Brando and Eva Marie Saint, directed by Elia Kazan.*
Kazan considers Brando as close to a genius as he has ever encountered among actors—a view that's widely shared by others, especially other actors. Many regard his performance in this movie as his best—emotionally powerful, tender, poetic. It won him his first Academy Award (best actor) as well as the New York Film Critics' Award and the British Oscar as best foreign actor—his third year in a row. Kazan was often surprised by his gifted protégé because he came up with ideas so fresh and arrived at in so underground a fashion that they seemed virtually discovered on the spot.   *(Columbia Pictures)*

In one form or another, improvisation has become a valuable technique in the contemporary cinema. Such filmmakers as Robert Altman, Rainer Werner Fassbinder, and Martin Scorsese have used it with brilliant results.

CASTING

Casting a movie is almost an art in itself. It requires an acute sensitivity to a player's type, a **convention** inherited from live theatre. Most stage and screen performers are classified according to role categories: leading men, leading ladies, character actors, juveniles, villains, light comedians, tragedians, ingenues, singing actors, dancing actors, and so on. Typing conventions are rarely violated. For example, even though homely people obviously fall in love, romantic roles are almost always performed by attractive players. Similarly, audiences are not likely to be persuaded by a player with an all-

8-26. *The End of Summer* **(Japan, 1961),** *directed by Yasujiro Ozu.*

A master of psychological nuances, Ozu believed that in the art of acting, less is more. He detested melodramatic excesses and demanded the utmost realism from his players, who frequently chafed at his criticism that they were "acting" too much. He avoided using stars and often cast against type so audiences would view the characters with no preconceptions. He usually chose his players according to their personality rather than their acting ability. Above all, Ozu explored the conflict between individual wishes and social necessity. His scenes are often staged in public settings, where politeness and social decorum require the stifling of personal disappointment. Ozu often instructed his players not to move, to express their feelings only with their eyes. Note how the two characters on the left are privately in worlds of their own, while still conforming superficially to the decorum of the occasion. *(New Yorker Films)*

8-27. *La Chinoise* **(France, 1967),** *with Juliet Berto, directed by Jean-Luc Godard.*

Though Godard was a pioneer in exploring the possibilities of realistic acting, after his conversion to Marxism in the late 1960s he came to repudiate this style of performance, dismissing it as "a bourgeois concept of representation." He was strongly influenced by the German dramatist Bertolt Brecht. Like Brecht, Godard believed that performers should act as *intermediaries* between the fictional characters they are playing and the spectators watching the movie. Instead of lulling viewers with an illusion of reality that pretends to be objective, actors should confront the spectators directly, acknowledging their presence and presenting them not with a vicarious emotional thrill but an analysis of how capitalist ideology works. In short, through the rejection of a realistic style of acting, the Marxist ideal of demystification is embodied on an aesthetic level within the movie itself. Instead of pretending that his images and actors are a "reflection of reality," the filmmaker frankly demonstrates how they can be manipulated, thus allowing the viewer to accept or reject the ideas in a more objective manner. See James Roy MacBean, *Film and Revolution* (Bloomington: Indiana University Press, 1975). *(Leacock Pennebaker, Inc.)*

American iconography (like Goldie Hawn) cast in European roles. Nor is one likely to accept a performer like Klaus Kinski as the boy next door, unless one lives in a very weird neighbourhood. Of course a player's range is all-important in determining his or her type. Some, like Glenn Close, have extremely broad ranges, whereas others, like Woody Allen, are confined to variations of the same type.

Typecasting was almost invariable in the silent cinema. In part, this was because characters tended toward allegorical types rather than unique individuals and often were even identified with a label: "The Man," "The Wife," "The Mother," "The Vamp," and so on. Blonde players were usually cast in parts emphasizing purity, earthy brunettes in erotic roles. Eisenstein insisted that players ought to be cast strictly to type and was inclined to favour nonprofessionals because of their greater authenticity. Why use an actor to impersonate a factory worker, he asked, when a filmmaker can use a *real* factory worker instead?

But trained actors tend to resent being typed and often attempt to broaden their range. Sometimes it works, sometimes it doesn't. Humphrey Bogart is a good example. For years he was stereotyped as a tough, cynical gangster, until he joined forces with director John Huston, who cast him as the hard-boiled detective Sam Spade in *The Maltese Falcon*. Huston weaned him even further from his type in *The Treasure of the Sierra Madre*, in which Bogart played a crafty paranoid, the prospector Fred C. Dobbs. The actor totally reversed his image in *The African Queen*, in which he played Charlie Allnut, a lovable and funny drunk whose vulnerability endeared him to audiences and won Bogart an Academy Award for best actor. But in *Beat the Devil*, Huston's celebrated casting instincts deserted him when he used Bogart in a role beyond his powers—as a sophisticated adventurer stranded with a shabby assortment of rogues and loons. The witty tongue-in-cheek dialogue fell flat in Bogart's self-conscious performance. A polished player like Cary Grant could have acted the part with much greater believability and grace.

"Casting is characterization," Hitchcock pointed out. Once a role has been cast, especially with a personality star, the essence of the fictional character is already established. In a sense, stars are more "real" than other characters, which is why many people refer to a character by the actor's name, rather than by the name of the person in the story. After working with Hitchcock on the script of *Strangers on a Train*, the novelist Raymond Chandler ridiculed the director's method of characterization. "His idea of character is rather primitive," Chandler complained ("Nice Young Man," "Society Girl," "Frightened Woman," and so on). Like many literary types, Chandler believed that characterization must be created through language. He was insensitive to the other options available to a filmmaker. For example, Hitchcock was a cunning exploiter of the star system—a technique that has nothing to do with language. For his leading ladies, for instance, he favoured elegant blondes with an understated sexuality and rather aristocratic, ladylike manners—in short, the Society Girl type. But there are great individual differences between such heroines as Joan Fontaine, Ingrid Bergman, and Grace Kelly, to mention only three of Hitchcock's famous blondes.

8-28. *Bicycle Thieves* (Italy, 1948), *with Enzo Staiola and Lamberto Maggiorani, directed by Vittorio De Sica.*
One of the most famous casting coups in film history is De Sica's selection of Maggiorani and Staiola as an impoverished labourer and his idolizing son. Both were nonprofessionals. Maggiorani actually was a labourer and had difficulty finding a factory job after this movie. When De Sica was trying to finance the film, one producer agreed to put up the money provided that the leading role was played by Cary Grant! De Sica couldn't imagine an elegant and graceful actor like Grant in the role, and the director wisely went elsewhere for his financing. *(Audio-Brandon Films)*

Hitchcock's casting is often meant to deceive. His villains were usually actors of enormous personal charm—like James Mason in *North by Northwest.* Hitchcock counted on the audience's good will toward an established star, permitting his "heroes" to behave in ways that can only be described as morally dubious. In *Rear Window,* for example, James Stewart is literally a voyeur, yet we can't bring ourselves to condemn such a wholesome type as Jimmy Stewart, the all-American boy. Audiences also assume that a star will remain in the movie until the final reel, at which point it's permissible—though seldom advisable—to kill him or her off. But in *Psycho,* the Janet Leigh character is brutally mur-

8–29a. *Romeo and Juliet* (U.S.A., 1936), *with Leslie Howard and Norma Shearer, directed by George Cukor.*
Cukor's version of Shakespeare's play is an example of the disasters that can befall a movie when a director casts against type. The lovers are a far cry from the youngsters called for in the original. Shearer was thirty-seven when she played the thirteen-year-old Juliet; Howard as Romeo was forty-four. At fifty-five, John Barrymore was preposterous as Mercutio, Romeo's firebrand friend. The spectacle of middle-aged adults behaving so childishly makes the whole dramatic action seem ludicrous.   *(MGM)*

8–29b. *Romeo and Juliet* (Britain/ Italy, 1968), *with Olivia Hussey and Leonard Whiting, directed by Franco Zeffirelli.*
Zeffirelli's version of the play is much more successful because he cast to type and awarded the roles to two teenagers. To be sure, Cukor's actors speak the lines better, but Zeffirelli's *look* truer. The differences between the ages of an actor and character are far more important on screen than on stage, for the cinematic close shot can be merciless in revealing age. Baz Luhrmann also cast young actors in his highly formalist *William Shakespeare's Romeo and Juliet* (U.S.A., 1996), updating the action to a modern city torn by ethnic violence and presenting it in a flamboyant music video style.   *(Paramount Pictures)*

8-30. *My Best Friend's Wedding* (U.S.A., 1997), *with Julia Roberts, Dermot Mulroney, and Rupert Everett; directed by P.J. Hogan.*
"Show me an actor with no personality, and I'll show you someone who isn't a star," Katharine Hepburn once observed. In the contemporary cinema, Julia Roberts radiates personality. She is beloved by the public, but not just for her spectacular good looks and captivating smile. At her best, she can transform even a manipulative schemer like this into an irresistible charmer, in an acting style that's so spontaneous it hardly looks like she's working
(TriStar Pictures)

dered in the first third of the film—a shocking violation of convention that jolts audiences out of their complacency. Sometimes Hitchcock cast awkward, self-conscious actors in roles requiring a note of evasive anxiety, like Farley Granger in *Rope* and *Strangers on a Train*. In cases such as these, bad acting is precisely what is called for—it's part of the characterization.

Many filmmakers believe that casting is so integral to character, they don't even begin work on a script until they know who's playing the major roles. Yasujiro Ozu confessed, "I could no more write, not knowing who the actor was going to be, than an artist could paint, not knowing what colour he was using." Billy Wilder always tailored his dialogue to fit the personality of his players. When Montgomery Clift backed out of playing the lead in *Sunset Boulevard,* Wilder rewrote the part to fit William Holden, who brought totally different character nuances to the role.

A change in the cast can profoundly alter the impact and meanings of a film even without changes in dialogue. In Atom Egoyan's *The Sweet Hereafter,* the

8–31. *The Crying Game* (Ireland/Britain, 1992), *with Jaye Davidson and Stephen Rea, written and directed by Neil Jordan.*
Unfamiliar performers enjoy an obvious superiority over stars—the public has no way of guessing what kind of people they're playing. Nonprofessional players and little-known actors can surprise us with astonishing revelations. In this movie, the character surprises send the story spinning into totally new directions. If the main characters had been played by personality stars, the audience would have guessed in advance what makes the characters tick, for the star system is a form of precharacterization. With actors like Davidson and Rea, we must judge the characters only as their bizarre tale unfolds.   *(Miramax Films)*

internationally known Canadian actor Donald Sutherland was originally cast as the lawyer who arrives in a small British Columbia community to persuade bereaved families to take legal action after their children have died in a school bus accident. Sutherland, who usually brings a nervous intensity to his performances, withdrew at the last moment, and Egoyan turned to British actor Ian Holm, whose restrained performance gives the role a powerful ambiguity that enhances the emotional impact of the film.

COSTUMES AND MAKEUP

The effect of an actor's performance also depends on the work of costume designers and makeup artists. Costumes and makeup aren't merely frills added to enhance an illusion, but aspects of character and theme. Their style can reveal class, self-image, even psychological states. Depending on their cut, texture, and bulk, certain costumes can suggest agitation, fastidiousness, deli-

8–32. *The Leopard* **(Italy, 1963),** *art direction by Mario Garbuglia, costumes by Piero Tosi, directed by Luchino Visconti.*

Visconti had the unusual distinction of being both a Marxist and an aristocrat (he was the Duke of Modrone). A master of the period film, he was exceptionally sensitive to the symbolic significance of costumes and décor. They are part of Visconti's political statement. For example, the clutter, texture, and florid patterns of the Victorian furnishings in this movie suggest a stifling, hothouse artificiality, sealed off from nature. The costumes, impeccably accurate to period, are elegant, constricting, and totally without utility. They were meant to be. Idle people of independent income—that is, income derived from the labour of others—rarely concern themselves with utility in clothing. *(Twentieth Century-Fox)*

cacy, and so on. A close-up of a fabric can suggest information that's independent even of the wearer. One of the directors most sensitive to the meanings of costumes was Sergei Eisenstein. In his *Alexander Nevsky*, the invading German hordes are made terrifying primarily through their costumes. The soldier's helmets, for example, don't reveal the eyes: Two sinister slits are cut into the fronts of the metal helmets. Their inhumanity is further emphasized by the animal claws and horns the officers have at the top of their helmets as insignia. The highly ornate armour they wear suggests their decadence and machinelike impersonality. An evil churchman is costumed in a black monk's habit: The sinister hood throws most of his hawklike features into darkness. In contrast, Nevsky and the Russian peasants are costumed in loose, flowing garments. Even their war armour reflects a warm, humane quality. Their helmets are shaped like Russian church onion domes and permit most of the features of the face to be seen. Their chain mail reminds the viewer of the fishing nets of the earlier portions of the movie, where the peasants are shown happiest at their work repairing their fishing nets.

Colour symbolism is used by Zeffirelli in *Romeo and Juliet*. Juliet's family, the Capulets, are characterized as aggressive parvenus: Their colours are appropriately "hot" reds, yellows, and oranges. Romeo's family, on the other hand, is older and perhaps more established, but in obvious decline. They are costumed in blues, deep greens, and purples. These two colour schemes are echoed in the liveries of the servants of each house, which helps the audience identify the combatants in the brawling scenes. The colour of the costumes can also be used to suggest change and transition. The first view of Juliet, for example, shows her in a vibrant red dress. After she marries Romeo, her colours are in the cool blue spectrum. Line as well as colour can be used to suggest psychological qualities. Verticals, for example, tend to emphasize stateliness and dignity (Lady Montague); horizontal lines tend to emphasize earthiness and comicality (Juliet's nurse).

Perhaps the most famous costume in film history is Charlie Chaplin's tramp outfit. The costume is an indication of both class and character, conveying the complex mixture of vanity and dash that makes Charlie so appealing. The moustache, derby hat, and cane all suggest the fastidious dandy. The cane is used to give the impression of self-importance as Charlie swaggers confidently before a hostile world. But the baggy trousers several sizes too large, the oversized shoes, the too-tight coat—all these suggest Charlie's insignificance and poverty. Chaplin's view of humanity is symbolized by that costume: vain, absurd, and—finally—poignantly vulnerable.

In most cases, especially period films, costumes are designed for the performers who will be wearing them. The costumer must always be conscious of the actor's body type—whether he or she is thin, overweight, tall, short, etc.—to compensate for any deficiency. If a performer is famous for a given trait—Dietrich's legs, Monroe's bosom, Schwarzenegger's chest—the costumer will often design the actor's clothes to highlight these attractions. Even in period films, the costumer has a wide array of styles to choose from, and his or her choice will often be determined by what the actor looks best in within the parameters defined by the milieu of the story.

During the Hollywood studio era, powerful stars often insisted on costumes and makeup that heightened their natural endowments, regardless of period accuracy. This was a practice that was encouraged by the studio bosses, who wanted their stars to look as glamorous as possible by suggesting a "contemporary look." The results are usually jarring and incongruous. Even prestigious directors like John Ford gave in to this tradition of vanity. In Ford's otherwise superb western, *My Darling Clementine* (1946), which is set in a rough frontier community, actress Linda Darnell, one of Twentieth Century–Fox's biggest stars, was allowed to wear glamorous star makeup and a 1940s-style hairdo, even though the character she was playing was a cheap Mexican "saloon girl"—a coy period euphemism for a prostitute. She looks as though she just stepped out of a Max Factor salon after receiving the Deluxe Treatment.

In realistic contemporary stories, costumes are often bought off the rack rather than individually designed. This is especially true in stories dealing with ordinary people, people who buy their clothes in department stores.

8-33. *Barry Lyndon* (U.S.A./Britain, 1975), *with Ryan O'Neal and Marisa Berenson (seated in boat), directed by Stanley Kubrick.*
"What I'm after is a majestic visual experience," Kubrick has said of his movies. The visual style of *Barry Lyndon*—the costumes, the sets, the photography—is modelled on the paintings of the eighteenth-century masters, especially Gainsborough and Watteau. One of the most exquisitely mounted movies in history, Kubrick's film is an exposé of the rotten morality that underlined the glacéed elegance of eighteenth-century Europe during "the Age of Enlightenment." The movie won Oscars for cinematography (John Alcott), art direction (Ken Adam, Vernon Dixon, and Roy Walker), and costume design (Milena Canonero and Ulla-Britt Soderlund).   *(Warner Bros.)*

When the characters are lower class or poor, costumers often purchase used clothing. For example, in *On the Waterfront*, which deals with dock workers and other working-class characters, the costumes are frayed and torn. Costumer Anna Hill Johnstone bought them in used-clothing stores in the neighbourhood adjoining the waterfront area.

Makeup in the cinema is generally more subtle than on stage. The theatrical actor uses makeup primarily to enlarge his or her features so they'll be visible from long distances. On the screen, makeup tends to be more understated, although Chaplin used stage makeup for the tramp character because he was generally photographed in long shot. Even the most delicate changes in makeup can be perceived in the cinema. Mia Farrow's pale green face in *Rosemary's Baby*, for example, was used to suggest the progressive corruption of her body while she is pregnant with the devil's child. Similarly, the ghoulish makeup of the actors in Fellini's *Satyricon* suggests the degeneracy and death-in-life aspect of the Roman population of the period. In *The Graduate*, Anne Bancroft is almost chalk white in the scene where she is betrayed by her lover.

8–34. *Terms of Endearment* (U.S.A., 1983), *with Jack Nicholson and Shirley MacLaine, written and directed by James L. Brooks.*
"Clothing is a wonderful doorway that most easily leads you to the heart of an individual," author Tom Wolfe has noted. "It's how characters reveal themselves." Costumer Ellen Miroj-nick concurs, adding that you can read 95 percent of a character entirely from visuals and body language. In this scene, for example, a womanizing former astronaut circles in on his next-door-neighbour, who is far from reluctant to receive his amorous hints. We don't need to hear what she says in response to his tentative probes. Her clothing and body language say it all.   *(Paramount Pictures)*

In *Tom Jones*, Richardson used elaborate, artificial makeup on the city characters like Lady Bellaston to suggest their deceitfulness and decadence. (In the eighteenth-century comedy of manners, cosmetics are a favourite source of imagery to suggest falseness and hypocrisy.) The country characters, on the other hand, especially Sophy Western, are made up more naturally, with no wigs, powder, and patches.

Cinematic makeup is closely associated with the type of performer wearing it. In general, stars prefer makeup that tends to glamourize them. Monroe, Garbo, and Harlow usually had an ethereal quality. Marlene Dietrich probably knew more about makeup than any star of her generation—glamour makeup, that is. Straight actors and actor stars are less concerned with glamour unless the characters they're playing are in fact glamorous. In an effort to submerge their own personalities, such performers often use makeup to disfigure the familiarity of their features. Brando and Olivier were particularly likely to wear false noses, wigs, and distorting cosmetics. Because Orson Welles was known primarily for playing strong domineering roles, he resorted to such tricks in makeup to maximize the differences between the roles. Nonprofessional players probably wear the least amount of makeup, because they're chosen precisely because of their interesting and authentic physical appearance.

Costume and makeup are especially important in constructing and maintaining a star image. A personality star will usually wear similar costumes and makeup from film to film, and these become an essential part of the performance. In certain cases—Chaplin's tramp outfit, for example—a recurring costume, supported by appropriate makeup, becomes totally fused with the star persona **(4–30)**. Actor stars, on the other hand, often take pride in their ability to change their appearance; costumes and makeup support the actor's physical skills. When Robert De Niro played an overweight retired boxer in *Raging Bull*, he put on weight to suit the part but also used costumes and makeup to show the character aging and the changes in his lifestyle **(1–7a)**. Even when nonactors wear what appear to be their own clothes and no makeup, these choices become part of the meaning of their performance.

FURTHER READING

BLUM, RICHARD A., *American Film Acting: The Stanislavski Heritage* (Ann Arbor, Mich.: UMI Research Press, 1984). History of Method Acting in America.

DMYTRYK, EDWARD, and JEAN PORTER, *On Screen Acting* (London: Focal Press, 1984). Practical emphasis.

DYER, RICHARD, *Stars* (London: British Film Institute, 1979). A systematic analysis, well-written.

NAREMORE, JAMES, *Acting in the Cinema* (Berkeley: University of California Press, 1988). Comprehensive.

OLIVIER, LAURENCE, *Laurence Olivier on Acting* (New York: Simon & Schuster, 1986).

ROSS, LILLIAN, and HELEN ROSS, *The Player: A Profile of an Art* (New York: Simon & Schuster, 1962). A collection of interviews with actors from stage, screen, and TV.

SCHICKEL, RICHARD, *The Stars* (New York: Dial Press, 1962). See also Richard Griffith, *The Movie Stars* (Garden City, N.Y.: Doubleday, 1970). Studies by two of America's best film critics.

SHIPMAN, DAVID, *The Great Movie Stars*, Vol. I, *The Golden Years* (New York: Bonanza Books, 1970); Vol. II, *The International Years* (New York: St. Martin's Press, 1972), Encyclopedic coverage, with sane, well-written evaluations.

WALKER, ALEXANDER, *Stardom, The Hollywood Phenomenon* (London: Penguin, 1974). Well-written history and analysis.

ZUCKER, CAROLE, *Figures of Light: Actors and Directors Illuminate the Art of Film Acting* (New York: Plenum Press, 1995).

NONFICTION FILMS | 9

National Film Board of Canada

You photograph the natural life, but you also, by your juxtaposition of detail, create an interpretation of it.
—JOHN GRIERSON

SUMMARY

Documentary as evidence and interpretation. The stages of documentary film history. The emergence of the classical documentary: Flaherty and Grierson. The early years of the National Film Board of Canada. Cinéma vérité in the United States. Direct cinema in Canada. Censorship and the problem of objectivity. Avant-garde cinema: visionary and structural films.

The term nonfiction film is most commonly applied to documentary cinema, but it has also been used to describe **avant-garde** films. These two filmmaking practices—documentary and the avant-garde—are the major alternative modes to the fiction films we normally expect to find in local cinemas and with which this book is mostly concerned. While they occupy opposite poles on the classification chart of styles and types of film (**1–1**), documentary **realism** and avant-garde **formalism** both start from a suspicion of the use of spectacle and narrative in fiction films to involve spectators in a world of fantasy and illusion. The distinction between fiction and nonfiction is not as easy to make as some filmmakers and theorists imply, but these alternative modes do raise important questions about the medium that need to be examined.

9-1.   *JFK* (U.S.A., 1991), *with Kevin Costner (centre), written and directed by Oliver Stone.*
As a number of historians have pointed out, "history" is actually a jumble of fragments, unsifted facts, random events, and details that no one thought were important enough to explain. This chaos is sorted out by a historian who superimposes a narrative over the sprawling materials. The historian excludes some facts, heightens others. Effects are provided with causes; isolated events are connected with other superficially remote events. In short, many modern historians would insist that the past contains various histories, not just one. Each history is the product of a person who assembles, interprets, and shapes the facts into a narrative. Oliver Stone's controversial depiction of the assassination of President Kennedy is told from the point of view of New Orleans D.A. Jim Garrison (Costner). The movie does what an historian does: It offers a possible explanation for a traumatic national tragedy that was never adequately resolved in the minds of much of the American public.   *(Warner Bros.)*

THE DOCUMENTARY MODE

The documentary mode depends on the basic assumption that film images provide evidence of a state of affairs that exists, or once existed, in the world outside the film. Documentaries deal with facts and claim to present these facts objectively, unlike fiction films which involve us with the subjective viewpoints of characters, even in stories based on actual events. Many filmgoers assume that documentaries must be dry and boring, at best a useful source of information; and there are, of course, many unassuming instructional documentaries. However, no documentary is simply an objective representation of facts, and the key question for the great documentary filmmakers has been how to create a convincing interpretation of reality without distorting the evidence.

If fiction films create meanings through narrative structure—the relations of **story** and **plot**—documentaries are structured more like essays. The raw images provide the evidence that is then organized to develop an argument. This argument is constructed largely through the way in which the images are **edited** together and through the way in which the images relate to the soundtrack. In the course of film history, documentary has evolved a number of different approaches to the relations of argument/interpretation to evidence/reality. These stages can be compared with the ways in which critics have classified **genre** movies (see Chapter 2):

1. *Primitive or formative.* This is the stage in which the idea of documentary emerged and the basic issues and conventions were established. It is usually associated with films made by Robert Flaherty during the 1920s.
2. *Classical.* In this phase the conventions were used and developed with an underlying confidence in their ability to express important truths about reality. This stage was most fully developed in the ideas and work of John Grierson during the 1930s.
3. *Revisionist or critical.* During this stage documentaries became less certain about their treatment of reality and began to question the conventions developed in the classical stage. In the 1950s and 1960s, this skeptical attitude was found in diverse movements, variously defined as **cinéma vérité** or **direct cinema**, that sprang up in many countries, especially France, Britain, the United States, and Canada.
4. *Parodic or reflexive.* Documentary films from this stage increasingly draw attention to the conditions in which they are made, reflecting the new sophistication of viewers in the television age and perhaps also a new sense that it is now often impossible to distinguish between image and reality.

These four stages suggest the range and complexity of the films and theory of documentary. Although we will focus on developments in the United States and Canada since the 1950s, we need to look briefly at the conventions of the classical stage since these provide a model against which later filmmakers have defined their own practices. (Of course, many documentaries continue to be made using the classical approach.)

9-2. *Roger & Me* (U.S.A., 1989), *with Michael Moore (centre), written, directed, and produced by Moore.*

The premise of this reflexive documentary is that if only Moore could get to talk to Roger Smith, the then-President of General Motors, perhaps Smith could explain GM's closing of its Flint, Michigan, plants in favour of cheap labour abroad. The premise is a pretext for showing us the harsh economic consequences of the close-down on the residents of Flint—a sad tale of desperation, resourcefulness, and despair. The movie is frankly one-sided and manipulative—a hard sell. But it's also compassionate, shrewd, and very funny.   *(Warner Bros.)*

GRIERSON AND THE CLASSICAL DOCUMENTARY

The first films made and screened by the Lumière brothers in 1895 **(6–2)** were brief segments of everyday life, often referred to as "actualities." Although fiction cinema soon emerged as the dominant mode, many newsreels, travelogues, and other nonfiction films continued to be made and shown in commercial cinemas. This period even saw the first controversies about the ethics of nonfiction filmmaking when actual events were re-created in the **studio** and passed off as newsreel coverage. However, despite these forerunners, most historians argue that the first true documentary was the work of Robert Flaherty, an American explorer who used a camera to record his travels in the Canadian Arctic and eventually released a feature film called *Nanook of the North* (1921) **(9–3)**.

The term "documentary" was first applied to film by John Grierson to describe Flaherty's second film, *Moana* (1925), made during a trip to Polynesia. Grierson was a Scottish sociologist who had visited the United States to study the social effects of the mass media, and he used Flaherty's films to argue his

9–3. *Nanook of the North* **(U.S.A., 1922),** *directed by Robert Flaherty.*
Often regarded as the first documentary, this film also raised some of the basic problems of documentary ethics. Flaherty was quite prepared to alter the reality in front of his camera to capture what he saw as the essential reality of the way of life of Nanook and his family. This way of life was fast disappearing, and Flaherty wanted to preserve it on film. Ironically, in doing so, he was helping to introduce the people to modern technology.

case that the influence of film should be used for social purposes, not just for the escapist fantasies of Hollywood cinema. He felt that Flaherty had shown the way but had not yet gone far enough, because he still organized his films around the exploits of an individual hero and tended to present a romantic view of exotic cultures.

Flaherty's attitude to the reality he depicted also raised problems. On the one hand, he stayed with the people he was filming for a considerable time to learn about their ways and to allow them to become comfortable in the camera's presence. The use of **long takes** and **deep focus** to preserve the duration and the space of the actual events added to the impression of authenticity, as critic André Bazin pointed out when he included Flaherty in his list of admired realist directors. On the other hand, Flaherty was quite prepared to interfere in the events to capture what he saw as the essence of reality. When Nanook was unable to find a seal to hunt, Flaherty had a dead seal flown in and filmed the hunter's epic struggle to land it in one impressive long take. He also persuaded Moana, the subject of his second film, to undergo a painful tattooing ceremony that was no longer practised by his people.

Flaherty's first two films were supported by Hollywood studios and **distributed** in commercial cinemas, but the **studio** executives were dismayed by the high **shooting ratios** that his approach entailed. Ironically, Grierson came to share the Hollywood response when he invited Flaherty to Britain to work on *Industrial Britain* (1932), which Grierson eventually finished himself. He thought that Flaherty was too concerned with making his images beautiful and not concerned enough with the social purposes of a film intended to demonstrate the benefits of industrial development.

By this time, Grierson was not just writing about documentary; he was putting his ideas into action. He directed only one film, *Drifters* (1929), about the North Sea fishing industry, in which he combined Flaherty's observational approach with a use of **montage** influenced by Soviet cinema. His major contribution to the future of documentary was made as a **producer** whose enthusiasm could convince governments and industry of the value of sponsoring films that would make people more aware of social issues. He set up film units in Britain, first at the Empire Marketing Board in 1927 and then at the General Post Office in 1933, and he was also responsible for the establishment of the National Film Board of Canada in 1939.

In his brief, but highly influential definition, Grierson referred to documentary as the "creative treatment of actuality." Although he often stressed the social objectives of documentary rather than its aesthetics, Grierson was well aware of the need for creative techniques to develop a convincing interpretation of actuality. Two of the most famous films produced by the GPO Film Unit—*Coalface* (1935) and *Night Mail* (1936)—included poetry by W.H. Auden and music by Benjamin Britten. More typically, however, Grierson's documentaries established the classical style in which the images are subservient to a verbal argument that has been scripted in advance. The commentary unifies the film and is spoken in a voice of authority. It is often referred to as a **voice-of-God commentary**, since the speaker is apparently omniscient and remains off screen and, for reasons that did not have to be justified at the time, the voice is always male.

Grierson's approach has been criticized for three major reasons:

1. He wanted to bring about social change, but his reliance on government and industrial sponsorship often meant that social criticism gave way to propaganda and advertising.
2. He argued that documentary was opposed to the "illusions" of the Hollywood dream factory, but the classical style, like its fictional counterpart, depended on the spectator not being aware of the filmmaking process and also on the assumption that this process in no way affected the filmed events.
3. The emphasis on the commentary meant that people were not allowed to speak for themselves, which ran contrary to Grierson's theoretical stress on documentary as a force for democracy.

Despite these criticisms, Grierson's energetic championing of the documentary cause firmly established its importance and continues to influence discussion today.

Grierson did produce one film that allowed the people involved to speak about social problems. The film was *Housing Problems* (1935), made to draw attention to living conditions in the urban slums of Britain and to promote the building of modern housing estates. It begins with a voice-of-God commentator who introduces the topic but then gives way to the voice of an expert, a local politician who describes examples of squalor and neglect. He remains off screen but speaks in a somewhat less polished style than the commentator. We are then shown some of the slum dwellers who stand in their homes as they describe what it is like to live in them. The working-class accents and colourful idioms used by these speakers give their testimony a powerful authenticity, but the very fact that they are on screen diminishes their authority, especially since they seem uncomfortable in the glare of the lights required by the location shooting (**9–4**).

Grierson later claimed that this film was the origin of cinéma vérité, but the framing of the slum dwellers' testimony by more official voices limits its impact. Since the film was sponsored by a gas company that would profit from the construction it was promoting, its social purpose coexists with a public rela-

9–4. *Housing Problems* **(Britain, 1935),** *directed by Arthur Elton and Edgar Anstey.*
Evidence of slum conditions is provided not only by the camera, which shows wallpaper peeling off the walls, but also by the people who describe the experience of living in such conditions. We are asked to identify with the victims and then to welcome the solution provided by the modern housing estate seen at the end of the film.

9–5. *Churchill's Island* **(Canada, 1941),** *directed by Stuart Legg.*
Legg, who was recruited by Grierson from the British documentary movement, was the master of the compilation film, editing archival footage to illustrate an argument forcefully delivered by a voice-of-God commentary. This film, released in the National Film Board's *World in Action* series, argued that Britain would win the war because of the determination of its people. It won the Oscar for best short documentary in 1941. *(National Film Board of Canada)*

tions function. This is not necessarily a problem, but it does perhaps suggest why the film does not tackle such issues as the effects of relocation on the community. *Housing Problems* is an early indication that the question of who is speaking in a documentary is never an easy one, even when interviews and other strategies seem to allow people to speak for themselves.

A more typical case of the role of the commentary in the classical documentary is found in a film produced by Grierson at the National Film Board in Canada. *Alexis Tremblay, Habitant* (1943) was directed by Jane Marsh, one of a number of women recruited to work at the film board during World War II, and was part of a project to promote awareness of the lives of people in different regions of the country. In this case, the film depicted a year in the life of a family in rural Quebec, but the English commentary, spoken by a male voice, effectively overrides the French voices of the film's subjects and the female voices of its makers.

Grierson's arrival in Canada coincided with the outbreak of war, and the early years of the NFB were devoted mainly to the production of documentaries in support of the war effort. These films were organized into two extended series, *Canada Carries On* and *World in Action*, and consisted mainly of archival footage (some of it captured from the enemy) selected to illustrate the argument put forward with great urgency by a voice-of-God commentator **(9–5)**. When Grierson resigned as commissioner in 1945, after becoming involved in a spy scandal, the young Canadian filmmakers at the NFB were uncomfortable with applying his methods to the less urgent but more complicated problems of the postwar period. Some attempted to expand the range of documentary through the use of dramatized reconstruction, but it was not until the 1950s that a new and distinctive approach emerged at the NFB.

AMERICAN CINÉMA VÉRITÉ

The documentary movement in general lost much of its momentum in the years after World War II, and it was only the development of lightweight equipment that led to a new approach to documentary in the 1950s. Cinéma vérité or direct cinema filmmakers set out to explore reality, insisting that the film should be shaped by what was found in the process of making it, and not "scripted" in advance. This exploration of reality was to be shared by the spectator, whose response would no longer be guided by an authoritative commentary.

Different versions of this new approach appeared at about the same time in several countries. In Britain, the Free Cinema movement, a loose-knit group of young filmmakers led by Lindsay Anderson, experimented with personal and poetic visions of the social environment. One of the most successful of these works is Karel Reisz's film about a working-class youth club, *We Are the Lambeth Boys* (1959). In France, the development of the new approach was closely linked to the needs of ethnographic filmmakers, who were looking for equipment that could be transported easily to the remote locations where they recorded the rituals and customs of the cultures they were studying. The key figure was Jean Rouch, an anthropologist who worked extensively in Africa and whose highly influential version of cinéma vérité was very sensitive to the influence of both the ethnographer and the camera on the events being recorded.

In the United States, the new approach to documentary was more directly linked to the arrival of television. Because of its need to capture news stories quickly, efficiently, and with minimal crew, television journalism was responsible for the development of a new technology, which in turn led eventually to a new philosophy of truth in documentary cinema. The technology included a range of hardware:

1. A lightweight 16 mm **handheld** camera that allowed the cinematographer to roam virtually anywhere with ease.
2. Flexible **zoom lenses** that permitted the **cinematographer** to go from 12 mm **wide-angle** positions to 120 mm **telephoto** positions in one adjusting bar.
3. New **fast film stocks** that allowed for scenes to be photographed without setting up lights. So sensitive were these stocks to **available lighting** that even nighttime scenes with minimal illumination could be recorded with acceptable clarity.
4. A portable tape recorder that allowed a technician to record sound directly in automatic **synchronization** with the visuals. This equipment was so easy to use that only two people—one at the camera, the other with the sound system—were required to bring in a news story.

The flexibility of this equipment permitted documentaries to redefine the concept of authenticity. This new aesthetic amounted to a rejection of pre-planning and carefully detailed scripts. A **script** involves preconceptions about reality and tends to cancel out any sense of spontaneity or ambiguity. Cinéma

9–6. *Law and Order* (U.S.A., 1969), *directed by Frederick Wiseman.*
Cinéma vérité prided itself on its objectivity and straightforward presentation. Of course, the documentarists realized that total neutrality is an impossible goal to achieve. Even Wiseman, among the most objective of documentarists, insists that his movies are a subjective *interpretation* of actual events, people, and places. He tries to be as "fair" as possible in presenting his materials. For example, he refuses to use off-screen narrators. The subjects of the film are allowed to speak for themselves, and the burden of interpretation is placed on the spectators, who must analyze the significance of the material on their own.   *(Zipporah Films)*

vérité rejected such preconceptions as fictional: Reality is not being observed; rather, it is being arranged to conform to what the script says it is. The documentarist is superimposing a **plot** over the materials. Re-creations of any kind are no longer necessary because crew members can be present at an event and capture it while it's happening.

The concept of minimal interference with reality became the dominant preoccupation of the American school of cinéma vérité. The filmmaker must not control events in any way. Re-creations—even with the people and places actually involved—were unacceptable. Editing was kept to a minimum, for otherwise it could lead to a false impression of the sequence of events. Actual time and space were preserved whenever possible by using lengthy takes.

Cinéma vérité also uses sound minimally. These filmmakers were—and still are—hostile to voice-of-God commentaries that tend to interpret images

9-7.   *Harlan County, U.S.A.* (U.S.A., 1977), *directed by Barbara Kopple.*
Cinéma vérité filmmakers in the United States have tended to seek out materials that are intrinsically dramatic, like crisis situations in which a conflict is about to reach its climax. For example, during the production of this documentary, which deals with a bitter coalminers' strike for decent working conditions, Kopple and her crew were repeatedly plunged into violence. In one sequence, they are actually fired on by a trigger-happy yahoo. The camera recorded it all. Implicit in the concept of documentary is the verb *to document*— to verify, to provide an irrefutable record of an event. In a nonfiction film, these privileged moments of truth generally take precedence over considerations of narrative.   *(Museum of Modern Art)*

for the spectators, relieving them of the necessity of analyzing for themselves. Some dispense with **voice-over** commentary entirely **(9–6)**.

An alternative tradition of formalistic or subjective documentaries can be traced back to the Soviet filmmaker Dziga Vertov. Like most Soviet artists of the 1920s, Vertov was a propagandist. He believed that the cinema should be a tool of the Revolution, a way of instructing workers about how to view events from an ideological perspective. "Art," he once wrote, "is not a mirror that reflects the historical struggle, but a weapon of that struggle."

Documentarists in this formalistic tradition tend to build their movies thematically, arranging and structuring the story materials to demonstrate a thesis, like the news stories on television's prestigious *60 Minutes*. In many cases, the sequence of shots and even entire **scenes** can be switched around with relatively little loss of sense or logic. The structure of the film is not based on chronology or narrative coherence, but on the filmmaker's argument **(9–8)**.

9–8. *Point of Order!* **(U.S.A., 1964),** *directed by Emile De Antonio.*
Materials that might seem politically neutral can acquire ideological significance when the footage is re-edited expressively. Many documentaries in the Vertov mould—like this exposé of the political immortality of Senator Joe McCarthy—were originally photographed by relatively impartial newsreel camera operators. The ideology is conveyed by the way in which this neutral material is restructured on the editing bench, providing a striking instance of how "plot" (or narrative structure) can radically alter "story." All montage films making use of newsreels descend from Vertov's theories. See also Jay Leyda, *Films Beget Films* (New York: Hill & Wang, 1964).   *(Continental Distributing)*

CANADIAN DIRECT CINEMA

Although the terms "cinéma vérité" and "direct cinema" have often been used interchangeably, they have also been used to distinguish between two different attitudes to the question of truth in documentary cinema:

1. The filmmaker tries to avoid interfering with reality in order to provide evidence of the way things really are, as in American cinéma vérité.
2. The filmmaker accepts that the presence of crew and equipment must affect the reality being filmed, and the film is a record of this intervention in the way things are.

Unfortunately, the terms have been applied somewhat inconsistently to describe each of these attitudes. In Canada, the American approach influenced some—mainly English-Canadian—filmmakers in the 1950s, but the emphasis has been on exploring the possibilities of the second approach, which is most commonly referred to in Canada as "direct cinema."

Another useful distinction has been made by Canadian filmmaker Michel Brault, whose innovative camerawork can be seen in many important Canadian documentaries. Brault distinguished between two kinds of direct cinema:

1. Films made with a telephoto lens, which enables actions to be filmed at a distance, often with a hidden camera.
2. Films made with a wide-angle lens, which enables the cinematographer to film people in intimate **close-ups**.

Of course, many films make use of both kinds of **lens**, and both can be used in the service of the two attitudes to documentary truth. The extreme alternatives of hidden camera (in which people are unaware that they are being filmed) and "in your face" filmmaking (in which people are unable to hide their emotions at moments of crisis) are quite familiar to the modern television audience. Both techniques involve making public what had previously been regarded as private experiences, altering the accepted boundaries between public and private life.

These developments were especially important in Canada in the 1950s, when there was virtually no production of fiction films. Documentaries were the national cinema, and it was the development of direct cinema that would eventually lead to a distinctive Canadian approach to fiction films in the 1960s (see Chapter 10). The movement had its origins in the work of Unit B at the NFB; under the leadership of producer Tom Daly, a group of young filmmakers, many of whom had worked with Norman McLaren in the **animation** department, started to make short documentaries. An emphasis on the precise editing of images for rhythmic effect was accompanied by a questioning tone far removed from the certainties of the classical documentary and from the crisis structures often used in American cinéma vérité.

Two of the earliest and most influential of these Unit B films were made in 1954. In Roman Kroitor's *Paul Tomkowicz: Street Railway Switchman*, a Polish immigrant is shown at work in the cold Winnipeg night, while the commentary consists of his own description of his feelings and experiences (the commentary was, in fact, re-recorded for intelligibility by a professional broadcaster). Colin Low's *Corral* was even more influential because it has no commentary and simply depicts a cowboy rounding up horses to the accompaniment of a solo guitar **(9–9)**.

Many of the Unit B documentaries did include commentary, but only sparingly and with a much less authoritative tone of voice than classical documentaries. They were often made for television, and many new ideas were tried out in a Canadian Broadcasting Corporation series called *Candid Eye*. The first film shown in this series was *The Days Before Christmas* (1958), for which a group of filmmakers roamed Montreal to find images and sounds that would capture the spirit of the pre-Christmas season. Its perspective is rather ambiguous, as

9–9.   *Corral* (Canada, 1954), *directed by Colin Low.*
At a fairly late stage in the editing, the filmmakers decided to dispense with commentary and to accompany the images of a round-up of wild horses with only a solo guitar piece. The result was a film that was, according to Quebec filmmaker Claude Jutra, "a precursor of all sorts of things to come."   *(National Film Board of Canada)*

sequences that stress festive good humour are set against others showing lonely people or commercial exploitation. In one sequence, which had an enormous impact on the documentary film community, Wolf Koenig picked up a camera and followed a security guard walking from inside a store to his van, maintaining a close-up of his gun in its holster.

One of the cameramen on *The Days Before Christmas* was Michel Brault, who would soon become a key figure in new developments at the French unit of the NFB and would be invited to France to work with Jean Rouch. The film board moved its headquarters from Ottawa to Montreal in 1956, and French-language production increased to meet the needs of television. Brault was credited as co-director of two of the most important early films produced by the French unit, *Les Raquetteurs* (1958), a short film in the wide-angle style on a snowshoers' convention, and *Pour la suite du monde* (1963), a beautifully shot feature-length film about a rural community on Île-aux-Coudres in the St. Lawrence River **(9–11, 9–12)**.

Because direct cinema films were not scripted in advance, administrators at the NFB now had less control over production, and French-unit film-makers could more easily deal with topics relating to Quebec's political and cultural concerns. They did, however, sometimes run into trouble after the films were completed. The most notorious case concerned Denys Arcand's *On*

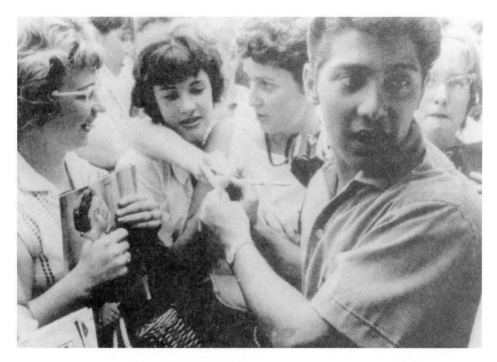

9-10. *Lonely Boy* **(Canada, 1961),** *directed by Wolf Koenig and Roman Kroitor.*
One of the most famous of the Unit B films, *Lonely Boy* deals with the effect of fame on Paul
Anka, the Canadian pop singer, as he performs in the United States. The title refers to one of
Anka's biggest hits, but it also describes Anka's personal life as the film depicts it. He is alone
among the frenzied fans, mainly young women, and very conscious of the need to maintain
a positive image. The film is often reflexive about its own role in the media circus, most
notably when Anka and the owner of a nightclub are asked to repeat an already very self-conscious embrace.   *(National Film Board of Canada)*

est au coton (1970); the title, an untranslatable pun on a colloquial phrase
meaning "We're fed up," implies a parallel between Quebec's status in Canada
and working conditions in the textile industry, the actual topic of the film.
After complaints from management, the NFB withdrew the film from circula-
tion on the grounds that it was not sufficiently objective. Since all of the workers shown in the film were francophone and many of the bosses anglophone,
this act of censorship was seen to be politically motivated, and many boot-
legged video copies were circulated among students and activists.

The vexed problem of documentary objectivity was not confined to
Quebec and has been an ongoing issue in the relations between documentary
filmmakers and the CBC. Allan King's *Warrendale* (1966) was produced for the
CBC but not shown, ostensibly because of the language used by some of the
emotionally disturbed children at the treatment centre that gives the film its
title. The decision was probably also influenced by the film's intense involve-

9–11. *Les Raquetteurs* **("The Snowshoers," Canada, 1958),** *directed by Gilles Groulx and Michel Brault.*
One of the first major works of the French unit at the NFB, this film was made on the initiative of the two filmmakers and almost consigned to the stock footage archive by producers who thought it insignificant. Brault's use of the wide-angle lens allowed him to mingle with the snowshoers at a convention in Sherbrooke, creating an affectionate if often ironic view of the events and initiating a series of direct cinema films about the collective rituals of ordinary people in Quebec. *(National Film Board of Canada)*

9–12. *Pour la suite du monde* **(Canada, 1961),** *directed by Pierre Perrault and Michel Brault.*
Perrault had already worked with the people of Île-aux-Coudres on radio programs that revealed his fascination with their language and speech. For this feature-length documentary, he persuaded the community to revive the long-abandoned practice of catching beluga whales with poles planted in the river bed. The film alternates close-ups of the inhabitants discussing the project and beautiful long shots of the men at work. As the French title suggests, the film explores the value of traditional culture in the modern world, but much of the point of the film is lost in *Moontrap*, the English-language version, which adds a commentary and eliminates most of the sequences in which the islanders speak for themselves. *(National Film Board of Canada)*

9–13. *Warrendale* **(Canada, 1966),** *directed by Allan King.*
As a documentary on a controversial method of treating emotionally disturbed children through holding and touching, *Warrendale* seeks to convey the spirit of this treatment to the spectator through its close-up involvement with its subjects. The film focuses on the children's reactions to the death of a cook which occurred during the shooting. Some critics objected to what they saw as the film's voyeuristic invasion of private space and its refusal to explain the issues, precisely the kinds of objection made to the treatment at Warrendale.   *(Allan King Associates)*

ment with the children, who are often shot in close-up, and its refusal to provide objective information about the controversial methods used at the centre **(9–13)**. King also created controversy with his next film, *A Married Couple* (1968), in which he and his crew virtually moved into a couple's home and observed their stormy relationship, giving rise to uncomfortable questions about whether it had in fact provoked the arguments that eventually led to the break-up of the marriage.

The CBC has also refused to show the films of Michael Rubbo, who was born in Australia but became one of the most innovative of the NFB documentary filmmakers. Rubbo appears on screen and provides the commentary in most of his films, which have sometimes been called "diary films." Since they depend on Rubbo's personal response to his subjects, the CBC insists that they do not meet its standards of objectivity. Indeed, these films issue a direct challenge to the concept of objectivity as they constantly remind us of the filmmaker's limited perspective. *Sad Song of Yellow Skin* (1970) opens with Rubbo ruminating on how his arrival in Vietnam changed his sense of the film he wanted to make, and *Waiting for Fidel* (1974) depicts his visit to Cuba for an interview with Fidel Castro that never takes place.

The issue of objectivity is one of the most vital in contemporary documentary practice. It has long been a key part of the professional codes of television journalism, not just at the CBC; and, of course, it is a basic principle of the classical style of documentary. Filmmakers like Rubbo and, more recently, Ross McElwee and Michael Moore in the United States **(9–2)** remind us that their perspective is personal even though the issues with which they deal exist independently and are not entirely within their control. Feminist critics and filmmakers have also challenged the standard of objectivity, arguing that it promotes an attitude to reality that excludes or devalues women's concerns.

9-14.   *Daisy: The Story of a Facelift* (Canada, 1982), *directed by Michael Rubbo.*
Rubbo has said that his main interest is in "character," a focus more usually associated with fiction films, but Rubbo argues that documentary is more interesting because the situations are "lived by a real person." He becomes a character in his own films, but his point of view is difficult to pin down. In *Daisy*, he uses the decision of a female colleague at the NFB to have a facelift as a springboard for a personal investigation into the role of appearances in our lives.   *(National Film Board of Canada)*

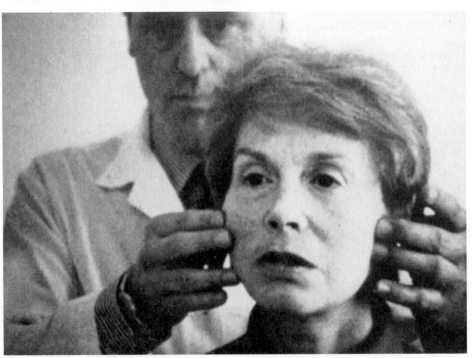

Through her work as a producer and director at the NFB, Anne Claire Poirier has tried to evolve new forms that can respond to these concerns. Her film on rape, *Mourir à tue-tête* ("*Scream from Silence*," 1979), used both fictional and documentary techniques to create a powerful emotional experience grounded in identification with the rape victim and awareness of the way women have been oppressed throughout history and in different cultures **(11–18)**. Bonnie Sherr Klein's *Not a Love Story* (1981) did not resort to fiction but was also designed to provoke feelings of outrage through its juxtaposition of women's personal responses to the pornography industry with the products of that industry **(9–15)**.

Poirier and Klein rely on the emotional impact of images of rape and pornography to convince spectators of the truth of their case, and both were accused of exploiting the degraded sexual imagery that they deplored. Both films are intensely personal, even though Poirier appears in her film only by proxy in fictional sequences in which a director works with her editor on a film

9-15. *Not a Love Story* **(Canada, 1981),** *directed by Bonnie Sherr Klein.*
Studio D, a women's film unit established at the NFB in 1974, produced many documentaries that explore contentious issues from a feminist perspective. Like Rubbo, Klein (right) appears in her own film, along with stripper Linda Lee Tracey, as they investigate the pornography industry. But unlike Rubbo, there is no doubt about Klein's point of view, as the film clearly endorses the perspective of those interviewees who argue that pornography should be censored because it leads to the degradation and abuse of women. Ironically, the pornographic images used by the film as evidence to support its argument led to the film being banned by the Ontario and Saskatchewan censor boards.   *(National Film Board of Canada)*

about rape. In these films, the personal involvement of the filmmaker is not just a matter of acknowledging that all viewpoints are personal, but of acting on the feminist principle that the "personal is political."

In the case of Alanis Obomsawin, an Abenaki singer and activist as well as filmmaker, personal involvement stems from a sense of solidarity with the cause of Aboriginal peoples. Although her work has been supported for many years by the NFB, the CBC remains uncomfortable with films whose committed stance implies the need to redress past misrepresentations. The standard of objectivity was again raised when the CBC demanded cuts to *Kanehsatake: 270 Years of Resistance* (1993), Obomsawin's feature-length documentary on the Oka crisis, and the full version was aired only after an impassioned public debate **(9–16)**.

These pressures on documentary objectivity are gaining momentum at a time when the antithesis between fiction and nonfiction can no longer be taken for granted. Fiction films like *JFK* and *Schindler's List* have borrowed documentary techniques, such as the **handheld** camera, to give their stories a sense of objectivity and authenticity **(9–1, 3–19d)**. Meanwhile, documentaries have tended to incorporate elements of fiction or performance, as in the hybrid category of the "**docudrama**," which is notoriously difficult to define.

9-16. *Kanehsatake: 270 Years of Resistance* **(Canada, 1993),** *directed by Alanis Obomsawin.* During the summer of 1990, a group of Mohawks occupied land in Oka, Quebec, that was sacred to their people but that the local authorities wished to use to expand a golf course. The result was a tense stand-off that involved the Quebec and federal governments and affected negotiations on a new constitution. Obomsawin and her crew spent most of the siege behind the barricades. As the film's title suggests, the stand-off at Oka is depicted not as an isolated incident but as the outcome of a long process in which Aboriginal peoples have been ignored and misrepresented.   *(National Film Board of Canada)*

The presence of actors in documentaries can have widely differing effects, as shown in two NFB productions from 1992. *The Valour and the Horror,* a documentary series that claimed to reveal the suppressed truth about Canada's involvement in World War II, was widely attacked when it was aired by the CBC. Its critics argued that the series was not factual or accurate and questioned the use of actors in sequences that viewers might not be able to distinguish from the more conventional documentary elements. Television audiences are probably more astute than this argument suggests, but this alleged problem certainly did not apply to *Forbidden Love,* in which fictional enactments of scenes from lesbian pulp fiction of the 1950s and 1960s are clearly distinguished from interviews with women who reveal how much this fiction meant to them in coming to terms with their own sexual identities **(9–17)**.

9–17. *Forbidden Love* (Canada, 1992), *directed by Lynne Fernie and Aerlyn Weissman.*
Many contemporary documentaries include re-enactments of events based on the testimony of witnesses. In this film, actors are used to re-enact not actual events but fictional episodes from the pulp novels that provided lesbians with secret pleasures in the 1950s and 1960s. The filmmakers use pastiche—a device of much "postmodern" art in which past styles are simulated with a knowing awareness that they are dated—not only to re-enact the fictional sequences but also to poke fun at documentary conventions. Fiction and documentary contaminate each other, and the film even presents itself as if it were pulp fiction.
(National Film Board of Canada)

AVANT-GARDE CINEMA

Whereas documentary has usually been defined in opposition to fiction, the **avant-garde** has tended to define itself in opposition to films that rely on narrative, at least on the coherent narrative structures of the classical style. Avant-garde films either do not tell stories at all or tell stories that are highly personal and simulate the fragmented patterns of inner thought. The objective is not to make statements about the world outside the film but to explore the formal properties of film as a medium and the ways in which these properties can be used to evoke the inner experience of artists and spectators.

With few exceptions, avant-garde films are not written out in advance. In part this is because the same artist usually shoots and edits the **footage** and is therefore able to control the material at these stages of the filmmaking process. Avant-garde filmmakers also value chance and spontaneity in their movies, and to exploit these elements they avoid the inflexibility of a script.

Maya Deren, an American avant-garde filmmaker of the 1940s, differentiated her kind of movie (which she called "personal" or "poetic") from mainstream commercial films primarily in terms of structure. Like a lyric poem, personal films are "vertical" investigations of a theme or situation. The filmmaker is concerned not so much with what's happening as with what a situation feels like or what it means. The film artist is concerned with probing the depths and meanings of a given moment.

According to Deren, fiction movies are like novels and plays, in that they're essentially "horizontal" in their development. Narrative filmmakers use linear structures that must progress from situation to situation, from feeling to feeling. Fiction directors don't have much time to explore the implications of a given idea or emotion, for they must keep the plot moving along.

Other avant-garde filmmakers disdain any kind of recognizable subject matter. Hans Richter and other early avant-garde artists in Europe totally rejected narrative. Richter was a champion of the "absolute film," which consists solely of abstract shapes and designs (see **6–6**). Insisting that movies should have nothing to do with acting, stories, or literary themes, Richter believed that film—like music and abstract painting—should be concerned with pure nonrepresentational forms. Many contemporary avant-garde filmmakers share these beliefs.

Richter began his experiments in abstraction in Germany in the early 1920s. An influential avant-garde movement also sprang up in France during the 1920s. The French filmmakers used recognizable but distorted images that suggested reality filtered through subjective vision. This approach provided the basis for the impressionist films of Jean Epstein (*The Fall of the House of Usher*, 1928) and Germaine Dulac (*The Smiling Madame Beudet*, 1923) as well as more shocking **surrealist** films, including *Un Chien andalou* (Luis Buñuel and Salvador Dali, 1928), which begins with a notorious sequence showing a razor blade slicing through an eyeball.

These French films deeply influenced later American avant-garde filmmakers such as Deren and Stan Brakhage who belonged to what P. Adams Sitney has called a tradition of "visionary film" (see **3–20**). The more abstract tradition re-emerged strongly in the 1960s in a movement known as "structural film." For the structural filmmakers, the form or shape of the film is a rigorous demonstration of a specific element of film language and its relation to the spectator's perceptual experience.

"Flicker films," for example, depend on the flickering of light as the frames of film move through the projector, an effect of which we are normally unaware but which becomes the central focus of these films (**9–18**). Structural films need not be entirely abstract: One of the most famous, *Wavelength* (1967), made by the Canadian artist Michael Snow, consists of a 45-minute zoom shot across a room and into a photograph of breaking waves on the opposite wall (**9–19**). A few events occur during the zoom, but they remain marginal and never add up to a coherent narrative.

9–18. *Razor Blades* **(U.S.A., 1968),** *directed by Paul Sharits.*

In Sharits's flicker film, two images (requiring separate screens and projectors) are simultaneously juxtaposed. Each filmstrip consists of irregularly recurring images—two or three frames in duration, interspersed by blank or colour frames—or purely abstract designs, like coloured stripes or circular shapes. The rapid flickering of images creates a mesmerizing stroboscopic effect, testing the audience's psychological and physiological tolerance. The content of the film is its structural form rather than the subject matter of the images as images.   *(Anthology Film Archives)*

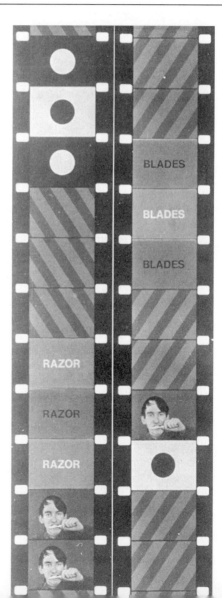

9-19. *Wavelength* **(Canada, 1967),** *directed by Michael Snow.*
Snow has been called "the most significant experimental filmmaker in the world." He is also a painter, sculptor, and musician. He has described *Wavelength* as "a continuous zoom which takes 45 minutes to go from its widest field to its smallest and final field." The zoom across a loft in New York, where Snow was living at the time, is accompanied by an electronic noise that rises in pitch as the wavelengths are continually shortened. We are occasionally distracted from these formal effects by fragments of narrative that add a touch of black humour to the film's meditation on the cinematic experience of space and time. *(Michael Snow)*

The structural approach has had a major impact on Canadian avant-garde filmmaking, encompassing the distinctive films of Joyce Wieland, David Rimmer, and Bruce Elder. In recent years, however, the avant-garde, in Canada and elsewhere, has tended to move away from exploring the specific qualities of film as a medium toward more hybrid forms that explore the implications of the diverse media images that have become part of our everyday experience, especially as they affect perception and identity. As with recent developments in documentary, the effect is to break down distinctions that had previously been taken for granted: Thus Kevin McMahon's *The Falls* (1991) can be described as an avant-garde documentary whose mixture of philosophy and humour makes it accessible to mainstream film and television audiences **(9–20;** see also **6–5).**

9-20. *The Falls* **(Canada, 1991),** *directed by Kevin McMahon.*
Documentary meets the avant-garde. As a female commentator muses on the different ways in which Niagara Falls has been "framed" in the course of history, the camera frames the Falls and the surrounding area in images that invite us to see them in new ways. Meanwhile, interviews are intercut to explore the contradictory realities of present-day Niagara Falls as tourist site, power source, and chemical waste dump.   *(Still courtesy of Primitive Features Inc.)*

FURTHER READING

BARSAM, RICHARD M., *Non-Fiction Film: A Critical History* (rev. ed.) (Bloomington: Indiana University Press, 1992). Good basic introduction to the field.

CORNER, JOHN., *The Art of Record: A Critical Introduction to Documentary* (Manchester: Manchester University Press, 1996). Thorough and accessible.

ELLIS, JACK C., *The Documentary Idea: A Critical History of English-Language Documentary Film and Video* (Englewood Cliffs, NJ: Prentice Hall, 1989). Thorough discussion of the evolution of documentary in many countries.

EVANS, GARY, *In the National Interest: A Chronicle of the National Film Board of Canada from 1949–1989* (Toronto: University of Toronto Press, 1991). Valuable historical survey.

GRANT, BARRY KEITH, and JEANETTE SLONIOWSKI, eds. *Documenting the Documentary: Close Readings of Documentary Film and Video* (Detroit: Wayne State University, 1998). Anthology of new critical essays on major documentaries.

JONES, D.B., *The Best Butler in the Business: Tom Daly of the National Film Board* (Toronto: University of Toronto Press, 1996). Biography that provides fascinating insights into the workings of the NFB.

MACDONALD, SCOTT, *Avant-Garde Film: Motion Studies* (Cambridge: Cambridge University Press, 1993). Critical analysis of selected films.

NICHOLS, BILL, *Representing Reality: Issues and Concepts in Documentary* (Bloomington: Indiana University Press, 1991). Useful and thorough exploration of documentary theory.

SITNEY, P. ADAMS, *Visionary Film: The American Avant-Garde* (New York: Oxford University Press, 1974). Major pioneering critical survey.

STEVEN, PETER, *Brink of Reality: New Canadian Documentary Film and Video* (Toronto: Between the Lines, 1993). Interviews with filmmakers.

CANADIAN CINEMA | 10

Bernard Lalonde

*I'm talking about Canada as a state of mind, as the space
you inhabit not just with your body but with your head.*
— MARGARET ATWOOD

SUMMARY

Arguments for and against national cinemas. Subsidies and quotas. Films as expressions of national identity. Impact of the global economy and independence movements. Canadian films as unfamiliar experience. English- and French-language production: two national cinemas or one? The four stages of Canadian film history. Early Canadian feature films. The Canadian Cooperation Project. The impact of the French New Wave on Canadian filmmakers. The creation of the Canadian Film Development Corporation. Cultural versus economic objectives. Adaptations of American genres. The Capital Cost Allowance Act. Films that conceal their Canadian origins. Telefilm Canada. Identity, image, and technology in recent Canadian films.

Hollywood films continue to dominate the world's screens. The glamour of the **star system** and high **production values** have enormous appeal for international audiences. Few locally produced films can match this appeal, and they must also compete with Hollywood's vast economic resources to be seen even by local audiences. Most Hollywood films have publicity budgets that equal or exceed their production budgets, and the publicity spills over national borders by means of modern communications media. Hollywood has also invested in the distribution system in many countries and has been able to exert considerable influence on governments seeking to protect national film industries. To argue for the need for national cinemas in other countries is not necessarily to argue against Hollywood cinema, but to suggest that these cinemas can provide different experiences that reflect and express distinct cultural identities.

NATIONAL CINEMA

When D.W. Griffith visited Toronto in 1925, he was the most famous filmmaker in the world. His films had done much to shape the **classical style** that gave Hollywood cinema its enormous international appeal. Canada had no film industry of its own, but Griffith told his Canadian hosts, "You should have your own films and exchange them with other countries." Twenty years later, the federal government asked John Grierson, as commissioner of the National Film Board, to advise on film policy. Not surprisingly, in view of his strong commitment to the documentary mode, Grierson's advice was very different from that of Griffith: He argued against government measures to encourage feature-film production in Canada. "What is the difference," he asked, "whether a film comes from Hollywood or Timbuktu or Saskatchewan as long as it is about the life of man as it is lived and dreamed in common everywhere?"

These two positions represent the opposite poles of the debate on national cinema. Hollywood films have an apparently universal appeal and set the norms against which other national cinemas have to define themselves. Most of these national cinemas—India and Japan are the major exceptions—have small domestic markets that cannot support a commercial film industry without some form of government aid. Although Grierson was far from alone

10-1. *The Apprenticeship of Duddy Kravitz* (1974), *with Zvee Scooler and Richard Drey-fuss, directed by Ted Kotcheff.*
The choice of an American actor to play the title role in this adaptation of Mordecai Richler's novel was highly controversial. After his recent success in *American Graffiti*, Dreyfuss was a rising Hollywood star, and his involvement ensured a much wider release than if Duddy had been played by a Canadian actor. Many Canadian productions have made similar choices, rarely with as much success as in this case. Dreyfuss's nervous intensity gives both energy and pathos to the depiction of the young Jewish entrepreneur, whose infectious charm masks a ruthless pursuit of success in business. He follows his grandfather's traditional advice that "a man without land is nobody" but, in doing so, he tramples on the feelings of all those who are close to him.   *(Paramount Pictures)*

in arguing that films should not reflect specific national cultures, virtually every nation in the world has accepted Griffith's position and has taken steps to protect its domestic film industry.

There are two basic approaches by which the state can intervene to assist filmmakers, although most nations have used a combination of the two:

1. Subsidies or tax incentives, which support production either through the investment of public money or by encouraging investment by private individuals.
2. Quotas, which target the distribution and exhibition of films by requiring that cinemas devote a certain percentage of screen time to domestic films, thus increasing the likelihood that these films will retrieve their production costs at the box office.

Both methods have been used successfully, but both have potential drawbacks. Subsidies can result in a national cinema whose films remain largely unseen because commercial screens are occupied by the latest Hollywood productions. Quotas may resolve this problem, but they can encourage the production of cheaply made films that nobody wants to see.

The issues are not just political or economic. As Margaret Atwood has argued, a nation is not just a political entity but also "a state of mind," and film critics have often explored the ways in which films express a sense of national identity. State intervention can lead to overt propaganda, as in the case of Leni Riefenstahl's *Triumph of the Will* (1935), commissioned by Adolf Hitler to express the Nazi view of a true German national identity. In a much less sinister way, the National Film Board was established in Canada in 1939 "to help Canadians in all parts of Canada to understand the ways of living and the problems of Canadians in other parts." More interesting than these conscious attempts to define (or construct) a national identity are the indirect, and often inadvertent, ways in which films reflect the traditions and cultures of the nations in which they are made.

10-2. *Highway 61* (1991), *with Valerie Buhagiar and Don McKellar, directed by Bruce McDonald.*
National identities do not exist in reality; they are myths—fictions that draw on reality but are necessarily selective. They can harden into stereotypes and can affect the behaviour of real people. Bruce McDonald's road film plays with, and disrupts, stereotypes of Canadian and American identity. Its Canadian hero, Pokey Jones (McKellar), a timid barber and part-time trumpet player, finds himself accompanying a gun-toting American (Buhagiar) down the legendary highway between Thunder Bay and New Orleans, pursued by a character who seems to be the Devil.   *(Shadow Shows)*

In discussions of national cinemas, critics look for common features and patterns of meaning that seem to express a sense of national identity, just as a **genre** critic might find evidence in westerns of deep-rooted assumptions about gender and community that have shaped American history. The risk involved in this kind of approach is that it can obscure the diversity of the national cinema, and it can lead to attempts to prescribe what films should be made rather than to describe or interpret the films that have been made. An adequate theory of national cinema cannot end up arguing that, for example, certain Canadian films are not *really* Canadian because they do not conform to a preconceived idea of the national identity.

The first major work of film criticism to focus on national identity was Siegfried Kracauer's *From Caligari to Hitler: A Psychological History of the German Film,* first published in 1948. Through close readings of German films, Kracauer argued that recurring **plot** structures and visual **motifs** express a fear of disorder and a desire for a strong authority figure, thus explaining why the Nazis had succeeded in mobilizing popular support. This book has been both influential and contentious, with its critics pointing to the circular argument it employs: The so-called national identity explains the films, while the films become evidence of the existence of this identity.

Yet there certainly are national myths that grow out of people's shared experience of history and geography and are then circulated and developed in the national culture. We are all influenced by these myths, whether we feel a close attachment to them or not, and they affect the choices made by both filmmakers and filmgoers. Because films can create such powerful effects of identification, a national cinema offers especially valuable insights into the working of these myths of national identity.

In recent years, discussions of national cinema have been complicated by political, economic, and technological changes that have deeply affected our understanding of national identity. On the one hand, the power of nation states has been challenged by the emergence of multinational corporations and by new alliances among nations, such as the European Union and the North American Free Trade Agreement. On the other hand, nations have been faced with internal pressures by demands for independence from minority groups, as seen in the violent fragmentation of the former Yugoslavia but also in the tensions created by the Quebec separatist movement in Canada.

The effects of these developments have been felt in the film industry. There has been a trend toward international co-productions in which investment from several nations allows films to be made with production values close to those that audiences have come to expect from Hollywood films. Despite some successes, the pressure to use actors from each participating nation means that this approach often results in films that lack a clear cultural identity. Movies produced through the European Union's fund to encourage co-productions have been called, disparagingly, "Europudding" films. Yet the emergence of this new global-image culture has provided outlets for low-budget film and video productions from nations or groups that previously lacked the resources to tell their own stories.

The political and technological challenges to the myths, and even the existence, of nation states, has left many countries in the world facing a crisis of national identity with which Canadians have long been familiar. In this volatile situation, Canadian cinema provides an especially relevant example of the issues at stake in approaching film through the study of national cinemas.

CANADA'S NATIONAL CINEMA(S)

According to Canadian filmmaker Patricia Rozema, "films are to society what dreams are to the individual." Unfortunately, few Canadians seem to feel that their dreams are reflected in Canadian films. Most Canadian films enjoy only short runs at cinemas in Montreal, Toronto, and Vancouver, and are rarely distributed at all in the rest of the country. When Canadians do see the products of their own national cinema, they often respond as if these were foreign films with unfamiliar conventions and cultural values. In Canadian video stores, Canadian films are most likely to be found in the "international" section.

In order to discover how and why this situation exists, we need to examine the economic and political aspects of the problem as well as the kinds of films that have been made. Economic factors obviously affect the choices made by filmmakers, but Canadian films exhibit distinctive qualities that cannot be accounted for only in economic terms. Nor should it be assumed that all Canadian films will exhibit the same qualities. We are dealing with a much larger number of films than most Canadians would assume, and with a great variety of different styles. Any attempt to define the national cinema must deal in tendencies rather than fixed categories.

Although a national cinema consists of all films produced within the national boundaries, most discussions focus on the feature films that tell the stories and develop the **iconography** that embody national myths. It is in the production of these films that the national cinema comes up most directly against Hollywood's cultural and economic power. Canada's geographical situation has made it especially vulnerable to this power, and Hollywood has historically insisted on treating Canada as part of its domestic market.

In Canada, films are produced in both of the nation's official languages, but the language barriers divide what is already a relatively small domestic market. French-language production, centred primarily in Quebec, is clearly distinguished from Hollywood cinema by linguistic difference, but anglophone filmmakers have to define themselves in relation to a dominant cinema that speaks the same language. In addition, English-language production is more geographically dispersed, with large centres in Toronto and Vancouver and production companies in almost every region of the country.

Some critics have argued that Canada's bilingual cinema is a sign of two cultures so distinct that we should really be speaking of two national cinemas, an argument that clearly parallels the political claims of Quebec separatists. The only way to judge the validity of such a claim is to examine the history of Canadian cinema in both languages, discussing the specific qualities of the films in the context of the policies and institutions that have attempted to build a national cinema. For our purposes, this history can be divided into four stages:

1. What might be called the prehistory of Canadian cinema, during which there was little feature-film production in Canada.

2. A period beginning in the early 1960s, when the production of a number of small-budget films resulted in the establishment of the Canadian Film Development Corporation (CFDC) to invest in feature-film production.

3. A period roughly from 1974 to 1984 in which the CFDC, with the help of the Capital Cost Allowance Act, emphasized commercial goals and the need for films that could compete in the international market.

4. The period since 1984, when the CFDC changed its name to Telefilm Canada and encouraged the development of smaller-budget films that have established several Canadian filmmakers as major figures in world cinema.

We will look at each of these stages in turn.

THE FORMATIVE YEARS

The first film screenings in Canada took place shortly after the Lumière brothers had perfected their invention in 1895, but Canada was a large but sparsely populated country that clearly lacked the resources to sustain its own film industry. Before Griffith's visit in 1925, there had been some sporadic feature-film production, beginning with *Evangeline* (1913), based on the poem by American poet Henry Wadsworth Longfellow dealing with the expulsion of the Acadians from Nova Scotia. Made by the Canadian Bioscope Company in Halifax, the film was directed by two Americans and had a largely American cast. A few more films followed, often produced under very difficult circumstances. The most notable of these were *Back to God's Country* (David M. Hartford, 1919) **(10–3)**, *Carry on Sergeant!* (Bruce Bairnsfather, 1928), and *The Viking* (George Melford, 1931).

The coming of sound added to the costs of filmmaking and virtually wiped out the production of feature-films in Canada for the next forty years. There were two short-lived bursts of activity that only highlighted the difficulties of Canada's situation:

1. When Britain introduced a quota system in 1927, Hollywood immediately took advantage of a loophole in the legislation that allowed films made in the British Empire to be counted as British films. The studios established branch-plant operations in British Columbia where they made so-called "quota quickies" on low budgets simply to fulfill the quota requirements. When the loophole was closed in 1938, this production boom came to an end.

10–3. ***Back to God's Country* (1919),** *with Nell Shipman, directed by David M. Hartford.*
Nell Shipman, who wrote, produced, and starred in the film, poses with a bear, one of the wild animals with whom the protagonist Dolores lives in harmony in an idyllic landscape ("God's country"). When the action moves to the "Great White North," an otherwise savage dog, Wapi, befriends Dolores and helps her save her husband from the villains. Although Shipman was born in Canada, *Back to God's Country*, shot on location in Alberta, was her only Canadian film, and the crew and cast were mainly imported from Hollywood. Her pioneering work has provoked a lot of interest among feminist film historians.

2. When the supply of French films to Quebec was curtailed by World War II, a number of domestic French-language films were produced. These films had the support of the Catholic Church and proved to be extremely popular. They were usually set in traditional rural communities but often dwelled on cruelty and perverse behaviour, pointing to serious tensions in Quebec culture **(10–4)**. The arrival of television in the early 1950s soon led to the closure of the Quebec studios.

When the Church and the conservative Union Nationale government gave their blessing to these Quebec productions, their intention was not just to provide supposed wholesome local alternatives to Hollywood films but also to counter the influence of the National Film Board. Under Grierson's guidance, NFB documentaries promoted a "pan-Canadian" viewpoint, stressing common concerns rather than regional differences and advocating the benefits of tech-

10–4. *La Petite Aurore l'enfant martyre* **(1951),** *with Lucie Mitchell and Yvonne LaFlamme, directed by Jean-Yves Bigras.*
Based on a successful play from the 1920s, this film was enormously popular with Quebec audiences. It relentlessly depicts the abuse of Aurore (LaFlamme) by her stepmother, Marie-Louise (Mitchell). Although she knows that Marie-Louise poisoned her mother, Aurore suffers in silence until she dies, despite the well-meaning efforts of the village priest. Some critics have suggested that the film provoked such intense identification because Aurore's plight reflected that of the people of Quebec before the Quiet Revolution.

nological progress. These attitudes alarmed the authorities in Quebec who wanted to preserve a traditional culture based on closeness to the land, but the NFB's perspective was shared by some younger people who were beginning the movement known as the Quiet Revolution that would lead to a period of rapid change in Quebec.

Although Grierson left Canada in 1945, he had already delivered his advice on the development of a national film policy. He urged the government to put pressure on Hollywood to live up to its "international obligations" and ensure that "a due proportion of their films are devoted to Canada." The government duly entered into negotiations with the Hollywood studios, and the result was the Canadian Cooperation Project, which came into effect in 1948. In return for the Canadian government's agreement not to introduce a quota system, the Hollywood studios agreed to ensure that Canada was mentioned as often as possible in Hollywood films in order to promote the tourist industry.

341

It seems likely that this agreement led to a reference to Canada in the Howard Hawks western *Red River* (1948). When a group of cowboys become lost, they fear that they will end up driving their cattle "across the icebergs in Canada." In addition to such rather questionable attempts to promote tourism, Hollywood did agree to make a few films set in Canada, the most distinguished of which was *I Confess*, Alfred Hitchcock's thriller made in Quebec City in 1952. The agreement remained in effect until 1958.

THE DIRECT CINEMA TRADITION

The ending of the Canadian Cooperation Project coincided with the international triumph of the French **New Wave**. Using techniques and equipment originally developed for documentary filmmaking, Truffaut and Godard and their colleagues showed a cheerful disregard for the rules of classical cinema and Hollywood production values. Their low-budget productions changed the economics of filmmaking and inspired young filmmakers in many countries to create or revive national cinemas. Several Canadian filmmakers rose to the challenge, and the early 1960s saw the production of a number of films made in difficult circumstances on shoestring budgets.

The young French filmmakers had paved the way for their own films by their work as film critics. Their Canadian counterparts, however, were deeply influenced by the Canadian documentary tradition, and many of them had been involved in the development of **direct cinema** at the NFB in the 1950s. Whereas the French films often paid **homage** to Hollywood **auteurs**, the Canadians could not share this enthusiasm. From a documentary perspective, Hollywood films had always been viewed with suspicion as mass-produced escapist fantasies. For Canadian filmmakers, Hollywood was too close for comfort, the source of popular films with which the domestic output would inevitably be compared. Hollywood was also associated with the new consumer culture which many Canadians saw as a sign of "Americanization." These early Canadian films explore all of these issues, but—like the NFB's direct cinema documentaries—they tend to raise questions rather than offer solutions.

Whereas the French New Wave had the advantage of belonging to an established national cinema and quickly achieved international recognition, the Canadian filmmakers were faced with the task of creating a national cinema virtually from scratch, at least as far as fiction films were concerned. This was a question not only of the lack of producers and production facilities but also of finding an audience. Canadian cinemas were controlled by the Hollywood studios, and the spectators who did see these new Canadian films were often puzzled by the unfamiliar experience that they offered.

There were some promising signs. A major breakthrough occurred in 1964 when two films, made under remarkably similar circumstances in Toronto and Montreal, were released. Both were, somewhat reluctantly, produced by the NFB despite its continuing commitment to documentaries. In Toronto, Don Owen used the budget for a half-hour documentary on juvenile delinquency to make *Nobody Waved Good-bye*, a largely improvised feature

10–5.   *Nobody Waved Good-bye* **(1964),** *with Julie Biggs and Peter Kastner (right), directed by Don Owen.*

Much of the enduring freshness of this film stems from its spirit of improvisation in both the dialogue and the filming of the action. At the end of the film, when Julie tells Peter that she is pregnant, Kastner had no idea what Biggs would be saying, and the look of surprise on his face is not acted. In the sequence illustrated, Peter plays chess with a French-Canadian youth (the actor was uncredited). He rejects the idea of a collective identity, which he thinks exists in Quebec, but he is not able to explain what his own values are. The sequence ends as his opponent says, "Your move, Peter." *(National Film Board of Canada)*

film on the same subject **(10–5)**. Meanwhile, in Montreal, Gilles Groulx managed to get approval to make to make a fiction film, *Le Chat dans le sac,* in which he sought to "eliminate the boundaries between documentary and fiction" **(10–6)**.

These two movies are often regarded as the founding films of a Canadian tradition of direct cinema fiction films, and critics have been divided over the implications of their similarities and differences. Groulx's film is more analytic and **formalist** in its style, in the manner of Godard's earlier films, while Owen's more observational and sometimes **lyrical** approach suggests the influence of Truffaut. Yet both films tell remarkably similar stories about adolescent males who rebel against the inadequate values of adult society.

10-6. *Le Chat dans le sac ("The Cat in the Bag,"* **1964),** *with Barbara Ulrich and Claude Godbout, directed by Gilles Groulx.*
As in *Nobody Waved Good-bye*, the young couple in this film share first names with the actors who portray them. The close relationship between actors and characters suggests that these fiction films could also be seen as documentaries about actors who have experienced similar situations in their own lives.   *(National Film Board of Canada)*

In *Nobody Waved Good-bye,* Peter is just finishing high school and engages in a self-destructive rebellion against the materialist values that his parents try to impose on him. In *Le Chat dans le sac,* Claude is trying to establish himself as a journalist and is more aware of the political context of his rebellion, reflecting the shift from a French-Canadian to a more confident Québécois identity associated with the Quiet Revolution. Yet even Claude is unable to translate this awareness into meaningful action, and declares, "I am Québécois; therefore I am searching."

Both films leave their heroes facing uncertain futures. Peter ends up alone on the road to nowhere in a stolen car after his girlfriend has just told him she is pregnant. Claude moves out of the city in an effort to simplify his life, effectively ending his complicated relationship with Barbara, a Jewish anglophone actress. He ends up standing in the snow, gazing at the distant figure of a young woman skating—an ambiguous ending that suggests the temptation to substitute an idealized image, associated with Quebec's rural past, for the messy reality of the modern urban world.

The break-up of a couple is also central to *A tout prendre* (*"The Way It Goes"*), Claude Jutra's first feature film, released in 1963, but virtually forgotten in the excitement generated by the two films of the following year **(3–22)**. In this case, the situation is more complicated because Johanne is black and Claude (played by Jutra himself) is an adolescent (in spirit, at least) who belatedly discovers that he is gay. The personal identity crisis of the male adolescent in all of these films can be seen as a metaphor for a country seeking to find terms on which it can develop a truly independent national identity. Other films in the same vein include Larry Kent's *Sweet Substitute* (1964) from Vancouver, David Secter's *Winter Kept Us Warm* (1965) from Toronto, and Pierre Patry's *Trouble-fête* (1964) from Montreal.

Two prolific Quebec directors also began their very different careers at this time. Gilles Carle made *La Vie heureuse de Léopold Z* (*"The Merry World of Léopold Z,"* 1965) at the NFB and went on to become a successful and often controversial director of films exploring the relations between sexuality and identity. Jean Pierre Lefebvre's *Le Révolutionnaire* (1965) was produced independently and was quickly followed by a series of low-budget personal films in which politics, lyricism, and humour are provokingly blended **(10–7)**. In their different ways, the films of Carle and Lefebvre draw on the direct cinema tradition but test the limits of its realist assumptions.

10–7. *Les Maudits sauvages* (*"Those Damned Savages,"* 1971), *with Pierre Dufresne, directed by Jean Pierre Lefebvre.*
In the opening sequence of Lefebvre's "almost historical film," Thomas Hébert (Dufresne) is seen trading with Aboriginal people in the year 1670. As he travels back from their camp, power lines and other signs of modernity begin to creep into the frame. At first, this seems like a terrible mistake, but then Hébert arrives in twentieth-century Montreal, and the film proceeds to use its anachronisms to explore the continuities and discontinuities over three centuries of Quebec history.   *(Cinak Ltée)*

The direct cinema films laid the groundwork for much later Canadian filmmaking. Filmed on location and with a great deal of improvisation on the part of actors and crew, they tended to rely on **long takes** and **jump cuts**, making no attempt to emulate the production values and smooth continuity of Hollywood cinema. Their loose narrative structures, fragmentary presentation, and **handheld shots** reflected the uncertainty and insecurity of their protagonists. They preferred open, and often downbeat, endings to the closed and happy endings of most Hollywood films.

Many of these qualities disturbed Canadian critics and audiences. *Nobody Waved Good-bye* was panned when it was first shown in Canada and quickly withdrawn but, after glowing reviews and a successful run in New York, it was re-released in Canada and celebrated as a promising beginning for a new Canadian cinema. *Le Chat dans le sac* was warmly received when it was first shown in Quebec but it was also boosted by praise from French critics. Although none of the direct cinema films was a huge box-office success, together they aroused enough public interest—at a time when the Montreal Expo of 1967 provoked reflection on a Canadian cultural identity—to encourage the federal government to enact legislation in support of a national cinema.

The Canadian Film Development Corporation was established in 1968 with a mandate "to foster and promote the development of a feature film industry in Canada." From the beginning, the CFDC was faced with two major problems:

1. Should its primary objective be cultural or economic? Should it support distinctively and visibly Canadian films (like the direct cinema films), or should it focus on films with high production values and "international" appeal?

2. How could it ensure that the films in which it invested were actually shown in cinemas when the government, under pressure from the Hollywood studios, would not introduce a quota system?

These problems are obviously interconnected and suggest more general questions that apply to all national cinemas: Are cultural and economic goals necessarily opposed? Does attention to local circumstances detract from the creation of films that will appeal to audiences in other countries?

The direct cinema filmmakers and their supporters insisted that the answer to both these general questions should be "no." A national cinema must be rooted in the reality of the nation and, in Canada's case at least, the reality of the various regions that make up the nation. Only films with a distinct cultural identity can deal with issues in ways that will allow audiences to relate them to their own cultural environment. If Canadian films tended to stress feelings of doubt and instability, that was because Canada had not yet achieved unity and a clear sense of national identity (or, in Quebec, because the Quiet Revolution was not really over and because the question of independence was still unresolved). If their films were rarely popular, it was because of a distribution system that ensured the expectations of Canadian audiences were shaped by Hollywood films.

The CFDC wavered between support for this line of argument and the desire to invest in films with more immediate prospects of commercial success. Yet there were some signs that the direct cinema insistence on cultural integrity might eventually pay off. The movement was encouraged by the critical and commercial success of Don Shebib's *Goin' Down the Road* (1970), a film about two young men from Cape Breton who come to Toronto in search of jobs, prove to be ill-equipped to handle the complications of life in the big city, and end up driving west in search of something better **(6–17)**. A little later, Claude Jutra's *Mon oncle Antoine* (1971), supported not by the CFDC but by the NFB, was hailed by several reviewers as "the great Canadian film," and it has since been repeatedly voted the best film ever made in Quebec and in Canada **(10–8)**. The NFB initially delayed the release of this bittersweet story of a male adolescent set in a Quebec mining community before the Quiet Revolution: Apparently the producers were disturbed by the unsettling mixture of charm and desperation that also marks Shebib's film.

10–8. *Mon oncle Antoine* **(1971),** *with Jean Duceppe and Jacques Gagnon, directed by Claude Jutra.*
Originally the film was to be called *Silent Night* (in English), a reference to both the Christmas setting and what Jutra called "Quebec's night which lasted so long." Set before the Quiet Revolution, the film centres on Bênoit (Gagnon) who lives at the village store with his Uncle Antoine (Duceppe). He observes his elders and sees how they have been ground down by the conditions in which they live, especially his uncle, who also runs an undertaking business despite his fear of the bodies. The film's apparently nostalgic tone is belied by Bênoit's critical perspective and by his own fears of death and sexuality.   *(National Film Board of Canada)*

The focus on young men who are unable or unwilling to assume the responsibilities of adult life led critic Robert Fothergill to write an article in 1973 in which he argued that Canadian cinema was populated by cowards, bullies, and clowns. He attributed this crisis in masculine identity to the pressures of trying to live up to the potent images of American popular culture. Yet there were female protagonists, also usually adolescent, in some of these films. Clarke Mackey's *The Only Thing You Know* (1971) places its heroine in a situation very much like that of Peter in *Nobody Waved Good-bye,* with subtly different effects that could be attributed to the gender difference. Paul Almond made a trilogy of English-language films in Quebec—*Isabel* (1968), *The Act of the Heart* (1970) **(8–6)**, and *Journey* (1972)—all starring Geneviève Bujold, whose bilingualism suggested that the troubled characters she played in some way represented Canada's divided culture.

There were also two films by women directors that anticipated future directions in Canadian cinema. In Sylvia Spring's *Madeleine Is...* (1970), filmed in Vancouver, a young woman finds herself caught between two men—her actual boyfriend, who is revealed to be a bully, and a gentle clown who might be a figment of her imagination. Mireille Dansereau's *La Vie rêvée* (*"Dream Life,"* 1972), deals with two young women who work for a film company where the males in authority treat women as objects **(10–9)**. Both films end with the

---

10–9. *La Vie rêvée ("Dream Life," 1972), with Véronique Le Flaguais (left), Liliane Lemaître-Auger, and Jean-François Guité, directed by Mireille Dansereau.*

Shot in super-16 mm and produced by a cooperative, this film focuses on two women employed by a commercial film company, contrasting their working lives with their fantasy lives. As Dansereau put it, in this film "the dreams are true and as real as reality." Jean-Jacques (Guité) becomes the object of their fantasies, as an imagined perfect lover, but when Isabelle (Lemaître-Auger) seduces him, he proves to be impotent. The film ends as the women tear from their walls the advertising images that have colonized their minds.   *(ACPAV)*

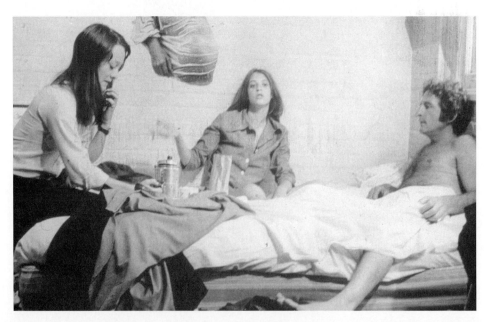

women breaking free of their dependence on men, and both introduce fantasy sequences that are sometimes difficult to distinguish from reality, adding to the effect of the blurring of the boundaries between fiction and documentary characteristic of direct cinema films.

While this direct cinema tradition continues to be a significant factor in Canadian cinema, other possibilities have emerged as a result of political and cultural changes since the 1970s. Direct cinema never really succeeded in finding an audience, and the difficult circumstances in which the filmmakers worked may have contributed to the negative dimension of their films. These films reflect a culture in search of its own norms that could provide a basis for personal and national identity. In cinema, the established norms had come from Hollywood and were often used to point to the deficiencies of Canadian films. But the "failure" to be "normal" is not necessarily negative, for either the filmmakers or their characters: It implies the possibility of a different culture and different ways of seeing.

CANADIAN GENRE FILMS

Recognizing the importance of genre in the success of Hollywood cinema, a number of Canadian filmmakers sought to adapt American genres to the Canadian situation. The two most successful English-Canadian examples were both released in 1973: Peter Pearson's *Paperback Hero*, in which a minor-league hockey player imagines he is the marshal of a small town in Saskatchewan **(10–10)**, and Don Shebib's *Between Friends*, which deals with an abortive armed robbery in a northern Ontario mining town. In both films, the American dream is betrayed by the Canadian context. Meanwhile, in Quebec, Denys Arcand directed a series of gangster films—*La Maudite galette* (1972) **(7–23)**, *Réjeanne Padovani* (1973), and *Gina* (1974)—in which political corruption and violent crime act as a metaphor for the tensions created by the independence debate and several terrorist bombings.

These, and other films like them, tried to inflect the codes of the American genres in distinctive ways that depend on their Canadian settings. Two other genre-based approaches proved more controversial, but also more commercial. In Quebec, a series of soft-core pornographic films was initiated by Denis Héroux's *Valérie* (1968), in which the heroine escapes from a convent, becomes a prostitute, and finally chooses to settle down with a painter and his young son. This film, which exploited new liberal attitudes to sexuality, was a huge box-office success and inspired many imitators. Héroux's production company, Cinépix, became identified with attempts to build a commercial cinema in Quebec based on the appeal of sex and violence. A more thoughtful treatment of these same topics is found in many of the films produced by a company founded by Gilles Carle and Pierre Lamy, most notably in Carle's own *La vraie nature de Bernadette* (*"The True Nature of Bernadette,"* 1971) and *La Mort d'un bûcheron* (1972) **(10–11)**.

The other controversial commercial success of these times was achieved by David Cronenberg, who became a key figure in the development of the mod-

10–10. *Paperback Hero* (1973), *with Keir Dullea, directed by Peter Pearson.*
In Pearson's Canadian western, the fantasies of Rick Dillon (Dullea) are never seen from his point of view, and his attempt to act like Matt Dillon, the hero of *Gunsmoke*, seems rather pathetic. Canadian reality constantly fails to match up to the American dream. In the final shoot-out, "Marshal" Dillon confronts the town's sheriff, but the tension evaporates as a farmer drives his tractor down the street and calmly wishes him "Good day." Although he is a bully and a clown, Dillon has a vitality lacking in most of the other characters in the film.
(BBS Productions, Inc.)

ern horror film. His first commercial film, known both as *Shivers* and *The Parasite Murders* (1975), was made with the support of the CFDC, and sparked a debate over whether public money should have been invested in a lurid story of sexual parasites that prey on the inhabitants of an apartment building. It proved to be the beginning of Cronenberg's successful career as a filmmaker whose "body horror" films reflect anxieties about the effects of modern technology on the human body.

Whether Cronenberg's films explore or exploit these anxieties has been a subject for debate, as has the question of their significance in relation to Canadian national cinema. They are often discussed as American genre films, but some critics see thematic similarities with the direct cinema films, especially in their concern with issues of identity and in their open endings. Their obsessive treatment of the relations between biology and technology has certainly influenced many younger Canadian directors whose films deal with similar issues outside the horror-film framework.

10–11. *La Mort d'un bûcheron ("Death of a Lumberjack," 1972), with Carole Laure, directed by Gilles Carle.*

The absent father is a recurring motif in Quebec literature and films, a reminder of pioneer times when men had to leave home to seek work, often in lumber camps. In Carle's film, Marie Chapdelaine (Laure)—named after the heroine of a classic Quebec novel—sets out in search of her father who disappeared in mysterious circumstances while working in a lumber camp. She frequently finds herself in situations where she becomes the object of men's gazes, as when she gets a job singing in a bar, and the film creates an uneasy tension between our condemnation of the male characters and the voyeurism we are invited to share. *(Les Films Gilles Carle, Inc.)*

Unlike several other Canadian filmmakers, Cronenberg has not left the country to pursue commercial success, but his films rarely draw attention to their Canadian settings. *The Dead Zone* (1983) is explicitly set in the United States, although filmed in Canadian locations. Cronenberg's remake of the classic horror film *The Fly* (1986) was filmed in Canada with two young Hollywood stars (Jeff Goldblum and Geena Davis) but it never identifies the city in which it takes place, even though the 1958 original, filmed in Hollywood, was explicitly set in Montreal, perhaps in deference to the Canadian Cooperation Project. Although *Videodrome* (1982), whose plot depends on cross-border television signals, has an explicitly Canadian setting **(2–22)**, the undistinguished cities of films like *Scanners* (1980) and *Dead Ringers* (1988) suggest that technology, based on the use of reason to control nature, has created an ordered and uniform environment which, among other things, eradicates any distinctive national characteristics.

These varied attempts to adopt and adapt Hollywood genres led the CFDC to place more emphasis on the economic than the cultural aspect of its mandate. This tendency was encouraged by the enactment in 1974 of the Capital Cost Allowance Act (CCA), which allowed investments in Canadian films to be claimed as a 100 percent tax shelter. Although there was an immediate increase in production activity, the need to attract investors who might be unfamiliar with Canadian cinema meant that many films were made with imported "**stars**" (usually young or aging Hollywood actors) and crew. Many films were never released because even these supposedly commercial films could not resolve the distribution problem and, in any case, they had already fulfilled their function of providing tax relief for the investors. While the complex regulations ensured that lawyers made profits, the Canadian direct cinema filmmakers were virtually excluded from these "boom" years.

Many of the films produced under the CCA were Canadian in name only; they masqueraded as Hollywood films, going to great lengths to conceal such identifying features as car licence plates. One of the more successful films of this period was *The Changeling* (1979), a horror film voted "best film" at the Canadian Film Awards, which had a British director (Peter Medak) and an American star (George C. Scott), and whose locations in Ontario and Vancouver were labelled in the film as northern New York State and Seattle. The biggest box-office hit, however, was *Porky's* (Bob Clark, 1981), an adolescent sex comedy set in Florida in the 1950s, whose cast included a few Canadian actors. On a more positive note, the CCA also supported *The Grey Fox* (Philip Borsos, 1982), an ironic and moving western about an aging American train robber who tries to settle down in Canada.

Despite a few isolated successes, the CCA failed to achieve its economic goals and certainly worked against the cultural distinctiveness of Canadian cinema. However, a number of films made at this time did show that the tension between economic and cultural objectives could have positive results. In 1974, Canadian filmmaker Ted Kotcheff, who been working in Britain since 1959, returned to direct *The Apprenticeship of Duddy Kravitz*, which—despite some protests against the casting of an American actor (Richard Dreyfuss) in the title role—proved to be a lively and engaging adaptation of Mordecai Richler's novel **(10–1)**. Silvio Narizzano also returned from Britain to direct *Why Shoot the Teacher* (1976), whose stunning images of the prairies in winter make up for its slightly sentimental story about a teacher from the east (played by American actor Bud Cort) who comes of age in Saskatchewan during the Depression. And it was an American director, Richard Benner, who made perhaps the **archetypal** film about Canadian identity in *Outrageous!* (1977): A female impersonator and a schizophrenic woman are outcasts in Canadian society but eventually triumph when they move to New York **(10–12)**.

During this period, Quebec cinema was subject to strong commercial pressures to make films in English. In marked contrast, some filmmakers made **low-key** intimate films depicting human relationships in a domestic context without much drama or action. Two early examples of this tendency were released in 1973: Jean Pierre Lefebvre's *Les Dernières fiançailles* (*"The Last*

10–12. *Outrageous!* **(1977),** *with Allan Moyle (left), Craig Russell, and Hollis McLaren, directed by Richard Benner.*
Based on short stories by Margaret Gibson, this engaging film deals with the relationship between a flamboyant female impersonator (Russell) and a timid schizophrenic (McLaren). Their crises of personal and sexual identity typify the resistance to being "normal" found in many Canadian films. They are both victims of "straight" society in Toronto, and the film's happy ending is made possible only when they move to New York. The film was commercially successful but its sequel, *Too Outrageous!* (1987), was less so, perhaps because of the dark shadow cast over it by the impact of AIDS in the intervening decade.   *(Bill Marshall)*

Engagement"), in which an old couple quietly live out their final days in their home and garden, and Jacques Leduc's *Tendresse ordinaire*, about a young woman awaiting the return of her husband from his job in the north. Two other important films which adopted this intimate manner, but with a more critical edge, were Jean Beaudin's *J. A. Martin, photographe* (1976) and Francis Mankiewicz's *Les bons débarras* (*"Good Riddance,"* 1979) **(2–27, 10–13)**.

CONTEMPORARY DEVELOPMENTS

In 1984, the CFDC changed its name to Telefilm Canada in recognition of the increasing importance of television as a medium in its own right and as a means of resolving the distribution problems that had always plagued Canadian cinema. Canadian content requirements (in effect, a quota system) had long been a condition of broadcasting licences in Canada, and television became an

10–13. *Les Bons débarras* **(*"Good Riddance,"* 1981),** *with Charlotte Laurier, directed by Francis Mankiewicz.*
The film centres on the ruthless efforts of Manon (Laurier) to keep her mother's love to herself. In the Quebec tradition, there is no father, but Manon is jealous of the retarded uncle who lives with them and of the local cop who wants to marry her mother. Réjean Ducharme, who wrote the screenplay, was already well known as the author of novels and plays about children who pursue their desires with an intensity that exposes the compromises and inhibitions of the adult world. Mankiewicz and his actors perfectly catch the spirit of the writer's vision.   *(Les Productions Prisma)*

increasingly important outlet for Canadian filmmakers. With the introduction of pay-TV and specialty satellite channels, the demand for program material has increased enormously, not just in Canada but worldwide, and the home video market has also proved to be a significant source of revenue.

Even if the screen is small, Canadian films are now being shown, and seen by more people, than ever before. Nevertheless, the economic basis of Canadian cinema remains precarious, and the problems of cultural identity are still unresolved, as they are in the nation itself. For contemporary Canadian filmmakers, questions of cultural and national identity merge into issues of ethnic, racial, and gender identity in the context of a media environment saturated in competing and contradictory images.

Of course, these concerns are far from unique to Canadian cinema, and audiences—in Canada as elsewhere—still prefer Hollywood films in which the complexity of modern life is addressed but usually contained within fairly conventional narrative structures. Since Canadian films are seen by only a small minority of the population, it is difficult to argue that they express what Kracauer called the "psychological disposition" of the people. Yet, as in earlier periods, there are motifs and patterns that recur in a variety of films and seem to express more than just the individual preoccupations of the filmmakers.

In particular, recent Canadian movies have extended the traditional Canadian concern with problems of identity to encompass an exploration of the relations of fantasy, memory, and technology. Although the influence of the direct cinema tradition is still apparent in many of these films, there has been a marked emphasis on fantastic, bizarre, and extreme images and stories. Canadian films have often faced censorship problems at home and abroad: The British attempt to ban Cronenberg's *Crash* (1996) is just one of the most notorious examples **(Colour Plate 12)**. Of course, the pleasure of watching car crashes is a staple of Hollywood cinema, and the perversity of films like *Crash* is that they raise disturbing questions about activities that are culturally accepted as "normal."

The revival of English-Canadian cinema during this period owed a great deal to the work of regional filmmakers. Two early successes were Anne Wheeler's *Loyalties* from Alberta and Sandy Wilson's *My American Cousin* from British Columbia **(11–21)**, both released in 1985. Both films work within the **realist** tradition, but two other regional directors made important contributions to the movement away from this tradition. The films of William MacGillivray, based in Nova Scotia, quietly undermine their realist surfaces with a reflexive concern with the way images work in our culture **(10–14)**; and,

10-14. *Life Classes* (1986), *with Jacinta Cormier, directed by William MacGillivray.*
MacGillivray's films are understated but deceptively complex character studies that explore the ways in which identity is shaped by environment and, increasingly in the modern world, by the media. *Life Classes* deals with a single mother who seeks her own independence and identity as an artist at a time when the electronic communications media are transforming both the remote Cape Breton community in which she lives and the values traditionally associated with high art. *(Picture Plant Ltd./David Middleton)*

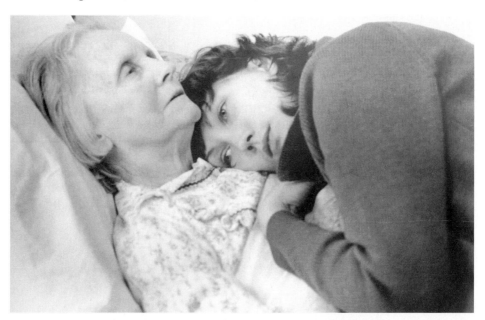

10-15. *Careful* (1992), *with Jackie Burroughs, Kyle McCulloch, and Brent Neale, directed by Guy Maddin.*
The convoluted plot of Maddin's third feature takes place in the shadow of the Alps, in a community where people are constantly being warned to be "careful" lest their raised voices cause an avalanche. Although Maddin is based in Winnipeg, his films seem far removed from the Canadian tradition of regional cinema. Nevertheless, it is difficult not to see this zany depiction of an inhibited community, living on the edge and toppling into absurdly tangled relationships, as a perverse parable about the conservative tendencies in Canadian culture.   *(Photo by Jeff Solylo)*

in Manitoba, Guy Maddin has made a series of films that create their own bizarre worlds, rejecting any form of realism **(10–15)**.

Canadian filmmakers also continue to make genre films but, apart from Cronenberg's horror films, few have achieved commercial or critical success. Indeed, many films suggest that American popular culture is no longer the potent rival that it was in earlier Canadian movies. Wilson's American cousin turns out be just as dominated by his parents as the film's Canadian heroine, and in many otherwise quite different films—including *La Ligne de chaleur* (*"The Heat Line,"* Hubert-Yves Rose, 1987), *Moody Beach* (Richard Roy, 1990), *Highway 61* (Bruce McDonald, 1991) **(10–2)**, and *North of Pittsburgh* (Richard Martin, 1991)—journeys south of the border reveal inhabitants as troubled and mixed up as the Canadian protagonists.

Two films did revive the use of the crime genre to reflect on the cultural and political tensions in Quebec, as Denys Arcand had done in the 1970s. They appeared at a time when the rejection of "sovereignty-association" in the

10-16. *Pouvoir intime ("Blind Trust,"* 1986), *with Marie Tifo and Pierre Curzi, directed by Yves Simoneau.*
Like all good heist films, this one begins with the careful planning of the robbery, but a guard's upset stomach disrupts the plans, setting in motion a series of events that result in a final bloody massacre. The use of English on the security van links the plot to the politics of language in Quebec, but also points to the betrayal of trust by the shady political figures who set up the robbery. At the end, two survivors meet in a ruined church to share the money, an ironic comment on Quebec's own betrayal of its past.   *(Les Films Vision 4)*

1980 referendum marked a setback for the independence movement, provoking a political climate of doubt and disillusionment. In Yves Simoneau's *Pouvoir intime (* "*Blind Trust,*" 1986), two government officials blackmail a gang into robbing a security van in an attempt to retrieve a compromising document **(10–16)**. Jean-Claude Lauzon's *Un Zoo la nuit (* "*Night Zoo,*" 1987) begins as a violent story about an ex-convict harassed by corrupt police officers, but gradually shifts its focus to his reconciliation with his dying father, culminating in an absurd but strangely moving sequence in which the son tries to fulfill his father's desire to kill a moose by taking him to a zoo, where he has to make do with shooting an elephant.

In these Quebec thrillers, the relations of gender and identity are viewed from a masculine perspective, but the revival of Canadian cinema has also seen the emergence of several important women directors. The films of Anne Wheeler and Sandy Wilson have already been mentioned, but it is Patri-

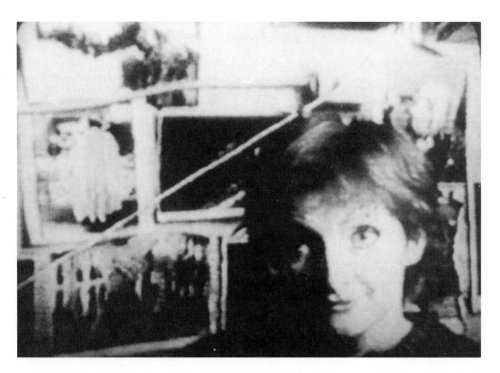

10-17.   *I've Heard the Mermaids Singing* (1986), *with Sheila McCarthy, directed by Patricia Rozema.*
The film begins when Polly turns on the video camera she has stolen from the art gallery where she works. She addresses it directly but places herself slightly off-centre, suggesting that she cannot see herself as the centre of even her own story. Verbally, Polly's clumsy attempts to explain herself contrast with the articulate but sterile language of the art world, just as her photographs of everyday reality (pinned to the wall behind her) contrast with the sublime painting she finds in the curator's house (and which is represented only by the bright glowing light that it emits).   *(Patricia Rozema)*

cia Rozema, Léa Pool, and Micheline Lanctôt who have gone furthest in developing a female perspective on the issues of identity that have long preoccupied Canadian filmmakers.

Rozema's first feature film, *I've Heard the Mermaids Singing* (1987), proved to be one of the most spectacular low-budget successes in Canadian film history. It was produced on a budget of $350 000, raised with great difficulty, but it went on to gross over $6 million worldwide. The film's appeal depends largely on its central character, Polly, a touchingly inept "person Friday" who becomes infatuated with the female art gallery curator for whom she works. The way the story is told gives the film its unusual flavour, as it weaves together video images of Polly's narration, **flashbacks** that illustrate her account of events, and fantasy sequences in which she defies gravity by flying above the city and walking on water **(10–17).**

10–18. *La Femme de l'hotel ("A Woman in Transit,"* 1984), *with (from left to right) Louise Marleau, Paule Baillergeon, and Marthe Turgeon, directed by Léa Pool.*
Pool's highly personal films deal with characters—usually, but not always, women—who feel out of place and who are unsure of their sexual identities. Baillergeon plays a filmmaker who has just returned to Montreal after a long absence, and encounters a woman (Marleau) who has left home and is wandering through the city. She brings this woman together with the actress (Turgeon) who is to play the main character in her film, and the three women develop a friendship in which they seem to form one composite character.   *(ACPAV)*

Léa Pool, a Swiss-born filmmaker now based in Quebec, achieved her first major success with *La Femme de l'hotel* (1984), a poetic film in which the identities of three women gradually merge into each other **(10–18)**. Micheline Lanctôt emerged as an accomplished director in the 1980s, after pursuing a successful career as an actress. Her film *Deux actrices* (*"Two Can Play,"* 1993), explores similar territory to *La Femme de l'hotel,* as we see Lanctôt herself working with two actresses whose personal identities merge with those of the characters they portray in the film within the film **(8–12)**.

While gender remains a key aspect of identity issues in Canadian cinema, ethnic and racial identities have also been added to the mix. The regional diversity of English-Canadian cinema has recently broadened even further to take in the multicultural dimension of Canadian culture. An official "policy of multiculturalism within a bilingual framework," announced in 1971 by the government of Pierre Trudeau, was intended to promote "national unity... founded on confidence in one's own individual identity." The effects of this policy never quite matched up to its intentions but it continues to influence the Canadian cultural outlook.

The NFB responded to the multiculturalism policy by producing numerous documentary and fiction films on various ethnic and racial groups, but these films, which tended to stress social problems and efforts to overcome them, have been described by critic Cameron Bailey as a "cinema of duty." More recently, filmmakers have been emerging from the groups themselves to extend and challenge the definition of Canadian national cinema. Srinivas Krishna's *Masala* (1991), for example, is a flamboyant satire on an official policy that sees the culture of ethnic communities as folklore to be preserved in museum conditions. As the director and in the role of the film's disaffected hero, Krishna is also critical of the Indian community, which goes along with this patronizing attitude. By mixing together many genres and stereotypes, Krishna suggests that we live in a world full of cultural contradictions in which it is no longer possible to believe that stories can make sense of the world **(11–31)**.

In view of Krishna's hostility to the idea of multiculturalism, it might be better to see his work as part of what has been called "diasporic" cinema, movies made by filmmakers from ethnic communities that have emerged in many countries as a result of the large-scale migrations characteristic of recent history. Such films exist in a fascinating but uneasy relationship with the national cinemas of which they become part. Krishna argues that his films have nothing to do with the Canadian direct cinema tradition, insisting that he should not be seen as part of the national cinema. Yet the disconcerting mixture of genres and stereotypes in *Masala* is a strategy very similar to that used by Gilles Carle in the 1970s.

Other key examples of this multicultural or diasporic cinema include Deepa Mehta's *Sam and Me* (1990), a gently comic film about a young Indian immigrant who gets a job caring for an old Jewish man whose family is unable to control him; Mina Shum's *Double Happiness* (1994), on the dilemmas of an aspiring actress who lives at home in Vancouver with her Chinese family; and Clement Virgo's mystical **film noir** *Rude* (1995), set in Toronto's Jamaican community **(2–13)**.

The situation in Quebec is rather different because the Québécois identity has been so tied to the French language and to Quebec's history that immigrants and ethnic communities seem to be excluded by definition. There is a widespread fear that immigration will lead to an erosion of Québécois identity, and the "ethnic vote" became a contentious issue in the 1995 referendum. The rapid growth of the Italian community, in particular, has caused an anxiety reflected in Lauzon's *Un Zoo la nuit*, in which the father's apartment is being gradually taken over by an expanding Italian restaurant. The relations between the Italian community in Quebec and the French majority have been explored from the Italian perspective in films by Paul Tana, notably *Caffé Italia Montréal* (1985) **(10–19)** and *La Sarrasine* (1991).

These new voices add to the range of issues and styles in Canadian cinema. Three veteran directors, Denys Arcand, André Forcier, and David Cronenberg, have also contributed important films that respond to new conditions and that have helped to shape new developments.

10-19. *Caffé Italia Montréal* **(1985),** *directed by Paul Tana.*
This film blends two sets of conventions, documentary and theatrical, to reflect the situation of many Italians in Quebec who find themselves caught between two cultures. Interviews with immigrants and their children and archival footage and photographs are intercut with theatrical scenes in which two actors of Italian descent (Pierre Curzi and Tony Nardi) dramatize the historical stages that led to their current situation. In the early years of immigration, Italian workers peer through the window of the café as their "godfather" holds court inside, taking bribes to secure them jobs on the Canadian Pacific Railroad.   *(ACPAV)*

After working in documentary and television during the CCA years, Arcand made a triumphant return to feature filmmaking with *The Decline of the American Empire* (1986), in which a group of women work out at a health spa and then enjoy an elaborate meal cooked by their male friends **(4–11)**. The film's gender reversals and its sexual frankness brought Arcand an invitation to direct an English-language remake in Hollywood (a project that eventually came to nothing). For the Quebec audience, an even more remarkable feature is that these characters are historians, but their witty conversation is marked by the virtual absence of any reference to Quebec's past or future, although one professor dismisses the prospects of independence in a lecture in a pre-credits sequence.

Arcand, who studied history at university, achieved another success with *Jesus of Montreal* (1989), in which an actor, attempting to modernize a traditional play, investigates the historical truth behind the story of Christ. The

10–20. *Jésus de Montréal* ("*Jesus of Montreal,*" 1990), *with Johanne-Marie Tremblay (left), Lothaire Bluteau, and Catherine Wilkening, directed by Denys Arcand.*
Following up on the international success of *The Decline of the American Empire*, which focused on the material pleasures of eating and sex, Arcand took on Quebec's spiritual state in this film. Daniel Coulombe (Bluteau) plays Jesus in a contemporary version of the Passion Play presented on Mount Royal. In his attempt to create a version of Jesus relevant to life in the modern city, Daniel runs into trouble with the law and the church, and finds himself enacting a series of events in his own life that uncannily mirror the original story.   *(Max Films Inc.)*

play's new version of the story restores the emotional power of Christ's message for many who see it, but it is rejected by church authorities and hilariously mis-interpreted by the critics who constitute the "church" of modern media. The film becomes an exploration of the relations between acting and truth, even as it depicts the exploitation of actors by a culture in which advertising and pornography are the major outlets for their talents **(10–20)**.

The relation of Quebec's history and religious traditions to the present is also central to *Le Confessional* (1995), the first feature film by the innovative stage director Robert Lepage. In the present, marked by international influences and political corruption, an artist tries to uncover the truth about his brother's illegitimate birth. Flashbacks gradually reveal the skeleton in the family's closet, a domestic melodrama that occurred in the 1950s, at the same time as the production of Hitchcock's *I Confess* was placing strains on the conservative Catholic culture of Quebec **(10–21)**.

10–21. *Le Confessional* (1995), *directed by Robert Lepage.*
At the end of his film, Lepage recreates the Quebec City première of Hitchcock's *I Confess* which was shot there in 1952 as part of the Canadian Cooperation Project. The negotiations between Hollywood and the Catholic Church provide a background to the moral dilemmas provoked by an illegitimate birth whose mystery is only unravelled almost fifty years later. In the present, the heritage of Quebec's past is placed in the context of international influences, of which the film itself is an example, since it was an official Canadian-British-French co-production.   *(Cinémaginaire Inc.)*

Less known outside Quebec than Arcand, Forcier directed his first film in 1967, and his darkly comic **surrealist** vision has arguably had more influence on younger filmmakers. His characters exist on the margins of society because they refuse to give up the personal fantasies and rituals that give their lives meaning. Whereas Forcier was once himself a marginal figure who did not fit easily into prevailing assumptions about Canadian cinema, his films of the 1980s and 1990s—*Au Clair de la lune* (*"Moonshine Bowling,"* 1982) **(10–22)**, *Kalamazoo* (1988), *Une Histoire inventée* (*"An Imaginary Tale,"* 1990), and *Le Vent du Wyoming* (*"A Wind from Wyoming,"* 1994) **(Colour Plate 10)**—are very much in tune with the work of younger filmmakers who increasingly make use of bizarre or shocking images to confront areas of experience that lie beneath the conscious workings of the mind.

The imagery in Jean-Claude Lauzon's extraordinary film *Léolo* (1992), for example, is certainly bizarre and often shocking **(10–23)**. Léo, a French-Canadian boy, understandably rejects his grotesque family and lives instead in

10-22.   *Au Clair de la lune* ("Moonshine Bowling," 1982), *with Guy L'Ecuyer (left) and Michel Côté, directed by André Forcier.*
Forcier has been called the "enfant terrible of Quebec cinema." His characters tend to live in fantasy worlds, but the boundaries between fantasy and reality are very difficult to define, as they are in the very different films of David Cronenberg. This film develops its surreal vision around the friendship between two homeless men: Albert (L'Ecuyer), a former bowling champion, and François (Côté), an albino from "Albinia" who dreams of returning to his own imaginary country.   *(Bernard Lalonde)*

a dream world in which he imagines his father as an Italian. His visions of a sun-drenched Sicilian landscape contrast with the dark Montreal slum in which he lives and imply that the Italian community has cultural roots that Quebec now lacks. Although Léo finally succumbs to the illness that afflicts his family and culture, the film celebrates the power of the imagination to transcend cultural limitations, largely through its mosaic style, mixing a few allusions to Quebec culture with a jumble of quotations that range from the chanting of Tibetan monks to Tom Waits.

While surrealism has long been a significant force in Quebec, it has not had a major impact on English-Canadian culture. The interest in imaginary obsessions and distortions in recent English-Canadian cinema owes much to the films of Cronenberg who, like Forcier, was once seen as a marginal figure in the context of the national cinema. In his most recent films, Cronenberg has moved away from the horror film but not from his concern with bodies and minds in the grip of irrational forces: Bill Lee's drug-induced hallucinations in

10–23.   *Léolo* (1992), *with Ginette Reno, directed by Jean-Claude Lauzon.*
In his dream life, Léo imagines that he is Italian, conceived when his mother (Reno) fell into a pile of tomatoes contaminated with the semen of a masturbating Sicilian farm worker. The film ends with Léo lying naked in a tub of ice cubes in the mental asylum that already houses most of his family, while his spirit takes refuge in the Italy of his imagination. Lauzon insisted that this apparently bleak ending is a celebration of "the power of the imagination," as expressed in Léo's writings, which are rescued from garbage cans by a character called the "Word Tamer." *(Alliance Communications)*

Naked Lunch (1991); René Gallimard's refusal to admit to himself in *M. Butterfly* (1993) that the Chinese actress he loves is really a man **(2–19)**; and the characters' obsessive desire to repeat the contact of metal and flesh in *Crash*.

Cronenberg's preoccupation with the relations between technology, bodies, and identity has influenced a number of younger English-Canadian directors. David Wellington's *I Love a Man in Uniform* (1993), for example, deals with an actor who gets a part in a TV cop show and starts to wear his uniform on the streets, gradually losing the ability to distinguish fiction from reality **(10–24)**. In some ways, this film resembles Pearson's *Paperback Hero* **(10–10)**, whose protagonist also masquerades as an authoritative male figure from an American genre; the difference is that Wellington draws us into his character's obsessions so that we often share his disorientation.

Cronenberg's perverse vision has also influenced the very different films of Atom Egoyan, the most prolific and important of the new generation of English-Canadian filmmakers. Egoyan's films are centrally concerned with the ways in which we use images in an effort to fix our identities. In many of the films, he contrasts the permanence and intensity of film images with grainy video images that can be more easily used for storing memories but are also subject to instant erasure. In *Next of Kin, Family Viewing* (1987) (**4–9**), and *Calendar* (1993), Egoyan draws on his own Armenian background to develop ironic and moving stories about the erosion of ethnic roots in modern urban environments. All of these films, as well as *Speaking Parts* (1989) (**3–4**), *The Adjuster* (1991), and *Exotica* (1993) (**10–25**), also explore the ways in which technology and media images affect sexual experience and people's fantasy lives.

In *The Sweet Hereafter* (**Colour Plate 16**), his first film not based on his own original screenplay, Egoyan seemed to be moving in a new direction. This film is based on a novel of the same title by American writer Russell Banks, and some critics found the film more "American" than Egoyan's previous work. It certainly seems a more realist film, with its stress on the natural beauty of British Columbia (to which Egoyan transferred the action) and its focus on the traumatic effects of a horrifying bus accident and an incestuous relationship. Yet the film also deals with the ways in which technology and the legal system

10–24. *I Love a Man in Uniform* (**1993**), *with Tom McCamus, directed by David Wellington.* As in *Jesus of Montreal*, the protagonist in this film is an actor who identifies with his role, with tragic results. As in *Paperback Hero*, the protagonist is a Canadian who adopts the masculine style of an American genre hero. Henry is torn between his desire to be an actor and the security of his job in a bank. When he gets a role in a TV cop show, made in Canada but made to look American, he finds that his fictional uniform gains him acceptance by real cops on the city streets. The city is clearly Toronto, but it comes to seem as anonymous and unreal as the location of the TV show.   *(Miracle Pictures)*

10–25.   *Exotica* (1994), *directed by Atom Egoyan.*
The Exotica nightclub is the perfect site for developing the tensions provoked by looking and touching in Egoyan's films. When the owner of the club uses a two-way mirror to watch over her dancers and clients, it reminds us of a similar mirror in the opening sequence through which customs officers spy on passengers at an airport. We are implicated in these acts of voyeurism and reminded that, as spectators in a cinema, like the audience at the club, we can see but cannot touch. The film is populated by lonely characters for whom looking is a substitute for touching, and obsession a substitute for lasting relationships.   *(Ego Film Arts/Johnnie Eisen)*

can separate us from reality. Despite the intense impact of the images and strong performances in the film, the movie takes on the appearance of a dream shaped by the disturbed imaginations of a young woman who is too close to her father and a middle-aged lawyer who is too far from his daughter.

In a world in which new developments in communications technology and politics are constantly changing our cultural environment, Egoyan's films, like many other recent Canadian movies, offer unsettling but rewarding experiences that provoke us into thinking about our own situations. These situations are often not specifically Canadian, and it is clear that discussions of national cinemas—and the development of national film and media policy—must take the international context into account. It is still too early to predict how the balance between global communications and local needs will be determined, but two recent films demonstrate some of the possibilities.

The Red Violin (1998) **(10–26)** was directed by Quebec filmmaker François Girard. As with Girard's earlier *Thirty-Two Short Films about Glenn Gould* **(6–5)**, the director collaborated on the script with Don McKellar, an English-Canadian actor, writer and director. The film was an official Canada/Italy/U.S.A./Britain co-production. Like several other Canadian films of the 1990s, including *Rude* **(2–13)** and *Eldorado* **(4–32)**, it depicts the intersecting lives of a disparate group of people, but here the narrative has a broad historical and geographical sweep. It traces the history of a violin made in Italy in the seventeenth century and includes segments filmed in Austria, Britain and China. There is an international cast, including black Hollywood star Samuel L. Jackson, who plays an expert called in by the auction company.

Girard insists that the film is rooted in Montreal even though it reflects the emergence of Marshall McLuhan's "global village." He also noted that, as a French Canadian, he felt that he belonged to a different culture from McKellar, but their collaboration revealed them to be part of the same global culture. McKellar appears in the film as the technician who restores the violin and, in

10–26. *The Red Violin* **(1998),** *with Carlo Cecchi and Irene Grazioli, directed by François Girard.* Music ties together the elaborate narrative structure and provides much of the pleasure in this highly cosmopolitan film. The score, by U.S. composer John Corigliano, captures the styles of the different periods and nations through which the violin travels from seventeenth-century Italy to contemporary Montreal. Each episode in this story uses actors from the nation in which it takes place speaking the appropriate language, although the present-day sequences in Quebec are almost entirely in English. In the Italian episode that begins the story, the violin maker (Cecchi) imbues the violin with his wife's spirit by staining it with her blood after she dies on the day he finishes making it.   *(Rhombus Media)*

10-27. *Last Night* (1998), *with Sandra Oh, directed by Don McKellar.*
McKellar wrote, directed and starred in his first feature film, for which he won the Prix de la
Jeunesse at the Cannes Film Festival. In his earlier films as an actor, such as Bruce McDonald's
Highway 61 **(10-2)**, he developed the persona of an insecure introvert who takes the bizarre
and illogical in his stride. As a director, he exploits this persona effectively by casting himself
as a man determined to confront the end of the world with quiet dignity but constantly having
to deal with other people responding to the disaster in their own ways. His most important
encounter is with a woman (Oh) who has made a suicide pact with her husband but is unable
to reach him in a city whose public services have come to a halt.   *(Rhombus Media)*

the same year, he also played the leading role in the first feature film he had
directed (he wrote it too). *Last Night* **(10-27)** originated out of a project in
which a French production company (Haut et Court) invited directors from
twelve different countries to make films about the upcoming millennium.

McKellar's film, co-produced by Canada's Rhombus Media, is not really
about the millennium but is instead a wry comedy about the end of the world.
Its narrative is much simpler than that of *The Red Violin*, covering a period of six
hours before the catastrophe during which the lives of several characters intersect in bizarre and revealing ways. Unlike such Hollywood blockbusters as
Armageddon and *Deep Impact*, this Canadian film eschews special effects and
offers no explanation for the disaster everyone knows is coming at midnight.
Whatever it is, nobody tries to stop it, and the characters wander the streets of
Toronto caught between their old routines and the desire to do something significant before the end.

In their different ways, these two films suggest the complex relations of local and international influences at work in Canadian cinema as it seeks to define its place in the postmodern media environment.

FURTHER READING

ARMATAGE, KAY, et al, eds., *Gendering the Nation: Canadian Women's Cinema* (Toronto: University of Toronto Press, 1999). Collection of historical and critical essays.

CLANDFIELD, DAVID, *Canadian Film* (Toronto: Oxford University Press, 1987). Useful short overview.

DORLAND, MICHAEL, *So Close to the State/s: The Emergence of Canadian Feature Film Policy* (Toronto: University of Toronto Press, 1998). Provocative analysis based on archival research.

FELDMAN, SETH, ed., *Take Two* (Toronto: Irwin Publishing, 1984). Collection of critical essays.

FELDMAN, SETH, and JOYCE NELSON, eds., *Canadian Film Reader* (Toronto: Peter Martin Associates, 1977). Early writings on Canadian cinema.

MAGDER, TED, *Canada's Hollywood: The Canadian State and Feature Films* (Toronto: University of Toronto Press, 1993). Thoughtful study of national film policy.

MORRIS, PETER, *Embattled Shadows: A History of Canadian Cinema 1895–1939* (Montreal: McGill-Queen's University Press, 1978). Key work on Canadian film history.

MORRIS, PETER, *The Film Companion* (Toronto: Irwin Publishing, 1984). Indispensable reference work, although somewhat out-of-date.

POSNER, MICHAEL, *Canadian Dreams: The Making and Marketing of Independent Films* (Vancouver: Douglas and McIntyre, 1993). Fascinating case studies.

VÉRONNEAU, PIERRE, and PIERS HANDLING, eds., *Self Portrait: Essays on the Canadian and Quebec Cinemas* (Ottawa: Canadian Film Institute, 1980). Collection of critical essays originally published in French.

THEORY | 11

The apparently simple act of spectating . . . involves theories of representation, of human nature, of morality, of the nature of reality, of the conditions for human happiness, etc. Similarly, for the filmmaker, however self-consciously intuitive the approach, there is inevitably a comparable set of theories underlying the production of a film. For the critic, or for anyone engaged in a discussion of cinema, judgements also involve theories . . . Those claiming to stand outside theory are simply unaware of the theory they are using.

—ROBERT LAPSLEY AND MICHAEL WESTLAKE

371

SUMMARY

Theoretical question: What is the essential nature of cinema? The three focus points: the work of art, the artist, the audience. Theories of realism: a mirror of the real world. The self-effacing artist. The values of discovery, intimacy, and emotional richness. The avoidance of artifice. Italian neorealism. Formalist film theories: imaginary worlds. A place of magic. The pleasure principle. The film artist: the auteur theory. *Cahiers du cinéma*. Structuralism and semiotic theories. The complexity of film: codified data in a deep structure. Thematic polarities and the nonlinear methodology of structuralism. Ideological and cultural theory. Feminist and queer theory. Race and ethnicity. Historiography: the assumptions and biases of writing histories. Aesthetic approaches. Technological approaches. Economic histories. Social histories.

Most theories of film are concerned with the wider context of the medium—its social, political, and philosophical implications. Theorists have also explored the essential nature of cinema—what differentiates it from other art forms, what its basic properties are. A theory is an intellectual grid, a set of aesthetic generalizations, not eternal verities. Some theories are more useful than others in understanding specific movies. No single theory can explain them all. For this reason, recent developments in the field have stressed an eclectic approach, synthesizing a variety of theoretical strategies **(11–1).**

Traditionally, theorists have focused their attention on three areas of inquiry: **(1)** the work of art, **(2)** the artist, and **(3)** the audience. Those who have stressed the work of art have explored the inner dynamics of movies—how they communicate, the language systems they use. Film theorists can be divided into **realists** and **formalists,** just as filmmakers tend to favour one style or the other. The most important artist-oriented approach is the **auteur theory,** the belief that a movie is best understood by focusing on its artistic creator, presumably the director. Structuralism and semiology were the dominant theories after 1970, and both tend to emphasize a synthetic approach, combining such concerns as **genre,** authorship, style, **iconography,** social context, and ideology. In the area of historiography—the theoretical assumptions underlying film history—recent trends have also emphasized an integrated approach.

THEORIES OF REALISM

Most theories of realism emphasize the documentary aspects of film art. Movies are evaluated primarily in terms of how accurately they reflect external reality. The camera is regarded as essentially a recording mechanism rather than an expressive medium in its own right. The subject matter is paramount in the cinema of realism, technique its discreetly transparent handmaiden. As we have seen in the case of André Bazin (Chapter 6), most theories of realism have a moral and ethical bias and are often rooted in the values of Islamic, Christian, and **Marxist** humanism.

Realist theorists like Cesare Zavattini and Siegfried Kracauer believe that cinema is essentially an extension of photography and shares with it a pro-

11-1. *The Maltese Falcon* (U.S.A., 1941), *with Humphrey Bogart, Peter Lorre, Mary Astor, and Sydney Greenstreet; directed by John Huston.*

Theory is the handmaiden of art, not vice versa. Movies can be explored from a variety of theoretical perspectives, each with its own set of values and parameters of inquiry. One's theoretical orientation will depend in large part on what one is looking for. For example, *The Maltese Falcon* can be placed in at least seven theoretical contexts: **(1)** An auteur critic would regard it as a typical Huston film. **(2)** It could also be analyzed as a Bogart vehicle, exploiting and expanding the star's iconography. **(3)** An industry historian would place the picture within its commercial context—as a superior example of the Warner Brothers product of its era. **(4)** A genre theorist would be interested in it as a classic example of the detective thriller, and one of the first of the so-called deadly female pictures that were so popular in the United States during World War II. **(5)** A theorist interested in the relationship of movies to literature might focus on Huston's script, based on Dashiell Hammet's celebrated novel of the same title. **(6)** A stylistic critic would analyze the picture within the context of film noir, an important style in the American cinema of the 1940s. **(7)** A Marxist might interpret the movie as a parable on greed, an implicit condemnation of the vices of capitalism. Each theoretical grid charts a different cinematic topography.   *(Warner Bros.)*

---

nounced affinity for recording the visible world around us. Unlike other art forms, photography and cinema tend to leave the raw materials of reality more or less intact. There is a minimum of interference and manipulation on the artist's part, for film is not an art of invention so much as an art of "being there."

Roberto Rossellini's *Rome, Open City* (**11–2**) inaugurated the Italian **neorealist** movement, one of the triumphs of the cinema of realism. The movie deals with the collaboration of Catholics and Communists in fighting the Nazi occupation of Rome shortly before the American army liberated the city. Technically, the film is rather crude. Good quality film **stock** was impossible to obtain, so Rossellini had to use inferior newsreel stock. Nevertheless, the technical flaws and the resultant grainy images convey a sense of journalistic immediacy and authenticity. (Many neorealists began their careers as journalists, and Rossellini himself began as a documentarist.) Virtually all the movie was shot at actual locations, and there are many exterior **shots** in which no additional lights were used. With the exception of the principal players, the actors were nonprofessionals. The structure of the movie is episodic—a series of vignettes showing the reactions of Roman citizens to the German occupation.

Rome, Open City is saturated with a sense of unrelenting honesty. "This is the way things are," Rossellini is said to have declared after the film premiered.

11–2. *Rome, Open City* **(Italy, 1945),** *with Marcello Pagliero, directed by Roberto Rossellini.* The torture scenes of this famous Resistance film were so realistic that they were cut out of some prints. In this episode, a Nazi SS officer applies a blowtorch to the body of a Communist partisan in an effort to force him to reveal the names of his comrades in the underground. The crucifixion allusion is deliberate, even though the character is a nonbeliever. It parallels the death of another partisan, a Catholic priest, who is executed by a military firing squad. The French critic André Bazin was a champion of Italian neorealism, applauding its moral fervour even more than its technical restraint. "Is not neorealism primarily a kind of humanism, and only secondarily a style of filmmaking?" he asked.   *(Pathé Contemporary Films)*

The statement became the motto of the neorealist movement. The film provided a rallying point for an entire generation of Italian filmmakers whose creative talents had been stifled by the repressive Fascist regime of the prewar era. Within the next few years, there followed an astonishing series of movies that catapulted the Italians into the front ranks of the international cinema. The major filmmakers of the movement were Rossellini, Luchino Visconti, and Vittorio De Sica and his frequent scriptwriter Cesare Zavattini.

There are considerable differences between these men and even between their early and later works. Furthermore, neorealism implied a style as well as an ideology. Rossellini emphasized the ethical dimension: "For me, Neorealism is above all a moral position from which to look at the world. It then became an aesthetic position, but at the beginning it was moral." De Sica, Zavattini, and Visconti also stressed morality as the touchstone of neorealism.

The main ideological characteristics of the movement can be summarized as follows: (1) a new democratic spirit, with emphasis on the value of ordinary people such as labourers, peasants, and factory workers; (2) a compassionate point of view and a refusal to make facile moral judgments; (3) a preoccupation with Italy's Fascist past and its aftermath of wartime devastation, poverty, unemployment, prostitution, and the black market; (4) a blending of Christian and Marxist humanism; and (5) an emphasis on emotions rather than abstract ideas.

The stylistic features of neorealism include: (1) an avoidance of neatly plotted stories in favour of loose, episodic structures that evolve organically from the situations of the characters; (2) a documentary visual style; (3) the use of actual locations—usually exteriors—rather than studio sets; (4) the use of nonprofessional actors, sometimes even for principal roles; (5) an avoidance of literary dialogue in favour of conversational speech, including dialects; and (6) an avoidance of artifice in the **editing,** camerawork, and lighting in favour of a simple "styleless" style.

Realists have shown a persistent hostility toward **plot** and neatly structured stories. For example, Cesare Zavattini more than any single individual defined the ordinary and the everyday as the main business of the cinema. Spectacular events and extraordinary characters should be avoided at all costs, he believed. He claimed that his ideal movie would consist of ninety consecutive minutes from a person's actual life. There should be no barriers between reality and the spectator, no directorial virtuosity to "deform" the integrity of life as it is. The artistry should be invisible, the materials "found" rather than shaped or manipulated.

Suspicious of conventional plot structures, Zavattini dismissed them as dead formulas. He insisted on the dramatic superiority of life as it is experienced by ordinary people. Filmmakers should be concerned with the "excavation" of reality. Instead of plots, they should emphasize facts and all their "echoes and reverberations." According to Zavattini, filmmaking is not a matter of "inventing fables" that are superimposed over the factual materials of life, but of searching unrelentingly to uncover the dramatic implications of these facts. The purpose of the cinema is to explore the "dailiness" of events, to reveal certain details that had always been there but had never been noticed.

11–3. *Reds* (U.S.A., 1981), *cinematography by Vittorio Storaro, directed by Warren Beatty.*
Realism is generally characterized by a plain style that doesn't call attention to itself. However, this stylistic austerity is by no means universal. For example, Beatty's movie contains many outbursts of visual lyricism to emphasize the intense emotions of the characters and their involvement in the 1917 Russian Revolution. This poetic, backlit shot produces a radiant sunburst effect, throwing the foreground materials into silhouette. *(Paramount Pictures)*

In his book *Theory of Film: The Redemption of Physical Reality,* the German-trained theorist Siegfried Kracauer also attacks plot as a natural enemy of realism. According to Kracauer, the cinema is characterized by a number of natural affinities. First of all, it tends to favour "unstaged reality"—that is, the most appropriate subject matter gives the illusion of having been found rather than arranged. Second, film tends to stress the random, the fortuitous. Kracauer is fond of the phrase "nature caught in the act," meaning that film is best suited to recording events and objects that might be overlooked in life. The realistic cinema is a cinema of "found moments" and poignant revelations of humanity. A third affinity that Kracauer notes is indeterminacy. The best movies suggest endlessness. They imply a slice of life, a fragment of a larger reality rather than a self-contained whole. By refusing to tie up all the loose ends at the conclusion of the movie, the filmmaker can suggest the limitlessness of reality.

Kracauer is hostile toward movies that demonstrate a "formative tendency." Historical films and fantasies he regards as tending to move away from the basic concerns of the medium. He also dismisses most literary and dramatic adaptations because he believes that literature is ultimately concerned with "interior realities," what people are thinking and feeling, whereas movies explore surfaces, exterior reality. He regards all stylistic self-consciousness as "uncinematic," because instead of emphasizing the subject matter, the filmmaker calls attention to *how* it is presented.

Theories of film realism are not very helpful in understanding the complexities of formalist movies—the works of an Eisenstein or a Steven Spielberg. On the other hand, they do help to explain the raw emotional power of such masterpieces of realism as *Bicycle Thieves,* which was directed by Vittorio De Sica and scripted primarily by Zavattini **(8–28).**

Bicycle Thieves was acted entirely by nonprofessionals and consists of simple events in the life of a labourer (played by Lamberto Maggiorani, who was an

11-4. *The Tree of the Wooden Clogs* (Italy, 1978), *directed by Ermanno Olmi.*
As a movement, Italian neorealism was pretty much over by the mid-1950s, but as a style and an attitude toward reality, its influence spread to many other countries. A number of present-day Italian filmmakers have continued in the tradition of neorealism. For example, Olmi's movies are steeped in the values of Christian humanism. In this film, which was shot on authentic locations with nonprofessional players, he celebrates the everyday lives of several peasant families around 1900. For them, God is a living presence—a source of guidance, hope, and solace. Their faith is childlike, trusting, like that of St. Francis of Assisi. In a series of documentarylike vignettes, Olmi unfolds their gentle drama, extolling their patience, their tough stoicism, their dignity. Above all, he exalts the sacredness of the human spirit. For Olmi, they are the salt of the earth.   *(New Yorker Films)*

actual factory worker). In 1948, when the film was released, nearly a quarter of the workforce in Italy was unemployed. At the opening of the movie, we are introduced to the protagonist, a family man with a wife and two children to support. He has been out of work for two years. Finally, a billboard-posting job opens up, but to accept it he must have a bicycle. To get his bike out of hock, he and his wife pawn their sheets and bedding. On his first day on the job, the bicycle is stolen. The rest of the movie deals with his attempts to recover the bike. The man's search grows increasingly more frantic as he crisscrosses the city with his idolizing son, Bruno. After a series of false leads, the two finally track down one of the thieves, but the protagonist is outwitted by him and humiliated in front of his boy.

Realizing that he will lose his livelihood without a bike, the desperate man—after sending his son away—sneaks off and attempts to steal a bicycle

11-5. *Closely Watched Trains* (Czechoslovakia, 1966), *with Václav Neckar and Jitka Ben-dová, directed by Jiri Menzel.*
One of the hallmarks of realism is intimacy—a sense of discovering a small private moment that might easily have been overlooked because it's not a big deal. These little nothings—a stolen kiss, a quick sidelong glance, an incongruous detail—are what make realism a celebration of the poetry of everyday life.   *(Museum of Modern Art)*

himself. But the boy observes from a distance as his father pedals frantically to escape a pursuing mob. He is caught and again humiliated in front of a crowd—which includes his incredulous son. With the bitterness of betrayed innocence, the youngster suddenly realizes that his dad is not the heroic figure he had formerly thought, but an ordinary man who in desperation yielded to a degrading temptation. Like most neorealist films, *Bicycle Thieves* doesn't offer a slick solution. There are no miraculous interventions in the final reel. The concluding scene shows the boy walking alongside his father in an anonymous crowd, both of them choking with shame and weeping silently. Almost imperceptibly, the boy's hand gropes for his father's as they walk homeward, their only comfort a mutual compassion.

11-6. *Ugetsu* (Japan, 1953), *with Masayuki Mori and Machiko Kyo, directed by Kenji Mizoguchi.*
Realistic critics and theorists tend to underestimate the flexibility of an audience's response to nonrealistic movies. To be sure, it's easier for a filmmaker to create the illusion of reality if the story deals with everyday events, for the world of the movie and the actual world are essentially the same. On the other hand, a gifted artist can make even fantasy materials "realistic." A movie like *Ugetsu,* which is set in the remote past and features spirits and demons, presents us with a self-contained magical universe which we are able to enter by temporarily forgetting the outside world of reality. In short, audiences are highly sophisticated in their responses to nonrealistic films. We can almost totally suspend our disbelief, partially suspend it, or alternate between extremes according to the aesthetic demands of the world of the movie.   *(Janus Films)*

FORMALIST FILM THEORIES

Formalist film theorists believe that the art of cinema is possible precisely because a movie is unlike everyday reality. The filmmaker exploits the limitations of the medium—its two-dimensionality, its confining **frame,** its fragmented time–space continuum—to produce a world that resembles the real world only in a superficial sense. The real world is merely a repository of raw material that needs to be shaped and heightened to be effective as art. Film art doesn't consist of a reproduction of reality, but a translation of observed characteristics into the *forms* of the medium.

Rudolf Arnheim, a gestalt psychologist, put forth an important theory of cinematic formalism in his book *Film as Art,* which was originally published in German in 1933. Arnheim's book is primarily concerned with the perception of experience. His theory is based on the different modes of perception of the camera on the one hand and the human eye on the other. Anticipating some of the theories of the Canadian communications specialist Marshall McLuhan, Arnheim insists that the camera's image of a bowl of fruit, for instance, is fundamentally different from our perception of the fruit bowl in actual life. Or, in McLuhan's terms, the information we receive in each instance is determined by the form of its content. Formalist theorists celebrate these differences, believing that what makes photography fall short of perfect reproduction is also what makes cinema an art, not just a species of xerography.

Formalists have pointed out many instances where divergences exist between the camera's image of reality and what the human eye sees. For example, film directors must choose which viewpoint to photograph a scene from. They don't necessarily choose the clearest view, for often this does not emphasize the major characteristics of the scene, its expressive essence. In life, we perceive objects in depth and can penetrate the space that surrounds most things. In movies, space is an illusion, for the screen has only two dimensions, permit-

11-7. *The Servant* **(Britain, 1963),** *with Wendy Craig, Dirk Bogarde (foreground), and James Fox, directed by Joseph Losey.*

A scene can be photographed in literally hundreds of different ways, but the formalist selects the camera setup that best captures its symbolic or psychological implications. In this shot, for example, a young woman (Craig) suddenly realizes the enormous power a valet (Bogarde) wields over her weak fiancé (Fox). She is isolated on the left, half-plunged in darkness. A curtained doorway separates her from her lover, who is so stupefied with drugs he scarcely knows where he is, much less what's really going on. The servant cooly turns his back on them, the camera's low angle further emphasizing his effortless control over his "master." *(Landau Distributing)*

ting the director to manipulate objects and perspectives in the **mise en scène.** For example, important objects can be placed where they are most likely to be noticed first. Unimportant objects can be relegated to inferior positions, at the edges or rear of the image.

In real life, space and time are experienced as continuous phenomena. Through editing, filmmakers can chop up space and time and rearrange them in a more meaningful manner. Like other artists, the film director selects certain expressive details from the chaotic plenitude of physical reality. By juxtaposing these space and time fragments, the filmmaker creates a continuity that doesn't exist in raw nature. This, of course, was the basic position of the Soviet **montage** theorists (Chapter 6).

Formalists are always concerned with patterns, methods of restructuring reality into aesthetically appealing designs. Patterns can be expressed visually, through the photography and mise en scène; or aurally, in stylized dialogue, symbolic sound effects, and musical **motifs.** Camera movements are often **kinetic** patterns superimposed on the visual materials, commenting on them in some heightened manner.

The problems with most formalist theories are the same as those with realists: There are too many exceptions. They are certainly useful in an appreciation of Hitchcock's works, for example, or Keaton's. But how helpful is the theory in explaining the films of Renoir or De Sica? We respond to their movies because of the similarities to physical reality, not the divergences from it. Ultimately, of course, these are matters of emphasis, for films are too pluralistic to be pigeonholed into one tidy theory.

THE AUTEUR THEORY

In the mid-1950s, the French journal *Cahiers du Cinéma* revolutionized film criticism with its concept of *la politique des auteurs*. This committed policy of authors was put forth by the pugnacious young critic François Truffaut. The auteur theory became the focal point of a critical controversy that eventually spread to England and North America. Before long, the theory became a militant rallying cry, particularly among younger critics, dominating such lively journals as *Movie* in Great Britain, *Film Culture* in the United States, and both French- and English-language editions of *Cahiers du Cinéma*. Although a number of writers rejected the theory as simplistic, auteurism dominated film criticism throughout the 1960s. The movement began as a defiant gesture of contempt toward the film establishment of the time.

Actually, the main lines of the theory aren't particularly outrageous, at least not in retrospect. Truffaut, Godard, and their critical colleagues proposed that the greatest movies are dominated by the personal vision of the director. A filmmaker's "signature" can be perceived through an examination of his or her total output, which is characterized by a unity of theme and style. The writer's contribution is less important than the director's, because subject matter is artistically neutral. It can be treated with brilliance or bare competence. Movies ought to be judged on the basis of *how*, not *what*. Like other formalists, the auteur critics claimed that what makes a good film is not the subject matter as such, but its stylistic treatment. The director dominates the treatment, provided he or she is a strong director, an *auteur.*

Drawing primarily from the cinematic traditions of the United States, the *Cahiers* critics also developed a sophisticated theory of film genre. Indeed, André Bazin, the editor of the journal, believed that the genius of the American cinema was its repository of ready-made forms: westerns, thrillers, musicals, action films, comedies, and so on. "The tradition of genres is a base of operations for creative freedom," Bazin pointed out. Genre is an enriching, not a constricting, tradition. The auteurists argued that the best movies are **dialectical,** in which the conventions of a genre are held in aesthetic tension with the personality of the artist.

The American auteurs that these critics praised had worked within the **studio** system, which had broken the artistic pretensions of many lesser filmmakers. What the auteurists especially admired was how gifted directors could circumvent studio interference and even hackneyed **scripts** through their technical expertise. The subject matter of Hitchcock's thrillers or Ford's westerns was not significantly different from others working in these genres. Yet both auteurs managed to create

---

11–8. *Fanny and Alexander* (Sweden, 1983), *with Bertil Guve and Pernilla Allwin, written and directed by Ingmar Bergman.*
The auteur theory works best with those film artists who control all the major creative decisions—both in subject matter and execution. A towering giant of the cinema, Ingmar Bergman has written almost all of his movies by himself. His films are often semiautobiographical, like *Fanny and Alexander,* one of his many masterpieces. In addition, Bergman worked with the same cast and crew for years, a virtual repertory company. In short, his movies are indisputably those of an auteur.   *(Svenska Filminstitutet and Embassy Pictures)*

great films, precisely because the real meanings were conveyed through the mise en scène, the editing, and all the other formal devices at the director's disposal.

The sheer breadth of their knowledge of film history permitted these critics to reevaluate the major works of a wide variety of directors. In many instances, they completely reversed previous critical judgments. Before long, personality cults developed around the most popular directors. On the whole, these were filmmakers who had been virtually ignored by the critical establishment of the previous generation: Hitchcock, Ford, Hawks, Lang, and many others. The auteur critics were often dogmatic in their dislikes as well as their likes. Bazin expressed alarm at their negativism. To praise a bad movie, he felt, was unfortunate; but to condemn a good one was a serious failing. He especially disliked their tendency to hero worship, which led to superficial a priori judgments. Movies by cult directors were indiscriminately praised, whereas those by directors out of fashion were automatically condemned.

The principal spokesman for the auteur theory in the United States was Andrew Sarris, the influential critic of the *Village Voice*. More knowledgeable about the complexities of the **star** and studio **system** than his French counterparts, Sarris nonetheless defended their basic argument, especially the principle of tension between an artist's personal vision and the genre assignments that these directors were given by their Hollywood bosses.

The most gifted American directors of the studio era were **producer– directors** who worked independently within the major studios. These tended to be the same artists the auteur critics admired most. But the lion's share of American fiction movies produced during this era were studio films; that is, the director functioned as a member of a team and usually had little to say about the scripting, casting, or editing. Many of these directors were skillful technicians, but they were essentially craftsmen rather than artists.

Michael Curtiz is a good example. For most of his career he was a contract director at Warner Brothers. Known for his speed and efficiency, Curtiz directed dozens of movies in a variety of styles and genres. He often took on several projects at the same time. Curtiz had no "personal vision" in the sense that the auteur theory defines it: He was just getting a job done. He often did it very well. Even so, movies like *Yankee Doodle Dandy* **(8–22a)**, *Casablanca*, and *Mildred Pierce* **(11–9)** can be discussed more profitably as Warner Brothers movies rather than Michael Curtiz movies. The same principle applies to most of the other Hollywood studios. In our day, it applies to films that are controlled by **producers** and financiers rather than artists.

Other films have been dominated by stars. Few people would think of referring to a Mae West movie as anything else, and the same holds true for the W.C. Fields comedies or the works of Laurel and Hardy. The ultimate in the star as auteur is the so-called **star vehicle**, a film specifically tailored to showcase the talents of a performer.

The auteur theory suffers from a number of other weaknesses. There are some excellent films that have been made by directors who are otherwise mediocre. For example, Joseph H. Lewis's *Gun Crazy* is a superb movie, but it's atypical of his output. Conversely, great directors do not always produce great

11–9. *Mildred Pierce* **(U.S.A., 1945),** *with Joan Crawford, directed by Michael Curtiz.*
Particularly during the golden age of the big-studio era (roughly from 1925 to 1955), most American mainstream movies were dominated by the imprimatur of the studio rather than the director, who was regarded more as an executor of a collaborative enterprise than a creative artist in his own right. *Mildred Pierce* has "Warner Brothers" written all over it. Typically tough and proletarian in emphasis, the movie features Joan Crawford as a self-made woman who kills a man. It was regarded as her comeback performance after many years as a glamorous star at Metro-Goldwyn-Mayer. The movie, based on James M. Cain's hard-boiled novel, was adapted by Ranald MacDougall, a studio scribe. It was directed by Michael Curtiz, Warners' ace director, who was known for his speed, efficiency, and versatility.   *(Warner Bros.)*

films. The works of such major filmmakers as Ford, Godard, Renoir, and Buñuel are radically inconsistent in terms of quality. The auteur theory emphasizes history and a director's total output, which tends to favour older directors at the expense of newcomers. Some artists have explored a variety of themes in many different styles and genres: Carol Reed, Sidney Lumet, and John Frankenheimer **(11–10)** are good examples. There are also some great filmmakers who are crude directorial technicians. For example, Chaplin and Herzog in no way approach the stylistic fluency of Michael Curtiz, or a dozen other contract directors of his era. Yet there are very few artists who have created such distinctively personal movies as Chaplin and Herzog.

Despite its shortcomings and excesses, the auteur theory had a liberating effect on film criticism, establishing the director as the key figure at least in the art of cinema, if not always in the industry. By the 1970s, the major battle had been won. Virtually all serious discussions of movies were at least partly couched in terms of the director's personal vision. To this day, the concept of directorial dominance remains firmly established, at least with films of high artistic merit.

STRUCTURALISM AND SEMIOLOGY

During the 1960s, the auteur theory dominated film studies, and even today much critical work is devoted to individual directors. Nowadays critics tend to pay more attention to the industrial and cultural contexts within which directors produce their films. In doing so, they reflect the impact of the attacks on the auteur theory by film scholars who demanded more rigorous methods. The new theorists were less concerned with expressing their enthusiasm for the films of their favorite directors and more interested in discovering the underlying principles of film language. *Structuralism* and *semiology* were attempts to introduce a new scientific approach, to allow for more systematic and detailed analyses of movies. Borrowing their methodology from such diverse disciplines

11–10. *The Manchurian Candidate* (U.S.A., 1962), *with Angela Lansbury and Laurence Harvey, screenplay by George Axelrod, based on the novel by Richard Condon, directed by John Frankenheimer.*

A weakness of the auteur theory is its tendency to gloss over the collaborative nature of the filmmaking enterprise. True, the director coordinates the contributions of others, modulating them into a unified whole. But some of these contributions are of major significance. For example, without slighting the brilliance of Frankenheimer's direction in this movie, much of its effect derives from the story and dialogue, not to speak of the fine cast. Frankenheimer has always insisted that cinema is a collaborative art. Furthermore, he has explored a variety of styles, genres, and themes. In short, he has no consistent "artistic signature"—a major concern of auteur critics. Frankenheimer was not one of their favourites.   *(United Artists)*

as linguistics, anthropology, psychology, and philosophy, these two theories first concentrated on the development of a more precise analytical terminology.

Structuralism and semiology have also focused intently on Hollywood cinema as the principal area of inquiry, for a number of reasons. In the first place, these theories have been dominated by the British and French, traditionally the most enthusiastic foreign admirers of the cinema of the United States. Hollywood movies also provided these critics with a stylistic norm—the **classical paradigm.**

In film, semiology (or *semiotics,* as it's also called) is the study of *how* movies signify. The manner in which information is signified is indissolubly linked with *what* is being signified. The French theorist Christian Metz was in the forefront in developing semiotics as a technique of film analysis. Using many of the concepts and much of the terminology of structural linguistics, Metz and others developed a theory of cinematic communication founded on the concept of signs or codes. The language of cinema, like all types of discourse, verbal and nonverbal, is primarily symbolic: It consists of a complex network of signs we instinctively decipher while experiencing a movie **(11–11).**

In most discussions of film, the shot was generally accepted as the basic unit of construction. Semiotic theorists rejected this unit as too vague and inclusive. They insisted on a more precise concept. Accordingly, they suggested that the sign be adopted as the minimal unit of signification. A single shot from a movie generally contains dozens of signs, forming an intricate hierarchy of counterpoised meanings. In a sense, this book, and especially the earlier chapters, can be viewed as a classification of signs, although necessarily more limited in scope than the type of identification and classification envisioned by Metz and other semiologists.

For example, each of these chapters is concerned with a kind of master code, which can be broken down into code subdivisions, which themselves can be reduced to even more minimal signs. Thus, Chapter 3 might be called a photography master code. This master could be broken down into subdivisions: shots, **angles,** lighting keys, colours, **lenses**, **filters**, optical effects, and so on. Each of these, in turn, could be subdivided again. The shots, for example, could be broken down to **extreme long, long, medium, close-up, extreme close-up, deep focus.** This same principle could be applied to other master codes: spatial codes (mise en scène), kinetic codes (movement), and so on. Codes of language would be as complex as the entire discipline of linguistics; acting codes would involve a precise breakdown of the various techniques of signification used by players.

As Metz pointed out, semiology is concerned with the systematic classification of types of codes used in the cinema; structuralism is the study of how various codes function within a single structure, within one movie. Structuralism is strongly eclectic and often combines the techniques of semiotics with other theoretical perspectives, such as auteurism, genre studies, ideology, stylistic analyses, and so on. For example, Colin MacArthur's *Underworld USA* is a structuralist analysis of gangster and crime films and the style known as **film noir.** MacArthur uses semiotic classifications in exploring the iconography of the genre films of such artists as Billy Wilder.

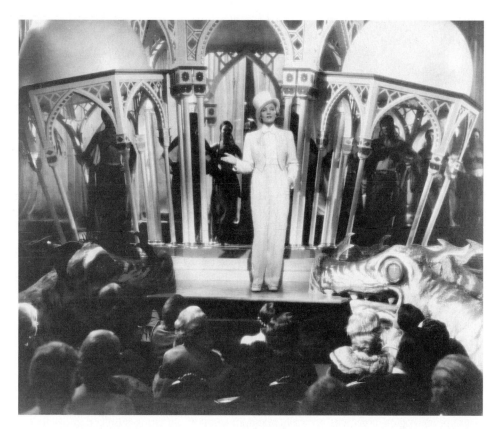

11-11. *Blonde Venus* **(U.S.A., 1932),** *with Marlene Dietrich, directed by Josef von Sternberg.*
Semiologists believe that the shot—the traditional unit of construction in film—is too general
and inclusive to be of much use in a systematic analysis of a movie. The symbolic sign, they
argue, is a more precise unit of signification. Every cinematic shot consists of dozens of signifying codes that are hierarchically structured. Using what they call the "principle of perti-
nence," semiologists decode cinematic discourse by first establishing what the dominant
signs are, then analyzing the subsidiary codes. This methodology is similar to a detailed
analysis of mise en scène, only in addition to spatial, textural, and photographic codes, semiologists would also explore other relevant signs—kinetic, linguistic, musical, rhythmic, etc. In
this shot, a semiologist would explore the symbolic significance of such major signs as Dietrich's white suit. Why a masculine suit? Why white? What does the papier-mâché dragon signify? The distorted perspective lines of the set? The "shady ladies" behind the archways? The
symbolism of stage and audience? The tight framing and closed form of the image? The protagonist's worldly song? Within the dramatic context, semiologists would also explore the
rhythms of the editing and camera movements, the symbolism of the kinetic motions of the
performer, and so on. Traditionally, critics likened the cinematic shot to a word, and a series
of edited shots to a sequence of words in a sentence. A semiologist would dismiss such
analogies as patently simple-minded. Perhaps an individual *sign* might be likened to a word,
but the equivalent to a shot—even a banal one—would require many paragraphs if not pages
of words. A complex shot can contain a hundred separate signs, each with its own precise
symbolic significance.   *(Paramount Pictures)*

11–12. *Les Ordres ("Orders," Canada, 1974),* with Jean Lapointe, directed by Michel Brault. During the October Crisis of 1970, when the Front de libération du Québec kidnapped a British diplomat and a Quebec cabinet minister, the Canadian government invoked the War Measures Act. Brault's film, based on the wave of arrests that followed, has been called "a perfect application of the theories of Brecht to cinema." Bertolt Brecht, a German dramatist, argued that spectators should not be drawn into the theatrical illusion but should be made aware of ideological processes normally taken for granted. Brault uses Brechtian distancing devices, such as having the actors introduce themselves and the roles that they will play, but does not attempt to provide a political analysis of the events. Instead, he evokes the nightmare experience of being arrested by police acting on orders from above, using black and white to depict everyday reality and colour for the intensity of perception created by the shock of imprisonment.   *(Les Productions Prisma)*

Structuralists and semiologists have been fascinated by the concept of a *deep structure*—an underlying network of symbolic meaning that is related to a movie's surface structure but is also somewhat independent of it. This deep structure can be analyzed from a number of perspectives, including Freudian psychoanalysis, Marxist economics, Jungian concepts of the collective unconscious, and the theory of structural anthropology popularized by the Frenchman Claude Lévi-Strauss.

The methods of Lévi-Strauss are based on an examination of regional myths, which he believed express certain underlying structures of thought in codified form. These myths exist in variant forms and usually contain the same or similar binary structures—pairs of opposites. By collapsing the surface (narrative) structure of myths, their symbolic motifs can be analyzed in a more systematic and meaningful manner. These polarities are usually found in dialecti-

11–13. *An Autumn Afternoon* (Japan, 1962), *with Chishu Ryu (right), directed by Yasujiro Ozu.* The films of Ozu were not widely seen in the West until the 1970s. Prior to this, his movies were regarded as "too Japanese" to be appreciated by foreign audiences, because he was a champion of traditional values, particularly that quintessential Japanese institution, the family. If Kurosawa is the artistic spokesman for modern values and the anguished individual, then Ozu speaks for the conservative majority, especially parents. But his movies are not mindless endorsements of family life, for Ozu was also an ironist, well aware of the gap between reality and the ideal—the principal source of his irony. In this film, for example, the protagonist (Ryu) is a gentle, aging widower who lives with his unmarried daughter in mutual devotion. His loneliness is assuaged by a few drinking buddies who spend much of their free time at the local bar. After hearing of the marriage of a friend's daughter, the widower decides that it's time for his daughter to move on as well. He arranges a marriage with a decent young man recommended by his friends. The movie ends on a bittersweet note of irony as the father muses contentedly on the success of his arrangements. He also realizes that he's getting on in years. And that he is alone. *(New Yorker Films)*

cal conflict: Depending on the culture analyzed, they can be agricultural (for example, water vs. drought), sexual (male vs. female), conceptual (cooked vs. raw), generational (youth vs. age), and so on. Because these myths are expressed in symbolic codes, often their full meanings are hidden even from their creators. Lévi-Strauss believed that once the full implications of a myth are understood, it's discarded as a cliché.

These structural techniques can be used to analyze a national cinema, a genre, or a specific movie. For example, the conflict between "traditional" and "modern" values can be seen in virtually all Japanese movies, and in Japanese society in general **(11–13)**. The roots of this conflict extend back to the late nineteenth century, when Japan transformed itself from a feudal country to a modern technological society patterned after the Western industrial states,

11–14. *Pretty Woman* (U.S.A., 1990), *with Julia Roberts and Richard Gere, directed by Garry Marshall.*
A film's narrative can be profoundly ideological, even when the movie purports to be light entertainment. Loosely based on the Pygmalion myth, *Pretty Woman* is about a love affair that develops between a ditsy hooker with the proverbial heart of gold (Roberts) and a rather cold and wealthy businessman (Gere) who hires her as a paid companion. Feminists were appalled by the film because it implicitly reinforces the notion of male supremacy and reduces the heroine to a sex object needing to be "rescued" by a Prince Charming who will make her life meaningful—a narrative pattern that feminists refer to as "the Cinderella syndrome." *(Touchstone Pictures)*

especially Britain and the United States. The Japanese are simultaneously repelled and attracted by both sets of polarities:

Traditional	*Modern*
Japanese	Western
Feudal	Democratic
Past	Future
Society	Individual
Hierarchy	Equality
Nature	Technology
Duty	Inclination
Self-sacrifice	Self-expression
Consensus	Diversity
Age	Youth
Authority	Autonomy
Conservative	Liberal
Fatalism	Optimism
Obedience	Independence
Form	Substance
Security	Anxiety

11–15. *The Searchers* (U.S.A., 1956), *with John Wayne, directed by John Ford.*
Personality stars frequently convey a ready-made ideology—a set of values that are associated with a given star because of his or her previous film roles. Their personas often incorporate elements from their actual lives as well. For example, John Wayne was associated in the public mind with a right-wing ideology. Most of his roles were military commanders, western heroes, law-and-order advocates, and authoritarian patriarchs. In private life he was an outspoken conservative, an America-first patriot who championed respect for authority, family values, and military supremacy.   *(Warner Bros.)*

A number of structuralists have explored genre films in a similar manner. For example, Jim Kitses, Peter Wollen, and others have pointed out how westerns are often vehicles for exploring clashes of value between East and West in American culture. By clustering the thematic motifs around a "master antimony" (a controlling or dominant code), a western can be analyzed according to its deep structure rather than its plot, which is often conventionalized (and less meaningful) in genre films. Such critics have demonstrated how each cultural polarity symbolizes a complex of positive and negative traits:

West	*East*
Wilderness	Civilization
Individualism	Community
Self-interest	Social welfare
Freedom	Restriction
Anarchy	Law and order

West	East
Savagery	Refinement
Private honour	Institutional justice
Paganism	Christianity
Nature	Culture
Masculine	Feminine
Pragmatism	Idealism

11–16.   *Une Affaire des femmes ("Story of Women,"* **France, 1988),** *with Isabelle Huppert, directed by Claude Chabrol.*

In realistic films especially, characterization is generally complex and ambiguous, filled with the contradictions of life. Based on an actual series of events that took place in France during the Nazi occupation, *Story of Women* deals with a working-class housewife (Huppert) who comes to the aid of a desperate girlfriend who feels trapped by an unwanted pregnancy. The Huppert character helps her by performing an illegal abortion. Later she helps another despairing woman who has had six offspring in seven years and is wracked with guilt because she no longer loves her children. Soon the protagonist is running a profitable abortion business, becoming coarser with each transaction. Eventually she is arrested, tried, and executed for her crimes by an all-male justice system. Our sympathies are torn. On the one hand, the protagonist is strong and independent, a loyal friend and a shrewd critic of the old-boy network that forces women to be baby machines for the state. On the other hand, as a result of her greed, she wrecks her marriage and destroys the lives of her own children, not to speak of her sleazy association with a Nazi collaborator who becomes her lover.

(An MK2/New Yorker Films Release)

West	East
Agrarian	Industrial
Purity	Corruption
Dynamic	Static
Future	Past
Experience	Knowledge
American	European

Semiotics and structuralism expanded the parameters of film theory considerably. Their pluralistic approach allows for much more flexibility, complexity, and depth in the critical enterprise. But these theories are merely tools of analysis. By themselves, they can tell us nothing of the *value* of signs and codes within a film. Like every other theory, then, these are only as good as their prac-

11–17. *High Hopes* **(Britain, 1988),** *with Ruth Sheen, Edna Dore, and Philip Davis, directed by Mike Leigh.*

British society has always been class conscious, especially during the 1980s under Prime Minister Margaret Thatcher. She dominated this decade in the United Kingdom just as her friend and fellow conservative Ronald Reagan dominated the political climate in America. Like many liberal English artists of his generation, Mike Leigh was sickened by the materialism of British society during this era. His satirical targets range over a wide spectrum and are richly deserving of their skewering. Only an eccentric hippie couple (Sheen and Davis) provide an island of decency in this sea of greed, pretentiousness, and conspicuous consumption.   *(Skouras Pictures)*

titioners. The writer's intelligence, taste, passion, knowledge, and sensitivity are what produce good criticism, not necessarily the theoretical methodology used.

IDEOLOGY AND CULTURE

The semiologists and structuralists argued that the meanings of films do not come from the reality to which they refer or from the intentions of their authors or even from the creative interpretations of their audiences. Since film language is a system of codes and signs, it is the way the different elements relate to each other that creates meaning. This language-based approach was soon taken further by theorists who applied its methods to the study of the social and psychological processes involved in making and viewing films.

11–18. *Mourir à tue-tête ("Scream from Silence,"* **Canada, 1978),** *directed by Anne-Claire Poirier.*

Poirier's powerful and controversial feminist film about rape uses a variety of techniques to make its point. A fiction film in which a young woman endures a particularly brutal rape is discussed by two women filmmakers who are editing it. Several documentary sequences—a ritual female circumcision in Africa, the shaving of women's heads in France after World War II—suggest that rape is the product of widespread and deeply ingrained cultural behaviour in which male violence is used to control female sexuality. The film also includes symbolic sequences, like the one shown here: An anonymous group of rape victims address a male judge who remains an off-screen voice (of God?), drawing attention to the extent of the rape problem and to the indifference of the legal system.   *(National Film Board of Canada)*

Drawing on the psychoanalytic theory of Jacques Lacan and the political philosophy of Louis Althusser, this new approach emerged in France during the social unrest of the late 1960s. It was a major influence on the discussions that accompanied the events of May 1968 when students and workers almost toppled the French government in an effort to achieve educational and social change. These events led many filmmakers to think about the political implications of their work, most notably Jean-Luc Godard. During the 1960s, Godard's films gradually became more formally challenging and politically radical (**2–3; 8–27**). For several years after 1968, he made his films as an anonymous member of the Dziga Vertov Cooperative, named after the Soviet documentary filmmaker (see Chapter 9). The former champion of the auteur theory thus protested against the idea of film as the expression of an individual artist and advocated the need for collective political action.

11–19.   *Thelma & Louise* (U.S.A., 1991), *with Susan Sarandon and Geena Davis, directed by Ridley Scott.*

Feminism was one of many liberation movements that rose to prominence in America and Europe during the 1960s. Virtually every powerful woman in the Hollywood film industry today has been influenced by the movement—not to speak of many male allies. *Thelma & Louise* explores the intimate bond between two best friends (pictured) whose weekend getaway unexpectedly takes them on an adventure across the United States. The movie explores such themes as marriage, work, independence, female bonding, and male chauvinism, often from a humorous perspective. Interestingly, the movie's structure is indebted to two traditionally male genres—the buddy film and the road picture.   *(MGM)*

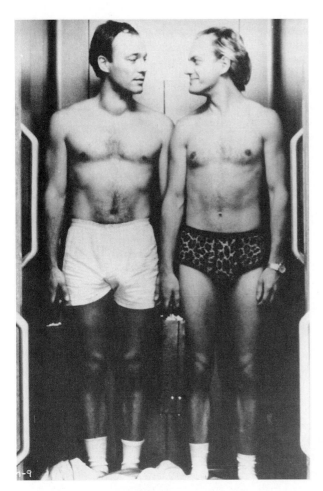

11–20. *Men* (Germany, 1985), *with Heiner Lauterbach and Uwe Ochsenknecht, directed by Doris Dörrie.*
A number of feminist film critics have written about "the male gaze," sometimes known simply as "the gaze." The term refers to the voyeuristic aspects of cinema—sneaking furtive glances at the forbidden, the erotic. But because most filmmakers are males, so too is the point of view of the camera: Everyone looks at the action through male eyes. The gaze fixes women in postures that cater to male needs and fantasies rather than allowing women to express their own desires and the full range of their humanity. When the director is a woman, the gaze is often eroticized from a female point of view, offering us fresh perspectives on the battle between the sexes, as well as among the same sex, as in Dörrie's good-natured social satire, *Men.*   *(New Yorker Films)*

Godard's new direction received support from the new editors of *Cahiers du cinéma*, which had also turned against its earlier commitment to the auteur theory. During the 1970s, these ideas became increasingly influential in film studies, despite many complaints against the high degree of abstraction and the jargon used by many theorists. The British film journal *Screen* published many important essays in this tradition, including translations from the French and new work by its own contributors.

These writers were especially concerned with the relations between film and ideology. In his interpretation of the writings of Karl Marx, Althusser defined ideology not just as a body of ideas but as the representation of "the imaginary relationship of individuals to their real conditions of existence." From this perspective, ideology works beneath the level of the conscious mind and persuades us to accept the values of our culture as if they were produced by nature. Beginning even before we are born, the workings of ideology provide us with "subject positions" through which we view the world and construct our identities. We may assume that these identities are personal and private, but they are actually shaped by social institutions and the mass media. We thus come to accept the "dominant ideology" even when its values do not work in our best interests.

As a medium that works primarily through images, film was seen as an ideal vehicle for ideology. Theorists influenced by Althusser were especially suspicious of classical narrative cinema with its stress on **continuity** editing and the subordination of style to narrative. They argued for new kinds of cinema that would call attention to the means by which the images were produced. Whereas classical narrative cinema aims to create an illusion of reality and encourages the spectator to identify with the main character, the new forms would require an active and critically detached audience. The models to which these theorists pointed included the Soviet montage school of the 1920s and various **avant-garde** traditions.

The key idea was that new ideas could not be conveyed by old forms. However, most audiences tended to reject these new kinds of film as unfamiliar and unpleasing. The theorists, of course, attributed this negative response to the ideological processes that represented classical narrative cinema as the norm against which all other films were judged. As we have seen, a similar argument was put forward in Canada to explain why Canadian audiences preferred Hollywood films to the work of Canadian filmmakers (see Chapter 10). Nevertheless the effect was that radical filmmakers produced films that did not communicate with the masses in whose interests they were supposedly made.

There are other problems with this kind of analysis. It attributes enormous power to ideology and often implies that it is virtually impossible to escape from its clutches, even if the theorists have somehow managed to do so. There is also no clear sense of what an alternative to ideology might be. More recent film theory suggests that spectators may be more active and creative than theories of ideology have claimed.

A number of theorists, especially those influenced by the work of David Bordwell, have put forward cognitive models of spectatorship that stress the conscious activity involved in responding to a film. These models suggest that even quite conventional films require an active response from their audiences. We draw on our previous experience of films that provide us with the schemas and templates that we need to decipher images and to construct a film's story from its plot (see Chapter 2).

Other theorists have turned to the work of Stuart Hall and the British Cultural Studies movement, which also calls into question the idea that audiences are "cultural dupes" at the mercy of an all-powerful ideological apparatus. This work draws on semiotic and ideological approaches but suggests that the processes of encoding and decoding cultural texts allow for a range of different responses. The stress is on what people do with texts rather than on what texts do to people. Instead of ideology, theorists within this tradition tend to speak of "hegemony," a term used by the Italian Marxist thinker Antonio Gramsci to describe how the dominant social class needs to win the consent of other classes to maintain its power. This is a dynamic process in which audiences are

11–21. *My American Cousin* (Canada, 1984), *with John Wildman and Margaret Langrick, directed by Sandy Wilson.*
Feminist critics have examined film history to draw attention to the contributions of women filmmakers. There have been few women directors or producers, a situation that is slowly changing in many countries. Women made major contributions to the revival of Canadian cinema in the 1980s and 1990s, one of the first being Sandy Wilson's small-budget autobiographical film, set in British Columbia in the 1950s, about a teenager's infatuation with her rebellious American cousin.   *(Fineline Productions)*

not completely controlled by the film industry nor completely free to make their own choices and construct their own meanings.

Contemporary film theory continues to explore specific questions of film language, but it is also increasingly interested in broader issues of culture and technology. Like the films themselves, film theory has been deeply influenced by the major social movements of the last few decades, including feminism, the gay liberation movement, and the politics of race and ethnicity. While historians have explored the unequal conditions in which women, gays, and racial and ethnic minorities have worked in the film industry, theorists have focused on the ways in which members of these groups are represented (or not represented) on screen.

Until recently, women directors and producers were rare in every major national cinema, and even today men far outnumber women in these positions of power. Feminist critics have drawn attention to the neglected work of women filmmakers **(11–21)**, while theorists have explored the images of women in the

11–22. *Lianna* **(U.S.A., 1983),** *with Linda Griffiths and Jane Hallaren, written and directed by John Sayles.*
An important subgenre of the gay cinema is the coming-out film—a young person's first experience with homosexual love. This movie concerns a browbeaten wife (Griffiths, left) who leaves her husband and has an affair with an older sophisticated woman (Hallaren). *(United Artists)*

one area of filmmaking in which they have been conspicuous: as actors and characters. In an enormously influential essay, first published in *Screen* in 1975, Laura Mulvey argued that classical narrative cinema assumes a "male gaze" of which women are the object. According to Mulvey, the male hero typically drives the film's action, while female characters exist only in relation to his desire—and that of the male spectator. Women connote "to-be-looked-at-ness."

Later theorists, and Mulvey herself, have questioned the psychoanalytic and ideological framework of her thesis. Although many films do conform to her model, critics have pointed to genres that address women's desires, such as the domestic melodrama or "woman's film" of the 1940s and 1950s. Theorists have also suggested that popular films do not always enforce traditional gender roles but often offer fantasies of escaping from these roles.

While feminist theory focused attention on representations of gender, most of the discussion, until recently, dealt with ideological constructions of femininity. As gender roles have gradually changed in society, however, tradi-

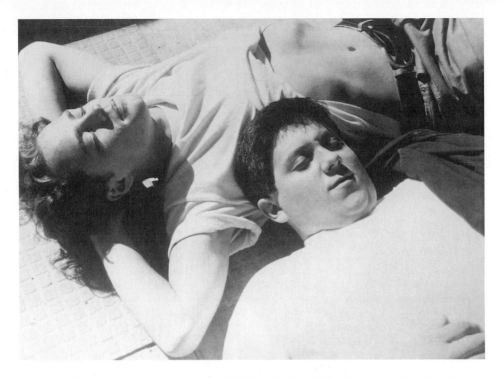

11-23. *The Hanging Garden* (Canada, 1997), *with Troy Veinotte and Joel S. Keller, directed by Thom Fitzgerald.*

An overweight adolescent (Veinotte) awakens to an awareness of his homosexuality and then hangs himself in the garden in which his father abused him as a child. At least this is what appears to happen in a film whose realism often becomes surrealist; but we have already seen William (played by a different actor) return to his rural Nova Scotia home from the city where he has lost weight and become secure and comfortable with his sexual identity. As the director puts it, the film shows that "no matter how much you hate your life and yourself in the current moment, it is possible to become the person you want to be." *(Alliance Atlantis)*

---

tional ideas of masculinity, once taken for granted, have been called into question. Theorists have begun to explore the different ways in which films have represented male identities, analyzing for example the ideological meanings of such masculine icons as Sylvester Stallone and Arnold Schwarzenneger in the context of the feminist movement **(1–7b; 11–24)**.

Feminist theory also called into question the heterosexual norms that governed the depiction of sexuality in films. The gay liberation movement also challenged these norms and the culture that created them. The film industry had always operated within a dominant ideology that prevented the overt expression of homosexual desire. Gay filmmakers in Hollywood and elsewhere had to conceal their sexual orientation, and gay characters could appear in films only in highly coded or negatively stereotyped ways.

Although gay characters now appear more frequently in Hollywood films, and even in television series, critics and theorists continue to debate whether these representations succeed in breaking with dominant ideological

11–24. *Rambo: First Blood Part II* **(U.S.A., 1985),** *with Sylvester Stallone, directed by George P. Cosmatos.*
Movies like Stallone's *Rambo* trilogy are marketed toward adolescent males—of all ages. The films earned huge grosses abroad, especially in the Third World, where American action films are very popular. The movies project a right-wing image of masculinity—tough, masterful, inexorable. This is an all-male world (the homoeroticism is largely subconscious) of sweat, hard pecs, and big guns.
(Tri-Star Pictures)

conceptions. The depiction of a young woman discovering her lesbian identity in *Lianna* **(11–22)** or a gay lawyer dying of AIDS in *Philadelphia* broke new ground for Hollywood cinema, but some critics argued that their good intentions were confounded by narrative structures that reaffirmed heterosexuality as the norm. Outside Hollywood, contemporary filmmakers like Rainer Werner Fassbinder and Derek Jarman dedicated careers to examining contemporary society from a gay perspective. In Canada important work in this direction has come from John Greyson **(5–3)** and Léa Pool **(10–18).**

Gay filmmakers have adopted a variety of styles, although many have been associated with a **camp** sensibility that involves the theatrical exaggeration and mockery of conventional stereotypes. More recently, queer theory has explored and celebrated films and filmmakers whose work expresses forms of subjectivity and sexuality that deviate from the established norms. Queer theorists have also found evidence of such deviations in mainstream films that on the surface seem to conform to those norms, thus suggesting that the experience of sexuality is much more complex and unstable than previously assumed.

Alongside the developments in society associated with the feminist and gay liberation movements, attitudes toward race and ethnicity have also changed. Film theorists have explored the implications for the medium of what Cornel West has called "the new cultural politics of difference," which seeks to break down the binary oppositions that structuralists identified as vital to the dominant ideology and classical narrative cinema. Instead of oppositions, such as us/them, white/black, in which one term is always preferred, the new approach advocates hybrid identities and hybrid forms to express a range of different possibilities (11–31).

Popular cinema has responded to these changes either by adapting to them or resisting them. While Hollywood films still dominate cinema screens in most parts of the world, the emergence of video, computer and satellite technology has made images and stories from other cultures more widely accessible. On the one hand, the emergence of the blockbuster movie in contemporary Hollywood depends on the use of publicity to generate a mass audience by appealing to as many groups in the potential audience as possible. On the other hand, the increased visibility of ethnic and lifestyle subcultures makes it possible to produce smaller-budget films for specific audience segments.

In culturally diverse countries like the United States and Canada, there are many subcultures—pockets of cultural values that coexist within the dominant ideology. Ethnic groups are distinct social communities within a larger cultural system that claim or are accorded special status (usually inferior) on the basis of such considerations as religion, language, ancestry, and race. In the United States, such groups include African Americans, Hispanics, Native Americans, and of course the many waves of immigration from abroad, especially those who have not been fully integrated into the American mainstream, like the Chinese Americans of *The Joy Luck Club* (11–25).

Movies that deal with ethnic issues usually dramatize the tensions between the dominant ideology and the cultural values of a minority community. For example, in the Australian cinema, a number of movies have dealt with the clash between the predominantly white, Anglo-Saxon power structure and the dark-skinned Aboriginal peoples, who have a long heritage of oppression and exploitation, as in *The Chant of Jimmie Blacksmith* (11–26).

African-American film historians have chronicled the sad, shameful treatment of blacks in American movies—a mean-spirited reflection of their treatment in American society as a whole. For the first fifty years of the American cinema, black characters were usually relegated to demeaning stereotypes. The title of Donald Bogle's history of blacks in American films says it all: *Toms, Coons, Mulattoes, Mammies & Bucks.* The most positive images of African Americans during this half-century were generally faithful servants, like the roles played by Hat-

11–25. *The Joy Luck Club* **(U.S.A., 1993),** *with Kieu Chinh, directed by Wayne Wang.*
Based on the best-selling novel by Amy Tan, this movie explores the conflict between the old-world ways of four Chinese-born women and the more liberal values of their American-born daughters. Movies that deal with ethnic issues often explore the theme of culture clash. *(Buena Vista Pictures)*

11–26. *The Chant of Jimmie Blacksmith* **(Australia, 1978),** *with Angela Punch and Tommy Lewis, directed by Fred Schepisi.*
This film is based on an actual series of events that took place around 1900. Jimmie Blacksmith (Lewis), half white and half Aborigine, is rescued from a life of misery by a Caucasian missionary couple. They raise him to be docile and respectful, to admire all that is white, despise all that is black. The Reverend Mrs. even advises the youth to marry a white farm girl, produce children, who in turn will produce children who would be "scarcely black at all." The roots of racism, Schepisi demonstrates, are both economic and sexual. Whites exploit Jimmie and other Aborigines as cheap labour and fear them as sexual threats. *(New Yorker Films)*

11–27. *Boyz N the Hood* (U.S.A., 1991), *with Cuba Gooding Jr., Larry Fishburne, and Ice Cube; written and directed by John Singleton.*
Ethnic filmmakers often use a realistic style to depict the authentic textures of everyday life. *Boys N the Hood* is a powerful coming-of-age drama set in the mean streets of the black ghettos of Los Angeles. Director Jóhn Singleton made this debut film on a small budget when he was only twenty-two years old. He was the youngest director in history to be nominated for an Academy Award in directing.   *(Columbia Pictures)*

tie McDaniel, the first black performer ever to win an Academy Award (for *Gone With the Wind* in 1939).

In the contemporary cinema, no African-American filmmaker has provoked more controversy than Spike Lee. Much of his criticism has been directed at people of his own race. In *Do the Right Thing*, Lee explores the smouldering tensions between black ghetto dwellers and an Italian-American family that owns a pizzeria in an inner-city neighbourhood (**7–11**). In *Jungle Fever*, Lee dramatizes the problems of an interracial couple. The story ends with the lovers calling it quits—defeated by the prejudices of their own communities as well as their personal failings.

The values and characteristics of the dominant groups in society are not normally regarded as ethnic, while the different values of so-called ethnic groups have often been represented in the media through negative stereotypes. It is often difficult for filmmakers to avoid confirming these stereotypes even if they set out to oppose them. Thus John Smith's National Film Board film *Sitting in Limbo*, which deals with the problems of teenagers in Montreal's Caribbean community, is often seen as reinforcing stereotypes because of its focus on a pregnant black woman and her unemployed boyfriend.

Members of ethnic groups have historically been faced with the choice of assimilating into the mainstream of society or attempting to conserve the group's cultural heritage. Canada's policy of multiculturalism was designed to offer a third option, in which ethnic groups could participate in the national culture while retaining their distinct identities (see Chapter 10). Although this policy had some unforeseen effects, it anticipated recent changes caused by increased mobility and the spread of electronic media in the modern world.

In his recent Canadian movie *Lulu*, Srinivas Krishna has explored many of these issues (**Colour Plate 5**). The title character is a Vietnamese woman who was introduced to her white Canadian husband on a videotape made in a Hong Kong refugee camp. Other characters include an Asian expelled from Uganda by Idi Amin, the husband's Caribbean friend, and an Arab refugee making a video documentary about the experience of ethnic minorities. The movie deals with the emergence of hybrid identities in what the husband calls a "mixed neighbourhood" and with the role of the media in this process. It draws on ethnic and gender stereotypes but constantly unsettles the assumptions on which they are based.

HISTORIOGRAPHY

Historiography deals with the theory of history—the assumptions, principles, and methodologies of historical study. Film history is a relatively recent area of inquiry—a hundred years is not a very lengthy period of study compared with that of the traditional arts. As in other areas of film theory, much of the best work in film historiography has taken place during the past two decades.

Film historians scoff at the naïve notion that there is *a* film history. Rather, they insist that there are many film histories, and each is defined by the historian's particular interests, biases, and prejudices. Theorists have chartered four different types of film history, each with its own set of philosophical assumptions, methods, and sources of evidence: (**1**) aesthetic film histories— film as art; (**2**) technological film histories—motion pictures as inventions and machines; (**3**) economic histories—film as industry; and (**4**) social histories— movies as a reflection of the audience's values, desires, and fears.

Most film historians regard cinema as too sprawling and complex to be covered by any single history. They view the field as a vast, infinite mass of data that needs to be sifted through and organized to be made coherent. Each historian concentrates on a given type of evidence, highlighting its significance while de-emphasizing or ignoring "irrelevant" data. Critics sometimes refer to this process of selection and emphasis as **foregrounding**—isolating fragments of evidence for the purpose of closer study. Foregrounding is always an implicit value judgment. Each type of film historian necessarily wrenches these fragments from their ecological context, thus presenting us with a somewhat skewed view of the whole. Each type of historian will also choose to focus on different movies, personalities, and events.

Aesthetic film historians concern themselves with a tradition of masterpieces and great filmmakers. Constantly subject to reevaluation, this tradition

11–28. *Short Cuts* (U.S.A., 1993), *with Lily Tomlin and Tom Waits, directed by Robert Altman.*

Aesthetic film historians and elitist critics tend to concentrate on such movies as *Short Cuts* because of their cultural prestige. Robert Altman is regarded as one of the great artists of the contemporary cinema, creator of such movies as *M*A*S*H, McCabe and Mrs. Miller, Nashville,* and *The Player.* Based on the short stories of Raymond Carver, *Short Cuts* is faithful to its source, including its tone of cynicism and bitterness. The film features an embarrassment of riches in the cast, many of them important stars who would have worked for Altman for nothing because of his enormous prestige within the world film community. Though widely praised by critics and nominated for a number of awards, the movie failed to arouse much interest with the general public, and its box-office revenues were small.   *(Fine Line Features)*

encompasses a broad consensus of critics, historians, and scholars. This is an elite form of history, ignoring the vast majority of motion pictures to concentrate on a relative handful of important works of art that have endured the test of time—that is, movies that are still great despite our viewing them in a totally different context. Aesthetic historians value a work primarily for its artistic richness, irrespective of whether the film was commercially successful. Thus, in most aesthetic histories, a huge popular success like *Home Alone* receives much less discussion than *Citizen Kane,* which failed at the box office.

Most college textbook histories—such as Gerald Mast's *A Short History of the Movies;* David A. Cook's *A History of Narrative Film;* and *Flashback,* by Louis

Giannetti and Scott Eyman—attempt to integrate as much as possible from technological, economic, and social film histories, but their main emphasis is on film as art. Opponents of this type of history have scoffed at its "Great Man" assumptions—that is, film history is largely the study of a few gifted individuals, not the dynamic matrix of social, industrial, and technological influences that inevitably affect all filmmakers, gifted or not.

The American scholar Raymond Fielding has put forth the philosophy of technological historians succinctly: "The history of motion pictures—as an art form, as a medium of communication, and as an industry—has been determined principally by technological innovations." Historians of this type are also concerned with "Great Men," such as W.K.L. Dickson, Thomas Edison, George Eastman, and Lee Deforest—inventors and scientists rather than artists or industry moguls. Technological historians are concerned with the implications—artistic, commercial, and ideological—of such innovations as portable cameras, **synchronous sound,** colour, improved film stocks, 3-D, stereophonic sound, steadycams, and so on **(11–29).**

11-29. *Medium Cool* (U.S.A., 1969), *with Robert Forster (at camera) and Peter Bonerz (sound), directed by Haskell Wexler.*
Technological film histories stress the importance of mechanical innovations in the evolution of the cinema. New technologies create new aesthetics. For example, in the late 1950s, television journalists needed simple, lightweight equipment to capture news stories quickly, while they were actually happening. The development of the so-called handheld camera (actually, usually mounted on a shoulder harness or tripod), portable sound equipment, zoom lenses, and more light-sensitive fast film stocks was in response to this need. In the 1960s, this new technology was appropriated by fiction filmmakers, allowing them to shoot movies more spontaneously and in actual locations and thus to create a more authentic style of realism.   *(Paramount Pictures)*

Cinema is the most expensive artistic medium in history, and its development has been largely determined by its financial sponsors—this is the thesis of most economic film histories, such as Benjamin B. Hampton's *History of the American Film Industry from Its Beginnings to 1931,* and Thomas H. Guback's *The International Film Industry: Western Europe and America Since 1945.* In most European countries the cinema in its early stages of development fell into the hands of artists who shared most of the values and tastes of the educated elite. In the former Soviet Union and other ex-Communist countries, film production was carefully regulated by the government, and the movies produced in those countries reflected most of the values of the political elite.

In the United States, the film industry developed within a capitalistic system of production. The Hollywood studio system was an attempt on the part of a handful of large corporations—MGM, Paramount, Warner Brothers, etc.— to monopolize the production of fiction films, and hence maximize their profits. For about three decades—roughly from 1925 to 1955—the major studios succeeded, producing about 90 percent of the fiction films in the United States, largely because the companies were **vertically integrated**; that is, they controlled all three phases of the industry: **(1)** production—the Hollywood studios; **(2)** distribution—financial headquarters in New York; and **(3)** exhibition—the large chains of big-city first-run theatres owned by the company.

During the era of studio dominance, virtually every filmmaker had to come to grips with this economic reality. The studio system was the only ballgame in town, and the **majors** were in business to make profits, the bigger the

11–30. *City of Hope* (U.S.A., 1991), *with John Sayles, written, edited, and directed by Sayles.*

Economic film histories concentrate on who pays the bills, who sponsors the making of a movie and why. Like many European filmmakers, Sayles finances his movies independently, guaranteeing him total artistic control. His goal is not the amassing of huge profits, but creative freedom. Most of his movies have been made on small budgets, with the same loyal crew of actors and technicians. This communal spirit has allowed them to produce nearly one movie a year. Though Sayles's films have not been huge hits, most of them were sufficiently profitable to maintain a constant cash flow. *(The Samuel Goldwyn Company)*

11-31. *Masala* **(Canada, 1991),** *with Madhuri Bhatia, Saeed Jaffrey (centre), and Les Porter, directed by Srinivas Krishna.*
Krishna is an independent Canadian filmmaker who argues that his films are not part of the Canadian tradition. "That kind of nation-state way of dividing culture is irrelevant to my personal experience," he insists. Just as a "masala," in Indian cooking, is a mixture of spices that combine to create a distinctive flavour, *Masala* uses a mixture of different styles, including musical numbers in the style of popular Indian movies, to explore the impact of living in a multicultural society on different generations of the Indian community. Although it pokes fun at official multiculturalism as embodied by the pompous Canadian minister (Porter), the film suggests that, in an increasingly globalized culture, identities are shaped by a mixture of influences and pressures.   *(Courtesy of Divani Films)*

better. In short, the profit motive has been the main driving force in the evolution of the American film industry, and movies tend to reaffirm the ideological values of their sponsors. However, even economic historians would concede that other motives have also figured in the production of American movies—the desire for prestige, artistic integrity, and so on. Likewise, movies made in Communist countries were occasionally critical of the social system that produced them. History—of any kind—is filled with contradictions.

Social histories are mainly concerned with the audience. They emphasize film as a collective experience, as a reflection of mass sentiments during any given era. These sentiments can be overtly articulated or subliminally insinuated by appealing to our subconscious desires. Social historians often turn to statistics and sociological data for supporting evidence. Books like Robert Sklar's *Movie-Made America* and Garth Jowett's *Film: The Democratic Art* are filled with revealing statistics about audience likes and dislikes.

Social historians have also devoted a great deal of attention to the American star system, arguing that popular stars are usually a reflection of audience values and anxieties. Unfortunately, these concerns do not lend themselves to quantitative analysis, and social historians are sometimes criticized for their intuitive leaps in logic. Historians of this sort are also interested in social stereotypes—how a movie portrays blacks, women, authority figures, and so on.

In *Film History: Theory and Practice,* Robert C. Allen and Douglas Gomery set forth the principal advantages and shortcomings of the various types of film history, arguing that a more integrated approach would minimize the dangers of distortion. Indeed, as in other areas of film theory, film history is increasingly being viewed as a monolithic ecological system that must be studied from various perspectives to be comprehensively understood.

FURTHER READING

ALLEN, ROBERT C., ed., *Channels of Discourse, Reassembled: Television and Contemporary Criticism* (Chapel Hill: University of North Carolina Press, 1992). Discussion of different theories, applied to television but also useful for film students.

ALLEN, ROBERT C., and DOUGLAS GOMERY, *Film History: Theory and Practice* (New York: Alfred A. Knopf, 1985). A provocative study of the problems of writing film history.

ANDREW, DUDLEY, *Concepts in Film Theory* (New York: Oxford University Press, 1984). A lucid exploration of the major areas of debate within the field.

———, *The Major Film Theories: An Introduction* (New York: Oxford University Press, 1976). A helpful and clearly written exposition of the theories of such figures as Arnheim, Eisenstein, Kracauer, Bazin, Metz, and others.

HOOKS, BELL, *Reel to Real: Race, Sex, and Class at the Movies* (New York: Routledge, 1996). Provocative essays on recent movies.

LAPSLEY, ROBERT, and MICHAEL WESTLAKE, *Film Theory: An Introduction* (Manchester: Manchester University Press, 1988). Thorough survey of the field.

MAST, GERALD, MARSHALL COHEN, and LEO BRAUDY, eds., *Film Theory and Criticism: Introductory Readings,* 5th ed. (New York: Oxford University Press, 1999). An excellent collection of articles from a variety of perspectives.

NICHOLS, BILL, *Ideology and the Image: Social Representation in the Cinema and Other Media* (Bloomington: Indiana University Press, 1981). Perceptive and copiously illustrated.

ROSEN, PHILIP, ed., *Narrative, Apparatus, Ideology: A Film Theory Reader* (New York: Columbia University Press, 1986). A collection of scholarly articles on and by contemporary film theorists.

SARRIS, ANDREW, *The American Cinema: Directors and Directions 1929–1968* (New York: Dutton, 1968). A basic document of the auteur theory.

RKO

The motion picture medium has an extraordinary range of expression. It has in common with the plastic arts the fact that it is a visual composition projected on a two-dimensional surface; with dance, that it can deal in the arrangement of movement; with theatre, that it can create a dramatic intensity of events; with music, that it can compose in the rhythms and phrases of time and can be attended by song and instrument; with poetry, that it can juxtapose images; with literature generally, that it can encompass in its sound track the abstractions available only to language.
—MAYA DEREN, FILMMAKER AND THEORIST

As Maya Deren's observation suggests, analyzing a movie is no easy task. Film is a more complex medium than the traditional arts because movies synthesize many language systems simultaneously, bombarding the spectator with literally hundreds of symbolic ideas and emotions at the same time, some of them overt, others subliminal. Of course, filmmakers rarely use each language system at full tilt. In every **scene**—indeed, in every **shot**—there is a principle of hierarchical subordination. The combinations are constantly in flux, like the couplings, divergencies, and recouplings of a group of dancers.

The French critic André Bazin described *Citizen Kane* as "a discourse on method" because of its encyclopedic technical range. The film, directed by Orson Welles (1915–1985), is an ideal choice to demonstrate how these various language systems interact dynamically within a single text. The following pages can only touch on the high points of this famous movie, but the analysis can serve as a guide for a systematic explication of any film.

Citizen Kane is the life story of a powerful newspaper magnate, Charles Foster Kane, who is as contradictory as he is controversial. The film is a fictionalized biography of the ruthless publishing baron William Randolph Hearst (1863–1951). Actually, the characters in the movie are composites, drawn from the lives of several famous American tycoons, but Hearst was the most obvious. Herman Mankiewicz, the co-author of the screenplay, knew Hearst personally and was a friend of the old yellow journalist's mistress, screen **star** Marion Davies. Davies was among the best-liked personalities in the film industry, and except for her fondness for alcohol and jigsaw puzzles, was quite unlike the Susan Alexander character in *Citizen Kane.*

The movie recounts the major events of the protagonist's lengthy life. Born in comparative obscurity, the eight-year-old Charles is sent away to boarding school after his mother inherits a huge fortune through a fluke. Kane's guardian throughout his youth is the banker Walter P. Thatcher, a pompous blowhard and political reactionary. After living a life of frivolous self-indulgence, Kane decides in his mid-twenties to become a newspaper publisher. Along with his close associates, the doggedly loyal Bernstein and the suave Jed Leland, he dedicates himself to championing the cause of the underprivileged and attacking corrupt institutions of power. At the height of his career, Kane marries the refined Emily Norton, niece of the president of the United States. But the marriage eventually turns stale, then rancid. In middle age, Kane consoles himself by secretly taking a mistress, Susan Alexander, a pretty but rather empty-headed shop worker with vague aspirations of becoming a singer.

Buoyed by his fame and popularity, Kane runs for governor of New York. His opponent, Boss Jim Gettys, attempts to blackmail him into withdrawing from the race by threatening to go public with the hypocrisy of Kane's marriage and to expose his cozy arrangement with Susan. Outraged, Kane refuses to capitulate, even though he knows that the scandal will publicly humiliate his wife, his son, and Susan. Kane loses the election and the respect of his best friend, Jed Leland. Emily divorces Kane, taking their young son with her.

Kane redirects his energies toward the career of a proxy, his new young wife, Susan Alexander Kane. He is determined to make her into a great opera star, despite the inconvenient fact that she has no discernible talent. Ignoring her objections indifferent to her public mortification, Kane pushes the talentless Susan to the brink of suicide. Thwarted again, he finally agrees to give up on his scheme to make her an opera star. Instead, he builds an enormous isolated palace, Xanadu, where he and Susan retire into semiseclusion. After years of being bullied into submission by Kane, Susan rebels and walks out on him. Finally, alone and embittered, the old man dies amidst the empty opulence of Xanadu.

MEDIUM

As critic David Bordwell has suggested, *Citizen Kane* is a film that celebrates "the two founts of cinema—the fantasy of Méliès and the reportage of Lumière." André Bazin used it to illustrate his arguments about **realism** and drew attention to the extensive use of **long takes** and **deep-focus** compositions. Other critics have shown that, far from respecting real space and time, many of the shots discussed by Bazin were actually created through special effects. The lighting and **editing** techniques also often draw on the **formalist** tradition, and the film certainly does not conform to the idea, shared by Bazin and **classical cinema**, that style should not call attention to itself. The often jarring combination of realist and formalist elements occurs at all levels of the film's style and helps to express the tensions that emerge in the film about the interpretation of Kane's life.

While critics have debated the relative importance of realism and formalism in the film's style, an even more impassioned argument has raged over the question of authorship. Bazin and his followers at *Cahiers du cinéma* regarded Welles as a great Hollywood **auteur** and treated the film as one expression of the director's personal vision that continued to develop in his later films. Some of these critics even preferred films, such as *Mr Arkadin* and *Touch of Evil*, on which Welles worked in more difficult conditions and managed to introduce his personal touch into routine narratives through his distinctive use of film language.

Pauline Kael, the influential American critic, was an outspoken opponent of the auteur theory and, in 1971, she published a long introduction to the *Citizen Kane* **screenplay** in which she disputed the assumption that Welles was responsible for the film's style and meanings.

Kael contended that Welles merely added a few polishing touches to Herman Mankiewicz's finished product. Mankiewicz was a Hollywood regular, a notorious drunk—charming, witty, and almost totally unreliable. When he approached Welles with the original idea for *American* (it was later called *John Citizen, U.S.A.*, and finally *Citizen Kane*), Welles asked his former partner, John Houseman, to help Mankiewicz write the screenplay, preferably in an isolated place, far removed from temptation.

Welles made extensive revisions on the first few drafts of the screenplay—so extensive that Mankiewicz denounced the movie because it departed radically from his scenario. Nor did he want Welles's name to appear on the screenplay credit, and he took his case to the Writers Guild. At this time, a director was not allowed any writing credit unless he or she contributed 50 percent or more of the screenplay. In a compromise gesture, the guild allowed both of them credit, with Mankiewicz receiving top billing.

When the controversy resurfaced in the 1970s, the American scholar Robert L. Carringer settled the case once and for all. He examined the seven principal drafts of the screenplay, plus many last-minute revision memoranda and additional sources. Carringer's conclusion: The early Mankiewicz drafts contain "dozens of pages of dull, plodding material that will eventually be discarded or replaced altogether. And most tellingly, there is virtually nothing in them of that stylistic wit and fluidity that is the most engaging trait of the film itself." In short, Mankiewicz provided the raw material; Welles provided the genius.

The script sparkles with surprises. The main characters are a far cry from the tired stereotypes of most movies of this era. Only Thatcher seems conventional, a variation of the 1930s tycoon. The writing is often tersely funny. During Kane's noisy marriage to Susan, for example, the couple is surrounded by pushy reporters. When asked what he's going to do now, Kane replies, "We're going to be a great opera star." Susan chimes in: "Charlie said if I didn't, he'd build me an opera house." The gallant Kane demurs: "That won't be necessary." Cut to a newspaper headline: KANE BUILDS OPERA HOUSE.

There are also moments of pure poetry, like Bernstein's surprising reply to Thompson after the reporter scoffs at Bernstein's suggestion that Rosebud might be a long-lost love. "You take me," the old retainer explains. "One day, back in 1896, I was crossing over to Jersey on the ferry, and as we pulled out, there was another ferry pulling in, and on it there was a girl waiting to get off. A white dress she had on. She was carrying a white parasol. I only saw her for one second. She didn't see me at all, but I'll bet a month hasn't gone by since, that I haven't thought of that girl." Welles always loved that speech—and wished that he had written it.

Thematically, *Kane* is so complex that only a brief itemizing of some of its themes is possible within these few pages. Like most of Welles's other movies, *Citizen Kane* might well be entitled *The Arrogance of Power*. He was attracted to themes traditionally associated with classical tragedy and the **epic**: the downfall of a public figure because of arrogance and pride. Power and wealth are corrupting, and the corrupt devour themselves. The innocent usually survive, but they are severely scarred. "All of the characters I've played are various forms of Faust," Welles stated. All have bartered their souls and lost.

Welles's sense of evil is mature and complex, seldom conventionalized. He was one of the few American filmmakers of his generation to explore the darker side of the human condition without resorting to a simplified psychology or to moralistic clichés. Though his universe is essentially doomed, it's shot through with ambiguities, contradictions, and moments of transient beauty. Welles considered himself a moralist, but his movies are never priggish or sanctimonious. Instead of facile condemnations, *Kane* laments the loss of innocence: "Almost all serious stories in the world are stories of a failure with a death in it," Welles stated. "But there is more lost paradise in them than defeat. To me that's the central theme in Western culture, the lost paradise."

There are literally dozens of symbolic **motifs** in the movie. Some of them are technical, such as the film's predominantly low camera **angles (12–10)**. Others are more content oriented, such as the series of fences the camera must penetrate before we are able to see Kane. There are also persistent motifs of stillness, decay, old age, and death. The two most important motifs in the movie are Rosebud and the fragmentation motif.

Rosebud turns out to be a favourite childhood possession. Scholars and critics have argued about Rosebud for decades. Welles himself described it as "dollar-book Freud"—that is, a convenient symbol of childhood innocence. The ideas of Freud gained wide currency in the American cinema of the 1940s, especially the centrality of a child's prepubescent life in determining his or her later character.

But Rosebud is also a more generalized symbol of loss. Consider: Kane is a man who lost his parents when he was a child. He was brought up by a bank. He lost his youthful idealism as a publisher. He lost in his bid to be governor. He lost his first wife and son. He lost in his efforts to make Susan an opera star. He lost Susan. Because it's much more than a mere object, more even than a symbol of Edenic innocence, the revelation of Rosebud to the audience delivers a powerful emotional impact.

12–1. *Citizen Kane, with William Alland and Paul Stewart.*
Near the end of the movie, Thompson (Alland) admits defeat. He never does find out what Rosebud means, and he describes his investigation as "playing with a jigsaw puzzle," while the camera cranes back and up, revealing thousands of crates of artwork, memorabilia, and personal effects—the fragmented artifacts of a person's life. "I don't think any word can explain a man's life," Thompson continues. "No, I guess Rosebud is just a piece in a jigsaw puzzle, a missing piece." *(RKO)*

12-2. *Citizen Kane, with Joseph Cotten.*
Jed Leland (Cotten) represents the moral conscience of the film, Kane's idealistic alter ego. Roles like this are difficult to play well, because they can easily degenerate into sentimental clichés of piety. Cotten toughens up the role by refusing to make Leland too likable. Although sensitive and intelligent, Leland is also a bit of a prig, "a New England schoolmarm," to use his own phrase. Like Bernstein, he loves Kane and is loyal to him when they are all young and committed to social reform. But when he finally recognizes Kane's ego for the destructive force it is, Jed pulls back, disillusioned.   *(RKO)*

12-3. *Citizen Kane, with Joseph Cotten and Everett Sloane.*
Kane's rampant consumerism is best illustrated by his mania for collecting European art treasures. Not because he enjoys art—indeed, he scarcely ever mentions it—but because of its value as a status symbol. His conspicuous consumption becomes a habit rather than a passionate interest. After a while, no one even bothers to uncrate his purchases—they're simply stored away with all his other possessions.   *(RKO)*

The fragmentation motif acts as a foil to the simpleminded notion that any single word could "explain" a complex personality. Throughout the movie, we are presented with images that suggest multiplicity, repetition, and fragments of a larger whole. Examples of this motif are the jigsaw puzzles, the profusion of crates, boxes, and artwork. The very structure of the movie is fragmented, with each narrator providing us with only a partial picture. In Raymond's **flashback** at the end of the film, the elderly Kane mutters "Rosebud" when he discovers a glass globe. Dazed, he walks down a corridor, the globe in his hand. As he passes a set of facing mirrors, we see his image multiplied into infinity. All of them are Kane.

STORY

The differences between **story** and **plot** can be best illustrated by comparing the narrative in chronological order with the restructured sequence of the plot. When Herman Mankiewicz approached Welles with the idea of the story, Welles was concerned that the materials would be too sprawling, too unfocused. To sharpen the story line and infuse it with more dramatic urgency, he suggested scrambling the chronology of events through a series of flashbacks, each narrated from the point of view of the person telling the story. Welles had used this multiple flashback technique in a number of his radio dramas.

He and Mankiewicz also introduced a note of suspense. In his final moments of life, Kane mumbles the word *Rosebud* **(12–4)**. No one seems to know what it means, and its significance piques the curiosity of a newspaper reporter, Thompson, who spends the remainder of the movie questioning

12–4. *Citizen Kane.*
Like a number of Welles's other movies, *Kane* begins with the end—the death of its protagonist when he is about seventy-five. In his final moments of life, the old man holds a small crystal ball containing a miniature scene that flurries with artificial snow when shaken. With his last dying breath, he utters the word "Rosebud." Then the glass ball crashes to the floor, splintering into a thousand fragments. The plot of the movie is structured like a search—for the meaning of this final utterance.
(RKO)

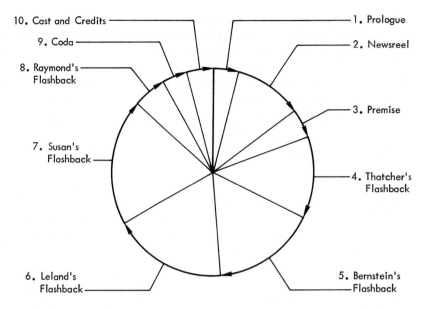

10. Cast and Credits
9. Coda
8. Raymond's Flashback
7. Susan's Flashback
6. Leland's Flashback
1. Prologue
2. Newsreel
3. Premise
4. Thatcher's Flashback
5. Bernstein's Flashback

12–5.   Approximate proportion of each plot unit in *Citizen Kane*.

Kane's former associates about this mystery, which he hopes contains the key to Kane's conflicting character.

Welles claimed that the Rosebud motif was merely a plot gimmick, intended to hook the audience on a dramatic question that's really a wild goose chase. But the gimmick works. Like the hopeful reporter, we too think that Rosebud will unlock Kane's ambiguous personality. Without this gimmick, the story would have remained rambling and unfocused. The search for the meaning of Rosebud shapes the narrative, providing it with a forward thrust, with a dramatic question we all want answered. This is what foreign critics mean by the American genius for storytelling.

The flashback structure of *Citizen Kane* allows Welles to leap through time and space, cutting to various periods of Kane's life without having to adhere to a strict chronology. To provide the audience with an overview, Welles introduced most of the major events and people of Kane's life in a brief newsreel shown early in the film. These events and people are explored in more depth in the individual flashbacks that follow.

Many critics have marvelled at the intricate, jigsaw-puzzle structure of the movie, with its interlocking pieces that don't click together until the final scene. The following plot outline sets forth the main structural units of the film and the principal characters and events of each:

1. *Prologue.* Xanadu. Kane's death. "Rosebud."
2. *Newsreel.* Death of Kane. Enormous wealth and decadent lifestyle. Contradictory political image. Marriage to Emily Norton. Exposé of "love

nest." Divorce. Marriage to Susan Alexander, "singer." Political campaign. Opera career. The Great Depression and Kane's financial decline. Lonely, secluded old age in Xanadu.

3. *Premise.* Thompson is instructed by his editor (12–7) to discover the mystery of Rosebud by questioning Kane's former associates. "It will probably be a very simple thing." False step: Susan refuses to speak to Thompson.

4. *Flashback: The Memoirs of Walter P. Thatcher.* Kane's childhood. Thatcher becomes guardian. Kane's first newspaper: *The Inquirer.* Introduction of Bernstein and Leland. Newspaper crusading years. Kane's financial decline in the 1930s.

5. *Flashback: Bernstein.* Early days at *The Inquirer.* "Declaration of Principles." Building a publishing empire. Engagement to Emily Norton.

6. *Flashback: Jed Leland.* Disintegration of marriage to Emily. Kane meets Susan. Political campaign in 1918. Exposé, divorce, remarriage. Susan's opera career. Final break between Kane and Jed.

7. *Flashback: Susan Alexander Kane.* Opera debut and career. Suicide attempt. Years of semiseclusion with Kane at Xanadu. Susan leaves Kane.

8. *Flashback: Raymond, butler at Xanadu.* Kane's final days. "Rosebud."

9. *Coda.* Revelation of Rosebud. Reverse of opening Prologue, producing closure.

10. *Cast and credits.*

When a story isn't told in a straightforward, chronological manner, something is lost and something is gained. What's lost is the suspense of any conventionally told tale, which usually asks: What does the protagonist want and how is he or she going to get it? In *Citizen Kane*, the protagonist is dead almost from the start. We are forced to piece together his life from the points of view of others. This technique of multiple narration forces us to gauge the biases and prejudices of each narrator. *Citizen Kane* is their story, too.

There are five storytellers, and each tells us a different story. Even when the events overlap, we view them from a different perspective. For example, Leland's account of Susan's operatic debut is coloured by his condescending attitude toward her. Her performance is viewed primarily from the audience, where Leland is sitting. When Susan recounts the same event, the camera is primarily on stage, and the tone of the sequence is no longer comic but agonized.

Welles's narrative strategy is something like a prism: The newsreel and the five interviewees each offer a unique view of the same man. The newsreel offers us a quick tour of the highlights of Kane's public life. Thatcher's account is tainted by his absolute confidence in the moral superiority of the rich and powerful. Bernstein's story is steeped in the gratitude and loyalty he felt for Kane when they were young. Leland offers a more rigorous perspective: He judges Kane by what he actually does, rather than what he says. Susan is the most victimized of the storytellers. Yet she is also the most compassionate and sensitive. Raymond, the butler, pretends to know a lot more than he does. His brief flashback merely concludes Thompson's investigation.

The ten sections of the film vary in length. A diagram charting the approximate proportion of each section is shown in Figure **12–5**.

PHOTOGRAPHY

Cinematographer Gregg Toland considered *Citizen Kane* the high point of his career. The veteran cinematographer thought he might be able to learn something from the "boy genius," whose accomplishments were mostly in radio and the Broadway theatre. Welles, used to setting up his own lights in the live theatre thought that movie directors were also responsible for the lighting. Intrigued, Toland let him go ahead, allowing Welles to determine the design of most of the lights but quietly instructing the camera crew to make the necessary technical adjustments.

Everyone saw at once that *Citizen Kane* didn't look like most American movies of its era. There is not an indifferently photographed image in the film.

12–6. Publicity photo of Orson Welles and cinematographer Gregg Toland during the production of *Citizen Kane* (U.S.A., 1941).

Toland, the most admired cinematographer of his generation, asked Welles if he could photograph the young director's first feature film. He was fascinated by Welles's bold theatricality, and he often suggested more effective ways of shooting scenes. They discussed each shot in the movie, which is eclectic in its visual style, integrating a variety of influences. Welles was strongly drawn to the lighting theories of such theatrical designers as Gordon Craig and Adolphe Appia and to many of the techniques of the German expressionist movement. Welles was also influenced by the moody low-key photography of John Ford's *Stagecoach*. Welles was so grateful for the help of the veteran cinematographer that he gave Toland a conspicuous credit title—unusual in this era.   *(RKO)*

Even the exposition scenes—normally dispatched with efficient **medium two-shots**—are startlingly photographed (**12–7**). Not that the techniques were new. Deep-focus, **low-key lighting**, rich textures, audacious compositions, dynamic contrasts between foregrounds and backgrounds, **backlighting**, sets with ceilings, side lighting, steep angles, epic **long shots** juxtaposed with **extreme close-ups**, dizzying **crane shots**, special effects galore—none of these was new. But no one had previously used them in such a "seven layer-cake profusion," to quote critic James Naremore.

Photographically, *Kane* ushered in a revolution, implicitly challenging the classical ideal of a transparent style that doesn't call attention to itself. In *Citizen Kane*, the stylistic virtuosity is part of the show. The lighting in the movie is generally in moderate **high key** in those scenes depicting Kane's youth and those dealing with his years as a crusading young publisher. As he grows older and more cynical, the lighting grows darker, more harshly contrasting. Kane's home, the palatial Xanadu, seems steeped in perpetual night. Only spotlight

12–7.   *Citizen Kane*.

Kane ushered in an era of flamboyant visual effects in the American cinema, and as such represented an assault on the classical ideal of an invisible style. Lights are often from below or other unexpected sources, creating startling clashes and abstract patterns and infusing the photographed materials with a sense of visual exuberance. There's nothing invisible about the lighting of this shot, for example. As written, the scene is merely exposition, setting up the movie's narrative premise. Some reporters are talking in a screening room, and while they talk, the light from the projection booth splashes into the darkened auditorium, flooding the silhouetted figures in a sea of undulating luminescence.   *(RKO)*

patches of light penetrate the oppressive gloom, revealing the contours of a chair, a sofa, yet another piece of heroic sculpture. But the pervasive atmosphere is dank, impenetrable. The darkness shrouds an unspeakable evil.

Spotlights are also used in closer shots for symbolic effects. The mixture of decency and corruption in Kane is suggested by the contrasting lights: Sometimes his face seems split in half, with one side brightly illuminated, the other hidden in darkness. What is concealed is often more important than what's revealed. In an early scene between the idealistic Kane and his two associates, for example, the protagonist tells Bernstein and Leland of his intention to publish a "Declaration of Principles" on the front page of his newspaper, promising his readers that he will be an honest and tireless champion of their rights as citizens and human beings. When Kane bends down to sign the document, however, his face is suddenly plunged into darkness—an ominous foreshadowing of Kane's later character.

12–8. *Citizen Kane, with Orson Welles and (at far end of the table) Joseph Cotten and Everett Sloane.*

Welles's deep-focus photography is meant to be admired for its virtuosity as well as its functionalism. André Bazin, an enthusiastic champion of deep-focus techniques, believed that it reduces the importance of editing and preserves the cohesiveness of real space and time. Many spatial planes can be captured simultaneously in a single take, maintaining the objectivity of a scene. Bazin felt that audiences were thus encouraged to be more creative—less passive—in understanding the relationships between people and things. In this photo, for example, we are free to look at the faces of over two dozen characters. "The public may choose, with its eyes, what it wants to see of a shot," Welles said. "I don't like to force it."   *(RKO)*

Gregg Toland had often experimented with deep-focus photography during the 1930s, mostly while working with director William Wyler. But the deep focus in *Kane* is more flamboyant than Wyler's use of this technique (12–8). Deep-focus photography involves the use of **wide-angle lenses**, which tend to exaggerate the distances between people—an appropriate symbolic analogue for a story dealing with separation, alienation, and loneliness.

Deep focus also tends to encourage the audience to actively mine a shot for its information. In a scene involving Susan Alexander's suicide attempt, for example, a cause–effect relationship is suggested in the opening shot. Susan has taken a lethal dose of medication and lies comatose on her bed in a semidarkened room. At the bottom of the screen, in **close-up** range, stands an empty glass and a bottle of medication; in the middle of the screen, in medium range, lies Susan, wheezing softly; in the upper portion of the screen, in long-shot range, Kane bangs outside the door, then forces it open and enters the room. The layering of the **mise en scène** is a visual accusation: **(1)** the lethal dose was taken by **(2)** Susan Alexander Kane because of **(3)** Kane's inhumanity.

Special effects are used throughout the movie for a variety of reasons. In some settings—such as the exterior shots of Xanadu—the special effects lend the locale a slightly phantasmagorical quality. In other scenes, such as the political rally, special effects provide a realistic facsimile of large crowds and a huge auditorium (12–9).

The American cinema of the 1940s was to grow progressively darker, both thematically and photographically, thanks in part to the enormous influence of *Citizen Kane*. The most important style of the decade was **film noir**—literally, "black cinema." It was a style suited to the times. Welles's style continued in a noir vein, especially in such movies as *The Lady from Shanghai* and *Touch of Evil*. Toland's death in 1948 at the age of forty-four was an irreparable loss to the American cinema.

MISE EN SCÈNE

Coming from the world of live theatre, Welles was an expert at staging action dynamically. Long shots are a more effective—and more theatrical—medium for the art of mise en scène, and hence the movie contains relatively few close shots. Most of the images are **tightly framed** and in **closed form**. Most of them are also composed in depth, with important information in the foreground, midground, and background. The **proxemic ranges** between the characters are choreographed balletically, to suggest their shifting power relationships. For example, an early scene in the movie shows Kane, Bernstein, and Leland taking over the staid offices of *The Inquirer*, the conservative newspaper young Kane has just bought because he thinks it might be fun to run a newspaper. While workers and assistants stream in and out of the frame, carrying equipment, furniture, and personal belongings, Kane carries on a whimsical conversation with the stuffy, soon-to-be ex-editor, Mr. Carter, a Dickensian study in spluttering comic exasperation.

12–9. *Citizen Kane, with Ray Collins.*

RKO's highly respected special-effects department consisted of thirty-five people, most of whom worked on Kane. Vernon L. Walker was in charge. Over 80 percent of the movie required some kind of special effects work, such as miniatures, matte shots, double and multiple exposures. Many scenes required reprinting—that is, combining two or more separate images onto one through the use of the optical printer. For example, this shot combines three separately photographed images—Boss Jim Gettys (Collins) standing on a balcony overlooking Madison Square Garden, with Kane down below delivering a campaign speech to a huge audience. The frame of the balcony masks the dividing line between the two areas. The auditorium area combines live action (stage) with a matte painting (audience); the balcony set consists of two walls. Welles was thus able to give the movie an epic scope, while keeping production costs relatively low. Total cost of the picture: just under $700,000—not lavish by the standards of 1941. *(RKO)*

Perhaps the best way of understanding the complexity of Welles's mise en scène is to analyze a single shot. The dramatic context of **12–11** is offered in the caption.

1. **Dominant.** Because of his central position within the frame and the high contrast between his dark clothes and the glaring snow, Charles tends to attract our eye first. He is also the subject of controversy in the foreground.

2. *Lighting key.* The interior is photographed in moderate high key. The exterior—consisting mostly of blinding white snow—is in extreme high key.

3. *Shot and camera proxemics.* This is a deep-focus shot, extending from a medium range in the foreground to an extreme long-shot range in the background. The camera is at a personal distance from Thatcher and Mrs. Kane, a social distance from Kane senior, and a public distance from Charles. The boy is playing happily, shouting disconnected phrases like "The Union forever!" Kane senior is stubbornly resisting

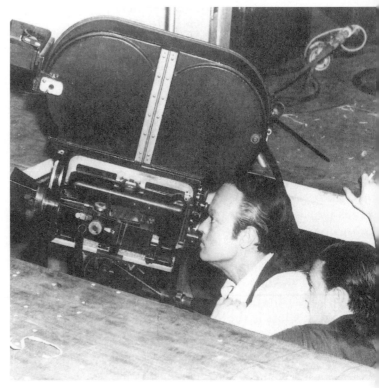

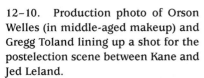

12–10. Production photo of Orson Welles (in middle-aged makeup) and Gregg Toland lining up a shot for the postelection scene between Kane and Jed Leland.

Welles used low-angle shots as a motif throughout the picture, especially to emphasize the awesome power of the protagonist. In this scene, the angle is so low that the floorboards of the set had to be torn away to allow for the camera's placement. Combined with the perspective-distorting wide-angle lens, such low-angle shots portray Kane as a towering colossus, capable of crushing anything that gets in his way.   *(RKO)*

their plans, while Thatcher and Mrs. Kane, more frigid than the outside weather, listen wearily.

4. *Angle.* The camera is at a slightly high angle, because more of the floor can be seen than the ceiling. The angle suggests a slight air of fatality.

5. *Colour values.* Not applicable: The film is in black and white.

6. ***Lens/filter/stock.*** Though it is difficult to discern in this photo, a wide-angle lens is used to capture its depth of field. The lens exaggerates the distances between the characters. No apparent filters. Probably slow stock requiring lots of lights.

7. ***Subsidiary contrasts.*** Our eye travels from Charles (the dominant) to Kane senior to Thatcher, Mrs. Kane, and the spotlighted document they are preparing to sign. On the small TV screen, Charles would probably be lost and Kane senior would then constitute the dominant.

8. *Density.* The image is densely packed with information, thanks to the high-key lighting and the richly textured details of the sets and costumes.

9. *Composition.* The image is split vertically in half, a tug of war, with two figures on the left, two on the right. The foreground table balances off the background table and rear wall. The composition segments and isolates the characters.

12–11.   *Citizen Kane, with Harry Shannon, Buddy Swan (in window), George Coulouris, and Agnes Moorehead.*

Almost all of the compositions in Kane are intricate and richly textured, at times baroquely ornate. But the visual complexity is not mere rhetorical ornamentation. The images are designed to reveal a maximum of information, often in an ironic manner. In this scene, for example, eight-year-old Charles plays with his sled outside in the snow while his future is being determined indoors by his mother and Thatcher. The boy's father watches impotently, sputtering a few feeble protests. The mise en scène is compartmentalized into twos, with the wall serving as the vertical dividing line. Kane senior and young Charles are grouped to the left in the upper portion of the frame; Thatcher and the severe Mrs. Kane dominate the right lower half, their pens poised to sign the contract that will soon separate Charles from his parents. Ironically, Mrs. Kane is motivated by love and self-sacrifice. She is sending Charles away to protect him from his father, a swaggering lout whose treatment of his son veers from forced jocularity to unpredictable outbursts of anger.   *(RKO)*

10. *Form.* The image is in closed form, its carefully coordinated components suggesting the self-containment of a stage setting enclosed by a proscenium arch.

11. ***Framing.*** The shot is tightly framed, with little latitude for movement. Each character seems confined to his or her own space cubicle. The

12-12. *Citizen Kane, with Dorothy Comingore (at lower left base of fireplace) and Orson Welles.*

In scenes depicting Kane as an old man, the camera is often far away, making him seem remote, inaccessible. Even when he is closer to the lens, as in this shot, the deep-focus photography keeps the rest of the world at a distance, with vast empty spaces between him and other people. We are often forced to search the mise en scène to locate the characters. In this photo, for example, Susan is dwarfed into insignificance by the enormous fireplace and the heroic sculpture behind her. She is a mere subsidiary contrast, not even as important as the statuary and much less important than the dominant, Kane. These static shots are so totally drained of intimacy and spontaneity that they're almost funny, if they weren't so sad.   *(RKO)*

excluded Charles is imprisoned within the frame of the window—an enclosure within an enclosure. His freedom is illusionary.

12. *Depth.* The image is photographed in four depth planes: **(a)** the foreground table and its occupants; **(b)** Kane senior; **(c)** the rear portions of the parlour; and **(d)** Charles playing outside in the distance.

12–13.   Artist's rendering of the interior set of Xanadu for *Citizen Kane*.
In the area of set design and décor, Welles was fortunate in his choice of studio, for RKO's art director, Van Nest Polglase, was among the best in the industry. Perry Ferguson, who actually designed the sets under Polglase's general supervision, shared his boss's preference for monumental sets with unusual sources of lighting and richly textured details.   *(RKO)*

13. *Character placement.* Charles and Kane senior occupy the upper portions of the image, Thatcher and Mrs. Kane the lower—an ironic placement, because those in the "inferior" positions actually control the situation. Husband and wife are maximally separated at the opposite edges of the composition, forcing Charles to be coupled in the centre with Thatcher—an intimacy both come to regret.

14. *Staging positions.* Kane senior is in the quarter-turn position, relatively intimate vis-à-vis the spectator. Thatcher is at full front, but his eyes are lowered, avoiding our gaze. Mrs. Kane is in the profile position, preoccupied with her spouse.

15. *Character proxemics.* Thatcher and Mrs. Kane are in intimate proximity. They are at an aloof social distance from Kane senior, and a remote public distance from Charles.

Welles's experience in the live theatre proved invaluable when he turned to making movies. He regarded film as essentially a dramatic rather than literary medium. As we have seen, the lighting style of *Citizen Kane* is more indebted to

12–14.   Exterior set of Xanadu for *Citizen Kane.*
The mist-shrouded tropic setting groans under the weight of the sprawling, towering Xanadu, unfinished and already beginning to decay, like a rotting mausoleum from the pages of Edgar Allan Poe. Although the palm trees sway as the wisps of fog drift past dreamily, the set was actually a matte painting, only a few feet high.   *(RKO)*

the stage than the screen, and Welles's use of lengthy takes is similarly derived from the need in the live theatre to stage the action in a unified space.

In the area of art direction too, Welles was able to save hundreds of thousands of dollars by showing only parts of sets rather than entire rooms. For example, the office set consists only of a desk and two walls, yet we seem to be in a huge luxurious office (**12–17**). Similarly, in the Xanadu scenes, Welles spotlit an oversized piece of furniture, a sculpture, or a fireplace, leaving the rest of the room in darkness—as though it were too enormous to be adequately illuminated. (The rooms are actually sparsely furnished.) When these techniques were insufficient, Welles was able to count on the RKO special effects department to create an epic canvas through such techniques as **animation**, **matte shots**, and **miniatures**.

MOVEMENT

From the very beginning of his film career, Welles was a master of the mobile camera. In *Citizen Kane*, camera movements are generally equated with the vitality and energy of youth. A static camera, on the other hand, tends to be associated with illness, old age, and death. These same **kinetic** principles apply to Kane's movements. As a young man, he is a whirlwind of energy, playfully gliding through life with scarcely enough breath to finish his sentences before his attention is distracted and he sweeps to another location. As an old man, however, he almost groans with each calculated step. Often he is photographed in stationary positions or sitting down. He seems bored and exhausted, especially in the Xanadu scenes with Susan (see **12–12**).

No one has used crane shots so spectacularly as Welles. But once again, the virtuosity is rarely indulged in for its own sake. The bravura crane shots embody important symbolic ideas. For example, after learning of Kane's death, a reporter attempts to interview Susan Alexander. The sequence begins in a torrential rainstorm. We see a poster and picture of Susan, advertising her engagement as a singer in a nightclub. As the soundtrack shudders with a rumble of thunder, the camera cranes up, up through the rain, up to the roof of the building, then plunges through a garish neon sign, "El Rancho," descends to the skylight where a blinding flash of lightning masks the camera's passage through the window itself, sweeps down to the deserted nightclub, where Susan is hunched at a table in a drunken stupor, prostrate with grief. (She is the only character in the film who is devastated by the news of Kane's death.) Both the camera and the reporter encounter numerous obstacles—the rain, the sign, the very walls of the building must be penetrated before we can even see Susan, much less hear her speak. The crane shot embodies a brutal invasion of privacy, a disregard for the barriers Susan has placed around her in her misery.

In Susan's opera debut, a travelling shot is used for comic effect, its payoff a virtual punch line. As she begins her first aria, the camera begins to rise, as if to ascend to the heavens. While she continues singing, her thin, watery voice grows progressively more feeble as the camera continues its upward journey, past sandbags, ropes, and platforms, until it finally comes to rest on two stagehands on the catwalk, looking down at the performance. They listen for a moment longer, then turn to face each other. One stagehand waggishly pinches his nose, as if to say, "She really stinks."

EDITING

The editing in *Citizen Kane* is a calculated display of virtuosity, leaping over days, months, even years with casual nonchalance. Welles often uses several editing styles in the same sequence. When Susan recalls her opera career, for example, the singing lesson with her exasperated voice teacher is photographed in a lengthy take. The backstage chaos prior to the curtain going up is edited in short bursts of fragmentary shots to emphasize the utter confusion of her opera debut. Welles used **parallel editing** to contrast Susan's terror on stage with Leland's contemptuous boredom in the auditorium. Kane's argument with Susan over her disastrous reviews is cut according to **classical** conventions. **Thematic montage** is used to condense her national tour on the road (**12–21**). The final scene of the sequence, Susan's suicide attempt, opens with a deep-focus lengthy take, as Kane crashes into Susan's hotel room and discovers her comatose in bed.

12–15. *Citizen Kane.*
In many respects, Kane is structured like a mystery story, a search to penetrate a great enigma. Welles is able to suggest this idea in the very opening sequence, through a series of dissolves and traveling shots. The movie begins with a sign: NO TRESPASSING. Ignoring it, the camera cranes up over the sign and over a wire fence. We dissolve from an ornate grill-work to an iron gate showing the letter "K." Xanadu is in the background, suffocating in mist, a solitary window light its only sign of habitation. Here lies the mystery. Here the search begins. *(RKO)*

It's difficult to isolate the editing in this film because it often works in concert with the sound techniques, not to speak of the fragmentation of the story. Often Welles used editing to condense a great deal of time, using sound as a continuity device. For example, to demonstrate Kane's gradual estrangement from his first wife, Emily, Welles features a series of breakfast scenes, using only a few lines of dialogue with each brief episode. Beginning with some honeymoon sweet-talk, the mood quickly shifts to slight irritation, then strained annoyance, bitter resentment, and finally silence and alienation. The sequence begins with the lovers sharing the intimacy of the same medium shot. As the marriage deteriorates, Welles **cross-cuts** to separate shots of each, even though they are sitting at the same table. The one-minute sequence ends with a long shot of the two at opposite ends of a lengthy table, each reading a different newspaper **(12–18).**

Welles used a similar technique in showing how Susan Alexander eventually becomes Kane's mistress. The first time he meets her, he is splashed with mud on the street. She offers him some hot water, if he wants to come up to her small apartment for it. While there, they become friends. She admits that she sings a little and he asks her to perform for him. While she begins to sing her song at an old piano, the image **dissolves** to a parallel shot, only now she is in a large, handsomely decorated apartment, where she finishes the song at a grander piano, dressed in an elegant gown. We don't need to be shown what happened "between" these two shots. We can infer what happened by Susan's much improved circumstances.

12–16. *Citizen Kane*, *with Everett Sloane, Orson Welles, and Joseph Cotten.*
As a young man, Kane is a dynamo of energy, and his youthful high spirits are often conveyed kinetically—with brisk travelling shots that parallel the protagonist's movements. In this scene, for example, he nervously lurches forward and backward, then forward again, the camera retreating and lunging back with him. *(RKO)*

12–17. *Citizen Kane*, *with George Coulouris, Orson Welles, and Everett Sloane.*
Welles frequently used lengthy takes in his staging, choreographing the movements of the camera and the characters rather than cutting to a series of separate shots. Even in relatively static scenes such as this, these lengthy takes provide the mise en scène with a sense of fluidity and dynamic change, while still entrapping the three characters within the same space. The setting is a large office in 1929. The Great Depression has dealt Kane a severe setback, forcing him to relinquish control over his publishing empire. The sequence begins with a close shot of a legal document, while Bernstein recites its contents. He lowers the document, thus revealing Thatcher, now an old man, presiding over the dissolution. The camera adjusts slightly, and we then see Kane, listening grimly. *(RKO)*

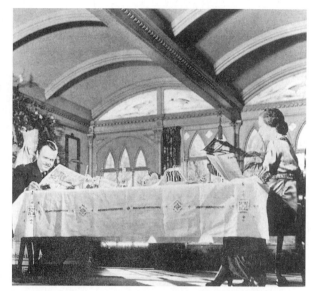

12–18. *Citizen Kane, with Orson Welles and Ruth Warrick.*
Welles often combined editing with another technique, which he used as a payoff. In the famous breakfast montage sequence portraying the disintegration of Kane's marriage to Emily, for example, he concluded with this final shot. The distance between the two says it all: They have nothing to say to each other. *(RKO)*

SOUND

Coming from the world of live radio drama, Welles was often credited with inventing many film sound techniques when in fact he was primarily a consolidator, synthesizing and expanding the piecemeal accomplishments of his predecessors. In radio, sounds have to evoke images. An actor speaking through an echo chamber suggests a visual context—a huge auditorium, for example. A distant train whistle suggests a panoramic landscape, and so on. Welles applied this aural principle to his movie soundtrack. With the help of his sound technician, James G. Stewart, Welles discovered that almost every visual technique has its sound equivalent. Each of the shots, for example, has an appropriate sound quality involving volume, degree of definition, and texture. Long and extreme long-shot sounds are fuzzy and remote; close-up sounds are crisp, clear, and generally loud. **High-angle shots** are often accompanied by high-pitched music and sound effects; **low-angle shots** by brooding and low-pitched sounds. Sounds can be dissolved and overlapped like a montage sequence.

Welles frequently leaped from one time period or location to another with a shocking sound transition. For example, the film's opening prologue concludes with Kane's death, which is accompanied by the gradual fading of the sound. Suddenly, we are almost assaulted with a **Voice-of-God** narrator booming out "News on the March!"—the beginning of the newsreel sequence. In another sequence, Jed Leland is delivering a campaign speech, in which he describes Kane as "the fighting liberal, the friend of the workingman, the next governor of this state, who entered upon this campaign . . ." Cut to Kane in Madison Square Garden, continuing ". . . with one purpose only . . ."

12-19.   *Citizen Kane,* with Orson Welles.
Budgetary considerations often determined the cunning editing strategies of the film, which
was edited by Robert Wise. In the political campaign sequence, for example, Welles cut from
long shots of Kane delivering his speech to closer shots of his family and associates listening
in the audience. These isolated fragments are intercut with reestablishing shots of the entire
auditorium (see **12–9**). The huge hall and its thousands of inhabitants weren't real: The cutting makes them *seem* real—by association.   *(RKO)*

Welles frequently overlapped his dialogue, especially in the comical
sequences where several people are trying to speak at the same time. In
Xanadu, the rooms are so huge that Kane and Susan must shout at each other
to be heard, producing an incongruous effect that's both sad and funny
(12–12). The Madison Square Garden facsimile is convincing in part because
we *hear* the shouts and cheers of the enormous crowds and hence imagine that
we see them as well.

Bernard Herrmann's musical score is similarly sophisticated. Musical
motifs are assigned to several of the major characters and events. Many of these
motifs are introduced in the newsreel sequence, then picked up later in the
film, often in a minor key, or played at a different tempo, depending on the
mood of the scene. For example, the poignant Rosebud motif is introduced in
the opening sequence, and when Rosebud is brought up during the course of

12-20.   Publicity photo of Orson Welles and composer–conductor Bernard Herrmann during a recording session for *Citizen Kane*.
Herrmann was the composer for Welles's Mercury Theatre of the Air, and when Welles went to Hollywood, he took Herrmann with him. *Citizen Kane* was his first movie score. The two worked closely together, Welles often cutting his film to accommodate the musical numbers, rather than vice versa, which was usually the case in Hollywood. Herrmann was present throughout the production, taking twelve weeks to compose the score, an unusually lengthy period of time. Difficult, intensely egotistical, an uncompromising perfectionist, Herrmann did most of his best work for Welles and Alfred Hitchcock, including the scores for *The Magnificent Ambersons, Vertigo, North by Northwest, Psycho,* and many others.   *(RKO)*

the investigation, a variation of the musical motif often underlines the dialogue. When Welles finally reveals to us—but not to the characters—the mystery of Rosebud, the musical motif swells powerfully into prominence, producing one of the most thrilling revelations in all of cinema.

Herrmann's score often parallels Welles's visuals. For instance, in the montage of breakfast scenes between Kane and his first wife, the disintegration of the marriage is paralleled by the variations in the music. The sequence opens with a soft romantic waltz, tenderly underscoring the fascination each feels for the other. This is followed by a slightly comical musical variation. As the relationship becomes more strained, the orchestration becomes harsher, more dissonant. In the final scene, neither one bothers to speak anymore. Their silence is accompanied by a brooding, neurotic variation on the opening musical theme.

In many scenes, Welles used sound for symbolic purposes. For example, he used a dissolve and montage sequence to show Susan on her disastrous operatic tour **(12–21)**. On the soundtrack, her aria can be heard, distorted into a screeching, dismal wail. The sequence ends with the gradual dimming of the light, to symbolize Susan's increasing despair. On the accompanying soundtrack, we hear her voice winding down to a wounded moan, as though someone pulled the plug on a record player in the middle of a song.

12-21. *Citizen Kane, with Dorothy Comingore.*

Kane demonstrates that virtually every kind of visual has its aural counterpart. This montage sequence is reinforced by an aural montage of Susan Alexander's shrieking arias, orchestral music, popping flash-bulbs, and the sounds of newspaper presses rolling. The pounding sounds are machinelike and inexorable, battering their sacrificial victim until she is stupefied by terror and exhaustion. *(RKO)*

ACTING

Welles had his own stable of writers, assistants, and actors, who worked with him in both radio and the New York live theatre. When he went to Hollywood, he took many of them with him, including fifteen actors. Except for Welles, none of these players was well known, and even Welles was known primarily as a radio performer. (He captured the imagination of the mass audience when his notorious *War of the Worlds* broadcast of 1938 panicked thousands of Americans, who believed the country was actually being invaded by creatures from Mars. Welles was delighted, of course. As a result of this cause célèbre, he got his picture on the cover of *Time* when he was only twenty-two years old.)

Citizen Kane boasts a first-rate cast. There are a few so-so performances, but none that is weak, and several that are outstanding, most notably those of Welles, Dorothy Comingore, Joseph Cotten, Everett Sloane, and Agnes Moorehead. Like most performers who are used to acting repertory-style, members of the cast work as an ensemble; the total effect is one of dramatic scenes that mesh seamlessly. The Mercury players look like seasoned film performers, not the young neophytes they actually were. For most of them, this was their first movie, yet they are always natural, sincere, and believable.

Even some of the cameo roles are performed with distinction. Because these parts are limited to only a few lines of dialogue, the actors must be able to convey the complexity of their characters—who are often contradictory—without appearing inconsistent. For example, Ray Collins performs Boss Jim Gettys as a cunning survivor. Streetwise and cynical, he is a man who has seen it all. Or at least he thought he had seen it all until he came up against Kane. Gettys seems quietly shocked that Kane, a supposedly high-class opponent, would be so low-class as to publish a doctored photo of Gettys "in a convict suit with stripes, so his children could see the picture in the paper, or his mother." We can't help but sympathize with Gettys's outrage, notwithstanding the fact that otherwise he is a creep.

Although she appears in only one scene, Agnes Moorehead as Kane's mother leaves an indelible impression. (Moorehead was to go on to an even more brilliant performance in Welles's next movie, *The Magnificent Ambersons*.) Moorehead's Mary Kane might almost have stepped out of a tale by Hawthorne: stern, puritanical, joyless. She is a woman who found out too late that she has married a fool. Trapped, she will endure the humiliation of her marriage, but she will not subject her son to the same fate. In her mind, he is meant for better things, even if that means she must part with the only person she loves. Mrs. Kane is a woman of few words, but her determination is communicated by her steely stoicism, her decisive movements, her ramrod-straight back. This is not a lady to mess with.

12–22. *Citizen Kane, with Dorothy Comingore.*

Comingore's brilliant performance as Susan provides considerable warmth to an otherwise cold and intellectual film. The few close-ups in the movie are reserved primarily for her, forcing us to become more involved with Susan's feelings. Like most of the major characters, she is a study in contradiction, screechy and pitiful at the same time. She can also be very funny. "A person can go crazy in this dump," she complains in her typical whining monotone. "Nobody to talk to, nobody to have any fun with. Forty-nine thousand acres of nothing but scenery and statues." *(RKO)*

a   b   c

12–23.   Three photos of Orson Welles as Charles Foster Kane at various periods in his life. Welles was required to age about fifty years during the course of the story. Thanks in part to the makeup artistry of Maurice Seiderman, Welles is completely convincing, whether playing Kane at twenty-five **(a)**, forty-five **(b)**, or seventy-five **(c)**. As Kane grows older, his hair grays and recedes, his jowls sag, his cheeks grow puffier, and the bags beneath his eyes grow more pouchy. Seiderman created a synthetic rubber body suit to suggest the increasingly flabby torso of an older man.   *(RKO)*

Everett Sloane and Joseph Cotten are flawless as Bernstein and Leland. Bernstein's uncritical hero-worship of Kane establishes him as the less intelligent of the two, a man who—unlike Leland—puts friendship above principle. But the endearing Bernstein is something of a comic innocent, so blinded by loyalty that he is incapable of seeing Kane's flaws, much less his vices. As an old man, Bernstein is still funny, a successful businessman, but no shallow materialist. "It's no trick to make a lot of money," he scoffs, "if all you want is to make a lot of money." He recognizes that Kane's motives ran deeper than the crassly entrepreneurial. He is still awed by the mysterious depths of Kane's inner spirit. And perhaps a bit saddened by the contrast with his own ordinary soul.

Welles's performance as Kane was lavishly praised. John O'Hara, reviewing the movie for *Newsweek*, said, "There has never been a better actor than Orson Welles." D.W. Griffith described it as the greatest film performance he had ever seen. Tall and imposing, with a deep, flexible voice capable of a wide spectrum of nuances, Welles was an astonishing technician, equally convincing as a brash young man, a rigid autocrat in middle years, and a burned-out, hulking septuagenarian. At twenty-five, Kane is charming and charismatic, with an insolent skepticism toward all forms of authority. Indeed, he is so charming that we hardly notice some of his questionable methods, his insistence on having everything his own way. As a middle-aged man, Kane is more somber. The element of threat is more brazenly paraded. He no longer argues

12–24. Publicity photo of Dorothy Comingore in opera costume for *Citizen Kane*. Bernard Herrmann composed the film's opera, *Salammbô*, in the style of nineteenth-century French "Oriental" operas. Edward Stevenson's costumes are in this same campy style of mockery. For example, Susan's outlandish regalia is a send-up of what the well-dressed French-Oriental opera queen might wear while suffering the agonies of unrequited love, torment, and despair. *(RKO)*

that the end justifies the means—he automatically assumes it, expecting others to acquiesce to his views. As an old man, Kane is among the walking wounded, a man who has repeatedly fought and lost.

Edward Stevenson's costumes adhere closely to the actual styles of each period. Because the movie traverses nearly seventy years and the events are not chronologically presented, the costumes had to be instantly recognizable for the audience to know the period of each scene. Kane's childhood has a nineteenth-century flavour—a cross between Charles Dickens and Mark Twain. The former can be seen in Thatcher's stiff collar and stovepipe hat; the latter in the plain frontier simplicity of the clothes of Mary and Jim Kane.

Costumes are symbolic as well as functional. As a crusading young publisher, Kane favours whites. He often removes his jacket and tie while working. Later in life, he is almost always in black business suits and ties. Emily's clothes look expensive, but with an understated elegance. She always looks like a well-bred young matron—fashionable, modest, and feminine. Susan favours simple clothes before meeting Kane. After meeting him, she is generally dressed in ritzy patterned dresses, sometimes sprinkled with sequins—like an aging show-girl parading her loot.

The following is an analysis of Susan's opera costume **(12–24)**, a triumph of irony and wit:

1. *Period.* Ostensibly nineteenth century, though in fact an amusing pastiche of various periods and "Oriental" influences.
2. *Class.* Royalty. The costume is profusely festooned with pearls, precious jewels, and other queenly niceties.

12–25.   Promotional poster for *Citizen Kane*.

Then as now, a studio's advertising emphasized a picture's commercial appeal and sex and violence were the most common ploys to lure the mass audience. The promotional campaign for *Citizen Kane* was somewhat classier. It stressed Welles's box-office appeal as the film's star and the controversy surrounding the picture's release. Posters and lobby displays also exaggerated the love angle, presumably to appeal to women patrons: "I hate him!" Susan proclaims. "I love him!" Emily counters. (Neither statement is in the movie, of course.) Interestingly, this poster crudely parallels the multiple points of view found in the film itself.   *(RKO)*

3. *Sex.* Female, with an emphasis on curved, swaying lines and peekaboo slits in the skirt. Only the turban provides a masculine touch, though it is whimsically inflected with fluffy white feathers.

4. *Age.* The costume is designed for a woman in her twenties, at the peak of her physical attractiveness.

5. *Silhouette.* Formfitting, unabashedly highlighting the wearer's curvacious contours.

6. *Fabric.* Silks, beaded ornamentation encrusted with jewels.

7. *Accessories.* Turban, pearl strands, incongruous Joan Crawford-style ankle-strap shoes.

8. *Colour.* The film is in black and white, but most of the fabric has a metallic sheen, suggesting gold and ebony.

9. *Body exposure.* The costume reveals and highlights such erotic areas as the breasts, midriff, and legs.

10. *Function.* The costume is totally without utility, difficult even to walk in. It is intended for a person who does not work, but is on display.

11. *Body attitude.* Tall and proud, with head and breasts held high, like a Vegas showgirl flashing her gaudy plunder.

12. *Image.* Every inch the opera queen.

THEORY

In the more than fifty years since the film was made, *Citizen Kane* has become an (almost) undisputed classic. It regularly tops the lists of best films whenever polls are conducted among critics or filmmakers. It is the most frequently screened film in film studies courses and it has been the subject of countless books, articles, and postgraduate theses. Not surprisingly, film theorists have also been attracted to the challenges of this complex and elusive film.

As we have already seen, realist and formalist theorists have claimed the film as a demonstration of the validity of their accounts of the medium, auteurists have discussed the thematic and formal qualities that *Citizen Kane* shares with Welles's later work. They suggest that Welles's personal vision emerges strongly despite the signifiant contributions of his collaborators, just as it did in genre films like *The Lady from Shanghai* (**1–26**) and *Touch of Evil* or in his independent productions like *Othello* (**12–27**) and *The Trial* which were made in often very difficult circumstances.

The film also lends itself to a structuralist analysis of its signifying systems. One theorist, drawing on the work of Christian Metz, produced an exhaustive and very lengthy sequence-by-sequence breakdown to show the different codes at work in the construction of the narrative. This kind of analysis has a primarily technical interest, but an approach that had its origins in linguistics is well suited to a film that depicts the search for the meaning of a word uttered at its beginning.

The mystery of Rosebud provides the enigma that sets the narrative going and encourages the spectator to decipher the evidence that Thompson

12–26. *The Magnificent Ambersons* (U.S.A., 1942), *with Dolores Costello, Agnes Moore-head, Joseph Cotten, and Ray Collins; directed by Orson Welles.*
Like most of Welles's movies, this, his favorite work, deals with the theme of a lost paradise. Unlike *Kane*, however, the tone is warm and nostalgic, the images more softly lyrical. Welles does not appear in the film, though he does narrate the story off screen. He concludes with a shot of a microphone on a swinging boom, accompanied by his spoken credit: "I wrote the picture and directed it. My name is Orson Welles."   *(RKO)*

uncovers as he interviews the witnesses. Whether or not we decide that the final revelation explains Kane's life, the discovery that the word refers to a sled allows us to feel that we have decoded the incomplete message with which the film began.

Of course, spectators react quite differently to this discovery, some finding it a disappointing outcome for such a complex narrative, while others feel that it is a powerful final image that connects up with many of the film's motifs. The film forces us to attend to its structure and leaves us wondering whether it has explained who Kane was or revealed the emptiness behind his bravado or simply shown that we can never fully understand another human being. After all, the first "sign" in the film is a "No Trespassing" warning.

Despite the suspicion that Rosebud is simply "dollar-book Freud," the film has proved a fertile source for psychoanalytic film theorists. Some of these theorists have explored the links between the sled and Kane's relations with his parents, in accordance with Freud's insistence that people's characters are

12-27. *Othello* (Morocco, 1952), *with Orson Welles and Suzanne Cloutier, directed by Welles.* In 1948, Welles, discouraged by a string of box-office failures, left for Europe and Africa, where he hoped to work as an independent producer–director. His first movie was this adaptation of a Shakespearean tragedy. The project was a nightmare. It was over three years in the shooting, and Welles had to interrupt production many times to seek additional funding. He lost several players in the process. There were three Desdemonas, four Iagos. Sequences had to be reshot time and again. But finally the movie was finished. On the Continent, it was enthusiastically praised and swept the Grand Prix at the Cannes Film Festival. But British and American critics complained of its crude soundtrack. This was to be the pattern of virtually all his subsequent work outside America.   *(RKO)*

determined by childhood experiences. The sled is first seen in the sequence in which his mother sends him away with Thatcher, apparently to protect him from his father. Thatcher becomes a substitute father but only as the representative of a bank, and Kane begins his career by rebelling against him.

Kane's fixation on the past, as signified by his final word, is most obviously associated with the loss of his mother. In many of Welles's films, characters seek power to compensate for losses in their past but eventually fail because they can never replace what has been lost. In *Citizen Kane,* the loss of his mother's love drives him to achieve the success that she wanted for him but also leads him to repeat the painful separation through his treatment of his two wives.

Some theorists have attempted to apply this psychoanalytic approach to Welles himself, pointing out that Kane shares as many biographical details with the filmmaker as with Hearst. In a sense, Welles's refusal to compromise on his first film was self-destructive, and he quickly ran into trouble with the studios. Although RKO had given him a free hand in making *Citizen Kane*, the studio re-cut his next film, *The Magnificent Ambersons* (**12–26**), and he never worked on a major Hollywood production again. Since Welles's parents died when he was young, his later behaviour may be attributed to a similar sense of loss to that of his character in his first film.

However, psychoanalytic theory is most productive not in its attempts to analyze Kane or Welles but in its illumination of the dream-like structure of the film itself. In Freudian theory, the unconscious communicates through dreams, but in an indirect and devious way that prevents the censorship of the conscious mind. *Citizen Kane* works like a dream in which a mass of conflicting and ambiguous information emerges under considerable pressure. It is as if the film (or Welles) is trying to reveal and conceal the truth at the same time. François Truffaut had this tension in mind when he wrote that "the films of Orson Welles are shot by an exhibitionist and cut by a censor."

The dream in the film is not just psychological; it is also the American dream. Kane's politics cannot be separated from his personal life and, in this respect, the film deals with the "imaginary" relations to reality that Althusser described in his theory of ideology. While we can usefully discuss the film in relation to Welles's own liberal political beliefs, theorists have tended to approach its ideological implications by exploring the tensions at work in its structure and its use of film language. The key question becomes whether the film ends up reinforcing the dominant ideology of the system in which it was made or whether its formal "excesses" enable it to expose the mechanisms on which the system depends.

One area in which this debate can be seen most clearly is in the development of feminist film theory. Initially, Welles came under attack as a misogynist whose work conformed to Hollywood's gender stereotypes. Molly Haskell, for example, complained that the women in *Citizen Kane* are "insignificant and no great credit to their sex." Some more recent theorists have argued that the central characters may be male but that the film offers a critical perspective on dominant gender codes. In her brief but penetrating study of the film, Laura Mulvey argued that, while it is a film that appeals to the spectator's voyeuristic impulses, it does not depend on the "erotic obsession with the female figure" that she identified in her 1975 essay as a key component in classical narrative cinema.

These theoretical perspectives on *Citizen Kane* have, at their best, enriched our understanding of the film, but they have been called into question by new developments in film studies. Cognitive theorists reject much of the linguistic and psychoanalytical framework used by structuralist and ideological theorists and stress the conscious processes involved in attributing meaning to films. From this perspective, we should focus on the ways in which the film deviates from the norms of classical narrative cinema and thus unsettles the viewer's responses to its depiction of Kane.

The cognitive approach tends to be formalist and to downplay the political effects of popular cinema. This tendency may, to some extent, be compensated for by the new interest in film history. By analyzing the data in film archives, historians may throw light on the conditions in which *Citizen Kane* was made and on the reactions of its audiences. This new information may place the issues that film theory has explored in a new light, but it is doubtful that the film's mysteries will ever be completely explained by historical research or theoretical analysis. What is certain is that, in the ongoing debates between film theorists, historians, and critics, *Citizen Kane* will pose some of the most important questions.

FURTHER READING

BAZIN, ANDRÉ, *Orson Welles: A Critical View* (New York: Harper & Row, 1978). Critical study by France's greatest film critic.

CARRINGER, ROBERT L., *The Making of Citizen Kane* (Berkeley: University of California Press, 1985). Definitive.

GOTTESMAN, RONALD, ed., *Focus on Orson Welles* (Englewood Cliffs, N.J.: Prentice-Hall, 1976). A collection of critical essays, filmography, and bibliography. See also Gottesman's *Focus on Citizen Kane* (Englewood Cliffs, N.J.: Prentice-Hall, 1971). Two excellent anthologies.

HIGHAM, CHARLES, *The Films of Orson Welles* (Berkeley: University of California Press, 1970). Critical study and psychobiography. Very well illustrated. See also Higham's *Orson Welles: The Rise and Fall of an American Genius* (New York: St. Martin's Press, 1985).

KAEL, PAULINE, *The Citizen Kane Book* (Boston: Little, Brown, 1971). Reading version and a cutting continuity of Kane, prefaced by Kael's controversial essay on the authorship of the script.

LEAMING, BARBARA, *Orson Welles: A Biography* (New York: Viking, 1985). Extensive interviews with Welles; somewhat idolatrous.

McBRIDE, JOSEPH, *Orson Welles* (New York: Viking, 1972). A perceptive critical study. Filmography. Stage, radio, television, acting credits.

MULVEY, LAURA, *Citizen Kane* (London: British Film Institute, 1992). Historical background and critical analysis.

NAREMORE, JAMES, *The Magic World of Orson Welles* (New York: Oxford University Press, 1978). Critical study.

THOMPSON, DAVID, *Rosebud* (New York: Knopf, 1996). A well-written biography, with sixty-nine photos.

GLOSSARY

A

actor star. See *star.*

aerial shot (T). Essentially a variation of the *crane shot,* though restricted to exterior locations. Usually taken from a helicopter.

aesthetic distance (C). Viewers' ability to distinguish between an artistic reality and external reality—their realization that the events of a fiction film are simulated.

A-film (I). An American studio era term signifying a major production, usually with important stars and a generous budget. Shown as the main feature on double bills.

aleatory techniques (C). Techniques of filmmaking that depend on the element of chance. Images are not planned out in advance but must be composed on the spot by the camera operator. Usually used in documentary situations.

allegory (C). A symbolic technique in which stylized characters and situations represent rather obvious ideas, such as Justice, Death, Religion, Society, and so on.

allusion (C). A reference to an event, person, or work of art, usually well known.

angle (G). The camera's angle of view relative to the subject being photographed. A high-angle shot is photographed from above, a low angle from below the subject.

animation (G). A form of filmmaking characterized by photographing inanimate objects or individual drawings *frame* by frame, with each frame differing minutely from its predecessor. When such images are projected at the standard speed of twenty-four frames per second, the result is that the objects or drawings appear to move, and hence seem "animated."

anticipatory camera, anticipatory setup (C). The placement of the camera in such a manner as to anticipate the movement of an action before it occurs. Such setups often suggest predestination.

archetype (C). An original model or type after which similar things are patterned. Archetypes can be well-known story patterns, universal experiences, or personality types. Myths, fairy tales, *genres*, and cultural heroes are generally archetypal, as are the basic cycles of life and nature.

art director (G). The individual responsible for designing and overseeing the construction of sets for a movie, and sometimes its interior decoration and overall visual style.

aspect ratio (T). The ratio between the horizontal and vertical dimensions of the screen.

auteur theory (C). A theory of film popularized by the critics of the French journal *Cahiers du cinéma* in the 1950s. The theory emphasizes the director as the major creator of film art, stamping the material with his or her own personal vision, style, and thematic obsessions.

available lighting (G). The use of only that light which actually exists on location, either natural (the sun) or artificial (house lamps). When available lighting is used in interior locations, generally a sensitive *fast film stock* must also be used.

avant-garde (C). From the French, meaning "in the front ranks." Those minority artists whose works are characterized by an unconventional daring and by obscure, controversial, or highly personal ideas.

B

backlighting (G). When the lights for a shot derive from the rear of the set, thus throwing the foreground figures into semidarkness or silhouette.

back lot (I). During the studio era, standing exterior sets of such common locales as a turn-of-the-century city block, a frontier town, a European village, and so on.

B-film (G). A low-budget movie usually shown as the second feature during the big-studio era in America. B-films rarely included important stars and took the form of popular *genres*, such as thrillers, westerns, or horror films. The major studios used them as testing grounds for the raw talent under contract.

bird's-eye view (G). A shot in which the camera photographs a scene from directly overhead.

blimp (T). A soundproof camera housing that muffles the noise of the camera's motor so sound can be clearly recorded on the set.

blocking (T). The movements of the actors within a given playing area.

boom, mike boom (T). An overhead telescoping pole that carries a microphone, permitting the *synchronous* recording of sound without restricting the movement of the actors.

C

camp, campy (C). An artistic sensibility typified by comic mockery, especially of the straight world and conventional morality. Campy movies are often ludicrously theatrical, stylistically gaudy, and gleefully subversive.

cels, also cells (T). Transparent plastic sheets that are superimposed in layers by *animators* to give the illusion of depth and volume to their drawings.

cinematographer, also **director of photography** or **DP (G).** The artist or technician responsible for the lighting of a shot and the quality of the photography.

cinéma vérité (C). A method of documentary filming using *aleatory* methods that don't interfere with the way events take place in reality. Such movies are made with a minimum of equipment, usually a handheld camera and portable sound apparatus.

classical cinema, classical paradigm (C). A vague but convenient term used to designate the style of mainstream fiction films produced in the United States, roughly from the midteens until the late 1960s. The classical paradigm is a movie strong in *story, star,* and *production values,* with a high level of technical achievement, and edited according to conventions of *classical cutting.* The visual style is functional and rarely distracts from the characters in action. Movies in this form are structured narratively, with a clearly defined conflict, complications that intensify to a rising climax, and a resolution that emphasizes formal closure.

classical cutting (C). A style of editing developed by D. W. Griffith, in which a sequence of shots is determined by a scene's dramatic and emotional emphasis rather than by physical action alone. The sequence of shots represents the breakdown of the event into its psychological as well as logical components.

closed forms (C). A visual style that inclines toward self-conscious designs and carefully harmonized compositions. The *frame* is exploited to suggest a self-sufficient universe that encloses all the necessary visual information, usually in an aesthetically appealing manner.

close-up, close shot (G). A detailed view of a person or object. A close-up of an actor usually includes only his or her head.

continuity (T). The kind of logic implied between edited shots, their principle of coherence. *Cutting to continuity* emphasizes smooth transitions between shots, in which time and space are unobtrusively condensed. More complex, *classical cutting* is the linking of shots according to an event's psychological as well as logical breakdown. In *thematic montage,* the continuity is determined by the symbolic association of ideas between shots, rather than any literal connections in time and space.

convention (C). An implied agreement between the viewer and artist to accept certain artificialities as real in a work of art. In movies, editing (or the juxtaposition of shots) is accepted as "logical" even though a viewer's perception of reality is continuous and unfragmented.

coverage, covering shots, cover shots (T). Extra shots of a scene that can be used to bridge transitions in case the planned footage fails to edit as planned. Usually *long shots* that preserve the overall continuity of a scene.

crane shot (T). A shot taken from a special device called a crane, which resembles a huge mechanical arm. The crane carries the camera and the *cinematographer* and can move in virtually any direction.

creative producer (I). A producer who supervises the making of a movie in such detail that he or she is virtually its artistic director. During the studio era in America, the most famous creative producers were David O. Selznick and Walt Disney.

cross-cutting (G). The alternating of shots from two sequences, often in different locales, suggesting that they are taking place at the same time.

cutting to continuity (T). A type of editing in which the shots are arranged to preserve the fluidity of an action without showing all of it. An unobtrusive condensation of a continuous action.

D

day-for-night shooting (T). Scenes that are filmed in daytime with special *filters* to suggest nighttime settings in the movie image.

deep-focus shot (T). A technique of photography that permits all distance planes to remain clearly in focus, from close-up ranges to infinity.

dialectical, dialectics (C). An analytical methodology, derived from Hegel and Marx, that juxtaposes pairs of opposites—a thesis and antithesis—to arrive at a synthesis of ideas.

direct cinema (C). A term often used as a synonym for *cinéma vérité*. In France and Canada, especially, it is used to designate an approach to documentary that stresses the relationship between filmmakers and their subjects. It is also applied to fiction films that use the equipment and techniques developed for documentary in the 1950s.

dissolve, lap dissolve (T). The slow fading out of one shot and the gradual fading in of its successor, with a superimposition of images, usually at the midpoint.

distributor (I). Those individuals who serve as go-betweens in the film industry, who arrange to book the product in theatres.

docudrama (C). A rather vague term often applied to various kinds of fictional reconstruction of actual events.

dolly shot, tracking shot, trucking shot (T). A shot taken from a moving vehicle. Originally tracks were laid on the set to permit a smoother movement of the camera.

dominant contrast, dominant (C). That area of the film image that compels the viewer's most immediate attention, usually because of a prominent visual contrast.

double exposure (T). The superimposition of two literally unrelated images on film. See also *multiple exposure.*

dubbing (T). The addition of sound after the visuals have been photographed. Dubbing can be either *synchronous* with an image or *nonsynchronous.* Foreign-language movies are often dubbed in English for release in this country.

E

editing (G). The joining of one shot (strip of film) with another. The shots can picture events and objects in different places at different times. In Europe, editing is called *montage*.

epic (C). A film *genre* characterized by bold and sweeping themes, usually in heroic proportions. The protagonist is an ideal representative of a culture—national, religious, or regional. The tone of most epics is dignified, the treatment larger than life. The western is the most popular epic genre in the United States.

establishing shot (T). Usually an *extreme long* or *long shot* offered at the beginning of a scene, providing the viewer with the context of the subsequent closer shots.

expressionism (C). A style of filmmaking emphasizing extreme distortion, *lyricism*, and artistic self-expression at the expense of objectivity.

extreme close-up (G). A minutely detailed view of an object or person. An extreme close-up of an actor generally includes only his or her eyes or mouth.

extreme long shot (G). A panoramic view of an exterior location, photographed from a great distance, often as far as four hundred metres away.

eye-level shot (T). The placement of the camera approximately one and a half to two metres from the ground, corresponding to the height of an observer on the scene.

F

fade (T). The fade-out is the snuffing of an image from normal brightness to a black screen. A fade-in is the opposite.

faithful adaptation (C). A film based on a literary original which captures the essence of the original, often by using cinematic equivalents for specific literary techniques.

fast motion (T). Shots of a subject photographed at a slower rate than twenty-four fps, which, when projected at the standard rate, conveys motion that is jerky and slightly comical, seemingly out of control.

fast stock, fast film (T). Film stock that's highly sensitive to light and generally produces a grainy image. Often used by documentarists who wish to shoot only with *available lighting*.

film noir (C). A French term—literally, "black cinema"—referring to a kind of urban American *genre* that sprang up after World War II, emphasizing a fatalistic, despairing universe where there is no escape from mean city streets, loneliness, and death. Stylistically, *noir* emphasizes *low-key* and *high-contrast* lighting, complex compositions, and a strong atmosphere of dread and paranoia.

filters (T). Pieces of glass and plastic placed in front of the camera lens that distort the quality of light entering the camera and hence the movie image.

final cut, also **release print (I).** The sequence of shots in a movie as it will be released to the public.

first cut, also **rough cut (I).** The initial sequence of shots in a movie, often constructed by the director.

first-person point of view. See *point-of-view shot.*

flashback (G). An editing technique that suggests the interruption of the present by a shot or series of shots representing the past.

flash-forward (G). An editing technique that suggests the interruption of the present by a shot or series of shots representing the future.

focus (T). The degree of acceptable sharpness in a film image. "Out of focus" means the images are blurred and lack acceptable linear definition.

footage (T). Exposed film *stock.*

foregrounding (C). When a critic isolates and heightens one aspect of a work of art from its context to analyze that characteristic in greater depth.

formalist, formalism (C). A style of filmmaking in which aesthetic forms take precedence over the subject matter as content. Time and space as ordinarily perceived are often distorted. Emphasis is on the essential, symbolic characteristics of objects and people, not necessarily on their superficial appearance. Formalists are often *lyrical,* self-consciously heightening their style to call attention to it as a value for its own sake.

frame (T). The dividing line between the edges of the screen image and the enclosing darkness of the theatre. Can also refer to a single photograph from the filmstrip.

freeze frame, freeze shot (T). A shot composed of a single *frame* that is reprinted a number of times on the filmstrip; when projected, it gives the illusion of a still photograph.

f-stop (T). The measurement of the size of the lens opening in the camera, indicating the amount of light that's admitted.

full shot (T). A type of *long shot* that includes the human body in full, with the head near the top of the *frame* and the feet near the bottom.

G

gauge (T). The width of the filmstrip, expressed in millimetres (mm). The wider the gauge, the better the quality of the image. The standard theatrical gauge is 35 mm.

genre (C). A recognizable type of movie, characterized by certain preestablished conventions. Some common American genres are westerns, thrillers, sci-fi movies, etc. A ready-made narrative form.

H

handheld shot (G). A shot taken with a moving camera that is often deliberately shaky to suggest documentary footage in an uncontrolled setting.

high-angle shot (T). A shot in which the subject is photographed from above.

high contrast (T). A style of lighting emphasizing harsh shafts and dramatic streaks of lights and darks. Often used in thrillers and melodramas.

high key (T). A style of lighting emphasizing bright, even illumination, with few conspicuous shadows. Used mostly in comedies, musicals, and light entertainment films.

homage (C). A direct or indirect reference within a movie to another movie, film-maker, or cinematic style. A respectful and affectionate tribute.

I

iconography (C). The use of a well-known cultural symbol or complex of symbols in an artistic representation. In movies, iconography can involve a star's *persona*, the preestablished conventions of a genre (like the shootout in a western), the use of *archetypal* characters and situations, and such stylistic features as lighting, settings, constuming, props, and so on.

independent producer (G). A producer not affiliated with a studio or large commercial firm. Many stars and directors have been independent producers to ensure their artistic control.

intercut (T). See *cross-cutting*.

intrinsic interest (C). An unobtrusive area of the film image that nonetheless compels our most immediate attention because of its dramatic or contextual importance.

iris (T). A *masking* device that blacks out portions of the screen, permitting only a part of the image to be seen. Usually the iris is circular or oval in shape and can be expanded or contracted.

J

jump cut (T). An abrupt transition between shots, sometimes deliberate, which is disorienting in terms of the continuity of space and time.

K

key light (T). The main source of illumination for a shot.

kinetic (C). Pertaining to motion and movement.

L

leftist, left-wing (G). A set of ideological values, typically liberal in emphasis, stressing such traits as equality, the importance of environment in determining human behaviour, relativism in moral matters, emphasis on the secular rather than religion, an optimistic view of the future and human nature, a belief in technology as the main propellant of progress, cooperation rather than competition, an identification with the poor and the oppressed, internationalism, and sexual and reproductive freedom.

lengthy take, long take (C). A shot of lengthy duration.

lens (T). A ground or moulded piece of glass, plastic, or other transparent material through which light rays are refracted so they converge or diverge to form the photographic image within the camera.

literal adaptation (C). A movie based on a stage play, in which the dialogue and actions are preserved more or less intact.

long shot (G). A shot that includes an area within the image that roughly corresponds to the audience's view of the area within the proscenium arch in the live theatre.

loose adaptation (C). A movie based on another medium in which only a superficial resemblance exists between the two versions.

loose framing (C). Usually in longer shots. The *mise en scène* is so spaciously distributed within the confines of the framed image that the people photographed have considerable freedom of movement.

low-angle shot (T). A shot in which the subject is photographed from below.

low key (T). A style of lighting that emphasizes diffused shadows and atmospheric pools of light. Often used in mysteries and thrillers.

lyrical (C). A stylistic exuberance and subjectivity, emphasizing the sensuous beauty of the medium and producing an intense outpouring of emotion.

M

majors (I). The principal production studios of a given era. In the golden age of the Hollywood studio system—roughly the 1930s and 1940s—the majors consisted of MGM, Warner Brothers, RKO, Paramount Pictures, and Twentieth Century–Fox.

Marxist (G). An ideological term used to describe any person or film that is biased in favour of *left-wing* values, particularly in their more extreme form.

masking (T). A technique whereby a portion of the movie image is blocked out, thus temporarily altering the dimensions of the screen's *aspect ratio*.

master shot (T). An uninterrupted shot, usually taken from a *long* or *full shot* range, that contains an entire scene. The closer shots are photographed later, and an *edited* sequence, composed of a variety of shots, is constructed on the editor's bench.

matte shot (T). A process of combining two separate shots on one print, resulting in an image that looks as though it had been photographed normally. Used mostly for special effects, such as combining a human figure with giant dinosaurs, etc.

medium shot (G). A relatively close shot, revealing the human figure from the knees or waist up.

metaphor (C). An implied comparison between two otherwise unlike elements, meaningful in a figurative rather than literal sense.

Method acting (C). A style of performance derived from the Russian stage director Stanislavsky, which has been the dominant acting style in the United States since the 1950s. Method actors emphasize psychological intensity, extensive rehearsals to explore a character, emotional believability rather than technical mastery, and "living" a role internally rather than merely imitating the external behaviour of a character.

metteur en scène (C). The artist or technician who creates the *mise en scène*—that is, the director.

mickeymousing (T). A type of film music that is purely descriptive and attempts to mimic the visual action with musical equivalents. Often used in cartoons.

miniatures, also **model** or **miniature shots (T).** Small-scale models photographed to give the illusion that they are full-scale objects. For example, ships sinking at sea, giant dinosaurs, airplanes colliding, etc.

minimalism (C). A style of filmmaking characterized by austerity and restraint, in which cinematic elements are reduced to the barest minimum of information.

mise en scène (C). The arrangement of visual weights and movements within a given space. In the live theatre, the space is usually defined by the proscenium arch; in movies, it is defined by the *frame* that encloses the images. Cinematic mise en scène encompasses both the staging of the action and the way that it's photographed.

mix (T). The process of combining separately recorded sounds from individual soundtracks onto a master track.

montage (T). Transitional sequences of rapidly edited images, used to suggest the lapse of time or the passing of events. Often uses *dissolves* and *multiple exposures.* In Europe, montage means the art of editing.

motif (C). Any unobtrusive technique, object, or thematic idea that's systematically repeated throughout a film.

multiple exposures (T). A special effect produced by the *optical printer,* which permits the superimposition of many images simultaneously.

N

negative image (T). The reversal of lights and darks of the subject photographed: blacks are white, whites are black.

neorealism (C). An Italian film movement that produced its best works between 1945 and 1955. Strongly *realistic* in its techniques, neorealism emphasized documentary aspects of film art, stressing loose episodic plots, unextraordinary events and characters, natural lighting, actual location settings, nonprofessional actors, a preoccupation with poverty and social problems, and an emphasis on humanistic and democratic ideals. The term has also been used to describe other films that reflect the technical and stylistic biases of Italian neorealism.

New Wave, Nouvelle vague (C). A group of young French directors who came to prominence during the late 1950s. The most widely known are François Truffaut, Jean-Luc Godard, and Alain Resnais.

nonsynchronous sound (T). Sound and image that are not recorded simultaneously, or sound that is detached from its source in the film image. Music is usually nonsynchronous in a movie, providing background atmosphere.

O

oblique angle, tilt shot (T). A shot photographed by a tilted camera. When the image is projected on the screen, the subject itself seems to be tilted on a diagonal.

oeuvre (C). From the French, "work." The complete works of an artist, viewed as a whole.

omniscient point of view (C). An all-knowing narrator who provides the spectator with all the necessary information.

open forms (C). Used primarily by *realist* filmmakers, these techniques are likely to be unobtrusive, with an emphasis on informal compositions and apparently haphazard designs. The *frame* is exploited to suggest a temporary masking, a window that arbitrarily cuts off part of the action.

optical printer (T). An elaborate machine used to create special effects in movies. For example, *fades, dissolves, multiple exposures,* etc.

outtakes (I). Shots or pieces of shots that are not used in the final cut of a film. Leftover footage.

overexposure (T). Too much light enters the aperture of a camera lens, bleaching out the image. Useful for fantasy and nightmare scenes.

P

pan, panning shot (T). Short for panorama, this is a revolving horizontal movement of the camera from left to right or vice versa.

parallel editing. See *cross-cutting.*

persona (C). From the Latin, "mask." An actor's public image, based on previous roles, and often incorporating elements from his or her actual personality as well.

personality star. See *star.*

pixillation, also **stop-motion photography (T).** An *animation* technique involving the photographing of live actors *frame* by frame. When the sequence is projected at the standard speed of twenty-four fps, the actors move abruptly and jerkily, like cartoon figures.

plot (C). The arrangement of story events in the order in which they appear in the film. For example, events that occurred in the past might be introduced at any point through *flashbacks* or dialogue.

point-of-view shot, also **pov shot, first-person camera, subjective camera (T).** Any shot that is taken from the vantage point of a character in the film, showing what the character sees.

process shot, also **rear projection (T).** A technique in which a background scene is projected onto a translucent screen behind the actors so it appears that the actors are on location in the final image.

producer (G). An ambiguous term referring to the individual or company that controls the financing of a film, and often the way it's made. The producer can concern himself or herself solely with business matters, or with putting together a package deal (such as script, stars, and director), or the producer can function as an expeditor, smoothing over problems during production.

producer–director (I). A filmmaker who finances projects independently, to allow maximum creative freedom.

production values (I). The box-office appeal of the physical mounting of a film, such as sets, costumes, props, etc.

prop (T). Any movable item that is included in a movie: tables, guns, books, etc.

property (I). Anything with a profit-making potential in movies, though generally used to describe a story of some kind: a screenplay, novel, short story, etc.

proxemic patterns (C). The spatial relationships among characters within the *mise en scène*, and the apparent distance of the camera from the subject photographed.

pull-back dolly (T). Withdrawing the camera from a scene to reveal an object or character that was previously out of *frame*.

R

rack focusing, selective focusing (T). The blurring of focal planes in sequence, forcing the viewer's eyes to travel with those areas of an image that remain in sharp focus.

reaction shot (T). A cut to a shot of a character's reaction to the contents of the preceding shot.

realism (G). A style of filmmaking that attempts to duplicate the look of objective reality as it's commonly perceived, with emphasis on authentic locations and details, *long shots, lengthy takes*, and a minimum of distorting techniques.

reestablishing shot (T). A return to an initial *establishing shot* within a scene, acting as a reminder of the physical context of the closer shots.

reprinting (T). A special effects technique in which two or more separately photographed images are rephotographed onto one strip of film.

reverse angle shot (T). A shot taken from an angle 180° opposed to the previous shot. That is, the camera is placed opposite its previous position.

reverse motion (T). A series of images are photographed with the film reversed. When projected normally, the effect is to suggest backward movement—an egg "returning" to its shell, for example.

rightist, right-wing (G). A set of ideological values, typically conservative in emphasis, stressing such traits as family values, patriarchy, heredity and caste, absolute moral and ethical standards, religion, veneration for tradition and the past, a tendency to be pessimistic about the future and human nature, the need for competition, an identification with leaders and elite classes, nationalism, open market economic principles, and marital monogamy.

rite of passage (C). Narratives that focus on key phases of a person's life, when an individual passes from one stage of development to another, such as adolescence to adulthood, innocence to experience, middle age to old age, and so on.

rough cut (T). The crudely edited footage of a movie before the editor has tightened up the slackness between shots. A kind of rough draft.

rushes, dailies (I). The selected footage of the previous day's shooting, which is usually evaluated by the director and *cinematographer* before the start of the next day's shooting.

S

scene (G). An imprecise unit of film, composed of a number of interrelated *shots*, unified usually by a central concern—a location, an incident, or a minor dramatic climax.

screwball comedy (C). A film *genre*, introduced in the 1930s in the United States and popular up to the 1950s, characterized by zany lovers, often from different social classes. The plots are often absurdly improbable and have a tendency to veer out of control. These movies usually feature slapstick comedy scenes, aggressive and charming heroines, and an assortment of outlandish secondary characters.

script, screenplay, scenario (G). A written description of a movie's dialogue and action, which occasionally includes camera directions.

selective focus. See *rack focusing*.

sequence shot, also ***plan-séquence*** **(C).** A single lengthy shot, usually involving complex staging and camera movements.

setup (T). The positioning of the camera and lights for a specific shot.

shooting ratio (I). The amount of film stock used in photographing a movie in relation to what's finally included in the finished product. A shooting ratio of 20:1 means that twenty feet of film were shot for every one used in the *final cut*.

shooting script (I). A written breakdown of a movie story into its individual shots, often containing technical instructions. Used by the director and his or her staff during the production.

short lens. See *wide-angle lens*.

shot (G). Those images that are recorded continuously from the time the camera starts to the time it stops. That is, an unedited strip of film.

slow motion (T). Shots of a subject photographed at a faster rate than twenty-four fps, which when projected at the standard rate produce a dreamy, dance-like slowness of action.

slow stock, slow film (T). Film stocks that are relatively insensitive to light and produce crisp images and a sharpness of detail. When used in interior settings, these stocks generally require considerable artificial illumination.

soft focus (T). The blurring out of focus of all except one desired distance range. Can also refer to a glamourizing technique that softens the sharpness of definition so facial wrinkles can be smoothed over and even eliminated.

star (G). A film actor or actress of great popularity. A *personality star* tends to play only those roles that fit a preconceived public image, which constitutes his or her *persona*. An *actor star* can play roles of greater range and variety. Barbra Streisand is a personality star; Robert De Niro is an actor star.

star system (G). The technique of exploiting the charisma of popular performers to enhance the box-office appeal of films. The star system was developed in America and has been the backbone of the American film industry since the mid-1910s.

star vehicle (G). A movie especially designed to showcase the talents and charms of a specific star.

stock (T). Unexposed film. There are many types of movie stocks, including those highly sensitive to light (*fast stocks*) and those relatively insensitive to light (*slow stocks*).

story (C). All the events that we see, hear about, or infer in a fiction film in the order in which they are supposed to have happened. The filmmaker constructs the *plot* from these events; the spectator reconstructs the story on the basis of the information supplied by the plot.

storyboard, storyboarding (T). A previsualization technique in which shots are sketched in advance and in sequence, like a comic strip, thus allowing the filmmaker to outline the *mise en scène* and construct the *editing* continuity before production begins.

story values (I). The narrative appeal of a movie, which can reside in the popularity of an adapted *property*, the high craftsmanship of a script, or both.

studio (G). A large corporation specializing in the production of movies, such as Paramount, Warner Brothers, and so on; any physical facility equipped for the production of films.

subjective camera. See *point-of-view shot.*

subsidiary contrast (C). A subordinated element of the film image, complementing or contrasting with the *dominant contrast.*

subtext (C). A term used in drama and film to signify the dramatic implications beneath the language of a play or movie. Often the subtext concerns ideas and emotions that are totally independent of the language of a text.

surrealism (C). An *avant-garde* movement in the arts stressing Freudian and Marxist ideas, unconscious elements, irrationalism, and the symbolic association of ideas. Surrealist movies were produced roughly from 1924 to 1931, primarily in France, though there are surrealistic elements in the works of many directors, and especially in music videos.

swish pan, also **flash** or **zip pan (T).** A horizontal movement of the camera at such a rapid rate that the subject photographed blurs on the screen.

synchronous sound (T). The agreement or correspondence between image and sound, which are recorded simultaneously, or seem so in the finished print. Synchronous sounds appear to derive from an obvious source in the visuals.

symbol, symbolic (C). A figurative device in which an object, event, or cinematic technique has significance beyond its literal meaning. Symbolism is always determined by the dramatic context.

T

take (T). A variation of a specific shot. The final shot is often selected from a number of possible takes.

telephoto lens, long lens (T). A lens that acts as a telescope, magnifying the size of objects at a great distance. A side effect is its tendency to flatten perspective.

thematic montage (C). A type of *editing* propounded by the Soviet filmmaker Eisenstein, in which separate shots are linked together not by their literal continuity in reality but by symbolic association. A shot of a preening braggart might be linked to a shot of a toy peacock, for example. Most commonly used in documentaries, in which shots are connected in accordance to the filmmaker's thesis.

three shot (T). A *medium shot,* featuring three actors.

tight framing (C). Usually in close shots. The *mise en scène* is so carefully balanced and harmonized that the people photographed have little or no freedom of movement.

tilt, tilt shot (T). See *oblique angle.*

tracking shot, trucking shot. See *dolly shot.*

two shot (T). A *medium shot* featuring two actors.

V

vertical integration (I). A system in which the production, distribution, and exhibition of movies are all controlled by the same corporation. In America the practice was declared illegal in the late 1940s.

viewfinder (T). An eyepiece on the camera that defines the playing area and the *framing* of the action to be photographed.

voice-of-God commentary (C). In documentary, the text spoken by an unseen, authoritative, and apparently all-knowing male commentator.

voice-over (T). A *nonsynchronous* spoken commentary in a movie, often used to convey a character's thoughts or memories.

W

wide-angle lens, short lens (T). A lens that permits the camera to photograph a wider area than a normal lens. A side effect is its tendency to exaggerate perspective. Also used for *deep-focus* photography.

widescreen, also CinemaScope, scope (G). A movie image that has an *aspect ratio* of approximately 5:3, though some widescreens possess horizontal dimensions that extend as wide as 2.5 times the vertical dimension of the screen.

wipe (T). An *editing* device, usually a line that travels across the screen, "pushing off" one image and revealing another.

women's pictures (G). A film *genre* that focuses on the problems of women, such as career versus family conflicts. Often such films feature a popular female *star* as protagonist.

Z

zoom lens, zoom shot (T). A lens of variable focal length that permits the cinematographer to change from *wide-angle* to *telephoto shots* (and vice versa) in one continuous movement, often plunging the viewer in or out of a scene rapidly.

INDEX